Transforming Inner Mongolia

To Tao, Xuan, Hao and Bojun

Transforming Inner Mongolia

Commerce, Migration, and Colonization on the Qing Frontier

Yi Wang

ROWMAN & LITTLEFIELD
Lanham • Boulder • New York • London

Published by Rowman & Littlefield
An imprint of The Rowman & Littlefield Publishing Group, Inc.
4501 Forbes Boulevard, Suite 200, Lanham, Maryland 20706
www.rowman.com

6 Tinworth Street, London SE11 5AL, United Kingdom

British Library Cataloguing in Publication Information Available

Library of Congress Cataloging-in-Publication Data

Names: Wang, Yi,– author.
Title: Transforming Inner Mongolia : commerce, migration, and colonization on the Qing
    frontier / Yi Wang.
Other titles: Commerce, migration, and colonization on the Qing frontier
Description: Lanham : Rowman & Littlefield, [2021] | Includes bibliographical references
    and index.
Identifiers: LCCN 2020054899 (print) | LCCN 2020054900 (ebook) | ISBN
    9781538146071 (cloth) | ISBN 9781538146088 (epub) | ISBN 9781538183670 (pbk)
Subjects: LCSH: Inner Mongolia (China)—History. | Migration, Internal—China—Inner
    Mongolia. | China—History—Qing dynasty, 1644-1912. | Borderlands—China—
    History. | Mongols—Ethnic relations. | Inner Mongolia (China)—Economic conditions.
Classification: LCC DS793.M7 W345 2021 (print) | LCC DS793.M7 (ebook) | DDC
    951.7/703—dc23
LC record available at https://lccn.loc.gov/2020054899
LC ebook record available at https://lccn.loc.gov/2020054900

Contents

Figures

Maps

Tables

Abbreviations

WL	Wanli (1572–1620)
SZ	Shunzhi (1643–1661)
KX	Kangxi (1662–1722)
YZ	Yongzheng (1723–1735)
QL	Qianlong (1736–1796)
JQ	Jiaqing (1796–1820)
DG	Daoguang (1821–1850)
XF	Xianfeng (1851–1861)
TZ	Tongzhi (1862–1874)
GX	Guangxu (1875–1907)
XT	Xuantong (1908–1912)
BB	Bordered Blue
BR	Bordered Red
BW	Bordered White
BY	Bordered Yellow
PB	Plain Blue
PR	Plain Red
PW	Plain White
PY	Plain Yellow
LF	Left Flank
LC	Left Center
LF	Left Front
LR	Left Rear
RF	Right Flank
RC	Right Center
RF	Right Front
RR	Right Rear

DSK   *Lümengshang Dashengkui* [Dashengkui, a trading firm in Mongolia], Zhongguo renmin zhengzhi xieshang huiyi Nei Menggu zhizhiqu weiyuanhui wenshi ziliao weiyuanhui, ed., Hohhot 1984.

JWJAD   *Jiaowu jiao'an dang* [The Zongli Yamen archives on Christian affairs and religious cases], Zhongyang yanjiuyuan jindaishi yanjiusuo, ed., Taipei 1974.

JKJYD   *Jüüngar khoshuun no jasag yamon no dangan* [Archives of administrative office of the Jüüngar banner], Sudebilige ed., Hohhot 2014

KWDA   *Qingmo Nei Menggu kenwu dang'an huibian* [Compilation of archives on reclamation affairs of Inner Mongolia in the late Qing], Nei Menggu dang'anguan ed., Hohhot 1999.

KWDC   *Qinming duban mengqi kenwu dachen dang'an* [Archives of imperial commissioner supervising reclamation affairs in Mongol banners], Nei Menggu dang'an guan, Record Group No. 433, 536 juan.

HQMG   *Hequ minjian gequ* [Folk songs of Hequ], Zhongyang yinyue xueyuan zhongguo yinyue yanjiusuo, ed., Beijing 1962.

IMAR   Inner Mongolia Autonomous Region

QHDSL   *Da Qing huidian shili* [Collected statutes and precedents of the Great Qing dynasty], Beijing 1991.

QSG   *Qing shi gao* [Draft history of the Qing dynasty], Zhao Erxun et al, eds., Beijing 1977.

QSL   *Da Qing lichao shilu* [Veritable records of the Great Qing], Beijing 1985.

SYTZG   *Suiyuan tongzhigao* [Draft of comprehensive gazetteer of Suiyuan], Suiyuan tongzhiguan, ed., Hohhot 2007.

YHTD   *Yihetuan dang'an shiliao* [Historical materials on the Yihetuan from the archives], Guojia dang'anju mingqing dang'anguan ed., Beijing 1959.

YHTDX   *Yihetuan dang'an shiliao xubian* [Sequel to historical materials on the Yihetuan from the archives], Zhongguo diyi lishi dang'anguan bianjibu ed., Beijing 1990.

Dynasties, Weights, and Measures

Dynasties of Imperial China

Qin   221–207 BCE
Han   206 BCE–220 CE
Sui   589–618
Tang   618–907
Song   960–1279
Yuan   1271–1368
Ming   1368–1644
Qing   1636–1912

Weights and Measures

Area
1 *qing* 頃 = 6.67 hectares (ha) = 16.47 acres
1 *qing* 頃 = 100 *mu* 畝
1 *mu* 畝 = 1/15 (0.067) ha = 1/6 (0.16) acre
1 *mu* 畝 = 240 square *gong* 弓
1 *niuju* 牛犋 = 270–280 *mu* 畝 ≈ 18 ha ≈ 45 acres
1 *niuju* 牛犋 = 120 *shang* 垧

Volume
1 *shi* 石 = 103 liters ≈ 2.9 bushels
1 *shi* 石 = 10 *dou*/peck 斗
1 *hu* 斛 = 5 *dou* 斗
1 *dou* 斗 = 10 *sheng* 升
1 *sheng* 升 = 10 *ge* 合
1 *tufang* 土方 ≈ 3 cubic meters

Length
1 *zhang* 丈 = 3.2 meters ≈ 10 feet
1 *zhang* 丈 = 10 *chi* 尺
1 *gong* 弓 = 1.667 meters
1 *li* 里 = 0.576 kilometers = 0.36 miles

Weight
1 *shi* 石 ≈ 77 kilograms ≈ 170 pounds
1 *dan*擔/picul = 100 *jin* 斤/catty ≈ 60–64 kilograms
1 *jin* 斤 = 0.6 kilograms = 1.33 pounds
1 *tun* 囤 = 180 *jin* 斤

Currency
1 silver *liang* 兩 = 1 tael ≈ 38 grams ≈ 1⅓ ounces
1 silver *liang* 兩 = 10 *qian* 錢
1 *qian* 錢 = 10 *fen* 分
1 *fen* 分 = 10 *li* 釐
1 *diao* 吊 = 1,000 *wen* 文/copper coins ≈ 1 silver liang 兩

Acknowledgments

During the many long years of bringing this book to completion, I have benefited enormously from the advice and assistance of many people. I thank all of them from the bottom of my heart.

To begin with, I am deeply grateful to the teachers who helped shape my path as a historian. The book would not have been possible without their guidance and unfailing support throughout the years. At the University of Chicago, Prasenjit Duara inspired me to study alternative history that challenges the dominant nationalist narrative, and guided me with wisdom, insights, and unstinting mentorship. Jacob Eyferth made me believe in myself and helped me articulate the ideas presented in this book with endless patience, enlightening questions, and crucial support. My other teachers, William Sewell and Dingxin Zhao, also gave me valuable advice and much-appreciated encouragement. John Garoutte of Sun Yat-sen University sparked a passion for frontier history early on through our memorable journey to Xinjiang and has urged me on over the years. Peter Perdue of Yale University and Timothy Brook of the University of British Columbia showed interest in the book project from its early stage and shared their profound expertise and insights on the Ming and Qing history.

The vibrant intellectual community in the History Department of Binghamton University made critical contributions to this book in terms of collegiality and support. Fa-ti Fan, John Chaffee, and Nancy Appelbaum have guided me in every possible way since I joined the department in 2014. Kent Schull, Meg Leja, and Alex Chase-Levenson read the entire manuscript and offered constructive comments and valuable suggestions. I thank Wendy Wall, Sean Dunwoody, Ana Candela, John Cheng, and Carl Gerderloos for their thoughtful feedback on early versions of the chapters. I am also grateful for the advice, encouragement, and group therapy provided by the members of Writing Life Workgroup: Sonja Kim, Katherine Martineau, and Giovanna Montenegro. Other colleagues also provided inspiration and support: Arnab Dey, Heather DeHaan, Heather Welland, Nancy Um, and the late Bat-Ami

Bar On. Our librarian, Julie Wang, has been ever supportive and willing to assist my book requests.

The research for this book was conducted mostly in China and Japan. I am indebted to many people in these two countries for sharing their knowledge and insights with me. In Hohhot, Baildagchi, Khasbaghana, and the late Jin Hai of Inner Mongolia University provided me with initial guidance about how to navigate through the field of Mongolian studies. I have received much advice and help over the years from Sodbilig and Erdenbaatar of Inner Mongolia University, whose friendships I deeply appreciate. In Ordos, Rev. Barisi and the late Msgr. Ma Zhongmu hosted my visits to Chengchuan (Boro-Balgasun) and offered invaluable information and hospitality. I also wish to thank Rev. Zhao Yanqing of Wuhai and the late Msgr. Liu Jingshan of Yinchuan for their time and assistance. In Wuyuan, Ren Xueyi helped me make the most of my visit to the historical canals. In Japan, I benefited from the expertise and advice of Ueda Makoto, Shidara Kunihiro, Kurahashi Keiko, and Igarashi Akio of Rikkyo University, Nakami Tatsuo of Tokyo University, Burensain Borjigin of Waseda University, Hirogawa Sahō of Hitotsubashi University, and Chimedyn Shinjilt of Kumamoto University. Li Altanjola taught me Mongolian and opened my eyes to the world of ethnic Mongols.

At the many forums where I presented some of the ideas contained in this book, I benefited from the thoughtful comments and criticisms received from Christopher Atwood, Sakura Christmas, Thomas DuBois, Peter Perdue, Sigrid Schmalzer, Nick Tackett, Patrick Taveirne, Xiaoxin Wu, Oyunbilig, Oyungerel, Wen-hsin Yeh, and Zhang Xianqing. Many thanks to the participants in workshops and conferences at the University of California, Berkeley; University of Toronto; University of British Columbia; Cornell University; Inner Mongolia University; Renmin University of China; and Association for Asian Studies, where parts of this book have been presented. I also want to thank TJ Hinricks, You-tien Hsing, Leo Shin, Lan Wu, Shellan Wu, and Yiching Wu for arranging for me to present my work at these forums. The material for chapter 4 first appeared in an essay entitled "Irrigation, Commercialization, and Social Change in Nineteenth-Century Inner Mongolia" in volume 59 of the *International Review of Social History* (2014) and is used by the permission of the publisher, Cambridge University Press.

The research and writing of this book was made possible by generous support from many institutions. A postdoctoral fellowship at the Center for Chinese Studies at the University of California, Berkeley, was crucial in developing the project to its present form. The Binghamton University Dean's Research Semester enabled me to prepare the manuscript for publication. I am grateful for the course release provided by the Institute for Advanced Studies in Humanities at Binghamton University and the Dr. Nuala McGann Drescher Leave Program offered by New York State and the United University Professions Joint Labor-Management Committees that helped bring the book to completion. I also wish to acknowledge the dedicated people at the following libraries and institutions: Inner Mongolia Archives; Center for Mongolian Studies at Inner Mongolia University; Inner Mongolia Autonomous Region

Library; Ordos Municipality Library; Ordos Municipality Archives; National Diet Library, Tokyo; Tōyō Bunko; the Institute for Advanced Studies on Asia (Tōbunken) of Tokyo University; and Staatsbibliothek zu Berlin. I give special thanks to Erdeni of Inner Mongolia University for his assistance and kindness in accommodating my research requests.

In addition, I am gratified to my editor Susan McEachern and her staff for granting this book a niche for publication, and for their patience and willingness to accommodate changes. I am indebted to the four anonymous readers at Cambridge University Press for their invaluable comments and insightful suggestions, which helped me correct many mistakes and clarify my arguments. Yuqing Huang prepared the maps with precision and responsiveness. Needless to say, I take sole responsibility for the views expressed in this book and for any errors, omissions, and misinterpretations it may contain.

Finally, I am most fortunate to have the constant support of my family. My parents and sister have been behind every step of my progress through the research and writing. The love, companionship, confidence, and support of my husband, Hao, has remained a source of inspiration throughout the years. The adoring presence of my son, Bojun, has made the writing process much more enjoyable and rewarding. This book is dedicated to them with much gratitude and love.

Introduction

In the nineteenth century, Wang Tongchun, an illiterate Chinese migrant in Inner Mongolia, experienced a career far more various than his humble origins might have suggested. Attracting the attention of both Chinese and Japanese researchers in the volatile decade of the 1930s, Wang was the subject of an academic biography penned by renowned historian Gu Jiegang and the inspiration for a group of Beijing-based academics to take a field trip to Hetao, a region located along the Yellow River and outside the Great Wall, where he had lived. Their findings were published in the semimonthly *Yu Gong* magazine, a leading journal of Chinese historical geography.[1] Wang again appeared in the publication of Zenrin kyōkai or Good Neighbor Association, a semi-official Japanese cultural organization aiming at promoting the Japanese imperial project in East Asia.[2] In these writings, Wang was credited as a pioneer of Chinese colonization (C: *kaifa* 開發, J: *kaitaku* 開拓) and dubbed a "national hero" because of his accomplishments in frontier development.[3] Wang also captured the folk imagination, in a distinct manner from the nationalist and imperialist narratives, and he was revered as a popular deity by the time of his death.[4]

Born in 1851 into an impoverished family in Zhili province of northern China, Wang arrived in Hetao in 1874, which was then a floodplain of the Yellow River inhabited largely by nomadic Mongols. Wang was employed as an irrigation canal overseer at a Chinese firm, and at the age of thirty, set out to build his own canal after renting land from a local Buddhist monastery. Within two decades, he completed four of the eight major irrigation canals of Hetao, which turned the area from a pastoral hinterland into the most prosperous agricultural colony outside the Great Wall. Wang became the wealthiest land-merchant and local magnate in Hetao, serving as chief executive, landlord, arbitrator, philanthropist, commander in chief of his private militia, and power contender against local Mongols and an expanding Catholic church. His irrigation domain crumbled, however, when the Mongol lands were put under reclamation by the Qing government, with all canals confiscated. During the early Republican era (1912–1949), Wang participated in several state-run irrigation projects in Hetao and elsewhere, yet he never regained his canals nor his influence.

1

Nevertheless, after his death in 1925, the local people in Hetao worshipped him as the River God in Hetao, dedicated a temple to him, and brought offerings on the anniversary of his death and during periods of natural calamity.

Wang's life story serves as an illustrative example of spontaneous Chinese migration into the Mongolian steppe, and the intricate interactions those migrants had with the Mongol indigenes, the environment, and the central state. It can be read as an epitome for the unprecedented Chinese expansion into non-Han peripheral regions, and the way in which such grassroots settler ventures were later subsumed by a broader set of state colonization projects that aimed at incorporating the Mongol frontier into the larger national and imperial formations. Indeed, the transformation of Hetao was by no means an isolated case. Starting from the eighteenth century, an influx of Han Chinese merchants and migrants from north China had ventured into the steppe. They established market towns, developed trading networks, and created belts of settlements across the Han-Mongol borderlands, just as their fellow countrymen expanded into southwest China, Taiwan, Manchuria, Southeast Asia, and the New World over roughly the same period. These migrants not only changed the demographic makeup of the local community, but they also significantly transformed the ecological, social, political, and cultural landscape of the destination society.

Transforming Inner Mongolia examines Chinese migration and settlement in Inner Mongolia from the eighteenth century through the early twentieth century, and it explores how changes in this border region shaped what has become the Chinese national state today. It tells a story of expansion, integration, collaboration, and confrontation in a periphery traditionally considered marginal and even antithetical to Chinese civilization. Rather than the usual tale of political domination and cultural assimilation, it presents a story from the bottom up, one in which migrants, capital, technologies, and organizational formats from China moved into the peripheries and interacted with pre-existing social and economic structures in these areas, ultimately transforming not just the borderland but the very concept of China as well.

This study treats Inner Mongolia not merely as a geographical locus where changes took place, but more importantly, as a nexus—in spatial and temporal terms—of cultural intersection, historical juncture, and multilevel integration. Spatially, it is located at the junction between the Central Eurasian steppe and northern China, part of which is an agro-pastoral ecotone where both pastoral and agricultural practices were possible. Temporally, Inner Mongolia in the Qing era existed at the intersection of two parallel processes of integration: first, the Qing territorial expansion and the incorporation of multiple non-Han peripheries into the imperial framework, and second, China's increasing absorption into the global framework of capitalism and nation-states. The overlapping of these processes eventually turned this historical borderland into both a Chinese and global periphery subject to forces of Chinese colonization as well as a hegemonic new world order imposed by the West. In the meantime, the cross-border flow of goods, people, capital, and technology gave rise to new economic practices, property regimes, and organizational formats that not only altered the frontier but had a lasting impact on core parts of China. Inner

Mongolia thus provides a unique vantage point to observe this multilevel integration across local, regional, national, and global scales.

This book demonstrates that border regions such as Inner Mongolia played a central role in China's transition from a multiethnic empire to a modern nation-state, and served as fertile ground for economic and administrative experimentation and the production of new templates that later became influential in core regions of China. The events in Inner Mongolia provide a window into the ways in which heterogeneous regions that came under the dominion of the Qing dynasty became interconnected with the larger global frameworks that reconfigured China as a multi-ethnic, territorial nation-state. In this study, I demonstrate that the periphery is no longer peripheral if we shift our perception from the imperial capital to a regional and global perspective. Instead, the borderlands stand out as a zone of possibility and experimentation where tendencies, latent elsewhere, were fully developed and as a "contact zone" where China's integration into a new global system is most visible.[5] In this sense, the periphery plays a significant role in expanding and enriching our understanding of early modern China and its political, economic, and social ramifications.

A MULTIFACETED FRONTIER

Among China's ethnic borderlands, Inner Mongolia stands out as an exception. Unlike Outer or Northern Mongolia, which proclaimed independence in 1911 after the fall of the Qing dynasty (1636–1912) and proceeded to found the Mongolian People's Republic in 1924, Inner or Southern Mongolia was integrally incorporated into the Chinese state.[6] The Inner Mongolia Autonomous Region (IMAR) founded in 1947 became the first minority administrative division under the People's Republic of China (PRC, 1949 to the present). Unlike Xinjiang and Tibet, which have seen growing separatist movements in response to religious and ethnic oppression in recent history, Inner Mongolia is viewed as a model of assimilation, and indeed the archetype of the Regional Ethnic Autonomy (*minzu quyu zizhi* 民族區域自治) system under the PRC.[7] Yet, the lack of significant political turmoil conceals a more uneasy picture. Despite being the titular nationality of the IMAR, the 4.22 million Mongols living in the region have become a minority in their historical homeland. They comprise only 17 percent of the 24.7 million people living there today, and the majority of the population are Han Chinese.[8] Rampant Chinese cultivation and a recent mining boom have resulted in a loss of grasslands, the marginalization of pastoralists, and environmental deterioration.[9]

Part of Inner Mongolia's exceptionality can be attributed to the geographical and historical traits of the region. Unlike Tibet and Xinjiang, which are physically isolated from core regions of China by high mountains and deserts and were annexed by the Qing dynasty only in the eighteenth century, nomads inhabiting today's Inner Mongolia had a long, entwined history of interaction with the sedentary Chinese in the south. As a significant contact zone at the frontier between the steppes and northern China, control of this region had alternated between Chinese dynasties and various nomadic regimes that used it as a base from which to extract resources from China.[10] The area saw the rise of the Mongols in the thirteenth century, who created the world's largest contiguous empire across Eurasia. As the first foreign regime to rule all of China, the Yuan dynasty (1271–1368) brought significant political, economic, and social integration that shaped its subsequent history.[11] The Mongols continued to play a crucial role during the Qing dynasty, as political allies of the ruling Manchus in the conquests of China and central Eurasia, or in the case of the Zunghars of western Mongolia, the Qing's most formidable opponent and rival empire-builder.[12]

Unlike Yunnan, Guizhou, and Taiwan, which were formally incorporated into the Chinese administrative system, the Mongol periphery remained largely separate from China proper until the twentieth century.[13] The Qing governed the Mongols through a distinct judicial and administrative system under the supervision of the Lifanyuan, the central agency overseeing the empire's Inner Asian dependencies.[14] Han Chinese were forbidden to cultivate or settle in Mongol territories, with intermarriage strictly prohibited, so as to protect the nomadic culture from Chinese influences.[15] This contrasted with the Qing policies that actively promoted Chinese settlement in other non-Han peripheries of the southwest and Taiwan, which can be partly explained by the different ecological and cultural environment of these regions. Compared with the well-watered river valleys and lowlands of the south, the vast regions north and west of China proper feature a desert-steppe ecotone, with too little precipitation to sustain large-scale sedentary agriculture. More importantly, the ruling Manchus, being part of the Tungusic peoples from the northeast, had shared a history of interactions and cultural affinity with the Mongols of the steppe as distinct from the groups of the southwest and Taiwan, which contributed to the development of distinct policies in these various regions.[16] Hence, the Qing segregation policy grew out of an attempt to preserve the Mongols as military allies, their distinct culture based on a pastoral lifestyle and the Buddhist religion, and their land as a "pure" ethnic homeland and a strategic frontier critical to the maintenance of the imperial order.[17]

Here we see that Inner Mongolia marks a dynamic, multivalent frontier space demarcated by natural, economic, geopolitical, ethnic, and cultural boundaries—steppe versus sown, pastoral nomadism versus sedentary agrarianism, nomadic confederation versus centralized agrarian state, Mongol versus Han Chinese, Shamanism/Tibetan Buddhism versus the syncretism of Confucianism, Daoism, and Buddhism. However, these overlapping boundaries were more fluid, messier, and "patchier" than such dichotomies suggest and left room for mutual accommodation, negotiation, and adaptation.[18] This was made possible by military conquests that radically expanded borderland spaces and by commerce and migration that generated flows of goods, people, ideas, and technologies, which gradually altered the equilibrium represented by the existing boundaries. Examples of such "patches" or ecologically distinct communities within wider landscapes of the steppe can be found in the Tümed plain near Höhhot, capital of Inner Mongolia, and the Ordos/ Hetao region along the Yellow River, where an agro-pastoral ecotone supported both pastoral habitats and sedentary communities. Since the late Ming period (1368–1644), the Tümed plain had been sprinkled with numerous agricultural settlements containing a Chinese population of over one hundred thousand, mostly abductees, deserters, and religious refugees. The Ordos/Hetao region has a history of government-organized military colonization (*tuntian* 屯田) that dates to the Qin dynasty (221–207 BCE). However, the Qing expansion of the seventeenth and eighteenth centuries allowed direct access to the steppe for the first time for Chinese individuals who were not military colonists, captives, or fugitives. By the early 1800s, it is estimated that around one million Chinese migrants inhabited Inner Mongolia. This number grew to 1,550,948 by 1912 and 3,719,113 by 1937.[19] Whereas the number was insignificant in terms of relieving the population pressures of China proper, it was nonetheless critical in overwhelming the indigenous inhabitants and ecology. By 1947, when the IMAR was founded, the Chinese population in Inner Mongolia had reached 4,696,000 and outnumbered the Mongols about six to one.[20] The wave of Chinese immigrants also had a devastating impact on the fragile environment of the steppe ecotone: causing land degradation and desertification.[21]

Boundaries were further crossed through intermarriages, linguistic and cultural borrowings, and acculturation that blurred the "ethnic" frontier. Pamela Crossley argues that the term "Mongol ethnicity" was a Qing construction to integrate the complex variety of cultures and economic milieux north of the Great Wall that defied easy categorization of nomadism, religion, or language.[22] Starting from the late Ming period, many Chinese who settled in the grassland took Mongolian names, married Mongolian women, and converted to Mongolian Buddhism. By the late Qing period, many of the Chinese traders who settled in the market towns of Mongolia had a Mongolian wife and children.[23] Meanwhile, some Mongol groups near the borders like the Kharachin and the Tümed practiced Chinese-style agriculture and borrowed Chinese cultural features such as words, grammatical structures, and deities. Over time, such incremental changes and cross-cultural exchanges reshaped the ecological, demographic, social, and cultural landscape of the region. However, compared with Chinese emigration to other frontier regions such as the southwest, Taiwan, and Manchuria, and to overseas areas such as Southeast Asia and the Americas, emigration to Inner Mongolia has received surprisingly little attention in English-language scholarship.[24]

This book historicizes the dynamics between core parts of China and its non-Han peripheries in order to reconstruct a multilayered narrative of the Han-Mongol borderland within the broader framework of the development and expansion of global capitalism and the nation-state system. It contrasts the process of Inner Mongolia's integration into China against northern Mongolia's path toward independence. First, I explore Inner Mongolia's role in China's transition from empire to nation-state. Second, I demonstrate how changes in the eighteenth and nineteenth centuries shifted the power dynamic between nomadic and settled populations permanently in the latter's favor, after two millennia of contestation. Finally, I investigate how changes in the Mongol periphery affected the core parts of China. To address these issues, this study explores the ways in which domestic factors such as population pressure and ecological crises interacted with the global forces of trade, capitalism, imperialism, and nationalism to fundamentally change frontier society. The parallel processes detailed here—an unprecedented Chinese expansion into the peripheries and an increasing integration of Greater China into global frameworks of capitalism and the nation-state—gave rise to new economic practices, property regimes, and political configurations that facilitated the integration of the heterogeneous periphery into the Chinese polity. This book approaches these historical conjunctures from a peripheral perspective by reconstructing the socioeconomic and cultural history of Inner Mongolia while addressing issues central to the understanding of late imperial and modern China.

BORDERLANDS IN PERSPECTIVE

Frontier studies have captured the interests of historians and social scientists since the publication of Frederick Jackson Turner's thesis in 1893, which highlighted the frontier experience as essential to the development of American culture. Turner viewed the frontier as an expansive line of settlement and the conjuncture between savagery and civilization. His theories have influenced numerous historians and social scientists since his time and have been applied to many other regions in the world. Turner's work has also drawn criticism because of his Darwinian approach and exclusive focus on Anglo-American settlers.[25] Recent scholarship on the American West and postcolonial studies promote a more inclusive approach by highlighting a contested, dynamic frontier experience of conflict, conquest, and adaptation. Historians now propose to replace the one-sided, simplistic Turnerian frontier with the notion of a "middle ground" or "contact zone" as a space of cultural negotiation and mutual accommodation.[26] Other theorists consider borderlands within the context of inter-colonial rivalry and state territorialization. By emphasizing the multisided and fluid boundaries between colonial empires, nation-states, and indigenous societies, they give more agency to borderland residents who participated in and challenged the state-dominated process of border-making.[27]

Within the context of these evolving multidisciplinary frontier studies, the Chinese frontier has assumed greater importance in China studies. Owen Lattimore's classical studies build upon Turner's interpretation of the frontier as a process rather than a fixed line, but assigns more active roles to the indigenous inhabitants as important agents in Chinese history, especially through their interactions with Chinese expansion and nomadic conquests of China. Lattimore develops a scientific model in explaining the formation, evolution, and interaction of human societies along frontiers. Rather than an absolute line of demarcation, he envisions the frontier as a broad margin that represents an "optimal limit of growth of one particular society" and a "reservoir" that marginal peoples utilized to maintain an equilibrium between Chinese political control and tribal conquests.[28] His structural approach considers ecological and geopolitical factors over the *longue durée* and offers a comparative framework for analyzing the evolution of frontiers in a regional and global context.[29] Lattimore's comparative approach is shared by Joseph Fletcher, whose extensive knowledge of multiple languages of East Asia and Inner Asia enabled him to trace common historical developments in economics, societies, and cultures across civilizational boundaries of Eurasia. He advocates a macro-historical paradigm of an "integrative history," which can chart the horizontal continuities and parallelisms of the early modern world.[30]

Drawing on these insights, this book examines the recent history of Inner Mongolia as an emerging "contact zone" or "middle ground" in which a spectrum of actors collaborated, contested, and negotiated as they created a new set of economic practices, property regimes, and organizational formats. This process helped incorporate the nomadic economy into the global market system without replicating the exact conditions that existed south of the borderland. Examples include the trading and banking firms of Shanxi merchants that dominated Mongolia by channeling the needs of Mongol and Manchu elites (chapter 2); cultural intermingling between Mongol and Chinese traditions as shown in some folk genres that developed from the migration experience (chapter 3); the booming irrigation communities of Hetao that combined merchant capital, irrigation technology, and wage labor (chapter 4); and the thriving Catholic enclaves that adopted an apostolic strategy of acquiring Mongol lands for attracting Chinese converts (chapter 5). As we will see, these interactions, which evolved on the local and trans-local levels, transformed the nomadic society well before the state colonization projects that would continue to incorporate Inner Mongolia throughout the twentieth century.

Transforming Inner Mongolia intersects with the history of Inner Asia by placing China and Inner Asia within the context of a transregional framework and as part of a global network of trade, capitalism, and imperialism. It responds to the growing scholarship by historians and anthropologists on Inner Asian peoples, empires, and nomadic-Chinese interactions. Instead of conventional paradigms of the tribute system that reinforced a hierarchical world order centered on assumptions of Chinese superiority, this scholarship depicts a complex picture of interdependence between nomads and agriculturalists over the *longue durée*, and reveals processes in which ecology, strategy, trade, technology, religion, and culture have all played a role.[31] To the extent that it suggests the preponderant importance of territorial specificity and economic and cultural exchange in mediating relations between China and the steppe, such work has been enormously helpful in the formation of my arguments. Yet, despite their lengthy chronological focus, such scholars have tended to sideline the nineteenth and twentieth centuries. Here, then, I have tried to rectify a relative historical elision and simultaneously integrate the history of Inner Mongolia with broader narratives in Chinese, imperial, and global history during a decisive period of integration.

This study responds to the "New Qing History," which uses newly accessible Chinese- and Manchu-language archives and texts to reassess Qing history. By emphasizing the Manchu identity of the Qing dynasty and its multiple and diverse experiences that drew equally from Chinese and Inner Asian traditions, the New Qing History scholars reject the assumption of Sinicization as the paradigm for explaining the Qing empire, while bringing in a global perspective that reexamines the Qing as one of the world empires in the early modern era.[32] This book builds on generations of path-breaking work on Ming and Qing frontiers that has established the borderlands as regions worthy of study in their own right and demonstrated their formative impact upon the history of modern China. Rather than viewing the non-Han peripheries as cradles of conflicts or passive receiver of Chinese civilization, such work elucidates the significance of border regions in shaping the governing rationale of the Ming and Qing rulers in terms of ideologies, politics, and ethnic relations, and calls attention to cross-boundary exchanges such as military conquest, migration, trade, and cultural interactions.[33] More recent scholarship on the Mongol frontier, notably the work of Johan Elverskog, David Bello, and Jonathan Schlesinger on Qing-Mongol relations and the environmental history of Han-Mongol interactions in Inner Mongolia, further challenge the China-centered paradigm in Qing frontier history by including multiple perspectives from both the periphery and the center, using multilingual sources, and highlighting the interconnection between ideology, identity, and environment.[34]

This book resonates with these major recent interventions that place the Mongol frontier within a larger framework of interconnectivity of the early modern world. Rather than looking at Qing empire-building as a top-down process emanating outward from the imperial center of Beijing, this study includes dimensions above and below the level of the nation-state. Instead of Manchu ruling elites, it focuses on a spectrum of local, regional, and transnational actors—merchants, migrants, missionaries, nobles, and lamas—whose agency is too often marginalized, if not entirely neglected, in existing historiography. In doing so, this book reorients the direction of research on China's borderlands from politics to multilayered socioeconomic and cultural history, and it places equal emphasis on broad macro-historical analysis and fine-grained micro-studies of particular regions and individuals.

CORE AND PERIPHERY

Transforming Inner Mongolia tells not just a story about Inner Mongolia, but also how the historical homeland of the Mongols was turned into a Chinese—and global—periphery. It relates how the dynamics of core and periphery have reshaped our perception of the frontier and indeed our conception of China itself. The core-periphery theory that emerged from the world-systems and dependency theory in the 1970s provided a spatial model of structured relations between an industrialized core and its less industrialized peripheries that explains the disparities caused by political influence, economic development, social status, and cultural hegemony.[35] Although this analysis is generally associated with the social and economic inequalities produced as various regions and states were integrated into the capitalist world economy, it is also useful in explaining the economic asymmetry and dependence that existed between a dominant core and one of its culturally distinct peripheries. The thesis of internal colonialism proposed by Pablo Gonzalez Casanova, Michael Hechter, and Harold Wolpe describes the regional inequalities and racial domination within one single state or policy, which parallel the relationship between metropole and colony in an imperial-colonial setting.[36] This approach provides an important framework for conceptualizing regional differences and interprets cultural hegemony as something perpetuated by the structural asymmetries that characterize the global economy. In a pre-industrial setting, such disparities were typically caused by the flow of capital and the subsequent commercialization of social relations.[37]

This discussion of core-periphery relations leads to further considerations about colonization, colonialism, and the applicability of these terms to the non-Western setting. The term "colonization," derived from the Latin word *colere* that means "to cultivate, to till; to inhabit," refers to the action or process of settling among and establishing control over the indigenous peoples of an area.[38] By extension, colonialism is defined as the practice of establishing colonies to extend a state's control over other peoples or territories.[39] The term is typically used with reference to the extension of European dominion over non-Western peoples and has a negative connotation that describes aggressive intrusion into the indigenous territory and active exploitation of economic, political, and cultural differences between the settlers and the indigenous population.[40] However, some recent scholarship has characterized Qing China as a colonial empire by situating it within a global context and exploring its similarities to other European contemporaries in terms of administrative apparatuses, symbolic configurations, and the use of technologies. Both the Qing and European empires went through unprecedented territorial expansion that led to enhanced political control over their diverse subjugated peoples, and both used technologies such as artillery and cartography to enforce their new claims to sovereignty.[41]

Transforming Inner Mongolia expands our understanding of colonialism beyond its negative connotations by revealing the multilayered patterns of domination and exploitation existing in the Qing peripheries and the complex relationships between colonization and regional and global integration. I identify two distinct but related historical processes: (1) the establishment of political control over the Mongols by the Qing empire and (2) the expansion of Chinese settlements in areas traditionally inhabited by the Mongols. The first process was accomplished through both military means and a set of bureaucratic apparatuses, including the institution of the Lifanyuan, the co-optation of local elites, and the maintenance of a separate administrative structure based on local tradition. Unlike its European counterparts until the early twentieth century, however, the Qing colonial administration of Mongolia did not involve the active planting of settlers, or, for that matter, any overt narrative of a "civilizing" project. This was partly due to the shared historical and cultural roots between the Manchus and Mongols and partly to the security concerns of protecting the northern frontier from potential nomadic challengers. Indeed, the Mongols, just like the Manchus, were located at the top of the imperial hierarchy. Therefore, they did not need civilization, but they did see a need to protect their traditional ways of life from Chinese influences.[42] The second process occurred as a result of population pressures in interior China and the rapid increase of the cross-border movement of goods, people, and capital, which led to the gradual replacement of the frontier's barter economy with the silver-based monetary economy of China. This process was initiated by Chinese merchants and migrants who were allowed restricted access to the northern frontiers and had no political control over the local population because of the separate administrative system and the spontaneous nature of their movement. The Qing court did not support this frontier expansion, but it backed indigenous privileges and their claims to land due to strategic concerns as well as due to the necessity of maintaining cultural boundaries within the empire. Such concerns for pluralism also differentiated the Chinese expansion from contemporary European settler colonialism.[43]

Although this study recognizes the colonial characteristics of the Qing administration over its various dependencies, the term "colonization" is used primarily in the context of the official campaign to open up Mongol lands for Chinese reclamation since the early twentieth century, as distinguished from the previous spontaneous movements of the Chinese population into Mongol territories, which are referred to more generally as "migration" or "immigration." Despite the close interrelation of these terms, "colonization" indicates a deliberate attempt by a nation to exert commercial, political, and social influences over another through systematic settlement and/or the establishment of political, economic, military, and cultural institutions. This deliberate action on the part of a nation's government is absent in "migration," which denotes leaving one's native land to move to a new area or country.

Only when the Qing abandoned its old protective policy toward the Mongols in favor of one that actively promoted Chinese immigration and state-centralization did these two processes begin to converge. The expropriation of Mongol land indicates a fundamental shift of Qing frontier policy from indirect rule to direct rule in the early twentieth century that coincided with the Qing dynasty's endeavors to transform itself into a modern nation-state in the face of surging Western imperialism.[44] In this sense, the Chinese colonization of Inner Mongolia was heavily conditioned by the threat of Western imperialism, as China proper functioned simultaneously as the Qing core and a globalized European periphery. Thus, the pastoral Mongols faced multiple levels of marginalization. Socially, they came under the mounting pressure of Chinese colonization and acculturation. Politically, they were absorbed into a centralizing and assimilating Chinese body politic. Culturally, nomadism was perceived as backward, anachronistic, a lower stage of development in the evolution of human societies, and the archetype of an archaic past that China sought to disengage from in its fervor to modernize. All this made Inner Mongolia a "periphery of the periphery" and subject both to the inequalities and domination imposed on a global scale by the capitalist world system and to regional disparities and cultural hegemony that reproduced those asymmetrical relations within a single nation-state. This inequality is unfolded through the layering of a palimpsest of colonial projects on top of one another, with each new project subsuming the previous ones—Chinese migrants, the Qing state, the Chinese state in the Republican and PRC eras, and more recently, the "Open Up the West" campaign (*xibu dakaifa* 西部大開發) launched in 1999 that aims to modernize the hitherto "underdeveloped" western hinterlands.[45]

COMMERCE, MIGRATION, AND INTEGRATION

Recent studies on the Qing frontiers have highlighted the role of trade and commerce as an important part of the Qing imperial project in the borderlands. The pathbreaking work of James Millward illuminates the role of Chinese merchants in financing the Qing military campaigns and administration of the newly incorporated territories of Xinjiang. Peter Perdue's magisterial volume on the Qing conquest of the Zunghars emphasizes logistics for supplying and sustaining the Qing expeditions and elucidates how trade relations and monetary exchanges helped foster economic integration within the Qing empire. C. Patterson Giersch's study explores the long-distance trade between China and Southeast Asia in shaping economic and social change in the borderlands of Yunnan. Kwangmin Kim's monograph examines the links between the political incorporation of Eastern Turkestan/Xinjiang into the Qing empire and its economic integration into the global capitalist economy. Kim particularly emphasizes the agency of local Muslim elites who formed alliances with the Qing court and transformed the oasis economy through commercial agriculture and trade.[46]

Adding to the growing literature, this book moves beyond a state-centered viewpoint to examine the correlations among commerce, empire building, and regional integration in Qing frontier history. The eighteenth-century expansion of the Qing empire provided unprecedented opportunities for Chinese merchants and artisans to penetrate the frontiers as suppliers of goods and services, taking commodities and techniques to the border regions, and bringing local products into the Chinese and global markets. On the one hand, strategic factors played a crucial role in the expansion of Chinese commerce into Mongolia, as merchants were mobilized to supply the Qing army during the Qing-Zunghar War (1690–1697). These merchants channeled the financial needs of the Manchu-Mongol ruling elites and monopolized the frontier trade with Russia at Kyakhta on the Sino-Russian border. Indeed, these activities broadly coincided with the Qing tendency to promote commerce as a means of expanding control over the steppe frontier. On the other hand, apart from such strategic factors, Inner Mongolia's geographical proximity to North China, coupled with the nomads' economic dependence on the sedentary Chinese, made the region susceptible to forces of commercialization, migration, and economic integration. The inflow of silver into China from the sixteenth century onward had tied

China ever more to the global market through the export of silk and porcelain, and by the eighteenth century, to the Mongol periphery as well through the trade of tea and through practices of moneylending based on silver, which were both conducted by Shanxi merchants. Involved in the lucrative long-distance trade were not only state-sanctioned trading firms that functioned as financial brokers and tax farmers for the Mongol upper classes, but also numerous itinerant traders who penetrated the market hierarchies down to the localities. As exemplified by the case of Wang Tong-chun in Hetao, these actors became important agents of change on the local level, as they engaged in moneylending, land brokerage, and capital investment in irrigation projects. Here, the relationship between commerce and frontier politics was a diverse one: whereas state policies and strategic concerns provided an indispensable precondition and context for commerce to expand, the long-term movement of goods and people transformed the local society through regional and global integration.

The growth of long-distance trade in the frontier regions also constituted an important—albeit overlooked—part of the debate over Chinese economic evolution during the Ming and Qing periods. Chinese historians since the 1950s have characterized developments in China's indigenous commercialization, such as the rise of managerial landlords, handicrafts workshops, and wage labor in the Jiangnan region as the "sprouts of capitalism." Here, in classical Marxist terms, capitalism is interpreted as a mode of production characterized by the private ownership of the means of production and a stage of historical development.[47] Western scholarship in the 1970s and 1980s adopted Malthusian and Smithian interpretations of China's economy, however, by arguing that urbanization and commercialization in China failed to bring technological breakthrough and capitalism, but rather led to a path of "high-level equilibrium trap" and "involution" due to population increase and declining labor productivity.[48] Despite their different positions, both interpretations hold the European model of modern industrial capitalism as the single standard against which the agrarian economy of China should be gauged.

More recently, a group of economic historians who have become known as the California School began to introduce a global and comparative perspective that refutes the Eurocentric model. Kenneth Pomeranz and Bin Wong argue that the level and trajectories of economic development were comparable in the most advanced regions of Europe and China as late as in 1800, and that both regions experienced Smithian growth in terms of market exchange and specialization while facing similar Malthusian constraints on growth.[49] This revisionist view of the economic potential of early modern China has stimulated a vigorous debate among historians and provided direction for new scholarship that looks beyond the East-West binary to consider economic development within the broader context of global interconnections and regional specificities.[50] Christopher Isett contributes to the debate by bringing frontier regions such as Manchuria into the sphere of Qing social and economic history. Isett asserts that the rural economy of Manchuria, like that of China proper, was locked in a Malthusian-Ricardo model of non-development rather than a Smithian market economy. Instead of mere Malthusian limits, Isett attributes the lack of development to the existing property and labor regimes such as the custom of partible inheritance, which perpetuated smaller land holding and prevented the formation of large estates.[51]

Transforming Inner Mongolia adds to the current debate by expanding the scope of investigation from the core regions of China to non-Han peripheries and demonstrating how response to economic change varies across regions and over time. Therefore, it is important to consider the temporal, spatial, and conjunctural variations before forming generalizations about China as a whole. The experience of Inner Mongolia, as this study shows, was diverse and heterogeneous. Whereas some areas developed agricultural and social patterns that were highly congruent with those of northern China, others displayed distinct features that departed from the mode of smallholder family farming dominant elsewhere in China proper. In Hetao in particular, the conjuncture of abundant arable land, merchant capital, and favorable irrigation conditions combined to generate a form of highly commercialized and capital-intensive agricultural production that resembled agrarian capitalism. Here I find David Faure's interpretation of capitalism in terms of "the application of the institutions which enabled capital to impact on the economy" particularly useful. Faure draws from Max Weber and Karl Polanyi and emphasizes the enabling effect of capitalist institutions on the development of a market economy.[52] In Hetao as well as other parts of Inner Mongolia, the expansion of transregional and cross-border trade gave rise to not only new business practices but also a set of mechanisms that enabled the accumulation and circulation of capital. These included institutions such as family firms, partnerships, joint ventures, native banks, and financial instruments such as shares, bonds, interests, contracts, and land deeds. In this sense, the "sprouts of capitalism" emerged in a Han-Mongol borderland where the grip of the Chinese agrarian regime was relatively weak rather than in the core regions of China, which made the region subject to the forces of double integration—that of the Mongol pastoral economy into the money-based economy of China and the larger processes of China's absorption into the global market system.[53]

The expansion of trade and changes in business practices led to migration flows across the borders. As mentioned earlier, a similar expansion also took place in other non-Han peripheries including the southwest, Taiwan, Xinjiang, and Manchuria, as well as in overseas areas such as Southeast Asia and the Americas. In each of these cases, the Chinese diaspora played a crucial role in reshaping social and economic lives in the destination societies, facilitating the development of capitalism, and integrating these frontiers into the Chinese and global market systems. This work thus resonates with the growing body of literature on the history of the Chinese diaspora that adopts a global historical approach to examine the role of Chinese migrations in the making of a worldwide trading system and modern nation-states. Philip Kuhn's masterly monograph presents a synthetic history of the long durée of Chinese emigration spanning five centuries and maps out a set of institutional and cultural practices of family, association, and communication networks that enable Chinese emigrants to fit into the venue society while maintaining ties with their native-place. Such "corridors" and "niches" connected overseas communities to the homeland, making the migration experiences simultaneously translocal and particular to specific regions within China. Kuhn highlights the role of overseas Chinese in facilitating European colonialism in Southeast Asia, serving as middlemen or tax farmers who mediated between the colonial regimes and indigenous populations. Wang Gungwu emphasizes the practice of "sojourning" as a fundamental Chinese emigrant pattern, which provides overseas Chinese a unique identity that differs from that of migrants who return to their homes or who assimilate into their new culture. Adam McKeown's study of Chinese diaspora communities across the Americas illuminates how transnational networks and institutions enabled the circulation of goods, people, money, and information across the Pacific Ocean.[54]

Whereas the bulk of the existing scholarship has focused on international migrations, this book calls attention to the frequently overlooked role of internal migrations within the context of translocal and transregional flows of capital, labor, and skills. The communities organized by Chinese merchants and migrants in Inner Mongolia shared much in common with the Chinese diaspora communities established by the Hokkiens, Teochius, and Hakkas in Malaya and Borneo in terms of the elaborate networks of trade and circulation and shared institutions such as native-place associations, professional guilds, self-governing corporations, and religious communities that linked the migrant communities to their native places south of the passes. Like their overseas counterparts, these migrants were driven into the frontier by economic opportunities as well as ecological pressures. The doubling of the Han population from roughly 150 million in 1700 to 300 million in 1800 and then to 450 million in 1850 impacted the densely inhabited regions of the north China plain as much as the provinces in the south. Such rapid population growth, coupled with recurrent natural disasters of drought and flood, triggered an unprecedented outflow of population into the grasslands beyond the passes, just as a similar movement occurred in the southwest, Taiwan, and Southeast Asia.[55] As in the other frontier regions, sojourning remained a dominant pattern that survived well into the twentieth century, partly due to the long-standing Qing restriction on Han settlement. Likewise, Chinese merchants in Mongolia played a crucial role as cultural brokers bridging the needs of Manchu and Mongol elites and ordinary nomads and facilitated Qing colonial enterprises in the Mongol frontier.

Integration of various kinds is the persistent focus of this study: Inner Mongolia's integration into the marketized agrarian regime of China and into a global capitalist economy, and the region's administrative integration into what would become the nation-state of China. These integrations arose not simply from top-down measures of imperial control and state formation, but also from cross-border movements of people, goods, services, and capital that led to a blending of culture and an exchange of products, ideas, and knowledge. They can be understood as part of the globalization processes that saw increasing interconnection among the world's economies and cultures as fostered through interregional trade and migrations. Although globalization can be traced back to the Silk Routes that linked the East and West in ancient and medieval times, the scale and volume of global flows greatly expanded with the creation of extensive Eurasian empires such as the Mongol and Ottoman empires after the thirteenth century and the European seaborne empires in the sixteenth century, which gave rise to elaborate networks of communication, migration, and interconnection.[56]

The case of Inner Mongolia is illustrative of the intersection of three events of integration since the sixteenth century. The first was the arrival in Asia of New World silver, which led to an expansion of commercial production and commodity trading and to the accumulation of merchant capital. The second event was the expansion of the Qing empire, which provided an overland system of political and economic integration (in particular through increasing trade with Russia). The third event was the expansion of European capitalist enterprises and military power in Asia, which institutionalized a world economy of capital accumulation centering on national states. This multileveled integration provided improved access to goods and services for the Mongol nomads and increased revenue and living standards for the aristocrats. However, it also resulted in the replacement of the region's barter economy of nomadic pastoralism with the new money-based economic regime of China and the incorporation of its formerly autonomous administration into the Chinese body politic. All this occurred at a time when China was being absorbed into the global system of capitalism and the nation-states.

My approach thus facilitates the conjoining of two major trends in the new Chinese historiography: new Qing frontier history and the history of migration. It combines a more interpretive concept of borderland as a place of multifaceted interaction and cultural exchange with a spatial model of regional and ethnic inequalities created by the world economic system, and it highlights the role that migration played in bridging these different spatial and social dimensions. In doing so, it links micro-studies of specific regions confined in time and space to macro-historical trends of ecological, socioeconomic, political, and cultural transformation.

SOURCES

This research is based on a wide range of Chinese, Japanese, and European language sources and Chinese translations of Mongolian sources, including archival materials, local gazetteers, travelogues, journals, newspapers, stele inscriptions, folk songs, and oral histories. Apart from official sources like legal codes, veritable records, and official historiography, it draws from archival materials from a number of central and local institutions, including the Zongli Yamen 總理衙門 (Office of General Management), the Office of Imperial Commissioner Supervising Reclamation Affairs in Mongol Banners (*Qinming duban mengqi kenwu dachen* 钦命督办蒙旗垦务大臣), and the administrative offices of Mongol banners or subdivisions. Many of these archives have not been used before in English-language works. The unpublished Archives of the Office of Imperial Commissioner Supervising Reclamation Affairs in

Mongol Banners (1901–1910, 536 *juan*) preserved in the Inner Mongolia Archives provides an invaluable source of information on the official reclamation campaign led by Imperial Commissioner Yigu and on the irrigation systems of Hetao and their developers. The Archives of the Administrative Office of Jüüngar banner (1739–1912, forty-two volumes), a selected proportion of which has been translated into Chinese, offer a rare Mongol perspective on issues like religious practice and land reclamation as well as on Han-Mongol encounters in general.[57] This study also utilizes the records and travelogues of Western missionaries, explorers, and diplomats, and reports of scientific surveys conducted by Chinese and Japanese governmental agents, research institutes, and academic societies, which provide first-hand observation and data about the region and peoples. Moreover, it draws on a rich repertoire of folk songs and oral histories to reconstruct the local history and daily experience of ordinary migrants. The study thus weaves together a tapestry of sources drawn from the local, regional, and global levels, and it reconstructs a multilayered and dynamic history of the Mongol borderland as reshaped by multiple forces of ecological pressure, commercialization, capitalism, imperialism, and state building.

Besides research, this study draws from the wide array of secondary Sinophone and Japanese scholarship on Qing borderlands in general and on Inner Mongolia in particular, which employ Manchu, Mongolian, and Japanese as well as Chinese sources. The literature includes general histories such as *Menggu minzu tongshi* [General history of the Mongolian nation] and *Nei Menggu tongshi* [General history of Inner Mongolia],[58] as well as monographs and journal articles that cover topics regarding Qing institutions, frontier policies, the Mongol economy, Chinese migration, and social transformation within Mongol society.[59] Among this work, the recent scholarship by a growing number of ethnic Mongol scholars merits special attention because of its use of unpublished Mongolian archival documents that provides a much-needed Mongol perspective on the socioeconomic changes brought by Chinese migration. To name a few, Khasbaghana's study on the regional history of the Ordos, Jusaal's research on the farming villages of eastern Inner Mongolia, and Uranchecheg's work on the treasury of the Tümed banners of Höhhot draw extensively from the hitherto unused materials from the administrative offices of Jüüngar, Tümed Left, and Kharachin banners, respectively. Additionally, Oyungerel's research on urbanization in Inner Mongolia and Burensain's study on sedentarization in eastern Inner Mongolia utilize the vast Japanese survey data taken of the area, especially surveys conducted by the Southern Manchuria Railway in the 1930s and 1940s.[60] Of the Japanese secondary scholarship, I draw mainly from the classic studies of Yano Jin'ichi and Tayama Shigeru; war-time surveys conducted by Anzai Kuraji, Gotō Tomio, and others on land reclamation and Chinese commerce[61]; as well as more recent scholarship on economic and social changes in modern Inner Mongolia.[62] These studies provide a wealth of information and nuanced interpretations of Inner Mongolia from local and regional perspectives.

CHAPTER SUMMARY

Chapter 1 provides an overview of the historical, geopolitical, and cultural background of the Eurasian steppe during the Ming-Qing transition that set the stage for Chinese expansion in the later periods. The chapter recounts the long-term nomad-sedentary interaction in the history of China and Inner Asia and outlines the state policies and security considerations regarding the Mongol frontier during the late imperial China (especially the new political arrangements ushered in by the Qing territorial expansion) including the decentralized rule of Mongol aristocracy, the territorialized banner and league system, and the segregation policies between nomadic Mongols and agrarian Chinese.

Chapter 2 explores the commercial penetration of the nomadic economy during the eighteenth and early nineteenth centuries, in particular the economic drive underlying the flow of money, credit, and people across the Han-Mongol border. Spearheading the economic expansion were merchants of Shanxi province, who channeled the financial needs of the Manchu-Mongol ruling elites and established flourishing market centers across the steppe. Using Dashengkui as a case study, I explore the role of Shanxi firms in incorporating the Mongol peripheries into the monetary system of China and into the global flows of trade. The financial domination of Chinese merchants caused widespread indebtedness among the Mongol upper classes and the impoverishment of Mongol commoners. Eventually, it resulted in the demise of the trading firms in the wake of the independence movement of the Khalkhas in the early twentieth century.

Chapter 3 investigates agricultural expansion into the Mongol periphery during the eighteenth and nineteenth centuries. It discusses the changes introduced by Chinese migrants to the Mongol periphery, including the transplantation of a centralized administrative system and the commodification of the Mongol land. Settlement trends, which favored agricultural exploitation, led to serious ecological deterioration by the second half of the nineteenth century. Such changes also resulted in the escalation of ethnic conflicts. Drawing on folk songs and oral histories, this chapter also reconstructs the daily experiences of ordinary migrants and their interactions with indigenous Mongol communities that would result in changes on both sides.

Chapter 4 examines the emergence of agrarian capitalism in the irrigation communities of Hetao on the northern bend of the Yellow River, which centered on massive capital accumulation, wage labor, and commercialized agricultural production. This process was dominated by a group of Chinese land merchants (exemplified by Wang Tongchun) who combined merchant capital and technical expertise to develop irrigation networks and establish managerial farms: thereby accelerating the commodification of Mongolian land. The process was furthered by the Mongol aristocracy, whose members held shares in the canals through land investment.

Chapter 5 investigates the expansion of the Roman Catholic church in Inner Mongolia on the back of Chinese migration, by focusing on the proselytizing activities of the Belgian missionaries from the Congregatio Immaculati Cordis Mariae

(CICM). The role played by the Western missionaries was complicated. Whereas their evangelistic strategy helped shelter many refugees from north China and eventually aided the administrative expansion of the centralizing state apparatuses into the Mongol periphery, their entanglement in land disputes and local politics accounted for the eruption of violence during the Boxer Uprising of 1900.

Chapter 6 examines the institutional and administrative expansion of the Qing state in the early twentieth century. It focuses on the official reclamation of Mongol pasturelands, which paved the way for the administrative incorporation of the Mongol periphery into the Chinese nation-state. The reversal of Qing segregation policy indicated a structural rupture that came as a result of various socioeconomic transformations from within the frontier, as well as in response to the pressures of imperialist powers from without. It also represented a major conceptual shift from a view of the frontier as a strategic buffer zone to a perception of it as a source of fiscal revenue. This shift unfolded over the same period in which the Qing state itself transformed from an empire that emphasized multiculturalism and differences into a nation-state that upheld unity and homogeneity. I show that the process was not a simple one of expropriation and marginalization, but one that entailed more complex and mediated changes in economic practices, property regimes, and political configurations.

Finally, the conclusion carries the story forward to the present day and discusses the political, ethnocultural, and ecological repercussions of Chinese settlement in the late twentieth and early twenty-first centuries, with special attention paid to ethnic tensions and ecological deterioration caused by capital investments, land grabs, and state-sponsored development projects.

NOTES

1. Gu Jiegang, "Wang Tongchun kaifa hetao ji," 2–10; Gu Jiegang and Feng Jiasheng, eds., "Houtao shuili diaocha zhuanhao."

2. Isobe, "Katō to ōdōshun."

3. Gu Jiegang, "Wang Tongchun kaifa hetao ji," 2; Xie Bingxin, *Pingsui yanxian lüxingji*.

4. Jia Hanqing, "Hetao shuili kenzhi," 11; Su Xixian, "Wang Tongchun," 59, 90.

5. Pratt, *Imperial Eyes*, 34.

6. Outer Mongolia was a historical term used to refer to the area that includes the independent state of Mongolia and the Republic of Tuva in Russia. Its area was roughly equivalent to the current Republic of Mongolia, formerly known as Mongolian People's Republic (1924–1992). It is largely inhabited by the Khalkha Mongols, who announced their independence from the Qing at the end of 1911 and established a monarchy under the Jebtsundamba Khutugtu (Bogdo Gegen). See Bawden, *The Modern History of Mongolia*, 187–237.

7. Bulag, "Inner Mongolia," 84–116.

8. Nei Menggu zizhiqu tongjiju, *2010 nian diliuci quanguo renkou pucha*.

9. Williams, *Beyond Great Walls*; Sneath, *Changing Inner Mongolia*.

10. Lattimore, *Inner Asian Frontiers of China*; Barfield, *The Perilous Frontier*; Di Cosmo, *Ancient China and Its Enemies*.

11. Morgan, *The Mongols*; Amitai and Biran eds., *Mongols, Turks, and Others*.

12. Bawden, *The Modern History of Mongolia*; Fletcher, "The Heyday of the Ch'ing order in Mongolia," 409–91; Di Cosmo et al., eds., *The Cambridge History of Inner Asia*.

13. On China's incorporation of Yunnan, Guizhou, and Taiwan, see Giersch, *Asian Borderlands*; Yang, *Between Winds and Clouds*; Herman, *Amid the Clouds and Mist*; Shepherd, *Statecraft and Political Economy on the Taiwan Frontier*.

14. Chia, "The Li-fan Yuan and the Inner Asian Rituals in the Early Qing (1644–1795)," 60–92.

15. Jagchid and Hyer, *Mongolia's Culture and Society*, 353–64; Lattimore, *The Mongols of Manchuria*, 37–87.

16. Barfield, *The Perilous Frontier*; Crossley, *The Manchus*; Rhoads, *Manchus and Han*; Rowe, *China's Last Empire*.

17. For the Qing-Mongol relations from a Mongolian perspective, see Elverskog, *Our Great Qing*. For the Qing segregation policy to preserve Mongolia and Manchuria, see Schlesinger, *A World Trimmed with Fur*, 5–8. For the politics of a "pure" land, see High and Schlesinger, "Ruler and Rascals," 289–304.

18. I use "patchy" following Winterhalder's definition of a "patch" as an ecologically distinct locality in the landscape that is used to measure the environmental variability and diversity in time and space. See Winterhalder, "Concepts in Historical Ecology," in Crumley ed., *Historical Ecology*, 17–41, 33; Bello, *Across Forest, Steppe, and Mountain*, 7.

19. Song Naigong, *Zhongguo renkou nei menggu fence*, 50–54.

20. The Mongol population dropped from around one million in the early 1800s to 831,877 in 1947. See Song Naigong, *Zhongguo renkou nei menggu fence*, 63.

21. Wang Guangzhi, "Jin shan meng jierangqu," 78–86; Xiao Ruiling et al., *Mingqing Neimenggu xibu diqu kaifa yu tudi shahua*.

22. Crossley, "Making Mongols," 58–82. For the comparative case of the Manchus, see Crossley, *A Translucent Mirror*, 281–336.

23. Borjigin, "The Complex Structure of Ethnic Conflict in the Frontier," 41–60; Pozdneyev, *Mongolia and the Mongols*, volume 1.

24. Lattimore, "Chinese Colonization in Inner Mongolia," 288–312; Cressey, "Chinese Colonization in Mongolia," 273–87.

25. Turner, "The Significance of the Frontier in American History," 1–18. For a critique of Turner's frontier thesis, see Limerick et al., *Trails*.

26. White, *The Middle Ground*.

27. Bolton, *The Spanish Borderlands*. For an overview of borderlands history through a theoretic and comparative lens, see Adelman and Aron, "From Borderlands to Borders," 814–41; Baud and Van Schendel, "Toward a Comparative History of Borderlands," 211–42.

28. Lattimore, *Inner Asian Frontiers of China*, 240, 489–91. For the concept of reservoir, see Lattimore, *Studies in Frontier History*, 113.

29. Lattimore, *Inner Asian Frontiers of China*, 469–91. For the *longue durée* approach of the French Annales School, see Braudel, *On History*.

30. Fletcher, "Integrative History," 37–57.

31. Rossabi, *China and Inner Asia*; Rossabi, ed., *China Among Equals*; Jagchid and Symons, *Peace, War, and Trade*; Barfield, *The Perilous Frontier*; Khazanov, *Nomads and the Outside World*; Di Cosmo, *Ancient China and Its Enemies*; Di Cosmo et al., *The Cambridge History of Inner Asia*.

32. For a general survey of the New Qing History scholarship, see Guy, "Who were the Manchus?"; Sen, "The New Frontiers of Manchu China"; Waley-Cohen, "The New Qing History." For an overview of the Sinicization thesis, see Ho, "The Significance of the Ch'ing Period in Chinese History"; Ho, "In Defense of Sinicization." For its rebuttal, see Rawski, "Presidential Address."

33. Recently published works on the Ming and Qing borderlands include the following: on Xinjiang and central Eurasia: Millward, *Beyond the Pass*; Perdue, *China Marches West*; Millward, *Eurasian Crossroads*; Kim, *Borderland Capitalism*. On Manchuria: Reardon-Anderson, *Reluctant Pioneers*; Isett, *State, Peasant, and Merchant in Qing Manchuria*; Bello, *Across Forest, Steppe, and Mountain*; Schlesinger, *A World Trimmed with Fur*. On Taiwan: Shepherd, *Statecraft and Political Economy on the Taiwan Frontier*; Teng, *Taiwan's Imagined Geography*; Andrade, *How Taiwan Became Chinese*; Hang, *Conflict and Commerce in Maritime East Asia*. On Guizhou and Yunnan: Hostetler, *Qing Colonial Enterprise*; Lee, *The Political Economy of a Frontier*; Herman, *Amid the Clouds and Mist*; Giersch, *Asian Borderlands*; Bin Yang, *Between Winds and Clouds*; Bello, *Across Forest, Steppe, and Mountain*. On Sichuan and Tibet: Dai, *The Sichuan Frontier and Tibet*; Wang, *China's Last Imperial Frontier*. On Guangxi: Shin, *The Making of the Chinese State*. On Muslims: Lipman, *Familiar Strangers*; Dillon, *China's Muslim Hui Community*.

34. Elverskog, *Our Great Qing*; Bello, *Across Forest, Steppe, and Mountain*; Schlesinger, *A World Trimmed with Fur*.

35. Friedmann, *Regional Development Policy*. For the world-systems theory, see Wallerstein, *The Modern World-System I, II, III*. For the dependency theory, see Frank, "The Development of Underdevelopment."

36. Casanova, "Internal Colonialism and National Development," 27–37; Hechter, *Internal Colonialism*; Wolpe, "The Theory of Internal Colonialism."

37. Skinner, ed., *The Cities of Late Imperial China*, 216. For a critique of Skinner's approach, see Sands and Myers, "The Spatial Approach to Chinese History," 721–46; Cartier, "Origins and Evolution of a Geographical Idea," 79–142.

38. For the definition of colony and colonization, see Online Etymology Dictionary http://www.etymonline.com/index.php?allowed_in_frame=0&search=colony.

39. For the definition of colonialism, see https://www.collinsdictionary.com/dictionary/english/colonialism.

40. Fieldhouse, *Colonialism 1870–1945*, 6.

41. Perdue, "Comparing Empires," 255–62; Di Cosmo, "Qing Colonial Administration in Inner Asia," 287–309; Adas, "Imperialism and Colonialism in Comparative Perspective," 371–88.

42. For an analysis of "civilizing projects," see Harrell, ed., *Cultural Encounters on China's Ethnic Frontiers*, 4. The Qing expansion in Inner Asia was quite distinct from its conquest of the southwest and Taiwan, which involved stronger presence of the central state, active Chinese immigration, and cultural assimilation of the indigenous populations. See Di Cosmo, "Qing Colonial Administration in Inner Asia," 293–94; Schlesinger, *A World Trimmed with Fur*, 6–7.

43. For differences between Qing and European imperialism, see Millward, *Beyond the Pass*, 245–49.

44. Reardon-Anderson, *Reluctant Pioneers*; Lan, "China's 'New Administration' in Mongolia"; Wang, *China's Last Imperial Frontier*; Relyea, *Gazing at the Tibetan Plateau*.

45. Goodman, "The Campaign to 'Open Up the West'," 317–34.

46. See Millward, *Beyond the Pass*; Perdue, *China Marches West*; Giersch, *Asian Borderlands*; Giersch, "Cotton, Copper, and Caravans," 37–61. Other recent publications on cross-regional trade in the frontiers include on Manchuria: Isett, *State, Peasant, and Merchant in Qing Manchuria*; on Sichuan, Dai, *The Sichuan Frontier and Tibet*; on Yunnan: Yang, *Between Winds and Clouds*; on Taiwan: Andrade, *How Taiwan Became*; Hang, *Conflict and Commerce in Maritime East Asia*.

47. For the "Sprouts of Capitalism" argument, see Shang Yue, *Zhongguo ziben zhuyi guanxi fasheng ji yanbian*; Zhongguo renmin daxue Zhongguo lishi jiaoyanshi, ed., *Zhongguo ziben zhuyi mengya*; Xu Dixin and Wu Chengming, *Zhongguo ziben zhuyi fazhan shi*, volume 1.

48. Elvin, *The Pattern of Chinese Past*; Huang, *The Peasant Economy and Social Change in North China*, chapters 4 and 11; Huang, *The Peasant Family and Rural Development in the Yangtzi Delta*; Chao, *Man and Land in Chinese History*; Perkins, *Agricultural Development in China*.

49. See Pomeranz, *The Great Divergence*; Wong, *China Transformed*. Likewise, Andre Gunder Frank foregrounds the role of silver in an effort to reorient the center of world economy from Europe to Asia from 1400 to 1800, and Li Bozhong provides the empirical assessment of the rural economy of the Jiangnan region that supports the divergence argument. See Frank, *Re-Orient*; Li, *Agricultural Development in Jiangnan*.

50. For the debate of involution versus development, see Huang, "Development or Involution in Eighteenth-Century Britain and China?"; Pomeranz, "Beyond the East-West Binary"; Brenner and Isett, "England's Divergence from China's Yangzi Delta."

51. Isett, *State, Peasant, and Merchant in Qing Manchuria*.

52. Faure, *China and Capitalism*, 12–14. For the discussion on capitalism, see Weber, *Economy and Society*; Polanyi, *The Great Transformation*.

53. Such "sprouts" were nonetheless vulnerable to external pressures. The economic growth in Hetao was cut short abruptly by the Qing official reclamation campaign, which shows that non-economic factors such as state making, social constraints, and legal propensity should be considered along with purely economic factors such as Malthusian limits when determining the reason for the failure of the "sprouts" to develop into full-blown capitalism.

54. Kuhn, *Chinese Among Others*, 43–52; Wang, "Sojourning," 1–14; McKeown, *Chinese Migrant Networks and Cultural Change*; Tagliacozzo and Chang, eds., *Chinese Circulations*. For a longue *durée* study of Chinese migrations, see Lary, *Chinese Migrations*. For a comprehensive overview of the migratory experience of overseas Chinese diaspora in the last millennium, see Wang, *The Chinese Overseas*. For the history of Chinese migration to the Americas, also see McKeown, *Melancholy Order*; Lee, *The Making of Asian America*.

55. The two phenomena were not unrelated, as the population increase created huge pressure on the limited arable lands and delicate environment of heartland China, which had already suffered from excessive deforestation and soil erosion that in turn caused frequent natural disasters. For discussions on the population growth and movement, see Rowe, *China's Last Empire*, 91–96.

56. For a long-term view of the history of globalization, see Frank and Gills, "The Five Thousand Year World System," 1–79; Frank and Gills, eds., *The World System*. Also see Flynn and Giráldez, "Born with a 'Silver Spoon'," 201; Flynn and Giráldez, "Cycles of Silver," 4.

57. For a brief survey of Mongolian language archives, see Jin Hai, "Menggu jindai lishi dang'an ziliao shulue," 97–99.

58. Bailadugeqi et al., *Menggu mingzu tongshi*; Taiyichiwuti Manchang, *Menggu zu tongshi*; Cao Yongnian, ed., *Nei Menggu tongshi*.

59. Some of these works shed light on the Qing institutions, frontier policy, and legal system in the Mongol borderlands. See Zhao Yuntian, *Qingdai menggu zhenjiao zhidu*; Zhang Yongjiang, *Qingdai fanbu yanjiu*; Du Jiaji, *Qingchao manmeng lianyin yanjiu*; Wulijitaogetao, *Qing zhi minguo shiqi menggu fazhi yanjiu*. Others elucidate the process of Qing territorialization through mapmaking and military institutions such as postal relay system and frontier guard post system. See Sun Zhe, *Kang yong qian shiqi yutu huizhi*; Liu Wenpeng, *Qingdai yichuan*; Baoyinchaoketu, *Qingdai beibu bianjiang kalun yanjiu*. Qi Meiqin and others' research on customs houses and border markets illuminate the changing role of commerce and trade in the Qing dynasty. See Qi Meiqin, *Qingdai queguan zhidu yanjiu*; Qi Meiqin, "Lun qingdai changcheng biankou maoyi," 73–86; Wu Meifeng, "*Qingdai de shahukou shuiguan*," 13–18. Other studies focus on Chinese migration and its social and ecological impact upon the Mongol borderlands. See Yan Tianling, *Hanzu yimin yu jindai Nei Menggu shehui bianqian yanjiu*; Zhang Shiming and Gong Shengquan, "Linglei shehui kongjian"; Wang Weidong, *Ronghui yu jiangou*; Liu Zhonghe, *Zou xikou lishi yanjiu*; Xiao Ruiling et al., *Mingqing Neimenggu xibu diqu kaifa*.

60. Hasibagen, *E'erduosi nongmu jiaocuo quyu yanjiu (1697–1945)*; Wurenqiqige, *18–20 shiji chu guihuacheng tumote caizheng yanjiu*; Zhusa, *18–20 shiji chu dongbu neimenggu nonggeng cunluohua yanjiu*; Wuyungerile, *Shiba zhi ershi shiji chu neimenggu chengzhen yanjiu*; Borjigin, *Kingendai ni okeru mongoru jin nōkō sonraku shakai no keisei*.

61. See Anzai, "Shinmatsu ni okeru suien no kaikon"; Anzai, "Mōkyō ni okeru tochi bunkatsu shoyūsei no ichi ruikei,"31–98; Gotō, "Kusachi ni okeru shina shōnin," 96–126; Isobe, "Katō to ōdōshun"; Kikuchi, "Orudosu kanjin shokuminshi."

62. Tetsuyama, "Uchi mōko no kindaika to chishō keizai"; Tetsuyama, *Shindai nōgyō keizaishi kenkyū*; Borjigin, *Kingendai ni okeru mongoru jin nōkō sonraku shakai no keisei*; Hirokawa, *Mōchi bujo*.

1

A Changing Frontier

Inner Mongolia in Context

For most Chinese living in the twenty-first century, Inner Mongolia (Mo: *Öbör Monggol* or *Dotood Monggol*, Ch: *Nei Menggu* 內蒙古) is more a political and geographical concept than an ethnic and cultural one. The Inner Mongolia Autonomous Region or IMAR (Nei Menggu Zizhiqu 內蒙古自治區) occupies the central part of North China: bordering Mongolia and Russia to the north and the provinces of Heilongjiang, Jilin, Liaoning, Hebei, Shanxi, Shaanxi, Ningxia, and Gansu to the east and south. It is distinct from Outer Mongolia (Mo: *Ar Monggol* or *Gadaad Monggol*, Ch: *Wai Menggu* 外蒙古), which was equivalent to the modern state of Mongolia plus the Republic of Tuva in Russia. With an area of 1,183,000 square kilometers (455,000 square miles), the IMAR is the third largest province in China, comprising 12.3 percent of the country's total area. The total population is 24.7 million, among which 80 percent are Han Chinese.[1] The capital city is Hohhot, which is situated in the south-central part of the region.

Compared to the relatively peaceful northern borders, the southern borders of the IMAR adjoining the Chinese provinces are more volatile. Throughout history, what is now central and western Inner Mongolia had been a contact zone that alternated in control between agrarian Chinese in the south and various nomadic groups of the north. The Great Wall, first built in the seventh century BCE, was a series of fortifications meant to protect the Chinese states against raids from the steppe. Stretching for over six thousand kilometers (thirty-seven hundred miles) from east to west, it delineated the physical and symbolic boundary between steppe and sown land for centuries. Today, large sections of the originally Mongol territories north of the Great Wall have been incorporated into Hebei, Shanxi, Shaanxi, Ningxia, and Gansu provinces, all of which share borders with the IMAR. The northward advance of Han-Mongol boundaries unequivocally testifies to the increasing integration of this borderland under Chinese control.[2]

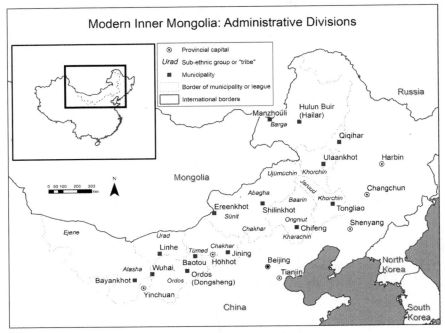

Map 1.1.   Modern Inner Mongolia: Administrative Divisions

Another indicator of change can be found in the demographics. Most of Inner Mongolia is located west of the Aihun-Tengchong Line (a.k.a. Hu Line), which is an imaginary diagonal line drawn by Chinese demographer Hu Huanyong in 1935 dividing China into two roughly equal parts, but with a striking difference in population distribution. The territory east of the line is densely populated, with 94 percent of the population (mostly Han Chinese) occupying 43 percent of the area. In contrast, the vast territory west of the line is inhabited mainly by non-Han people and comprises 57 percent of China's area but only 6 percent of its population.[3] Besides demographic differences, the Aihun-Tengchong Line also represents significant geographical, economic, and social disparities that help explain the flow of people, capital, and goods from east to west.

Table 1.1 shows the population growth in Inner Mongolia from the late sixteenth through the early twenty-first century. Han Chinese began to settle at the court of Altan Khan (1507–1582) of the Tümed Mongols during the late Ming period and numbered between five hundred thousand and one million. These Chinese were prisoners of war and religious, economic, and military refugees who served as craftsmen, spies, and counselors, and they built Höhhot and palaces and temples of Altan Khan. Many of them settled as farmers and founded villages called *baishing* (Ch: *bansheng* 板升).[4] There is also evidence of Han Chinese living among the Kharachin

Table 1.1. **Population Growth of Inner Mongolia, 1570–2010**

Period	Mongols	Han Chinese	Total
Late 1500s	1,090,000	705,000	1,795,000
Early 1800s	1,030,000	1,000,000	2,150,000
1912	877,946	1,550,948	2,403,179
1937	864,429	3,719,113	4,630,576
1947	831,877	4,696,000	5,617,000
2010	4,226,093	19,650,687	24,706,321

Sources: Song Naigong, *Zhongguo renkou nei menggu fence*, 46–63; Nei Menggu zizhiqu tongjiju, *Nei menggu zizhiqu 2010 nian diliu ci quanguo renkou pucha zhuyao shuju gongbao*, 2011. http://www.stats .gov.cn/tjsj/tjgb/rkpcgb/dfrkpcgb/201202/t20120228_30397.html.

Mongols in eastern Inner Mongolia, and indications of the Kharachin Mongols practicing agriculture and living in Chinese-style houses as early as in the sixteenth century.[5] The Chinese population in the grasslands continued to grow from one million in the early 1800s to 1.55 million in 1912.[6] In contrast, the Mongol population dropped from over one million in the early 1800s to 830,000 just a century later.[7] Existing historiography in both China and Mongolia have attributed this decline to the practice of sending male children to Buddhist monasteries, which absorbed over one-third of the male population.[8] However, the great majority of the monks were "steppe lamas" or novices who were married and lived as herders outside the monastery, and only went to the monastery when rituals were performed.[9] Hence, historical accounts that point to Buddhist monasticism as being largely responsible for the decline of the Mongol population should be revised. In this chapter, we will show that the population decline caused by the interplay of a set of political, social, and cultural practices during the Qing period led to economic degeneration and the siphoning off of Mongolian wealth.

The population disparity between the Mongols and Chinese was drastically amplified over the course of the twentieth century owing to the official reclamation policies implemented in the periods of the late Qing, Republic of China, and People's Republic of China (PRC). By 1947, when the IMAR was founded, the Chinese in the region had reached 4.7 million and outnumbered the Mongols six to one.[10] Large-scale migration and reclamation of Mongol lands persisted through the PRC period. By 2010, the Chinese population had surpassed 19.6 million, a fourfold growth from 1947. The impact of such a sharp increase of immigrant population upon the social and cultural landscape of the Mongol society and its fragile ecological environment cannot be overstressed.

TERMINOLOGY

The Chinese term *Menggu*, a transliteration from *Monggol* in Mongolian, can be used to indicate both the people and the state. Thus, the term is imbued with an ambiguity not found in English, in which the semantic signification of the people and the state is clearly differentiated: a "Mongol" is defined as (1) a member of any of the traditionally nomadic peoples of Mongolia and (2) a native or inhabitant of Mongolia, whereas "Mongolia" is described as (1) an ancient region of east-central Asia comprising modern-day Inner Mongolia and the country of Mongolia and (2) formerly Outer Mongolia, a country of north-central Asia between Russia and China.[11] These definitions tend to prioritize the territory over the people, despite every historical trace that suggests the opposite. In fact, there had never been a unified "Mongolia" with fixed and commonly recognized boundaries until modern times. Outer Mongolia proclaimed independence from the Qing dynasty in 1911, and the Mongolian People's Republic (now the Republic of Mongolia) was established in 1924. Today, there are more Mongols living beyond the borders of Mongolia than within them, including in Inner Mongolia, Qinghai, and Xinjiang of China and in the Republics of Buryatia and Kalmykia of Russia.

Despite its geographical associations, the notion *Menggu* was foremost an ethnopolitical reference denoting the nomadic people inhabiting the Central Eurasia plateau since no later than the eighth century.[12] The term became an umbrella name for many Mongolian-speaking "tribes" (Mo: *aimag*, Ch: *bu* 部) united under the rule of Chinggis Khan (1162–1227) during the thirteenth century. Whereas historians traditionally characterize the Mongolian society as kinship-based "tribes" or "tribal confederacies," recent scholarship shows that the Mongols were organized not as patrilineal clans or lineages, but rather as political-territorial units that Christopher Atwood calls "appanage communities," which were based on a system of aristocracy dominating commoner subjects.[13] After the disintegration of the empire, the Mongols were split up into *tümens* ("ten thousand households") and *otogs* ("places") that functioned as basic administrative units, each ruled by a single nobleman. Such units became the locus of unity and personal loyalty, as members shared affiliation to a hereditary noble and common ownership of pasture and natural resources despite their lack of kinship ties. Today, many ethnic Mongols continue to refer to themselves by their aimag or tribal names, unlike the Han Chinese who customarily associate with their native place.

Indeed, the term *Menggu* did not acquire its geographical connotations until the late nineteenth century. At that time, Western explorers launched a series of geographical and scientific expeditions, which were intended to construct scientific and systematic knowledge about distant places through accurate observation and description.[14] By means of the production of topographical and cartographical knowledge, the physical landscape of the region was represented as Mongolia with a new objectivity that had been absent in the indigenous discourse. It gave rise to a new epistemology that sought to define a people by the territorially demarcated geographical and political space, and by doing so, it put both the people and territory under state control. Therefore, it can be said that *Menggu* in the sense of a geographically based "Mongolia" was a European concept rather than a Chinese or Mongolian one. In this sense, the priority placed on the territory/state over the people resulted from a sleight of hand as manifested by the nation-state system that focuses on the centralized, sovereign, territorial state as the central actor of world politics.

The shifting connotations of *Nei Menggu* from an ethnic marker to a geographical concept indicated the processes by which the Mongols were redefined, reorganized, eventually displaced, and marginalized, as they were incorporated into the framework of the territorial empire followed by the nation-state. There are at least three moments of rupture associated with such a transformation. To begin with, the subjugated Mongols were organized into a set of territorial-based subdivisions called banners and leagues, which were each attached to a given territory with fixed boundaries, and the crossing of borders by banner subjects was strictly forbidden. It thus added a fixed territorial dimension to the nomadic traditions of the Mongols, as each aimag was divided into a group of fiefdoms ruled by hereditary Mongol princes (*jasag noyan*), with boundaries demarcated between them. Second, the influx of Chinese migrants helped establish a centralized state apparatus in decentralized Mongol territories, which was instrumental in legitimizing Chinese migration in Mongolia and displacing the personal jurisdiction of Mongol aristocracy with the territorial jurisdiction of Chinese bureaucratic units. It paved the way for the eventual integration of Inner Mongolia into the Chinese polity and along with it the alienation of the indigenous Mongols from their native land. Finally, such alienation became aggravated during the PRC period, when the term *Nei Menggu* had shed its original tribal connotations and become associated with geographical or political indicators such as "region" or "autonomous region." Similarly, the term *Menggu* lost its self-sufficiency as a tribal reference and became affiliated with such ethnic qualifiers as *minzu* 民族 (nationality) or simply *zu* 族 in conformity to their status as one of the twenty-six officially recognized minority ethnic groups of China. These semantic changes were accompanied by large-scale Chinese migration and state-organized colonization of the steppe and resulted in the uprooting and marginalization of the Mongols in the national quest for modernization and industrialization. Therefore, unstable connotations and the appropriation of the nomenclature reflect the changing politics of representation associated with both the people and the land.

Apart from these semantic alterations that reflected the changing politics of representation, it is also important to be aware of the Sino-centric perspective embedded in the terminology of Inner/Outer Mongolia. Geographically, the pair roughly corresponded to the Ming notions of *Monan Menggu* 漠南蒙古 and *Mobei Menggu* 漠北蒙古, as demarcated by the geographical location of these territories to the south or north of the Gobi Desert.[15] Derived from the Manchu terms "*dorgi/tulergi Monggo*," the distinction of *Nei Menggu* (*Dotood Monggol*) versus *Wai Menggu* (*Gadaad Monggol*) indicates both the geographical-administrative demarcation of the Mongols and their varied political affiliations with the Qing court. *Nei Menggu* is the abbreviation of *Nei zhasake Menggu* 內扎薩克蒙古 (Mo: *Dotood Jasag Monggol*), which referred to the twenty-four aimags that allied with the Manchus between 1621 and 1664 in the Qing conquest of China and the suppression of major revolts. *Wai Menggu* is abbreviated from *Wai zhasake Menggu* 外扎薩克

Map 1.2.   Qing Empire, c. 1820

蒙古 (Mo: *Gadaad Jasag Monggol*), which denotes the Khalkha and Oirat aimags of western Mongolia, Qinghai, and Xinjiang that were subjugated after 1689. The modern usage of Wai Menggu, however, indicates the four Khalkha aimags, the Khobdo region, and the Manchu-ruled Tannu Uriankhai (present Republic of Tuva in Russia) that became independent in 1911.[16]

Due to the political embeddedness of the "Inner/Outer" division, the terms are often replaced by "Southern/Northern Mongolia" (Mo: *Öbör/Ar Monggol*, Ch: *Nan/Bei Menggu* 南/北蒙古) in the contemporary setting, which implies the unity and self-sufficiency of Mongolia as a geo-body and spatial entity detached from Manchu or Chinese control. In Mongolian, *öbör* means "south," "inner," "front," or "bosom" in contrast to *ar* that denotes "north," "outer," "rear," or "back."[17] This study utilizes the conventional term of Inner Mongolia for convenience sake, while being fully conscious of its implication of cultural and linguistic hegemony.

NOMADS OF THE STEPPE

At the foot of Yin Shan	敕勒川
Lies the Chi Le Plain	陰山下
The sky is like a great yurt	天似穹廬
Covering the steppe in all bounds	籠蓋四野
Blue is the sky	天蒼蒼
Vast is the wilderness	野茫茫
Where the wind bends the grass	風吹草低
The cattle and sheep show[18]	見牛羊

The beloved "Song of Chi Le" (*Chile ge* 敕勒歌), a folk song of the ancient nomadic Xianbei people, depicts vividly the vast, open landscape and rich pastures on the steppe. It is one of the most celebrated imageries of the Mongolian steppe, as the endlessly stretching horizon of extensive grassland is typical of the Chinese imagery of Mongolia even today. However, rather than a broad expanse of continuously unchanging terrain as depicted in the popular view, the area known as Inner Mongolia is marked with topographical diversity. Situated on the southern edge of the Mongolia Plateau, with an elevation of over one thousand meters (3,280 feet) above sea level, Inner Mongolia forms a long belt aligned east to west. The backbone of the area is the Yin Mountain system that stretches from the densely wooded slopes of the Khingan (Xing'an) Mountains in northeast China to the dry desert at the foot of the Mt. Altai in Xinjiang. The eastern portion is formed by watersheds of the Amur River (Heilong Jiang) and Liao River, both of which originate in the Khingan Mountains. The northwestern portion constitutes part of the Gobi desert, an expansive arid zone stretching from Mongolia to the Taklamakan in Xinjiang. Much of the central region is dominated by rolling grasslands and steppes, bounded by rugged mountains and intersected by river valleys.[19] The Yellow River flows through the south-central region, making a great loop that delimits the Ordos region and provides irrigation for the area.

Travelers to Mongolia in the nineteenth and early twentieth centuries often complained about the monotony of the landscape and the severity of the weather. It is a dry, arid area with a typical continental climate that is cut off from monsoon circulations. It has a long and cold winter, and a summer with intense heat and little precipitation. The spring and autumn seasons are short. Throughout the year, it has a predominant and severe northwest wind, which is strongest in the spring. In general, the coldness and the meager rainfall determine that the main vegetation of this area is grass, making it a natural ranching land for a range of livestock. In adjusting to the natural restrictions of this country, its inhabitants became nomadic shepherds who wandered with their flocks in search of pasturage. Agriculture is carried out in the river valleys and the alluvial plain along the Yellow River, where irrigation is possible.[20]

The area now called Inner Mongolia has been the cradle of many nomadic peoples belonging to three large Central Asiatic ethnic groups: the Tungus, Turks, and Mongols. Archaeologists have discovered a number of Paleolithic and Neolithic sites in various parts of Inner Mongolia, indicating that human activity in this region can be traced back to as far as seventy thousand years ago.[21] During the Bronze and Iron Ages from two thousand BCE to the third century BCE, the inhabitants had formed primitive agricultural communities in the fertile river basins, established tribal alliances, and came in contact with early China.[22] Chinese chronicles show that ancient nomads interacted with the Chinese from the Xia and Shang dynasties (c. 1550–c. 1030 BCE) onward, who were categorized under the Rong or Di. These "old barbarians" fought in small groups on foot and should be distinguished from the horse-riding "new barbarians" that began to appear after the fourth century BCE (generally referred to as the Hu).[23] The invention of cavalry gave the mounted nomads a distinctive advantage of mobility over the settled communities. It eventually resulted in the predominance of nomadic pastoralism in the Eurasian steppe replacing the mixed hunter-gatherer and agricultural economy.[24]

Among these, the Xiongnu people, who inhabited the Central Eurasian steppe between the third century BCE and the fifth century CE, had frequent interaction with the Qin (221–207 BCE) and Han (206 BCE–220 CE) dynasties in the south. As the first unified empire across the Eurasian steppe, the Xiongnu empire served as a prototype for many to follow, including the Turk, Uighur, and Mongol empires. The Han dynasty historian Sima Qian (145–90 BCE) depicts the Xiongnu as a pastoral nomadic people who "move about in search of water and pasture and have no walled cities or fixed dwellings, nor do they engage in any kind of agriculture." They "herd their flocks in times of peace and make a living by hunting, but in times of crisis they take up arms and go off on plundering and marauding expeditions."[25] This mobile life distinguished them from the sedentary, agrarian Chinese who lived in fixed dwellings in walled cities. For this reason, they were often referred to as a "moving state on horseback" (*mashang xingguo* 馬上行國).[26] Nonetheless, archaeological evidence shows that "Xiongnu" does not denote an ethnic or racial category, but rather a political community that comprised diverse ethnolinguistic groups and economic circumstances. The extensive empire established by the Xiongnu stretched from western Manchuria to the Pamirs and covered much of present Siberia and Mongolia, and it was the first of its kind on the Eurasian steppe to encompass vast territories and diverse regions. Its relationship with the Chinese dynasties, one that alternated between military conflict and more peaceful exchanges of tribute, trade, and marriage treaties, was viewed as the archetype of the interaction between steppe and sown that dominated the Chinese history for two millennia. The Great Wall system, first built along the northern borders of the Chinese states to ward off the invading Xiongnu, stood as a demarcation of two distinct territorial and cultural spaces, however penetrable they might have been.[27]

Historians have provided a number of reasons for the long and troubling history of interaction between China and pastoral nomads. Traditional Chinese historiography, drawing from the moral and cultural perceptions centering on the *hua/yi* or cultured/barbarian distinction, attribute the aggression of nomads to their greedy and predatory nature. As Sima Qian remarks, "Their only concern is self-advantage, and they know nothing of propriety or righteousness."[28] Modern historical and anthropological studies demonstrate that the boundary separating the two was primarily an economic and political one. The mobile lifestyle of the nomads turned out most sustainable and adaptive to the fragile ecology of the steppes, whereas the limitation of extensive pastoral economy made them dependent upon their sedentary neighbors for the supply of necessities such as grain, cloth, and metal. In explaining the motivation for nomadic invasions, some historians attribute it to ecological factors such as climatic desiccation and population increase that affected the patterns of life on the steppe, whereas others point to trade imbalances with neighboring sedentary societies from whom the nomads obtained essential commodities.[29]

Sechin Jagchid presents the "trade or raid" thesis arguing that trade was the single determinant of peace or war along China's northern borders and war broke out only as a result of the failure of the existing mechanisms of tribute, bestowals, and intermarriage arrangements.[30] Anthropologists Anatoly Khazanov and Thomas Barfield share the notion of the economic dependence of pastoral nomads on sedentary societies while emphasizing the formation of nomadic state structures as a systematic means of extracting wealth from the settled Chinese.[31] This "dependency theory" is challenged by Nicola Di Cosmo, whose work reveals a more complex process of multifaceted interactions on China's northern frontier that transcends the "steppe versus sown" or "Chinese versus barbarian" dualism. Drawing from archaeological evidence, Di Cosmo shows that the Xiongnu empire possessed a substantial agrarian base and maintained a complex network of economic, political, and diplomatic relations with other populations of Inner Asia. Accordingly, areas conventionally considered purely "nomadic" were actually economically diverse regions. Di Cosmo further argues that the formation of the "supratribal" nomadic state involved both internal and external factors, and more specifically, a social response to a state of environmental or political crisis rather than rising out of the economic need to extract resources out of sedentary societies.[32]

Di Cosmo's research convincingly demonstrates the coexistence of multilayered ecological, territorial, political, and ideological boundaries in the nomad-China interaction and the role played by the historian in creating an ideologically loaded "master narrative" of polarity that overshadows fluid and multifaceted processes. This nonbipolar approach is shared by Wang Mingke, whose comparative work on the Xiongnu, Xiqiang, Xianbei, and Wuhuan during the Han dynasty aims at revealing the "historical reality" underneath the various historical events, political structures, human actions, and human choices that he refers to as "historical representations." In this sense, "trade and raid," just like "tribute or conquest," can be seen as expressions of political strategies utilized by nomads to expand their resources. Moreover, the very notion of China emerged out of the reciprocities in the long-term interactions with its nomadic neighbors.[33]

From the twelfth century on, the inhabitants of the steppes have been the Mongols, who unified several Mongol-Turkic groups under the leadership of Chinggis Khan (r. 1206–1227) and established the largest contiguous land empire in world history. Like the pastoral nomads that preceded them, the Mongols derived their strength and power from their ability to move fast, which conditioned their socio-organization and political structure. To ensure efficient mobilization across a vast space, the Mongols organized their scattered population around the decimal organization of tens, hundreds, thousands, and ten thousand households that functioned as the basic military and administrative unit. Such units were then integrated and consolidated into a "state" (*ulus*), which was an imperial polity organized under an elected supreme chief (*khan*). Grazing domains and subjects were distributed among these fief-like units, which were ruled by a class of nobility (*noyan*) whose rank was established on a hereditary basis. The highest ranked individuals were descendants or blood relatives (*altan-urugh*, "golden descendants") of Chinggis Khan.[34]

This feudal-like system of the Mongol Empire persisted through the Qing period, which centered on the fidelity between lord and vassal.[35] However, the empire brought together by the personal authority of the khan faced fragmentation at his death, as ensuing succession problems inevitably led to internecine competition and even civil war. After the fall of the Yuan dynasty and the retreat of the Mongols to the steppe, factional wars between the Chinggisid Eastern Mongols and the non-Chinggisid Oirats in the west led to many institutional changes on the steppe. Following his reunification of Mongolia, Dayan Khan (r. 1479–1517) reorganized the Mongols into six administrative domains called *tümen* ("ten thousand"): Chakhar, Uriyankhan, Khalkha, Tümed, Ordos, and Yöngshiyebü (Kharachin). These domains were then subdivided into petty realms called *otog* or *khoshuun* (banners), which were ruled by an individual lord.[36]

This new hierarchical administrative structure caused decentralization of the imperial rule. The six *tümens* faced competition from other Mongolian-speaking groups that remained relatively autonomous, including the Four Oirat confederation (Choros, Dörbed, Torghut, Khoshut), the Khorchins ruled by descendants of Chinggis' brother Khasar in the northeast, and the Buryats in the far north. By the time of Lighden Khan (r. 1603–1634), the last Chinggisid Khan, the power of the Great Khan was significantly weakened. The Khorchin first formed alliances with the Manchus from 1612 to 1624, and the Eastern Mongols were subsequently incorporated into the Qing as Inner and Outer Mongolia in 1635 and 1691, respectively. The Buryats were formally annexed by Russia after 1689. Only the Oirats under the Zunghar confederation actively resisted the Qing until finally eliminated in 1758.[37]

With this deep historical context in mind, the rest of this chapter examines how the processes of Qing empire building and Chinese immigration ushered in determinant changes to the political and physical landscape of the steppe. This unprecedented Chinese migration into the Mongol periphery resulted from a complex interplay of internal and global changes in economic relations and political contexts that led to the decline of the Mongols' military power and nomadic economy. Three factors combined to reinforce the transformation that foreshadowed and paved the way for Chinese migration: (1) the political division of the Mongols, (2) the religious dominance of Tibetan Buddhism, and (3) the introduction of a dual administration system.

A SYSTEM OF DIVIDE AND RULE

By the early seventeenth century, the unity of the eastern Mongols maintained under Dayan Khan and his grandson Altan Khan had given way to tribal antagonisms and rivalries. The unpopular reign of Lighden Khan who attempted to consolidate power through centralization generated violent opposition from the other tümens. They formed a coalition with the Manchus in a set of campaigns against him. The Khorchins, Kharachins, and some of the Khalkhas were the first to declare allegiance to the Manchus and were incorporated into a separate banner hierarchy under Manchu command.[38] Following Ligden's defeat and subsequent death in 1634, his son Ejei Khan surrendered to the Manchus, thus ending the rule of the Borjigin clan in Mongolia. In April 1636, forty-nine nobility of the sixteen southern Mongol aimags held the Kurultai assembly in Mukden (present Shenyang, Liaoning province). They recognized Hong Taiji, khan of the Later Jin, as the Great Khan (Bogd Sechen Khan) of the Mongols and emperor of the Great Qing empire, and dedicated the imperial seal of the Yuan dynasty to him. The Güshi Khan of the Khoshut Oirats of the west who later established rule in Tibet nominally acknowledged their allegiance to the Qing in 1637, and the Khalkha of the north had maintained friendly relations with the Manchu court since 1638 through the tribute of "nine whites." The invasion of Tüshiyetü Khanate in 1688 by Galdan Boshughtu Khan, the leader of the Zunghar Oirats, forced the Khalkhas to seek help from and submit to the Qing at the Dolonnuur Assembly in 1691. The Zunghars remained recalcitrant until conquered by Qing troops in 1757.[39]

The Qing governed the Mongol dependencies indirectly through a special bureau called the Mongol Office (Mo: *Monggol jurghan*, Ch: *Menggu yamen* 蒙古衙門) staffed exclusively by Manchu and Mongol officials. Renamed Lifanyuan 理藩院 or "Ministry Ruling the Outer Provinces" (Ma: *tulergi golo-be dasara jurgan*, Mo: *Gadaad monggol-un törü-yi jasakhu yabudal-un yamun*) in 1638, its authorities included the supervision of ennoblement and court audiences of natives, tributes and gifts, border disputes, league conventions, military and justice, house registers and taxes, postal stations, trade, and religion. Later, the ministry's function was extended to managing various groups of Inner Asian peoples in Tibet, Qinghai, Xinjiang, and the southwest, and it became the central agency in charge of the administration of non-Han borderlands as well as the dynasty's relations with Russia.[40] A collection of precedents, laws, and ordinances of the Lifanyuan was promulgated in 1815 as the *Lifanyuan zeli*, which was based on the *Menggu lüli* (Mongol Statutes and Precedents) first promulgated in 1643, and served as the legal foundation of Qing governance over Mongolia.[41] The aim was to keep the Mongols as political allies and a military reserve for the Qing emperor and to mobilize their armed forces as the need arose.

After the submission of the southern Mongols in 1635, a new compartmentalized system of leagues and banners was implemented to organize them, which was based on the pre-existing *tümen* and *otog* divisions but with important new geopolitical reconfigurations. The southern Mongols were organized into a multitude of territorial-based subdivisions called "banners" (Mo: *khoshuu/khoshuun*, Ch: *qi* 旗),

which mixed characteristics of the Manchu banner system with the aristocratic traditions of the Mongols and functioned as the basic unit of local administration and military organization of Mongol society. Each banner was ruled by a hereditary prince (Mo: *jasag*, Ch: *zhasake* 扎薩克) in charge of his territory and subjects. Under the jasag was a hierarchy of banner officials and staff, including two senior administrators (Mo: *tusalagchi*, Ch: *xieli taiji* 協理台吉) from the noble lineage, and an adjutant (Mo: *jakirugchi janggi*, Ch: *guanqi zhangjing* 管旗章京) and two deputy adjutants (Mo: *meirenü janggi*, Ch: *meilin zhangjing* 梅林章京) staffed by commoners. Within each banner, the population was organized on the basis of a military system and divided into a number of sub-units called "arrows" (Mo: *sumu/sumun*, Ch: *zuo* 佐) originally designed to each consist of 150 adult men and their families. Their actual number varied from banner to banner. The banners were in turn grouped into conventional princely assemblies called "leagues" (Mo: *chuulghan*, Ch: *meng* 盟). The leagues were often named after the place where they held their triennial assemblies with representatives of the Lifanyuan, the highest agency overseeing the Mongol affairs. A league governor (Mo: *chuulghan darugha*, Ch: *mengzhang* 盟長) was appointed from among the banner jasags, whose authority included arbitrating disputes between banners and transmitting orders or decisions made by the central government, especially concerning military mobilization. The institution was designed to weaken the tribal organization and foster more centralized control.[42]

By 1670, the twenty-four aimags of southern Mongols were organized into forty-nine jasag banners and six Inner Jasag leagues, which were as follows:[43]

1. The Jerim League comprised four aimags and ten banners: Khorchin (six), Ghorlos (two), Dörbed (one), and Jalaid (one).
2. The Josotu League comprised two aimags and five banners: Kharachin (three) and Tümed (two).
3. The Juu Uda League comprised eight aimags and eleven banners: Aokhan (one), Naiman (one), Baarin (two), Jaruud (two), Aru Khorchin (one), Ongniut (two), Keshigten (one), and Khalkha (one).
4. The Shilinghol League comprised five aimags and ten banners: Üjümchin (two), Khauchit (two), Sünit (two), Abagha (two), and Abaghanar (two).
5. The Ulaanchab League comprised four aimags and six banners: Dörben Keüked (one), Muumingghan (one), Urad (three), and Khalkha (one).
6. The Yekhe Juu League comprised one aimag and seven banners: Ordos (seven).

Following the Dolonnuur Assembly in 1691, the Khalkhas were incorporated into the Qing and divided into fifty-seven banners (increased to eighty-six in 1765) that comprised four leagues: Jasagtu Khan, Sayin Noyan Khan, Tüshiyetü Khan, and Sechen Khan. By the mid-eighteenth century, the jasag system had been extended to the submitted or conquered Oirats in central Eurasia. These included the two banners of west Hetao (Alasha Khoshut and Ejene Torghut, which were created in 1697 and 1753, respectively), the twenty-nine Upper Mongol (*Deed monggol* a.k.a.

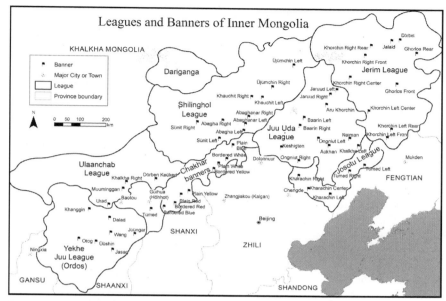

Map 1.3. Leagues and Banners of Inner Mongolia, c. 1900

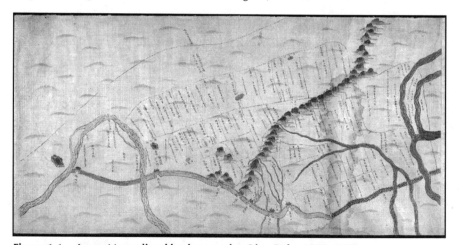

Figure 1.1. Inner Mongolian *khoshuus* under Qing Rule, 1689–1722.
Courtesy of the United States Library of Congress

Khökhe Nuur monggol) banners of Qinghai established in 1724, the nineteen banners of Khobdo in 1753, and the thirteen banners of the returned Torghut and Khoshut from Russia in Ili in 1771.[44] These administrative divisions, along with the Khalkhas, constituted the Outer Jasag. Both the Inner and Outer jasags were under the supervision of the Lifanyuan. After the 1730s, the Mongol banners were also subordinated to military governors (*jiangjun* 將軍) or imperial ambans (*banshi dachen* 辦事大臣) appointed to major regional centers of Mongolia, Qinghai, Xinjiang, and Tibet.

The territorial banner and league system was designed to coopt Mongol elites while undermining existing confederation ties and preventing the reemergence of strong nomadic power in the steppe. Elverskog points out that the Manchu integration of the Mongols was not just a process of political subjugation or military conquest, but also one of conceptual and political reconfiguration. He highlights the conceptual framework of the *ulus* ("community") and *törö* ("state") as central to the sociopolitical order in which the Mongols viewed themselves and the world, as well as a locus of communal identification and political legitimacy. By transforming the semiautonomous Mongol *ulus* into an inalienable part of the Qing state, the banner system served to redefine the Mongol boundaries of communal identification and subscribe them with the logic of empire.[45] It was a process of "deterritorialization and reterritorialization" of the pre-existing Mongol sociopolitical structure so as to fit it into the Manchu imperial project, just like the Qing itself was forced into a new global order by the Western imperialist powers two centuries later.[46]

This deterritorialization and reterritorialization were achieved through various political, cultural, and symbolic means. On the one hand, the Mongol aristocracy were bound to the Qing emperor by a vassal-overlord relationship, which was sustained through the bestowal of titles and ranks, intermarriage, and an institution of alternate-year attendance (*nianban* 年班) to the imperial court in Beijing. The granting of titles and ranks, or "ornamentalism" as Elverskog puts it, served as a key apparatus of the incorporation of Mongol local elites by recognizing their local authority while enlisting their loyalty to the Qing through the discourse of imperial grace.[47] The Mongol nobles were to attend the imperial audience in Beijing and pay tribute to the Qing emperor on a rotational basis. In return, they received honorary titles and ranks, rich stipends, and generous gifts. This system was designed to enhance the vertical connections between Mongol aristocracy and the imperial center.[48] The bonds were further strengthened through marriage alliances between the imperial family and Mongol nobles of the Khorchin, Khalkha, and Khoshut aimags.[49]

On the other hand, the political authority of the Mongol nobles was significantly weakened by the fragmentation caused by the banner system. The once powerful aimags were divided into multiple banners, each consisting of an inseparable unit of the jasag, the people, and their grazing areas. Virtually all jasags were of Chinggisid lineage, and their position was hereditary. The jasags enjoyed territorial autonomy and relative political independence in their domains, with administrative and judicial authority over matters such as banner administration, the collection of taxes, the adjudication of crimes, the regulation of trade, and military mobilization. A jasag was free to allocate pasturelands to his banner subjects (Mo: *albatu*, Ch: *qiding* 旗丁). To him alone, these subjects owed taxes, service obligations, and nontransferable loyalty. This system succeeded in isolating the banners from one another and preventing the development of greater supratribal power under one single leader.[50]

Even more important was the fact that the compartmentalization of realms greatly compromised the mobility that was the source of nomadic power. Unlike the old *otog* that was an administrative sub-unit of mobile people, banners were delineated by fixed boundaries. Neither the jasag nor his subjects were allowed to transgress their assigned boundaries unless authorized to do so by the imperial court. All lands and natural resources—pasture, water, forests, salt and soda lakes, etc.—were communally owned and freely accessed by members of the community. Often jealously guarded, these resources became the source of many intra-banner disputes that frequently required the arbitration of the Lifanyuan.[51] By assigning a rigid territorial identity to each banner, the Manchu ruler succeeded in transforming mobile Mongol aimags into petty fiefdoms with solid boundaries while exercising a tight control over each of them.

Apart from "Outer-vassal Mongolia" (Mo: *Gadaad Monggol*, Ma: *tulergi goloi monggo*, Ch: Waifan Menggu外藩蒙古) that was indirectly ruled by the Qing government, there were aimags classified under the category of "Internal Mongolia" or "Court Mongolia" (Mo: *Dotood Monggol*, Ch: *Neishu Menggu* 內屬蒙古) that were under the direct jurisdiction of the Qing government.[52] These aimags were deprived of their hereditary jasags owing to revolt against the Qing dynasty or to their relatively small sizes and lack of contribution to the dynasty. They were organized into a system of amban banners (Mo: *amban khoshuu*, Ch: *zongguan qi* 總管旗) under the administration of a Mongol or Manchu *amban* ("high official," Ch: *zongguan* 總管) who was dispatched by Beijing.[53] The lands of amban banners were subject to centralized deployment for garrison usages or military colonization, whereas their adult male members were responsible for fulfilling military conscription or corvée labor for the Qing government or imperial family whenever the need arose.

Despite their similar organization, both indirectly ruled jasag banners and directly ruled amban banners were inherently distinct from the Mongol Eight Banners (Mo: *Monggol naiman khoshuu*, Ch: *menggu baqi* 蒙古八旗). The former was a basic unit of local administration and military organization in Mongol society, inhabiting either the steppe homeland or designated grazing areas in Mongolia (in cases of the Chakhar and Barghu), whereas the latter was composed of hereditary military households subordinated to the Manchu Banners of the same color and garrisoned in Beijing and the provinces. These came from the old allies of the Manchus and enjoyed privileges of the Qing ruling elite including hereditary land allotments and promotion to high position within the military and civilian hierarchies via the civil service examination.[54]

Apart from secular banners, a total of seven autonomous "ecclesiastical banners" (Mo: *lamayin khoshuu*, Ch: *lama qi* 喇嘛旗) were set up throughout Mongolia. Each ecclesiastical banner was composed of large monasteries with over eight hundred lamas. In charge of these were officially recognized reincarnated lamas, who had administrative and judicial authorities over their domain and subjects just like their secular counterparts.[55] The compartmentalization of the Mongols into a multitude of mutually independent banners and temple areas exemplified the principle of "divide and rule" designed to maximize Qing control over them.

RELIGIOUS PATRONAGE

In addition to political division of the Mongols, the Qing also formed an intimate alliance with Tibetan Buddhism, the dominant religion in Tibet and Mongolia, in order to gain political and ideological control over the nomadic populations in these regions. Founded in the late fourteenth century by Tsong-kha-pa (1357–1419), the Gelugpa (dGe-lugs-pa, "Virtuous Way") or the Yellow Hat Sect highlighted monastic discipline, including the enforcement of celibacy, the wearing of yellow robes, and adherence to a rigorous routine, so as to distinguish it from the older Nyingmapa (rNying-ma-pa) or Red Hat sect. In 1578, Altan Khan of Tümed invited the head of Gelugpa, Sonam Gyatso, to Lake Kokonor and conferred on him the title of Dalai Lama, which marked the conversion of the Mongols to Tibetan Buddhism and the beginning of an alliance between the Mongols and Tibetan religious leaders.[56] After that, the Yellow Hat sect spread rapidly across Mongolia and became widely accepted by the elite and the masses alike. It wielded great influence on both the ecclesiastic and secular life of Mongolia. The highest rank in the Buddhist hierarchy was the reincarnating lama called *khubilghan* (*tülku* in Tibetan or *huofo* 活佛 in Chinese). The most important Mongolian incarnation was the Jebtsundamba Khutugtu of Urga, the supreme head of the Khalkhas.[57] The institution of reincarnation was instrumental in maintaining a consistent religious leadership and securing the alliance between monastic and political power, as shown in the centuries of intertwinement between the Chinggisid lineage and the line of Great Lamas and the mutual conferring of titles between representatives of ecclesiastical and secular authorities.[58] The ties between religion and politics were so close that the high lamas were considered equal to or higher in rank than the lay nobility, and together the two groups were referred to as the "twin pillars of feudalism" of Mongolian society.[59]

After the Qing consolidated power in China, the Manchus intended to emulate the Mongols' precedent by reproducing the lama-patron relations with the Tibetan religious leader while supplanting the Mongols as the new universal Buddhist ruler.[60] In 1651, the Shunzhi emperor invited the Fifth Dalai Lama, who was the leader of the Gelugpa Sect and a newly unified Tibet under the military support of Güshi Khan of Khoshut Mongols, to Beijing and offered his patronage and protection.[61] Meanwhile, the Zunghar leader Galdan Boshughtu Khan (1644–1697) had been a Yellow Hat lama in Tibet, and his close ties with the Fifth Dalai Lama was instrumental to his ascension to power in 1688.[62] The rivalries between the Qing and Zunghars for the Dalai Lama's political influence and spiritual authority over the Mongols eventually led to the prolonged Qing-Zunghar war, which ended in the establishment of Qing rule in Tibet in 1720, the consolidation of control in Amdo and Kham in 1724, and the conquest of Zungharia in 1757. In this sense, the patronage over Tibetan Buddhism can be seen as an integral part of the Qing imperial expansion in Inner and Central Asia.

The Qing court patronized Tibetan Buddhism by granting titles and privileges to high lamas, funding the construction of monasteries throughout Mongolia, and sponsoring the translation and circulation of Buddhist scriptures. Three imperial Gelugpa monasteries were erected by the order of the Kangxi and Yongzheng emperor and funded by the imperial treasury: Khökhe süme ("Blue monastery," built in 1712); Shira süme ("Yellow monastery," 1731) of Dolonnuur; and Amur-Bayasqulangtu keyid ("Monastery of blessed peace," 1736) of northern Khalkha. They were dedicated to the two great lamas, the Jangjiya and the Jebtsundamba Khutugtu, who were religious heads of Inner and Outer Mongolia, respectively.[63] The eighteenth and nineteenth centuries witnessed a boom in the number of monasteries and lamas. By the late nineteenth century, there were over twelve hundred monasteries in Inner Mongolia alone, many of which were built with imperial funds. Among the 243 incarnate lamas registered with the Lifanyuan, 157 resided in Inner Mongolia.[64] The Mongolian translation activities also flourished. Between 1650 and 1911, the Qing emperors sponsored translations of over 230 Buddhist works into Mongolian, including the 108-volume Buddhist canon, the Kanjur, and its multivolume commentaries, the Tenjur (Mo: Danjuur), which were printed in Beijing and distributed throughout Mongolia.[65]

The Qing codes granted the lamas legal, political, and economic privileges. The four main ranks of lamas were exempt from military and fiscal duties, and the upper lamas enjoyed many feudal privileges, as did their secular counterparts. In charge of the monastery-turned "ecclesiastical banners" were the reincarnated lamas, who had authority over administrative and judicial matters, house registers, and taxes concerning their domain and subjects, just like the lay jasags over his banner. The monasteries held property in the form of land and livestock, all of which was donated by the lay community, nobility, and commoners. They also owned serfs or lay disciples (Mo: *shabinar*, C: *miaoding* 廟丁), who were bestowed by the banner rulers and were personally bonded to the monasteries in the same way as the banner subjects were to their lords. These lay disciples were responsible for grazing herds for the lamas and running all sorts of errands in the temples. While the high clergy maintained an extravagant lifestyle, the economic burden fell upon ordinary banner subjects, who not only paid taxes and performed services for their lords, but also made contributions in the form of lavish gifts and sacrifices to cover the ritual expenses of the monasteries. With the temporal wealth they amassed, the monasteries soon gained formidable economic power in Mongolia in addition to their enormous religious and political influence.[66]

The diffusion of Tibetan Buddhism brought about decisive changes to the Mongolian society and economy. On the one hand, the spread of the religion greatly advanced the development of arts, medicine, astronomy, astrology, and education among the Mongols while producing a rich literature in both Mongolian and Tibetan. By the nineteenth century, the religion had penetrated deeply into Mongolian culture and functioned as the anchor point of Mongolian cultural identities, nobles and commoners alike. On the other hand, the creation of the monasteries as separate economic units brought profound impact upon the nomadic economy of the Mongols. The expansion of monasteries drained the wealth of the people, and

the privileged position of the lamas, especially the high clergy, caused the stratification of the society, which eventually led to the economic decline of the Mongol
society. Meanwhile, the existence of a large number of lamas as an institutionalized,
unproductive class curtailed both economic and human productivity. Virtually
every Mongol family would voluntarily send at least one son to the monasteries for
religious merits. By the late nineteenth century, from one-third to one-half of the
male population entered the monastic institution and became part of the consuming
class.[67] Whereas a great majority of lamas were novices who did not take the precepts
of celibacy, many of those who did take them lived lives of debauchery and became
one of the worst perpetrators of spreading syphilis across the countryside. This venereal disease was widely attributed to be a major factor for the low birth rates and high
child mortality rates in Mongolia.[68]

Further, the proliferation of monasteries facilitated urbanization and the expansion of Chinese traders across Mongolia. Almost all Mongolian cities grew on the
sites of monasteries. The construction work and creation of works of religious art
brought large numbers of Chinese artisans into the steppe, and the fixed structure
of monasteries provided not only a marketplace for mercantile activities, but also
a shelter for sojourning traders and a storage space for their goods. Over time, the
monasteries were developed into market towns populated by lamas, merchants,
and artisans, and they became centers of social life, economic activities, and cultural exchanges on the steppe. Moreover, as owners of extensive landed properties,
the monasteries also directly participated in financial activities, with the lamas
serving first as patrons of Chinese firms and later as partners and shareholders in
the firms.[69]

Meanwhile, the Qing court used Tibetan Buddhism as a form of social-political
control. The monasteries were under the supervision of the Lifanyuan, and legal
codes were applied to regulate their expansion. Each lama had to be registered with
the Lifanyuan and was prohibited from traveling without a passport. Like the lay
nobility, the high lamas were obliged to attend imperial audience in Beijing through
the *nianban* or annual rotation system and were divided into six rotas. Reincarnation
of Khutugtus among the Mongol nobility was discouraged in order to contain the
expansion of ecclesiastical power and prevent its alliance with the secular authority of
the lay nobility. Due to the expanding power of Jebtsundamba Khutugtu among the
Khalkha Mongols, the Qianlong emperor (r. 1736–1796) changed the rules so that
the incarnating Khutugtu was to be found only among the Tibetans and thus outside
the Chinggisid family and the Mongol nobility.[70] Further, two separate ecclesiastical
systems were maintained in Inner and Outer Mongolia. Each were placed under the
authority of one of the Khutugtus to avoid the emergence of a single unified Mongolian church. Between the two Khutugtus, the Jangjiya Khutugtu of Inner Mongolia
was supported largely by the Qing as a counterweight to contain the influence of the
Jebtsundamba Khutugtu.[71]

DUAL ADMINISTRATION

Following the Mongols' submission in the 1630s, it was the Qing policy to preserve the nomadic characteristics of the Mongol culture from Chinese influences so as to keep them as political allies and military reserves for the ruling Manchus. The Mongols and Chinese were physically segregated, as their territory was demarcated and intermarriage was strictly prohibited. Administratively, the Mongols were under the jurisdiction of the Lifanyuan, which held an equivalent rank to the Six Ministries that governed the eighteen provinces of China proper. Judicially, the legal code promulgated in Mongolia, *Menggu lüli*, was based on Mongolian customary laws and was distinct from *Da Qing lüli*, which was the code for China proper.

Throughout the seventeenth and eighteenth centuries, the Qing court issued a set of imperial edicts and regulations attempting to restrict Chinese migration to Manchu and Mongol territories, known as the "closing off" (*fengjin* 封禁) policy. The ban was reiterated in legal codes such as *Menggu lüli* and *Lifanyuan zeli*, which prohibited Chinese migrants from cultivating Mongol lands, deforesting them, or exploiting the mineral reserves of Mongol banners. It also prohibited the Mongols from accommodating or recruiting Chinese cultivators.[72] Those Chinese who had settled beyond the passes for trade or cultivation were forbidden to marry Mongolian women, bring their families, construct permanent buildings, adopt Mongol names, or register as members of Mongol banners. In addition, they were obliged to return to their native place after the fall harvest each year.[73]

Despite the official prohibition, Chinese peasants continued to travel outside the Great Wall due to several factors. First, the territorial expansion of the Qing led to an increasing demand for grain supplies on the steppe for the Manchu and Mongol bannermen troops and for grain reserves for the Mongol banners. Following the Qing conquest, the new dynasty established numerous "official" and "imperial estates" (*guanzhuang* 官莊, *huangzhuang* 皇莊) along the Great Wall, which Chinese farmers were recruited to cultivate. Many of these official farms were located in Jehol directly north of the Great Wall and in the Tümed area near Höhhot.[74] The demand for grains was intensified during the Qing military campaigns against the Zunghars with growing numbers of garrison troops, postal stations, and imperial functionaries stationed in Mongolia. Consequently, the court modified its policy to control the number of migrants through a licensing system by registering them and obliging them to return by the end of each year.[75]

Second, the relaxation of the ban was partly due to the necessity of coping with population pressure and ecological crises in north China. During frequent natural disasters of flood, drought, and famine, the Qing court decided to accommodate the northward movement of Chinese refugees into the Mongol territory as a means of relief.[76] In 1724, the Yongzheng emperor (r. 1723–1735) issued the decree of "Borrow Land to Feed People" (*jiedi yangmin* 借地養民), which permitted Chinese refugees to settle in the Josotu and Juu Uda leagues and exempted them from state taxes while allowing the Mongols to collect rent from Chinese tenant-farmers. This inconsistency of policy reflected the contradictory tasks facing the Manchu rulers: namely, to maintain the political and cultural integrity of the Mongols, and to cope with the challenges facing the expanding empire that demanded a more integrative allocation of resources.

Third, there had been a definite Mongol demand for the resources, labor, and income brought by Chinese immigrants. Cultivation by Chinese settlers was largely accommodated or even encouraged by the Mongol nobility. Apart from supplying the grain products and labor, they provided extra revenue in the form of rentals for the Mongol upper classes, whose growing taste for luxuries also made them dependent on the mortgage of land as a source of profit. In many ways, the financial interests of the Mongol nobility and clergy facilitated and accelerated the flows of Chinese immigrants. This explains why many legal codes and imperial decrees against illegal cultivation in the mid-eighteenth and early nineteenth century targeted the Mongol ruling classes and punishment was meted out in painstaking details in cases of violation.[77]

By the eighteenth century, there were sizable patches of cultivated land in the Mongol banners stretching from Jehol to Hohhot and ever advancing northward. The spread of Chinese migration had brought about the interpenetration of Chinese and Mongol cultures. Despite the Qing prohibition, many Chinese migrants married Mongol women and were added to the Mongol registers of the banners.[78] Meanwhile, the Mongols living in these regions also started to practice sedentary farming and shifted to a semi-pastoral and semi-agriculturalist lifestyle. In some areas, the influx of Chinese immigrants became so overwhelming that pasturelands greatly shrank, forcing the Mongols to give up animal husbandry altogether for full-time farming. The Kharachins of Jehol and the Tümeds of Höhhot were the first to settle down and adopt Chinese-style farming, and by the nineteenth century, most of them had lost their native language and become acculturated to the Chinese style of living.[79]

The influx of Chinese migration outside the passes and the rise of disputes and lawsuits involving migrants and locals posed a challenge to the Qing policy of separating the Mongols from the Han Chinese. Among others, the principle of personal jurisdiction under which the Mongol banners operated was distinct from the principle of territorial jurisdiction adopted in the Chinese provinces. While the Mongols were ruled by their hereditary jasag, his authority could not be extended to the Chinese migrants residing in his domain, as they retained household registration in their native province. The ever-expanding migrant communities across the Han-Mongol border regions thus called for a higher level of official intervention.

In his analysis of the administrative hierarchies of Chinese government, G. William Skinner divides their functions into four levels below the imperial capital. The highest level was the eighteen provinces (*sheng* 省), which were subdivided into seventy-seven circuits (*dao* 道). A circuit was a lower-tier division in charge of surveillance and military defense typically found in the fringes of the empire. The next level comprised three prefecture-level units: (1) prefectures (*fu* 府), (2) autonomous departments (*zhili zhou* 直隸州), and (3) autonomous sub-prefectures (*zhili ting* 直隸廳). The lowest level was counties (*xian* 縣), ordinary departments (*sanzhou* 散州, or *shuzhou* 屬州), and ordinary sub-prefectures (*santing* 散廳, or *shuting* 屬廳), which were subordinate to prefectures. The distinction between same-level units can be explained by their different locations, population densities, and political functions. Compared with more populous prefectures and counties that were found in regional centers, autonomous departments and sub-prefectures were usually located in the sparsely populated border regions. These were directly subordinate to the central government, provinces, or regional military governors, and maintained a degree of flexibility and autonomy. Whereas the key function of prefectures and counties was revenue collection, departments and sub-prefectures focused on security and defense.[80]

Skinner's model is pertinent in explaining the spatial layout of administrative hierarchies of the Chinese government. Yet, it does not address the temporal changes reflected by the altering status within the administrative hierarchy. Such alterations were particularly discernible in the newly incorporated non-Han border regions during the eighteenth century. As Masui Yasuki and others point out, the autonomous department and sub-prefecture system was institutionalized around 1770 and reflected the increasing incorporation of these peripheries in the wake of the *gaitu guiliu* 改土歸流 policy that replaced local chieftains with state-appointed officials in the southwest, followed by the military conquest of Xinjiang during the Qianlong (1736–1796) era.[81] Both were accompanied by large-scale Chinese migration and cultivation, either through state-sponsored military colonies (*tuntian* 屯田) or through ecologically driven migration that was encouraged or accommodated by the Qing government. The enhanced centralized control can be seen through not only the proliferation of bureaucratic units, but also through the vertical elevation of these units from autonomous sub-prefectures and departments to county or prefecture, which indicated both an increasing population density and expanding demands of revenue collection in these regions.

During the eighteenth century, the Chinese administrative system was extended beyond the Great Wall in order to manage the growing Chinese population living there.[82] Table 1.2 contains a list of centralized administrative units set up in Inner Mongolia. These units had reached fifty by 1911 and covered all the Inner Mongol leagues except Shilinghol. Among these, eighteen units were established before 1800, mostly in the amban banners of Jehol, Chakhar, and Tümed regions. A second wave of bureaucratic expansion came after 1902, when jasag banners of Manchuria and western Inner Mongolia were opened for Chinese colonization.

Table 1.2 shows that all twenty administrative divisions established outside the Great Wall prior to the early 1800s were sub-prefectures, including seven in Jehol, five in Chakhar, six in Tümed, and two in Manchuria. By 1778, all seven sub-prefectures of Jehol had been abolished and elevated to prefectures, departments, or counties, indicating full incorporation of the region into the administrative system of China proper. A second wave of Qing administrative expansion came during the Guangxu reign (1875–1908), following the lifting of the official ban against Chinese migration to Manchuria in 1860. Out of the thirty-one new units established,

Table 1.2. Centralized Administrative Divisions in Inner Mongolia, 1723–1908

Name	Unit	Year	Banner	League	Division	Province
Jehol	*santing*	1723	Kharachin R*	Josotu	Bachang *dao*	Zhili
(Chengde)	*zhou*	1733			Chengde *fu*	
	fu	1778				
Bagou	*ting*	1729	Kharachin R	Josotu	Bachang *dao*	
(Pingquan)	*zhou*	1778			Chengde *fu*	
Zhangjiakou	*ting*	1724	Chakhar RF	—	Koubei *dao*	
Dolonnuur	*ting*	1732	Chakhar LF	—	Koubei *dao*	
Dushikou	*ting*	1734	Chakhar LF	—	Koubei *dao*	
Siqi	*ting*	1736	Chakhar LF	—	Bachang *dao*	
(Fengning)	*xian*	1778			Chengde *fu*	
Tazigou	*ting*	1740	Kharachin L	Joşotu	Chengde *fu*	
(Jianchang)	*xian*	1778				
Khara Khota	*ting*	1742	Kharachin R	Josotu	Chengde *fu*	
(Luanping)	*xian*	1778				
Sanzuota	*ting*	1774	Tümed R	Josotu	Chengde *fu*	
(Chaoyang)	*xian*	1778				
	fu	1903				
Weichang	*santing*	1876	Kharachin R	Josotu	Chengde *fu*	
Fuxin	*xian*	1903	Tümed L	Josotu	Chengde *fu*	
Suidong	*xian*	1903	Khüriye Lama	Josotu	Chengde *fu*	
Ulaan Khada	*ting*	1773	Ongniut L, R	Juu Uda	Chengde *fu*	
(Chifeng)	*xian*	1778				
	zhou	1908				
Jianping	*xian*	1903	Aokhan	Juu Uda	Chengde *fu*	
Kailu	*xian*	1908	Aru Khorchin, Jaruud L, R	Juu Uda	Chengde *fu*	
Linxi	*xian*	1908	Baarin R	Juu Uda	Chengde *fu*	
Guihua	*ting*	1723	Tümed	—	Datong *fu*	Shanxi
	ting	1741			Guisui *dao*	
Suiyuan	*ting*	1739	Tümed	—	Guisui *dao*	
Sarachi	*ting*	1760	Tümed	—	Guisui *dao*	
Qingshuihe	*ting*	1760	Tümed	—	Guisui *dao*	
Khoringer	*ting*	1760	Tümed	—	Guisui *dao*	
Togtokhu	*ting*	1760	Tümed	—	Guisui *dao*	
Fengzhen	*santing*	1750	Chakhar RF PY,	—	Datong *fu*	
	ting	1884	RF PR		Guisui *dao*	
Ningyuan	*santing*	1750	Chakhar RF BR,	—	Shuoping *fu*	
	ting	1884	RF BB		Guisui *dao*	
Taolin	*ting*	1903	Chakhar RF BR, RF BB	—	Guisui *dao*	
Xinghe	*ting*	1903	Chakhar RF PY, RF PR	—	Guisui *dao*	
Wuchuan	*ting*	1903	Dörben Keüked, Muumingghan, Khalkha R	Ulaanchab	Guisui *dao*	

Table 1.2. *(continued)*

Name	Unit	Year	Banner	League	Division	Province
Wuyuan	*ting*	1903	Urad, Dalad, Khanggin	Ulaanchab & Yekhe Juu	Guisui *dao*	
Dongsheng	*ting*	1907	Wang, Jasag	Yekhe Juu	Guisui *dao*	
Changchun	*ting*	1800	Ghorlos F	Jerim	Changchun *fu*	Jilin
	fu	1889				
Nong'an	*xian*	1889	Ghorlos F	Jerim	Changchun *fu*	
Changling	*xian*	1908	Ghorlos F	Jerim	Changchun *fu*	
Dehui	*xian*	1910	Ghorlos F	Jerim	Changchun *fu*	
Changtu	*ting*	1806	Khorchin LR	Jerim	Changtu *fu*	Shengjing (Fengtian)
	fu	1877				
Fenghua	*xian*	1877	Khorchin LC	Jerim	Changtu *fu*	
Huaide	*xian*	1877	Khorchin LC	Jerim	Changtu *fu*	
Kangping	*xian*	1880	Khorchin LF, LC, LR	Jerim	Changtu *fu*	
Liaoyuan	*zhou*	1902	Khorchin LF, LC, LR	Jerim	Changtu *fu*	
Fakumen	*ting*	1906	Khorchin LF, LC, LR	Jerim	Changtu *fu*	
Zhangwu	*xian*	1903	Khorchin LF	Jerim	Xinmin *fu*	
Taonan	*fu*	1904	Khorchin RF	Jerim	Taonan *fu*	
Kaitong	*xian*	1904	Khorchin RF	Jerim	Taonan *fu*	
Jing'an	*xian*	1904	Khorchin RR	Jerim	Taonan *fu*	
Anguang	*xian*	1905	Khorchin RR	Jerim	Taonan *fu*	
Liquan	*xian*	1909	Khorchin RC	Jerim	Taonan *fu*	
Zhendong	*xian*	1910	Khorchin LR	Jerim	Taonan *fu*	
Dalai	*ting*	1904	Jalaid	Jerim	Heilongjiang *dao*	Heilongjiang
Zhaozhou	*ting*	1906	Ghorlos R	Jerim	Heilongjiang *dao*	
Anda	*ting*	1906	Ghorlos R, Dörbed	Jerim	Heilongjiang *dao*	
Hulun	*ting*	1908	Solon, Oirat, N Barghu, O Barghu	—	Hulun *dao*	
Lubin	*fu*	1908	Manzhouli	—	Hulun *dao*	
Total						**51**

Source: Yilinzhen et al, *Nei menggu lishi dili*; *Daqing yitongzhi*.
* R = right, L = left, RF = right flank, LF = left flank, PY = plain yellow, PR = plain red, BR = bordered red, BB = bordered blue, F = front, R = rear, RR = right rear, RF = right front, RC = right center, LR = left rear, LC = left center, LF = left front, N = new, O = old.

twenty-six were located in Mongol jasag banners, including eighteen in the Jerim league of western Manchuria, five in the Josotu and Juu Uda leagues north of Jehol, three in the Yekhe Juu and Ulaanchab leagues north and west of Höhhot, and only five in the directly ruled amban banners. Twenty of these units were created as counties, prefectures, and departments, in contrast to eleven autonomous sub-prefectures. The expansion shows that the advance of Chinese cultivation from the fringes to the heartland of the steppe had resulted in increasing integration of the Mongol frontier into the Chinese administrative system, and it also shows the changing focus of the government in these regions from security and defense to revenue collection.

The expansion of centralized bureaucracy marked the development of a dual administrative system in the Mongol territory, in which centralized prefectures and counties coexisted and competed with decentralized banners and leagues. The intrusion of territorial-based bureaucratic power, which began as an expedient way to manage Chinese migrants outside the passes, helped legitimize Chinese settlement in the steppe and set the stage for incorporating the Mongol periphery into the centralized bureaucracy of China. Meanwhile, the dual administrative system eroded the self-rule of Mongol banners and became the source of endless disputes involving the local and migrant communities. It caused ethnic conflicts such as the Jindandao Incident of 1891 and eventually contributed to the rise of Mongolian nationalism and movements for independence and autonomy among the Mongols in the twentieth century.

CULTIVATION IN CULTURAL CONTEXT

We have mentioned that although the majority of Mongol tribes maintained a nomadic lifestyle, agriculture had been well practiced in the river valleys and loam basins of the steppe since ancient times. For most parts of the steppe, however, the high altitude, extreme fluctuation of temperature, long winters, and low precipitation provided limited potential for agricultural development. Moreover, ecological limitations affected its inhabitants' cultural perceptions and beliefs, which shaped certain social practices and taboos regarding their physical environment. We can identify a number of cultural factors that shaped the different perceptions of cultivation between the Mongols and their Chinese neighbors.

To begin with, the Mongols viewed the land differently from the Han Chinese.[83] For the latter, the land was the source of wealth and the basic territorial unit of administration. This was because the agricultural civilization was based on intensive land use and population concentration, which determined the landlocked nature of Chinese culture. It further gave rise to a concept of bounded spatiality represented by walls and cities. In contrast, the Mongols lived a pastoral life based on an extensive economy and the seasonal change of pasture. For them, mobility was the very essence of nomadic power. The need to move their flocks regularly according to the availability of grassland resources gave rise to a concept of space that was expansive and boundless in character. The land was perceived mainly as the pasturage for livestock, and therefore only of secondary significance. Similar bifurcation also found expression in their distinct vocabulary used to signify cultivation, which implies different attitudes toward the utilization of land. The Chinese term for land reclamation is "opening up wasteland" (*kaihuang* 開荒), which associated untilled virgin land with the idea of unproductive land utilization. Untilled land was therefore representative of a primitive, uncivilized state of social development. In contrast, the Mongols referred to the same activity as "breaking/shattering the land" (*ghajir khagalakhu*), which carries a negative connotation.[84]

Second, traditional Mongolian society cultivated a deep cultural prejudice against the sedentary lifestyle of farmers and their intensive land use, which in many ways matched the Han distaste for "barbarians." Jagchid and Hyer mention the sense of privilege that the Mongols felt about their own lifestyle of herding and hunting on horseback, as compared to the farmers' toiling with the soil for a living.[85] This explains why even after agriculture was well established in Mongolia in the mid-Qing period, most Mongols tended to maintain their privilege as herdsmen and employ Han migrants to cultivate their land for them. Lattimore also reported the deep pride that the nomads held in being a "barbarian," which meant freedom from artificial lifestyle and excessive luxuries brought by settled life. He notes that the Mongol farmers who adopted agriculture were not men of wealth and success, but those who, after long years of garrison service or attendance to their princes, had lost touch with the pastoral life and become dependent on the settled life. It was thus viewed not as an upgrade in civilization, but rather as a "makeshift" or descent to the lower level of living of the Chinese.[86] In contrast to the distinction of *hua/yi* that was maintained by the orthodox Confucian political philosophy to uphold the moral supremacy of the Chinese, the Mongols adopted a completely different set of codes and criteria in affirming nomadic lifestyle as superior to its alternative. In the Mongolian vocabulary, the "hard" (*jakirag*) Mongols were contrasted with the "soft" (*buurai*) Chinese, in the sense that the physically virile and morally strong nomads living in the saddle and camps were infinitely superior to the physically and morally weak farmers who were dependent on the land or merchandise.[87]

Third, the reluctance to dig up the pastures may also be associated with the indigenous and shamanist beliefs among the peoples of northern Asia and the Ural-Altaic, which was characterized by pantheism and the worship of all natural phenomena.[88] According to this tradition, the entire earth (*gazar*) was animated by personifications of natural spirits and deceased ancestors. The cult of the earth was manifest in the veneration of the *Etügen Ekhe* ("Earth Mother"), which protected all and bestowed on all. It was one of the oldest cults among the Mongols and secondary only to that of the *Möngkhe Tengri* ("Eternal Heaven"). The worship also extended to mountains, rivers, and lakes, which were considered the dwelling places of local deities, and *oboos* or ceremonic rock piles or cairns were erected to pay homage to these local spirits.[89] After the introduction of the Tibetan Buddhism in the second half of the sixteenth century, these folk beliefs were incorporated and reinforced by the Buddhist belief that land should be preserved in its natural form. To cultivate the soil, therefore, harms the surface of the world and the "skin of the earth," which will anger the local deities and bring ill luck to the people.[90] Such indigenous beliefs and practices reflected the influence of the natural environment upon the cultural perceptive of the Mongols.

Despite the cultural prejudices and taboos against cultivation, agriculture had a long history among the nomads. As mentioned earlier, archaeological data show that agricultural activities existed in the river valleys of Manchuria and Mongolia since around 2000 BCE. Even after animal husbandry became predominant from the sixth century BCE onward, agriculture as an auxiliary economic form did not disappear from the steppe.[91] In 1594, Xiao Daheng observed in his work *Beilu fengsu*:

> The ways in which various tribes plough and sow are no different from the people of our frontiers. Their farming tools include oxen and plough, and seeds include wheat, millet, beans, and broomcorn millet. These all have a long history, rather than of recent origin. Only produces like gourd, squash, eggplant, mustard, green onion, and chives were introduced after they began to send tribute. While they do plough and sow, their farms depend on the heaven rather than manpower. They sow the seeds in the spring and harvest in the autumn. Instead of toiling laboriously to double the yield, they farm extensively and the harvest is meager. This is what we call "planting recklessly, and reckless is the return."[92]

Here, Xiao describes an extensive form of ley farming (Mo: *namug tariya*, Ch: *mansazi* 漫撒子) that has been practiced in Mongolia as a supplement to the nomadic economy. It involved no plowing, weeding, fertilizing, or irrigating of the land as Chinese farmers customarily did. The traditional crops included wheat, millet, beans, and broomcorn millet. The harvest depended solely on the weather, and the yield was usually small.[93] The Kangxi emperor (r. 1662–1722) commented on this form of Mongol cultivation, which he observed during his excursions to Mongolia: "The Mongols are by nature indolent. After sowing the seeds in the soil, they move their herds about and do not harvest the crops even though they ripen. When frosts hit and the ears of grain fall off, rather than reaping them, they call it a crop failure."[94] These remarks were made in a 1698 edict, as the emperor dispatched officials to the Aokhan and Naiman banners of the Juu Uda league to teach the Mongols farming techniques as a means of state disaster relief. The Qianlong emperor also depicted the Mongols' "fields depending on heaven" (*kao tian tian* 靠天田) in details in his poem "Wilderness Fields" (*Huang tian* 荒田), written in 1754 after his tour to Jehol, Khorchin, and Jilin:

Originally a land of riding archers and herders,	本是射生遊牧地
Now it also gradually began to value farmland.	即今漸亦重農田
Not knowing diligence of tilling and weeding,	耤耘未識各勤力
Fat or lean years, it is said, all relied on Heaven.	豐歉惟云總賴天
All summer they are out pursuing grass and water,	出逐草泉長夏裡
Up until autumn they return to pick up the sickles.	歸臨銍艾九秋前
Planting recklessly, and reckless is the return;	耕而鹵莽報鹵莽
It is indeed true now seeing farming on the steppe.[95]	塞稼觀餘始信然

Here, the characterization of Mongol "indolence" contrasted with Han "diligence" is striking. Like his grandfather, the Qianlong emperor also labeled the Mongols as "reckless" (*lumang* 鹵莽) cultivators, a word directly quoted from Xiao Daheng, and the Mongol fields as "wilderness" (*huang* 荒), a derogatory term used to refer to uncultivated land in orthodox Confucian discourse. In another poem "Mongol Fields" (*Menggu tian* 蒙古田), written in 1782, the emperor described the transition to Han-style intensive farming among the Mongols:

In the past as the Mongols tilled their fields,	蒙古昔種田
They sowed the seeds and then departed.	撒種委之去
Calling it "a harvest depending on Heaven,"	謂曰靠天收
In autumn they returned to reap the crops.	秋成返刈獲
Their departure was not without reason,	其去非無因
Some for hunting, others to attend their herds.	或獵或考牧
Now they do it in a different way;	而今則不然
All are used to affairs of tilling and weeding.	均習耘耨務
Measuring the days of rain and sunshine,	課雨與量晴
Their worries are no different from farmers.	不殊三農慮
Yet it means abandoning herding and hunting;	然實廢牧獵
This is indeed forgetting their own origin.[96]	斯亦忘其故

Here, the Qianlong emperor lamented the fact that many Mongols had taken up Chinese-style farming and abandoned their nomadic roots, which testified to the advance of what David Bello calls an "imperial arablism" in the Mongol borderlands during the second half of the eighteenth century. By arablism, Bello means not only agricultural activities, but also the embedded environmental relations between nature and culture that defined the ethnocultural identity of the inhabitants.[97] For the emperor, the influx of Chinese migration and the expansion of intensive agriculture had not only altered the pastoral landscape of Mongolia, but it had also threatened to alter the nomadic identity of the Mongols centering on herding and hunting.

The Mongols' *namug tariya* or extensive farming is often treated by Han Chinese as an inferior mimicry of Han-style farming that is "extremely simple and coarse" and "no different from wilderness."[98] Obviously, the contempt toward *namug tariya* stemmed from a Sino-centric prejudice derived from the hegemony of agricultural economy as well as an age-old disdain for non-Han peoples due to cultural differences and historical feuds. It further gathered momentum with the dominance of the Marxist discourse that considers human society as progressing through successive stages of development from hunting to pastoral, agricultural, and industrial economies. As farming is deemed a step higher than herding on the evolutional ladder, *namug tariya* is regarded a transitional form between pastoralism and full-fledged agriculture and is considered inferior, just like the herders who are depicted as "irrational," "immature," and "backward."[99]

To be sure, *namug tariya* was a hybrid form of farming that emerged in the pastoral-agricultural ecotone of Inner Mongolia. Yet it must be understood in the context of its supplementary nature to the pastoral economy, so that it did not hinder or handicap the herding that was the primary concern of the Mongols. Also, locations of farming had to be kept away from the best pasturage. There were no agricultural activities throughout the summer so as not to interfere with the grazing of livestock. Instead, they were limited to the spring and fall seasons.[100] Moreover, unlike the Han farmers who were tied to a money economy and produced cereals for market, *namug tariya* was meant to provide grain provisions for familial consumption. There was little demand to increase the output that necessarily involved more time and labor. In short, agriculture was considered little more than a subsidiary production of minor significance to the herders, which explained the meager resources invested in it.

To conclude, rather than a particular stage in a universal process of progressive evolution, *namug tariya* was a form of economic production shaped by the unique environmental relations and living experiences of the agro-pastoral ecotone. In this sense, the unprecedented influx of Han migration and the spread of Chinese-style farming, as a direct result of Qing policies to incorporate Inner Mongolia, not only brought grave consequences to the delicate ecology of the steppe such as land degradation, but also transformed the environmental relations of its inhabitants, which caused an abandonment of the nomadic lifestyle among the Kharachin and Tümed Mongols.

CONCLUSION

This chapter has chartered developments within Inner Mongolia across both time and space. It explored the geographical, social, political, religious, economic, and cultural contexts that laid the foundation for processes we will examine in detail throughout the rest of this book. A semiotic examination of the nomenclatures associated with the Mongols and Mongolia has shown the shifting connotation of the term *Menggu* from the ethnically defined "Mongol" to the territorially bounded "Mongolia." This was not a mere shift in local linguistic usage, but instead it reflects the impact of much broader global patterns that affect the region. It speaks to a new world system of nation-states centered upon distinct territories, as well as a new epistemology that sought to produce "objective" knowledge for the purposes of political control.

This chapter has focused on the set of structural changes brought to the steppe by Manchu supremacy, including the division of the Mongols into a multitude of territorially bounded banners and leagues, the spread of Tibetan Buddhism as the dominant religious and economic institution in the region, and the introduction of a dual system of administration that eroded the autonomy of the Mongols. These strategies succeeded in maintaining frontier security by keeping the Mongols as political subordinates and junior partners of the Manchu rulers while preventing the rise of powerful tribal confederations on the steppe. At the same time, the stringent containment of the Mongols and the privileges enjoyed by their upper classes resulted in the decline of nomadic society and made them vulnerable to external influences brought by an influx of migrants and a monetized economy. Eventually, these transformations paved the way for unprecedented Chinese migration and colonization in the nineteenth and twentieth centuries, which would completely alter the physical and social landscape of the steppe.

The chapter, then, provided an overview of long-term nomad-sedentary interactions and the evolving political systems of the Mongols that set the stage for the changing interrelations between Mongol nomads, Chinese migrants, and the Qing state from the eighteenth through twentieth centuries. Unlike traditional Chinese historiography, which centers on a culturalist paradigm of the *hua/yi* dichotomy, recent scholarship offers a more integrative paradigm of analysis that emphasizes the interplay of economic structure, political organization, and military power between China and the steppe, with a focus on the internal dynamic of the steppe's history. It is this integrative approach that I have taken here: highlighting the historical legacy of the Mongol empire in the constitution of the Manchu Qing dynasty and the PRC. It is impossible to consider China as the territorial and multicultural entity as we now know without recognizing how its inheritance from the Mongol empire produced important apparatuses, institutions, and legitimizing tools that would continue to be employed outside of the borderlands.

NOTES

1. Nei Menggu zizhiqu tongjiju, *Nei menggu zizhiqu 2010 nian diliuci quanguo renkou pucha*.

2. Hao Weimin, *Nei menggu zizhiqu shi*, 84–85, 132–35; Song Naigong, *Zhongguo renkou nei menggu fence*, 1.

3. Hu Huanyong, "Zhongguo renkou zhi fenbu," 43. For an updated exposition of the Hu-Line, see Hu Huanyong, "Zhongguo renkou de fenbu, quhua, he zhanwang," 139–45.

4. These Chinese built Höhhot and the palaces and temples of Altan Khan, and also patronized Tibetan Buddhist temples such as the Huayansi/Buzimiao. Altan Khan's first palace was called Yekhe Baishing (Ch: Da Bansheng 大板升, "the Great town/building"). See Serruys, "Chinese in Southern Mongolia during the Sixteenth Century," 26–66. Huang Li-Sheng studies the Chinese stone inscription that described the Chinese patronization of the Huayansi/Buzimiao. See Huang Li-Sheng, *You junshi zhenglue dao chengshi maoyi*, 308.

5. Wada, *Mingdai Menggu shi lunji*; Serruys, "Chinese in Southern Mongolia," 75–76.

6. Until 1878, the Qing policy had forbidden Han women from migrating outside the passes. As of 1912, the male:female ratio in Suiyuan was estimated to be 145.10:100. See Song Naigong, *Zhongguo renkou nei menggu fence*, 54. In addition, it was common for early Han migrants to become "Mongolized" by marrying Mongols and taking a Mongolian name, which partly explained the low growth rate of Han population before the twentieth century. See Serruys, "Chinese in Southern Mongolia," 75–76.

7. See Song Naigong, *Zhongguo renkou nei menggu fence*, 46–50. This estimation is likely right, as other figures show that by the mid-seventeenth century, the estimated Mongol population in Inner Mongolia (including Manchuria) was about 1,104,750. Due to lack of census

figures, the statistics were calculated on the basis of the number of units (*sumu* 蘇木) in each banner. A *sumu* was the basic military unit consisting of 150 able-bodied men, and therefore administrated 150 households, theoretically. A household was calculated on an average of five. See Huang Fenshen, *Mengzang xinzhi*, volume 1, 87; Jagchid and Hyer, *Mongolia's Culture and Society*, 320. Joseph Fletcher estimated the total Mongolian-speaking population in 1800 to be as high as 3,500,000, including 2,600,000 in Inner Mongolia. However, there seems to be little evidence to support this, as this would result in too abrupt a decline to a population of less than one million in just a century's time. See Fletcher, "Ch'ing Inner Asia c. 1800," 48.

8. Prevalent venereal diseases such as syphilis among the lamas and ordinary Mongols also contributed to the population decline. It is reported that by 1947, over three-fifths of the pastoral population in Inner Mongolia suffered from syphilis. See Li Narangoa, "Sōryo dōin to bukkyō kaikaku."

9. It is generally estimated that only one-third of the Mongol lama population observed the vow of celibacy. See Charleux, *Nomads on Pilgrimage*, 212. For information on these "steppe nomads," see Pozdneyev, *Religion and Ritual in Society*.

10. The Han figures included all those subject to regular county administration, including the Hui Muslims, whereas the Mongol figures include all those subject to banner administration. See Song Naigong, *Zhongguo renkou nei menggu fence*, 50–54. Nagata Shigeshi estimated the population of Suiyuan province to be 2,275,072 in 1932, of which the Han immigrants counted for 2,056,322. This accords with the previous figure as it excluded the population in Chakhar and Rehe provinces. See Nagata, *Mōkyō konshoku to taishi imin*, 43–44. Huang Fensheng gave a more conservative estimation of the Mongol population, which was 580,880 in 1936, based on the statistics of Jehol, Chakhar, and Suiyuan. He estimated the total Mongol population of all leagues, banners, and aimags to be 986,068, which included those living in the three northeastern provinces (Heilongjiang, Jilin, and Fengtian) and Ningxia. See Huang Fensheng, *Mengzang xinzhi*, 98–99.

11. See http://www.thefreedictionary.com/Mongol and http://www.thefreedictionary.com/Mongolia.

12. Early references to various Chinese renderings of *Mongghol* in Chinese records date back to the Tang (618–907) period, such as *Mengwu* 蒙兀 in *Jiutangshu* [Old Book of Tang], *Menggu* 萌古 in *Liaoshi* [History of Liao], and its variation 朦骨 in *Jinshi* [History of Jin]. See Yano, *Kinsei mōkoshi kenkyū*. Jagchid and Hyer also discuss various theories concerning the origin of the term "Mongol." See Jagchid and Hyer, *Mongolia's Culture and Society*, 6. Also see Han Rulin, "Menggu mingcheng," 151–52.

13. For a rebuttal of the tribal model of Mongolian society, see Sneath, *The Headless State*; Atwood, "Banner, *Otog*, Thousand," 1–76.

14. The pioneers in exploration of Mongolia were French and Russians. French Lazarist priests Evariste Régis Huc and Joseph Gabet made a memorable journey from Beijing to Lhasa in 1844–1846, and Armand David traveled to Mongolia in 1866 on a mission delegated by the Museum of Natural History in Paris. Geologist Nikolai M. Przhevalski made four major expeditions to Central Asia and led the way in mapping, measuring, and defining Mongolia in scientific terms. Anthropologist Alexei M. Pozdneyev traversed both Inner and Outer Mongolia in 1892–93. See Huc and Gabet, *Travels in Tartary, Thibet and China*; David, *Abbé David's Diary*; Prejevalsky, *Mongolia, the Tangut Country, and the Solitudes of Northern Tibet*; Pozdneyev, *Mongolia and the Mongols*.

15. As Zhang Yongjiang points out, *Monan Menggu* is primarily a geographical concept and differs from either modern "Inner Mongolia" or "Inner Jasag Mongols" of the Qing period. See Zhang Yongjiang, "Lun qingdai monan menggu qiqu de eryuan guanli tizhi," 29.

16. Borjigin, "The History and the Political Character of the Name of Nei Menggu," 60–66.

17. Uradyn Bulag discusses the connotations of "Inner/Outer" versus "Southern/Northern" and their relationship to the rise of nationalism in modern Mongolia. See Bulag, *Nationalism and Hybridity in Mongolia*, 179–80. For the political connotations of the names of Dotood/Gadaad Mongol versus Öbör/Ar Mongol, see Borjigin, "The History and the Political Character," 61, 74.

18. The lyric in its original tongue was lost and only the Chinese version, which dates to the Northern Qi period (550–577), has been preserved.

19. See Chang Yin-T'ang, *The Economic Development and Prospects of Inner Mongolia*, 3–5; Jagchid and Hyer, *Mongolia's Culture and Society*, 9–13.

20. Chang, *The Economic Development*, 12–16; Jagchid and Hyer, *Mongolia's Culture and Society*, 13.

21. These include the Sjara-osso-gol (Sharusunghol, Ch: Salawusu) Culture of southwestern Mongolia and the Shuidonggou Culture of Ningxia, both discovered in 1922, featuring the fossilized mammalian teeth and antlers of the Ordos/Hetao man, and the Dayao culture near Hohhot, discovered in the late 1970s. See Derevyanko and Lü, "Upper Paleolithic Cultures," 103–26. The fossil tooth of the Ordos/Hetao man was dated to at least thirty-five thousand years ago in the 1980s. However, recent studies show that it should be dated back to between seventy thousand and 140,000 years ago. See Shang Hong et al., "Guanyu salawusu yizhi diceng," 82–86.

22. Using archaeological evidences from the Xiajiadian site of the Chifeng region and the Zhukaigou site of the Ordos region, Di Cosmo argues for the coexistence of both agriculturalists and pastoralists in the early nomadic societies. See Di Cosmo, "Ancient Inner Asian Nomads," 1096–100; Di Cosmo, *Ancient China and Its Enemies*; Wang Mingke, *Youmuzhe de jueze*.

23. The "old barbarians" included Guifang 鬼方, Xunyu 獯鬻/葷粥/薰育, Xianyun 玁狁/獫狁, and Rong and Di, whose appearance in Chinese chronicles dates back to the Shang Dynasty. The "new barbarians" included Loufan 樓煩, Linhu 林胡, and Donghu 東胡, who were active during the Warring States Period (475–221 BCE). See Lattimore, *Inner Asian Frontiers of China*, 60–61; Barfield, *The Perilous Frontier*, 28–30.

24. For the rise of pastoral nomadism in the steppe, see Lattimore, *Inner Asian Frontiers*, 58–66; Barfield, *The Perilous Frontier*, 28–30. Wang Mingke's work provides an overview of the environmental, archaeological, and historical research related to the rise of pastoral nomadism in the steppe. See Wang Mingke, *Youmuzhe de jueze*, 69–78.

25. Sima Qian, *Shiji* 110, *Xiongnu liezhuan* 50, 2879. The translation is cited from Sima Qian, *Records of the Grand Historian of China*.

26. See Sima Qian, *Shiji* 123. This notion of "moving state" was also used to characterize the nomadic Mongols during the Qing period. The terminology that the Qing scholar Lin Qian used to describe the Mongols apparently resonated with that of Sima Qian: "The Tatar Mongols were the general name of a variety of nomadic groups. They have no cities and palaces; people live in yurts and wander about in search of water and grass. They were called the moving states." See Lin Qian, *Guodi yiming lu*, volume 1.

27. For more illustration of the role of Great Wall as the frontier zone, see Lattimore, "Origins of the Great Wall of China," 529–49. For a historical account on the making of the Great Wall, see Waldron, *The Great Wall of China*. More recently, Di Cosmo argued that wall-building efforts of the Chinese states, rather than defensive reaction against nomadic attacks, served as an offensive strategy of territorial expansion and reclamation of nomadic lands. See Di Cosmo, *Ancient China and Its Enemies*, 155–58, 186; Temule, "The Great Wall as Perilous Frontier for the Mongols in 16th Century," 121–56.

28. Sima Qian, *Shiji* 110, 2879.

29. For a survey of theories for explaining the nomadic invasions of sedentary societies, see Tao Jing-shen, "Bianjiang minzu zai zhongguo lishi shang de zhongyaoxing," 190–201; Hsiao Ch'i-ch'ing, "Beiya youmu minzu nanqin gezhong yuanyin de jiantao," 303–22. Di Cosmo groups these theories into two main categories—the "greedy" theory and the "needy" theory; see Di Cosmo (1994), 1092–93. For discussion on the steppe versus the sown paradigm, see Lane, *Daily Life in the Mongol Empire*, 25; Temule, "The Great Wall as Perilous Frontier," 121–23.

30. Jagchid and Symons, *Peace, War, and Trade Along the Great Wall.*

31. Khazanov, *Nomads and the Outside World*, xxxi–xxxii; Barfield, *The Perilous Frontier.*

32. For example, the establishment of the Xiongnu empire was a direct result of the crisis created by the Qin invasion of the Ordos, the nomadic homeland. See Di Cosmo, *Ancient China and Its Enemies*, 169–73, 186. For the role played by crisis in the formation of nomadic state, see Di Cosmo, "State Formation and Periodization in Inner Asian History," 14–16.

33. Wang Mingke, *Youmuzhe de jueze*, especially chapters 3–6. Wang adopts the reciprocity framework presented by cultural anthropologist Marshall Sahlins in interpreting the nomad-sedentary relations, by identifying three types of reciprocity in human exchange—generalized, balanced, and negative reciprocity. The tribute payments and gift pattern occurring in Chinese court can be considered as generalized reciprocity, trade at border markets as balanced reciprocity, and raids and military invasions as negative reciprocity. See Wang Mingke, *Youmuzhe de jueze*. For Sahlins's typology, see Sahlins, *Stone Age Economics*, 193–95. For the formation of Chinese identity and its distinction from the borderlands, also see Wang Mingke, *Huaxia bianyuan*, chapter 10.

34. Traditional scholarship on the social system of the Mongols describes a transition from pre-Chinggisid tribe-clan model of *obog* and *aimag* that was based on kinship into a supratribal state polity centered on the khan. See Vladimirtsov, *Menggu shehui zhidu shi*, 17, 47–48, 82–97, 100–11; Tayama, *Shin jidai ni okeru mōko no shakai seido*; Jagchid and Hyer, *Mongolia's Culture and Society*, 56, 245–96; Fletcher, "The Mongols," 16–24. However, Sneath and Atwood's recent work show that the Mongols were not a kinship society but one that was centered on aristocratic power over common subjects. See Sneath, *The Headless State*, especially chapter 2. Also see Atwood, "The Administrative Origins of Mongolia's 'Tribal' Vocabulary," 7–45.

35. Vladimirtsov is the first to describe the Mongolian social system as "nomadic feudalism." Tayama divides the two stages of "feudal state" (*hōken kokka*) from the thirteenth to mid-fourteenth century, and "feudal monarchy" (*hōken ōsei*) from mid-fourteenth to mid-seventeenth century. Jagchid, however, is cautious of both the European origin of "feudalism" and the distorted Marxist use of the term, and chooses to call it a "nomadic quasi-feudalism." See Jagchid and Hyer, *Mongolia's Culture and Society*, 263–64.

36. Vladimirtsov, *Menggu shehui zhidu shi*, 121–28, 144–48, 166–69; Tayama, *Shin jidai ni okeru mōko no shakai seido*, 22–63; Jagchid and Hyer, *Mongolia's Culture and Society*, 269–74.

37. For background on Mongolia in the early Qing, see Bawden, *A Modern History of Mongolia*; Fletcher, "Ch'ing Inner Asia c. 1800"; Zhao Yuntian, *Qingdai menggu zhangjiao zhidu*, 1–21; Chia, "The Li-fan Yüan in the Early Qing Dynasty"; Crossley, "Making Mongols," 58–82.

38. Beginning in the 1620s, the Manchus had incorporated allied and conquered Mongols into the Eight Banner system, and the separate Mongol Eight Banners were created in 1635. These Mongol forces joined the Manchu and Chinese Eight Banners (created in 1642) in the conquest of China and Inner Asia. See Elliot, *The Manchu Way*, 73–74.

39. For the Qing-Zunghar war, see Perdue, *China Marches West*.

40. For the history, organization, and function of the Lifanyuan, see Zhao Yuntian, *Qingdai menggu zhengjiao zhidu*, 45–69; Chia, "The Li-fan Yuan in the Early Ch'ing Dynasty"; Chia, "The Lifanyuan and the Inner Asia Rituals," 60–92.

41. The earliest legal codes of the Mongols dated back to the *Jasag* promulgated by Chinggis Khan, which consisted of a series of moral injunctions and laws. Before the Qing conquest, various Mongol tümens drew up their own codes, such as the Altan Khan Code of the Tümed Mongols, and Tumen Khan Code of the eastern Mongols. The *Menggu lüli* was first promulgated in 1643 as the *Menggu lüshu* and based on the Mongol customary law, and its revised version appeared in 1741 as a special code for Mongolia. *Lifanyuan zeli* was first published in 1696, as a systematization of the Mongolian indigenous law with added content regarding Tibet and Russia, and its final revision was promulgated in 1815. See Wuyunbilige et al., *Menggu minzu tongshi*, volume 4, 273–78; Dalizhabu, "'Menggu lüli' ji qi yu 'Lifanyuan zeli' de guanxi," 1–10.

42. On the banner and league institutions, see Jagchid and Hyer, *Mongolia's Culture and Society*, 278; Woodhead and Bell, *The China Year Book*, 611; Barfield, *The Perilous Frontier*, 275–76; Atwood, *Young Mongols and Vigilantes in Inner Mongolia's Interregnum Decade*, 23–34.

43. For details of distribution of the banners and aimags, see Chang, *The Economic Development and Prospects of Inner Mongolia*, 60–62; Zhang Yongjiang, "Lun qingdai monan menggu diqu de eryuan guanli tizhi," 31; Borjigin, "The History and the Political Character of the Name of Nei Menggu," 64; Di Cosmo et al., eds., *The Cambridge History of Inner Asia*, 341.

44. *Da Qing huidian shili* (hereafter QHDSL), 970–72. The Oirat groups that formed the two banners of west Hetao had been driven from Xinjiang into Ningxia and Gansu areas by the Qing-Zunghar conflict from the 1680s to early 1700s. Though not part of Inner Mongols, these banners became incorporated into present-day Inner Mongolia. For the incorporation of these banners, see Zhang Mu, *Menggu youmu ji*, 264–65, 374–78.

45. Elverskog, *Our Great Qing*, 17–39.

46. Elverskog, *Our Great Qing*, 39. The terms deterritorialization and reterritorialization are coined by Gilles Deleuze and Felix Guattari to characterize the process of removal of social, political, and cultural practices from a place or territory, and the reconstruction of such practices under the new spatial reconfiguration. James Hevia employed the terms to emphasize the displacement of Qing political, legal, and cultural order by European powers and its integration into the emerging global system. See Hevia, *English Lessons*.

47. Elverskog, *Our Great Qing*, 65–75.

48. The *nianban* system was in some ways similar to the *sankin kōtai* (参勤交代) system of Tokugawa Japan. Both involved regular attendance of feudal lords in the capital, and both contributed to the rise of a money economy which increasingly connected the feudal domain to a national market and eventually undermined the feudal order. However, in the latter case, it was basically a hostage system that required each *daimyo* or his family to reside in Edo for periods of time as a means of effectively constraining his political autonomy. The *nianban* system, however, was designed as a means of pacifying the feudal lords and princes of the Qing dependencies through imperial audience, in which tributes were paid in exchange for the favors and gifts from the emperor. It was meant to be a privilege as well as a duty. The Mongol princes stayed in Beijing for only a short period of time, usually from the end of year through the first month of the new year. The *nianban* audience was restricted to those who were immunized from measles. For those who had not had measles yet, they were required to take turns in joining the emperor in the yearly hunting at the imperial hunting ground (*weichang* 圍場) in Jehol in each fall. This was called *weiban* 圍班 (hunting attendance). See Lu Minghui, *Qingdai beibu bianjiang minzu jingji fazhan shi*, 388–89. For more discussion on the *sankin kōtai* system, see Vlastos, *Peasant Protests and Uprisings in Tokugawa Japan*.

49. Marriage alliance between the Manchu and Mongols had been established as a policy since the time of the first Qing emperor, Hong Taiji (1592–1643). Throughout the Qing period, altogether thirty-two Manchu princesses were married to Mongol nobles, and many Qing emperors took Mongol wives and concubines. See Wuyunbilige et al., *Menggu minzu tongshi*, volume 4, 66. For a comprehensive study on the intermarriage between Manchu and Mongolia, see Du Jiaji, *Qingchao manmeng lianyin yanjiu*, 600–20.

50. See Jagchid and Hyer, *Mongolia's Culture and Society*, 274–78. For more discussions on the Mongolian social system in the Qing period, see Tayama, *Shin jidai ni okeru mōko no shakai seido*; Jagchid and Hyer, *Mongolia's Culture and Society*, 289–92.

51. See, for example, the border disputes between Üüshin and Otog banners that were detailed in the accounts of missionary scholars of the Boro-Balgasun church. See Van Hecken, "Une dispute entre deux bannières mongoles," 276–305; Serruys, "A Question of Land and Landmarks between the Banners Otog and Üüsin (Ordos)," 215–37.

52. *Waifan Menggu* included both Inner and Outer Jasags. *Neishu Menggu* included the Chakhar of Zhili province, the Tümed of Guihua (Höhhot) of Shanxi province, the Dariganga pasture under the amban of Chakhar, the Oirat of Jehol, the Tannu Uriankhai under the military governor of Uliasutai, the Altai Uriankhai and Altai Nuur Uriankhai of Khobdo, the Myanghad, Zakhchin, and Oirat of Khobdo, the Barghu of Heilongjiang, the Chakhar and Oirat of Ili, and the Dam Mongols of central Tibet. See Wuyunbilige et al., *Menggu minzu tongshi*, volume 4, 245. Bello differentiates the two categories as administratively distinct between what he calls the Manchu state "gūsa" banners and Mongol local "khoshuu" banners. See Bello, *Across Forest, Steppe, and Mountain*, 50.

53. As Christopher Atwood points out, this amban should be distinguished from the ambans (*baqi dutong* 八旗都統) who served as military commanders of Manchu banner garrisons in various Qing forts, and the ambans (*dachen* 大臣) who served as imperial residents or agents appointed to major Inner Asian political centers of Outer Mongolia, Qinghai, and Tibet. See Atwood, *Young Mongols and Vigilantes*, 24, footnote 12.

54. Di Cosmo, "The Qing and Inner Asia: 1636–1800," in *The Cambridge History of Inner Asia*, 340; Atwood, *Young Mongols and Vigilantes*, 34–35.

55. Wuyunbilige et al., *Menggu minzu tongshi*, volume 4, 245.

56. On the rivalry between the Yellow Hat and Red Hat schools, see Fletcher, "Ch'ing Inner Asia c. 1800," 99. On the Mongols' conversion to Tibetan Buddhism, see Elverskog, *The Jewel Translucent Sūtra*.

57. Bawden, *The Jebtsundamba Khutukhtus of Urga*; Miaozhou, *Mengzang fojiao shi*, 147–79.

58. For example, the Fourth Dalai Lama Yonten Gyatso was born in Mongolia as the great-grandson of Altan Khan, and the son of the Tüshiyetü Khan Gombojorji was recognized as the first Jebtsundamba Khutukhtu in 1650. See Bawden, *The Modern History of Mongolia*, 33–34; Heissig, *The Religions of Mongolia*, 28–31.

59. Jagchid and Hyer, *Mongolia's Culture and Society*, 183.

60. For the lama-patron relations between Tibetan Buddhism and Qing imperial politics, see Grupper, "Manchu Patronage and Tibetan Buddhism," 47–75; Hevia, *Cherishing Men From Afar*, 39–42; Chia, "The Lifanyuan and the Inner Asian Rituals," 60–92; Hevia, "Lamas, Emperors, and Rituals," 243–78; Waley-Cohen, "Religion, War, and Empire-Building," 336–52.

61. On the relationship between the Dalai Lama and the Emperor of China, see Schwieger, *The Dalai Lama and the Emperor of China*.

62. Hyer, "The Dalai Lama and the Mongols," 7; Perdue, *China Marches West*.

63. Pozdneyev, *Mongolia and the Mongols*, volume 1, 16; volume 2, 193. For a detailed study on these monasteries, see Charleux, "Qing Imperial Mandalic Architecture for Gelygpa Pontiffs".

64. Heissig, *The Religions of Mongolia*, 1.

65. Heissig, *The Religions of Mongolia*, 33.

66. Bawden, *The Modern History of Mongolia*, 37.

67. The lama population in the late Qing and early Republican period was estimated at over one hundred thousand. Other statistics show that the lamas may have comprised about 25 to 40 percent of the entire male population. See Wuyunbilige et al., *Menggu minzu tongshi*, volume 4, 370. Fletcher estimates an even higher percentage, that between 30 to 65 percent of the male population of Inner Mongolia took vows, but it is yet to be verified. See Fletcher, "Ch'ing Inner Asia c. 1800," 54. Also see Yao Minghui, *Menggu zhi*; Heissig, *The Religions of Mongolia*, 1.

68. Lattimore, "Inner Mongolia: Chinese, Japanese, or Mongol?" 65; Jagchid and Hyer, *Mongolia's Culture and Society*, 177, 299.

69. Fletcher, "Ch'ing Inner Asia c. 1800," 54–56; Lattimore, *Inner Asian Frontiers of China*, 94; Jagchid and Hyer, *Mongolia's Culture and Society*, 299.

70. Miaozhou, *Mengzang fojiao shi*, 163–67, 391–401; Bawden, *The Modern History of Mongolia*, 33; Jagchid and Hyer, *Mongolia's Culture and Society*, 185.

71. Miaozhou, *Mengzang fojiao shi*, 180–200; Heissig, *The Religions of Mongolia*, 33.

72. QHDSL 153, 288.

73. The Kangxi emperor first issued an imperial edict in 1683 that prohibited Han migrants from marrying Mongolian women. See QHDSL 978 and 979; *Qinding Lifanbu zeli*, 297–306.

74. Lattimore, *The Mongols of Manchuria*, 73, 84; Lu Minghui, *Qingdai beibu bianjiang*, 77–79.

75. QHDSL 978; Yano, *Kinsei mōkoshi kenkyū*, 114–18.

76. QSL, KX, 269. The drought of 1719 and 1720 in Shanxi and Shaanxi, the flood of 1723 in Henan and Hebei, and the drought of 1743 in Shandong and Henan caused a large

flow of refugees into the Jehol and southern Manchuria. See Wuyunbilige et al., *Menggu minzu tongshi*, volume 4, 235.

77. For example, in 1749, two Lifanyuan officials were appointed to supervise the implementation of a prohibition decree. According to the law, accommodating Han illegal immigrants would be treated as hiding wanted criminals. Jasags who violated the law would be deprived of one year's stipend, and lower-level officials would be punished with a heavy fine of livestock and a hundred lashes. In 1806, jasags and other nobilities who accommodated up to fifty illegal Han immigrants would be fined up to five year's stipend. Those who received over fifty illegal cultivators would be permanently dismissed from office. Lower-level officials without an annual stipend would be fined with various number of livestock and in case of repeated violations, punished with corvée at post stations. See Wuyunbilige et al., *Menggu minzu tongshi*, volume 4, 289.

78. Zhou Tiezheng, ed, *Chaoyang xianzhi 26, zhongzu.*

79. Lattimore, *The Mongols of Manchuria*, 84–87.

80. Skinner, "Cities and the Hierarchy of Local Systems," in Skinner, ed., *The Cities of Late Imperial China*, 302–22.

81. Masui, "Qingdai 'zhiliting' yu 'santing'"; Masui, "Kenryūki ni okeru chokureichō." For discussions on the establishment of the sub-prefecture system in general, also see Fu Linxiang, "Qingdai fuminting zhidu"; Xi Huidong, "Qingdai tingzhi chutan."

82. For detailed discussion on centralized administrative units of *ting/xian* and *zhou/fu/ dao* in Inner Mongolia, see Wuyungerile, *Shiba zhi ershi shiji chu neimenggu chengzhen yanjiu*, 66–77.

83. Lattimore, *Inner Asian Frontiers of China*; Barfield, *The Perilous Frontier*; Jagchid and Symons, *Peace, War, and Trade Along the Great Wall*; Di Cosmo, "Ancient Inner Asian Nomads"; Williams, *Beyond Great Walls.*

84. Khan, "Who Are the Mongols?" 128.

85. Jagchid and Hyer, *Mongolia's Culture and Society*, 316.

86. Lattimore, *The Mongols of Manchuria*, 69.

87. Lattimore, *The Mongols of Manchuria*, 65.

88. Shamanism is a religious practice that involves a shaman ("one who knows") practitioner who intermediates between this world and the spirit world for healing or other purposes. The tradition is spread among the Tungusic groups of northern Asia, including Tibetans, Mongols, and Manchu, as well as indigenous peoples living in North and South America, Africa, and Oceania. For overview of shamanism, see Heissig, *The Religions of Mongolia*, 6–23. Humphrey suggests that the shamanistic tradition is more powerful in the western, northern, and eastern peripheries of the steppe where grasslands are interspersed with forests, mountains, great rivers, and lakes. See Humphrey, "Chiefly and Shamanist Landscapes in Mongolia," 140.

89. Heissig, *The Religions of Mongolia*, 101–04; Jagchid and Hyer, *Mongolia's Culture and Society*, 163. For the worship of *Möngkhe* Tengri and *Etügen Ekhe and oboo* rituals, see Humphrey, "Chiefly and Shamanist Landscapes in Mongolia," 142–43, 146–48, 149.

90. Jagchid and Hyer, *Mongolia's Culture and Society*, 310.

91. Di Cosmo, "Ancient Inner Asian Nomads."

92. Xiao Daheng, *Beilu fengsu*, 12. For more discussion on Xiao's work, see Serruys, "Peilou fong-sou," 141–42.

93. See Lattimore, *Inner Asian Frontiers of China*; Jagchid and Hyer, *Mongolia's Culture and Society*, 316; Di Cosmo, "Ancient Inner Asian Nomads," 1100–04; Lu Minghui, *Qingdai beibu bianjiang minzu jingji fazhan shi*, 91–93.

94. QSL, KX 37/12/17. Also see Lattimore, *Inner Asian Frontiers of China*; Jagchid and Hyer, *Mongolia's Culture and Society*, 316; Di Cosmo, "Ancient Inner Asian Nomads," 1100–04; Yoshida, "Uchi mongoru ni okeru dentō nōgyō to kanshiki nōgyō no jyuyō."

95. Gugong bowuyuan, ed., *Qing gaozong yuzhi shi*, volume 4, 265.

96. Gugong bowuyuan, ed., *Qing gaozong yuzhi shi*, volume 14, 167–68. On the two poems, also see Bello, *Across Forest, Steppe, and Mountain*, 45–46.

97. Bello, *Across Forest, Steppe, and Mountain*, 15.

98. He Yangling, *Chasui mengmin jingji de jiepou*, 30; Xu Chonghao, ed., *Monan menggu dili*, 83; Yoshida, "Uchi mongoru ni okeru dentō nōgyō," 2.

99. For the attributes of peripheral peoples associated with the civilizing projects, see Harrell, "Introduction: Civilizing Projects and the Reaction to Them," 3–36.

100. Yoshida, "Uchi mongoru ni okeru dentō nōgyō," 3.

2

Merchants, Monetization, and Networking

Chinese Commercial Expansion in the Steppe

Until fairly recently, the area we call Inner Mongolia today was a land of nomads. For over two millennia, their interactions with the settled Chinese as conquerors or as the acculturated Other were a central theme of Chinese history. Yet, prior to the modern times, no specific name for this vast territory existed in the Chinese language. It was referred to by generic terms such as "beyond the pass" (*kouwai* 口外), "beyond the frontier fortress" (*saiwai* 塞外), and "beyond the borders" (*bianwai* 邊外), which partly reflected its status as a nonentity within the spatial conceptualization of the Chinese.[1] The terms "pass," "fortress," and "border" invariably refer to the Great Wall, which demarcated the physical border between China and the steppe and the socioeconomic border between the two distinct civilizations and societies of pastoral nomadism and sedentary agriculture. Constructed in the wake of military tension between the Ming Dynasty (1368–1644) and invading Mongols, the Great Wall exemplified a physical and symbolic demarcation between "interior" (*nei* 內) and "exterior" (*wai* 外) and "cultured" (*hua* 華 or *xia* 夏) and "barbarian" (*yi* 夷). Such distinctions were of utmost significance for the Confucian cosmological order, as the nomads not only posed a real threat on the defensive frontier of the Chinese, but for mainstream Confucianism, they also constituted the cultural Other against which the Chinese civilization defined itself.[2]

Like most boundaries that existed not just to delineate and differentiate, but to connect and unite, the boundary delimited by the Great Wall was never as fixed and stable as it appeared. The eighteenth and nineteenth centuries witnessed a steady flow of Chinese migration from the northern provinces of Shanxi and Shaanxi into the fringe of the steppe. This mass migration was locally referred to as *zou xikou* 走西口 ("going beyond the western pass"). Although the term *zou xikou* appeared rather late, partly due to a folk song bearing the same name that gained popularity in the nineteenth century (see chapter 3), its origin can be traced back to the itineraries of Chinese traders who first gained access to the steppe as military contractors during the Kangxi emperor's expeditions against the Zunghars (1690–1697).[3] Later, they were established near garrison stations, Buddhist monasteries, and the headquarters of Manchu administrators, where new market towns emerged and expanded. Riding on the military and territorial expansion of the Qing empire, these merchants managed to penetrate Mongolia with flows of goods, money, credit, and people. Their economic activities not only redefined the boundaries between the sedentary Chinese and the nomadic Mongols, but they also brought about far-reaching repercussions to the socioeconomic, demographical, and cultural landscapes of the two societies.

This chapter focuses on the penetration of Chinese trade into Mongolia and shows how trade flows and the money economy changed Mongol society long before it was transformed by massive settlement. In particular, it explores the initiatives of Shanxi merchants in establishing buzzing market centers and elaborate trade networks across the Central Eurasian steppe and their interactions with the Manchu government and Mongol authorities. Dashengkui, the leading trading conglomerate in Mongolia, exemplified a novel form of frontier commercialism based on massive capital accumulation through long-distance trade and usurious moneylending. By providing goods and services to the remotest corners of the grassland, these merchants successfully incorporated the Mongol periphery into the market system of China proper as well as the global capitalist framework. Thereby, the merchants paved the way for large-scale Chinese agricultural settlement during the nineteenth and twentieth centuries and the eventual administrative integration of Inner Mongolia into China. On the other hand, the deep embeddedness of this frontier commercialism in political power also distinguished it sharply from Western capitalism based on the free market and clearly defined property rights. The financial domination of the Chinese merchants caused widespread indebtedness among the Mongol upper classes and the impoverishment of the commoners. Eventually, it would result in the demise of the trading firms in the wake of the independence movement of the Khalkha Mongols in the early twentieth century.

THE WESTERN PASS

The connotation of *xikou* is open to debate. It is often used interchangeably with the Shahukou Pass located in Youyu county of Shanxi province. Some Chinese historians pinpoint *xikou* as Höhhot, the burgeoning Mongolian town beyond the Great Wall, whereas others identify it as a general name for a cluster of passes lying to the west of Kalgan (a.k.a. Zhangjiakou) or the Eastern Pass.[4] The semantic ambivalence of the term in many ways mirrors the dual roles played by the Great Wall as a barrier of strategic defense and a channel of cultural and economic exchange. Constructed by the Ming dynasty in 1473, the wall was a product of high military tensions on the Ming-Mongol borders. It was primarily a defense line that protected China against the invading Mongols. Moreover, it marked the distinction between the *yi* and the *xia*, the distinction of which became hardened after centuries of foreign conquest and military antagonism. Nonetheless, since its construction, the Great Wall had functioned as the channel of contact between the two economies of sedentary Chinese and nomadic Mongols. Over time, its strategic role as a stronghold of defense and demarcation gave way to its economic role as the locus of border markets and tax ports.[5] The word *kou* was thus characterized by its multiple connotations of strategic "passage" (*guankou* 關口) as well as "marketplace" (*shikou* 市口) or "trading port" (*kou'an* 口岸).

Underlying the turbulent Ming-Mongol relations were the evolving macroeconomic dynamics between China and its nomadic neighbors of the north. As mentioned in chapter 1, the limitation of the extensive pastoral economy centered on animal husbandry made the nomads dependent upon agrarian societies for the supply of agricultural and handicrafted products. Meanwhile, China's great need for horses for its cavalry, as well as for other domestic animals for drafting and transportation purposes, should not be overlooked. Throughout Chinese history, the northern nomads adopted various strategies alternating between war and peace to extort wealth or increase trade with China.[6] The Chinese dynasties in their turn channeled its economic and diplomatic relations with neighboring states through the framework of the tribute system (*chaogong* 朝貢). This system was a form of state-subsidized monopoly trade disguised in the formality of symbolic subordination, as a means of exerting political influences and instigating frontier pacification.[7] It was designed to grant trade privileges in exchange for recognition of the symbolic power of the Chinese emperor. Under the pretense of the elaborate ceremonial demonstration of Chinese superiority and prestige lay economic motives centering on the nomads' subsistence needs. When such peaceful relations were not established, or when the volume of trade allowed by the Chinese was not sufficient to meet their needs, the nomads resorted to military means such as plundering and even war, to gain what they needed.[8]

During the early Ming period, the Ming court maintained tribute relations with a number of frontier groups by allowing them to send annual or biannual tribute missions to Beijing.[9] These missions supplied the tribal elites with food provisions and luxuries such as silk and satin. The missions were supplemented by periodical horse fairs (*mashi* 馬市) held at strategic locations along the border such as Liaodong and Datong.[10] More restrictions were placed upon the Eastern and Oirat Mongols inhabiting the territories in-between Liaodong and Datong, and tribute relations with them were often marred by border raids that sometimes led to open war. For example, frictions over tribute missions with the Oirats caused the latter to raid the Ming borders, resulting in the Tumu debacle of 1449 in which the Ming troops were annihilated and the Zhengtong emperor captured.[11] In its aftermath, the Ming shifted to a more defensive policy in favor of wall building, with all tribute relations with the Mongols terminated and the border markets shut down.

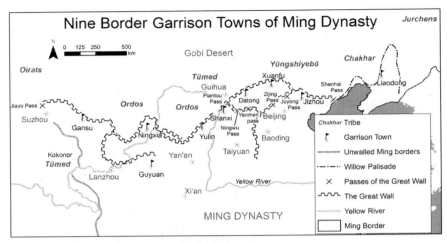

Map 2.1.   Nine Garrison Towns of Ming Dynasty

The construction of the Great Wall proved of little avail in containing the Mongols. When the request for trade by Altan Khan, leader of the Tümed Mongols, was repeatedly denied, he raided the border areas and besieged Beijing in 1550, causing great disarray in the Ming court.[12] Peace was not established until the border markets were reopened along the Great Wall in 1571 when Altan Khan received the title "Shunyi Wang" (Obedient and Righteous Prince) from the Longqing emperor (r. 1567–1572) and was allowed to exchange horses for textiles. Twenty markets were opened between the garrison towns (*zhen* 鎮) of Xuanfu and Gansu, including twelve horse fairs and eight monthly markets (*xiaoshi* 小市, or *yueshi* 月市). These markets served as supply centers for both the nomads and the Ming court. Through them, the nomads could obtain everyday commodities such as cotton fabrics, cooking pots, grains, coarse silk, and a restricted amount of iron cauldrons and ploughshares, and the Ming court could obtain much-needed warhorses. In addition to the official markets, there was also considerable private trade (*sishi* 私市, or *minshi* 民市) involving Chinese merchant capital.[13]

The Shahukou Pass 殺虎口, located 120 kilometers northwest of Datong *zhen*, was one such fort turned into a market. First fortified in 1544, it lay at the juncture of the inner and outer walls of the Ming defense system and bordered the Tümed plain in the north that was the home base of Altan Khan. Its original name, Shahubu 殺胡堡 ("kill-barbarian-fortress"), was indicative of the hostility across the border. After 1571, it was turned into the site of a monthly market under the administration of Datong *zhen*. The trade was so prosperous that a new fort named Pingjibu 平集堡 ("peace-market-fortress") was built to its south. Shops were established in the walled space between the two forts.[14] The juxtaposition of these two names captured the tensions embedded in these fortress-markets and the paradoxical roles they played in the Ming-Mongol relations.

The necessity to trade with nomadic states in the north gave rise to a new business structure in the latter part of the Ming dynasty. The cross-border exchange contributed to the emergence of a flourishing internal market, the expansion of the production of consumer items, a growing merchant class, and more importantly, a brisk money economy in China that developed from the sixteenth century onward.[15] The border trade was conducted by a special group of government-contracted merchants who emerged out of the necessity of sustaining an extensive defensive system for the Ming dynasty. As early as 1370, a contracting system called *kaizhongfa* 開中法 was developed, under which private traders were contracted to transport grain and necessities from inland China to the frontier in return for participating in the state monopolized salt trade.[16] Most of these traders were natives of Shanxi province due to their geographic proximity to the frontier and a long merchant tradition that traced back to the Song Dynasty (960–1279). Following the reopening of border trade in 1571, they began to play a key role not only in state-run horse fairs, but also in private markets that exceeded the official ones in terms of volume of trade.[17] As it turned out, the Shanxi border traders became the forerunners of the Chinese merchants who dominated trade and commerce in Mongolia from the seventeenth century to the twentieth century.

The Ming-Qing transition brought about significant change to the strategic and symbolic roles associated with the Great Wall. The Manchu conquest in the seventeenth century created a multi-ethnic empire that was double the size of its predecessor, and it unified territories on both sides of the Great Wall. In particular, the Khalkha Mongols who dwelt in the vast territories north of the Gobi Desert pledged allegiance to the Qing in 1691.[18] In that same year, the Kangxi emperor turned down an official request to repair the Great Wall: citing its high cost and ineffectiveness in terms of defense.[19] As the emperor put it,

> Of old, the Qin heaped up earth and stones and erected the Great Wall. Our dynasty has extended its mercies to the Khalkha and set them to guard the northern territories. They will be even stronger and firmer than the Great Wall.[20]

For the Qing emperor, the Khalkha provided far more effective protection of the northern frontier than any defensive walls possibly could. Meanwhile, the Great Wall also shed much of its symbolic implication as the emblem of Chinese civilization. As a frontier people of non-Han origin, the Manchu rulers sought to downplay the *yi/xia* distinction by relativizing the interior and exterior through such rhetoric as "one family under the heaven" (*tianxia yijia* 天下一家) and "impartiality of within and without" (*zhongwai yishi* 中外一視).[21] As an indication of such a strategic and symbolic shift, the Qing rulers took pains to alter the place names along the borders that were reminiscent of Han-Mongol antagonism. For example, the derogative term "barbarian" (*hu* 胡) was replaced by the more neutral "tiger" (*hu* 虎) in the naming of Shahukou.[22] Although the Great Wall remained an ethnopolitical delineation separating the Mongols and Chinese, its old function as a boundary line for exclusion and discrimination increasingly gave way to that of a gateway that facilitated cross-border exchange and economic integration.

Into the Qing period, Shahukou emerged as a crucial nexus connecting the steppe to China proper. The new communication system of five-route postal relay stations (*wulu yizhan* 五路驛站) was completed in the wake of the Qing campaigns against the Zunghars in 1690 and the subsequent submission of the Khalkhas at the Dolonnuur Assembly in 1691. It ran through the five major passes of the Great Wall: Zhangjiakou, Dushikou, Gubeikou, Xifengkou, and Shahukou, thereby linking the steppe to Beijing as never before. Apart from facilitating military supplies and governmental transportation, the post roads also served as the designated passageways for the tributary missions of peripheral peoples as well as the annual rotations of Mongol princes and high lamas to Beijing.[23] Later, the postal relay system was extended to the Khalkha-Russian borders and further to Ili and Tarbagatay of Xinjiang. As it turned out, the communication network designed to sustain long-distance logistic transportation greatly facilitated the caravan trade between China proper and the Central Eurasia steppe.

In addition to its strategic importance, Shahukou was also distinguished for its economic status as a major tax port and outlet of passenger and freight traffic across the Han-Mongol border. A customs house set up in 1651 was put in charge of levying taxes on all merchandise in and out of Mongolia. From 1735 on, Shahukou became one of the three ports of admission for Chinese merchants entering Mongolia, together with Pantaokou and Gubeikou, where official permits (*bupiao* 部票) were issued upon duty payment. The taxes were used to cover expenses incurred by the military campaigns against the Zunghars and support the garrison troops. Until 1768, Shahukou remained under the direct jurisdiction of the Board of Revenue and was staffed by Manchus and Mongol officials dispatched from Beijing. After that, the administration of Shahukou was turned over to the governor of Shanxi. This transfer showed the decline of the pass in terms of military and economic significance after the elimination of the Zunghar power in the mid-1700s.[24]

The transformation of Shahukou from a minor fort-market to one of the most important transportation hubs and tax ports showcased the changing power dynamics along the Han-Mongol borders during the Ming-Qing transition. Although the wall-building strategies of the Ming were unable to hold back the northern nomads who demanded trade on penalty of war, the military expansion of the Qing empire facilitated the commercial penetration of Chinese merchants into the steppe that would change the nomadic world forever. Thus Shahukou may be seen as lying at the juncture of various distinct historical interactions ranging from Mongol military excursions to peaceful border markets and Chinese commercial expansion. All this made Shahukou a natural candidate for *xikou*, which simultaneously separated the steppe from China proper and linked it to China proper. Nevertheless, by the mid-1700s, Shahukou's unique status was challenged by Höhhot, the buzzing frontier town north of the Great Wall.

EXPANDING FRONTIER TRADE

The Qing handled frontier trade differently from their predecessors. Unlike the antagonist relations between the Ming and its northern neighbors, the relationship between the ruling Manchus and Mongols was one between overlord and vassal based on military and political alliance. Border trade resumed soon after the submission of the Mongols in the mid-1630s. At first, trade was allowed only at designated places near the border such as Höhhot, Kalgan, Gubeikou, and Shahukou. Later, eight more trading sites were established in the border regions of Jehol and the Ordos in the late 1690s, as a token to reward these aimags for their loyalty and service during the Ming-Qing and Qing-Zunghar wars.[25] Compared with the Ming period, frontier trade in the Qing was carried out on more flexible terms and across a greater geographical space so as to meet the economic needs of the Mongols.[26]

Another change was the organization of imperial pastures outside the Great Wall, which led to the decline of Ming-style horse fairs. Beginning in 1644, four imperial herds (Mo: *süreg*, Ch: *muqun* 牧群) were established in the Chakhar region north of Xuanfu and Datong, which were responsible for supplying military horses and dairy products for the Qing court. These imperial herds included the Shangdu/Dabsun Nuur herds administered by the Ministry of Imperial Stables, Herds, and Carriages (*shangsiyuan* 上駟院); the cattle and sheep herds of the Bordered Yellow, Plain Yellow, and Plain White banners under the Office of Imperial Pasturages (*qingfengsi* 慶豐司), both under supervision of the Imperial Household Department (*neiwufu* 內務府); and the Taipusi Left Flank and Right Flank herds administered by the Court of Military Stud (*taipusi* 太僕寺). Together, they produced over a hundred thousand horses for military usage and utilization at the imperial court.[27] The horse fairs were formally abolished in 1696. This change marked the withdrawal of state intervention from cross-border trade and paved the way for the advance of private merchant capital.

Nonetheless, as new rulers of China, the Manchu authorities continued to employ tribute relations as a means to pacify autonomous nomadic powers that posed potential challenges to their rule. In 1655, the Khalkha khans began to present the annual tribute of "nine whites" (Mo: *yesun chaghan-u alban*, Ch: *jiu bai gong* 九白貢) comprising one white camel and eight white horses, to the Manchu emperor in Beijing.[28] The Qing also accepted the request of the Zunghar leader Galdan to send tribute to Beijing shortly after his rise to power in 1677. These measures were taken to gratify the desires of the nomadic rulers while preventing their commercial alignment with Russia. These tribute missions were allowed to trade at the border markets of Höhhot and Kalgan, with restrictions applied regarding the routes and frequency of these missions, so as to limit the resources obtainable through trade and thereby contain the military power of these autonomous aimags. In an edict of 1683, the Kangxi emperor prescribed that no more than two hundred members of the tribute missions sent by Galdan as well as other Oirat tribal leaders were permitted in Beijing. The rest of the members were directed to trade in Kalgan and Höhhot. Nevertheless, Galdan ignored the edit and sent a mission of over three thousand members in the following year. Upon Galdan's invasion of Khalkha in 1687, all tribute relations with the Zunghars were cut off.[29] Here we can see that tribute and trade continued to function as an important strategy to secure border control during the Qing period.

At the turn of the eighteenth century, a more adaptive mode of trade began to emerge on the steppe, with the rise of the so-called firms traveling in Mongolia (*lümengshang* 旅蒙商), which allowed more mobility and flexibility than the government-designated border markets. Granting Chinese merchants direct access to the steppe was a Qing innovation that marked a distinctive departure from the traditional pattern of trade based on tributary missions and frontier markets. It was made possible by a complex set of interactive forces that reshaped the power dynamics between the steppe and China proper.

First, the Qing military campaigns against the Zunghars provided opportunities for Chinese merchants to penetrate into the Mongolian steppe as never before. During the Kangxi emperor's expedition of 1696, these merchants accompanied the Qing army across the Gobi Desert and into the Khalkha territories as contracted military suppliers. They provided provisions and other necessities to the troops, while trading tea and cotton cloth with the nomads for livestock and other pastoral products.[30] During the Yongzheng Emperor's campaign against Galdan Tsering (r. 1727–1745), the Manchu forces were settled at Uliasutai, which became a pivotal military and administrative base in the Khalkha region. A military governor (*jiangjun* 將軍) of Uliasutai was appointed in 1733 to oversee the four Khalkha aimags and Khobdo. Later, two offices of Imperial Resident (Ma: *amban*, Ch: *banshi dachen* 辦事大臣) were created in Urga (modern Ulaanbaatar) and Khobdo that were subordinate to the Uliasutai military governor.[31] The maintenance of a large number of military and administrative personnel in the heartland of the steppe necessitated the cooperation of a commercial organization that served their needs. For this reason, Chinese traders were mobilized to transport grain and goods from south of the Great Wall. They established encampments in the outskirts of military camps and administrative centers of Manchu *ambans* and conducted barter trade with Mongol nomads in the nearby areas.

Second, the spread of Tibetan Buddhism across Mongolia and the Qing subsidization of monasteries further aided the penetration of Chinese merchants. The monasteries as an institution played a significant role in the economic life of Mongolia. They owned serfs, land, and cattle; organized temple fairs and trade caravans; produced religious and nomadic artifacts; lent money; and rented cattle and arable land.[32] The monasteries were usually situated near summer pastures with easy access to water and grass, in order to accommodate the large number of herders and animals that assembled. Annual temple fairs and Buddhist festivals were of paramount importance in the economic and cultural life of the Mongols.[33] During the summer season, when temple fairs were held, the monasteries were converted into buzzing marketplaces that attracted many itinerant merchants from south of the passes, whereas their fixed structures provided ready shelter and storage space for the merchants.[34] The monasteries ran their own camel caravans that participated in the tea trade between trade centers. They also rented camels to the Chinese.[35]

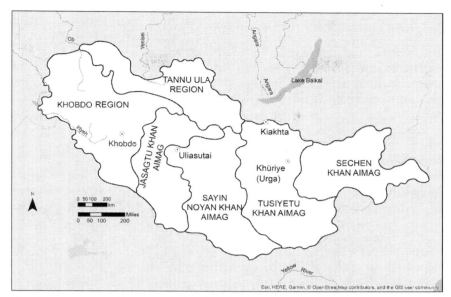

Map 2.2. Northern Mongolia during the Qing

Figure 2.1. Panorama of Urga by Mongolian painter Jugder in 1913. The large circular compound in the middle is the Jüün-Khüriye temple-palace complex. The circular compound to the left is Gandan temple complex. Between the two compounds is the Baruun Damnuur-chin markets. To the far bottom right is the Maimaicheng district.
Courtesy of The Bogd Khaan Palace Museum, Ulaanbaatar

The great monasteries became nodes of commercial activities. Urga (originally Örgöö, meaning "palace, yurt"), known as Yekhe Khüriye ("the great circle") to the Mongols and Da Kulun 大庫倫 to the Chinese, was the largest monastic center of Khalkha. Established in 1641, it was the residence of Jebtsundamba Khutugtu, head of the Gelugpa Sect of Mongolia. Chinese merchants first came to Urga in the late seventeenth century, and gathered near the Khüriye or monastery where they established shops, living quarters, and warehouses. Joining the traders were also carpenters, painters, braziers, shoemakers, curriers, etc., who set up craft workshops near the monasteries. Their rapid expansion caused much distress to the religious authorities, so that in 1810, they were ordered to set up a separate trading district in the eastern part of the city called Maimaicheng 買賣城 (Mo: Maimaachin, a.k.a. Maimaa Khota "the market city"), away from the monastic area.[36] Likewise, Dolonnuur (present Duolun county, Inner Mongolia, a.k.a. Lamamiao 喇嘛廟), the site of the 1691 Assembly, grew into the religious and commercial center of Inner Mongolia.[37] As the Kangxi and Yongzheng emperors issued the order to erect two monasteries, Khökhe süme and Shira süme, in 1691 and 1727, the construction work was commissioned to some Shanxi merchants who were allowed to lease unoccupied chambers from the monasteries for stores and warehouses. Later, Dolonnuur became the metalwork center of Mongolia (specializing in the production of Buddhist bronze statues) as well as the largest distribution center of livestock.[38]

A third force that contributed to the economic expansion of Chinese merchants in Mongolia was the booming frontier trade with Russia. The Russian Cossacks began to move across Siberia to areas east of Lake Baikal in the early seventeenth century, and they established fortified settlements in Nerchinsk and Selenginsk where they engaged in barter trade with the Mongols. In 1654, a Russian embassy led by Baikov

Figure 2.2.   Detail of Maimaicheng (right) and Russian Consulate (left) in Jugder's 1913 painting.
Courtesy of The Bogd Khaan Palace Museum, Ulaanbaatar

Figure 2.3.   The old center of Urga, engraving from a photograph by Nikolay A. Charushin in 1888.
From *World Illustration Magazine*, T. 46, No. 1178, 132–133, St. Petersburg, 1891

opened the trade route from Russia to China via Zungharia and the Gobi Desert of Mongolia.[39] In 1689, the Qing and Russia signed the Treaty of Nerchinsk that defined the borders and regulated trade and diplomatic relations between the two empires. The Treaty of Nerchinsk was the first treaty signed by China with a Western nation. Between 1689 and 1727, eleven state caravans were sent from Russia to Beijing, and non-official traders were also allowed to trade in Urga and Nonni of Manchuria.[40] In 1727, the Treaty of Kyakhta further established trade agreements between the two countries by allowing a Russian state caravan to travel to Beijing every three years by way of Mongolia. Private trade was permitted in two places along the Sino-Russian

Figure 2.4.   A general view of Kiakhta, showing the "Neutral Ground."
From George Kennan, *Siberia and the Exile System*, Volume 2, New York: The Century Co., 1891

borders, Kyakhta and Tsurukhait near Nerchinsk, where merchants from both countries were free to conduct business.[41]

On the Chinese side of the border opposite Kyakhta, a trading emporium or Maimaicheng (present Altanbulag of Mongolia) was built, which had over two hundred compounds and several hundred permanent residents by 1770.[42] The most important items of China's exports were silks, cotton, tea, porcelain, tobacco, and rhubarb, which were traded for furs, peltry, hides, leather, fabrics, glassware, hardware, and cattle from Russia.[43] The Kyakhta trade became so prosperous that it soon eclipsed the triennial state caravans to Beijing, which were terminated in 1762. The volume of Sino-Russian trade soared from three hundred thousand rubles in the 1730s to 8,384,000 rubles in 1800 and reached 19.86 million rubles in 1854.[44] Throughout the eighteenth century and much of the nineteenth century, the route between Kalgan and Kyakhta via Urga remained the exclusive channel for Sino-Russian trade. Kalgan became the "central point" of Chinese trade with Russia, with all Russian cloths, textiles, and fur goods coming first to its storehouses and dispersed from there to China proper via its wholesalers. Here the main warehouses of Chinese goods for firms conducting business in Kyakhta and Mongolia were also concentrated.[45] Only after the 1850s did traffic through Kyakhta began to fall off, as the Treaty of Kulja (Ili) in 1851 opened Xinjiang to Russian trade, followed by the Treaty of Tianjin in 1860 that opened the entire Sino-Russian frontier to Russian traders. These treaties provided an alternative and cheaper way to the trade exchange between the two countries.[46]

Figure 2.5. The Russian-Chinese tea trade in Kiakhta.
Courtesy of Museum: Russian State Historical Library, Moscow

EMERGING CENTRAL PLACES

The rise of frontier towns across the Mongolian steppe represented a new trend of urbanization and settlement that paved the way for Chinese commercial expansion. Trading centers emerged where military, political, and religious power concentrated. They were often located near military camps, residences of Manchu *ambans*, and Buddhist monasteries, where Chinese merchants set up settlements called *maimaicheng* and extended their networks linking Russia, Mongolia, Xinjiang, and interior China.[47] These urban settlements were in turn organized into a hierarchy of central places differentiated by their geographic location within the transport network as well as their function within the economic system.[48] At the highest level were metropolitan centers like Höhhot, Kalgan, and Urga, which were centrally situated within the transport system and had crucial wholesaling and distributing functions. At a lower level were regional administrative and transit centers such as Uliasutai, Khobdo, Kyakhta, and Dolonnuur. At the lowest reach were periodical markets held at designated border areas, local monasteries, or headquarters of banner princes, which were characterized by their peripheral locations and sporadic occurrence.[49]

It is within this economic and political hierarchy that the role of Höhhot as the "West Gate" should be understood, which simultaneously linked the steppe to China proper and separated the two areas. Located about one hundred kilometers northwest of Shahukou, Höhhot or the "Blue Town" was the capital city of the Tümed Mongols. Founded by Altan Khan in 1572, it was built in the style of the thirteenth-century Mongol capital Daidu (modern Beijing). Its Chinese name, Guihuacheng 歸化城 ("city of allegiance to civilization"), was bestowed by the Wanli emperor in 1575.[50] Its mixed population included many Chinese, mostly prisoners of war and religious, economic, and military refugees including members of the outlawed White Lotus sect who had fled there to escape the persecution in China. Agriculture was practiced on the Tümed plain since the 1540s, when Altan Khan encouraged Han refugees to settle in *baishing* villages.[51] Meanwhile, the construction of Höhhot coincided with the Mongols' conversion to Tibetan Buddhism in the 1570s. Having since served as the religious center of Inner Mongolia, the city was prominent for the extraordinary number of monasteries it housed.[52]

Into the Qing period, Höhhot continued to serve as the civil and military administrative center of western Inner Mongolia, as it was the residence of a Manchu vice lieutenant governor (Mo: *meiren-ü janggi*, Ch: *fudutong* 副都統) who oversaw the Tümed Mongols of Höhhot. The Tümed Mongols were organized in two special banners in the similar fashion to the Manchu Eight Banners.[53] In 1739, a new walled fort-city named Suiyuancheng 綏遠城 ("city of pacifying the remote areas," hereafter Suiyuan) was built 2.5 kilometers to the northeast of Höhhot and served as the headquarters of the Manchu garrisons moved there from Shahukou. A military governor was appointed to oversee the defense matters of western Inner Mongolia.[54] Suiyuan soon replaced Shahukou as the new frontier military center beyond the Great Wall. Populated primarily by Manchu bannermen, bureaucrats, Mongol bannermen and

Figure 2.6. Inscription on the screen wall facing the Residence of Suiyuan Military Governor in Höhhot. Inscription reads *Pingfan shuomo,* or "screen and fence of the Gobi Desert."
Photo by the author

their households, it remained physically separate from Höhhot, which functioned as the religious, economic, cultural, and administrative center of Inner Mongolia.

Just as the military importance of Shahukou was displaced by Suiyuan in the early 1700s, its economic role was also eclipsed by the growing commercial weight of Höhhot. The frontier town began to acquire much economic significance during the early 1630s, as it was the designated marketplace for the Inner Mongols that submitted to the Manchus. Later, tribute missions of Khalkha and Zunghar Mongols were also allowed to trade here with the Chinese en route to Beijing. According to Zhang Penghe, special imperial envoy to Khalkha who stopped by Höhhot in 1688, there was considerable development of agriculture and trade in the city:

> [Höhhot] is a walled city with mud-made houses. Agriculture is widely practiced; chicken and pigs are raised, and crops such as hemp, corn, soybean, wheat, green onion, and chives are grown. Foreign merchants gathered here to trade; all sorts of goods from China and abroad can be found. It is indeed a place of crucial importance.[55]

Zhang's observation was shared by fellow traveler, French Jesuit Jean-Francois Gerbillon, who provided the earliest European witness report of the Blue Town:

[Guihuacheng] is now a very small Town, tho' we were inform'd that it was heretofore a Place of great Trade, and much frequented whilst the Western Tartars [i.e. Mongols] were Masters of China. . . . There is nothing remarkable in the Town except the Pagodas and the Lamas, several of the former being better built, finer and more ornamented than the greatest part of those I have seen in China. Most of the Houses are but Huts of Earth, . . . and there is a greater number of Inhabitants. The Western-Tartars and the Chinese live promiscuously in this Quarter, and the Emperor of China hath his Officers here, who govern by his Authority. . . I was told that it is but two good Days Journey, that is, about eighteen Leagues from this Place to the Entrance into the Province of [Shanxi], with which the Town of [Guihuacheng] drives its chief Trade, which as yet is not very considerable.[56]

Gerbillon's account shows that Höhhot in the 1680s was above all a monastic center. Although a fair number of Chinese inhabited there, the amount of trade was not yet substantial.

This was soon to change, however, because of the Qing military expansion into the Central Eurasian steppe followed by the opening of Kyakhta trade with Russia. With the completion of the postal relay system in the 1690s, Höhhot was to rise as a major market center and trading depot beyond the passes due to its central location on the trade routes to northern Mongolia and Russia, and later to Xinjiang and Qinghai as well. The areas surrounding major monasteries like Yekhe Juu and Shireetü Juu were soon turned into buzzing business districts where merchants from Shanxi congregated. A customs house was established in Höhhot in 1761, which exceeded the Shahukou Customs in terms of tax revenues by the early 1800s.[57] Beginning in 1777, the official licenses required of all Chinese merchants entering Mongolia were no longer issued at the major passes of the Great Wall, but were made available for purchase at the Manchu governor or amban's office in Höhhot, Kalgan, Dolonnuur, and Urga.[58] Thus, by the eighteenth century, Höhhot had surpassed Shahukou to the south as the new *xikou* or primary gateway linking the steppe to China proper.

When the Russian scholar A. M. Pozdneyev (1851–1920) visited Höhhot in 1893, he was somewhat perplexed by the ambivalence of the frontier town. It was located outside the Great Wall in a historical land of the Mongols, and yet its Chinese population was subject to the same taxation applicable to China proper. He cited the words of a local Manchu official:

"Of course, we could not move the very stones of the Great Wall over here," he said, "but ever since duties were first imposed in [Guihuacheng], it has belonged to inner China. It became just what [Kalgan] is now; so in official language we refer to it not only by the old Ming name [Guihua] or the Manchu one 'Kuke Khoto' but also by a new name, [Xikou], that is 'West Gate' (to inner China), just as we call Kalgan [Dongkou], that is 'East Gate.'"[59]

For the Manchu official, the establishment of the customs house in Höhhot had marked it a de facto frontier replacing the Great Wall in delimiting China proper from the steppe. Pozdneyev also saw the name Xikou addressed in government

Figure 2.7.   Shireetü Juu of Höhhot, Inner Mongolia.
Photo by the author

Figure 2.8.   An inscribed board donated by Shanxi firm Dashengkui to Shireetü Juu of Höhhot in 1724. Inscription reads *Yinshan gusha*, or "Ancient monastery of Mt. Yinshan."
Photo by the author

consignments and displayed in the military insignia of the garrison in Höhhot, and he came to the conclusion that Höhhot was now changing its former name.[60] This assertion was confirmed in several nineteenth-century local gazetteers, in which Xikou was unanimously referred to as an equivalent for Höhhot.[61] Apparently the colloquial term Xikou, with a predominantly economic rather than military connotation, had found a way into the official discourse by the nineteenth century.

The emergence of Höhhot was illuminating, as it exemplified the rise of multicultural frontier cities outside the Great Wall that testified to the impact of Manchu territorialization and empire building in reorganizing the power structure on the steppe. These cities functioned as compartmentalized communities of officials, soldiers, lamas, traders, craftsmen, and temporary laborers, all of whom were immigrants extraneous and heterogeneous to the nomadic order of Mongolian society. The new immigrant communities were self-governing, through occupational guilds (*hangshe* 行社), native-place networks (*huiguan* 會館), and religious societies centered on folk religious temples (*miao* 廟).[62] Over time, the forces of these urban societies succeeded in expanding and infiltrating the outlying regions, and eventually incorporating Mongolia into the money economy of China as well as the global economic order dominated by silver.

MECHANISMS OF MONETIZATION

Earlier studies have shown that the influx of silver from the New World during the sixteenth century facilitated the integration of local and regional markets in China while tying China to the world economy. Dennis O. Flynn and Arturo Giráldez illuminate how the global trade of silver created a world market and transformed the local ecologies of China by augmenting the exports of silks and other products, spurring the specialization of production, and restructuring the Chinese economy from a paper-money system to a silver-based economy.[63] Takeshi Hamashita demonstrates the ripple effect that China's conversion to silver had created in East Asia and Southeast Asia, and by extension, other neighboring trading zones such as India, the Islamic region, and Europe because of China's tributary system.[64] Throughout the late Ming and early Qing periods, however, the non-Han peripheral regions remained largely outside of the money economy of China proper, where barter trade prevailed. It was not until the second half of the eighteenth century that the Mongolian steppe became financially linked to the core areas of China through a series of military-political mechanisms, which greatly facilitated transregional communication and the controlled circulation of people, goods, and resources across the steppe, while at the same time subjecting the Mongols to the financial control of Chinese merchants.

The first apparatus was the postal relay system (Mo: *örtöö*, Ch: *yizhan* 驛站 or *taizhan* 台站) built across the steppe to facilitate military liaison and logistic supply during the Qing-Zunghar war. Modeled after the thirteen-century Yam (a.k.a. *jam*, "route") system of the Mongol empire and established at intervals of around one hundred *li* (fifty seven kilometers), the relay stations were responsible for providing food, shelter, and spare horses for traveling Manchu officials, officers, and government runners; transporting grain, weapons, and salaries for the military bases; and escorting criminals and captives.[65] Following the construction of the postal system in Inner Mongolia in 1692–1693, the postal system of northern Mongolia was completed in the 1750s and further extended to Ili and Tarbagatay of Xinjiang by the 1770s. The postal system of northern Mongolia comprised four main routes that linked the garrison towns of Uliasutai and Khobdo, Urga, Kyakhta, and the Khalkha-Russian borders, with one hundred and twenty relay stations dispersed along the routes.[66] The completion of the relay station system facilitated transregional trade and traffic by creating a transport network that linked the frontier territories to China proper. The caravan routes of Han merchants typically ran parallel to the official post roads, which provided them easy access to water and shelter as well as a sense of security in the wilderness across the Gobi Desert.

A second institution was the frontier guard posts (Mo: *kharuul*, Ch: *kalun* 卡倫) system established across Mongolia following the conclusion of the Treaty of Kyakhta with Russia, so as to maintain frontier control and prevent communications between the Mongols and Russians.[67] By 1765, a total of seventy-three frontier guard posts had been set up along the Khalkha-Russian borders.[68] In Inner Mongolia, guard posts and cairns (Mo: *oboo*, Ch: *ebo* 鄂博) were established to demarcate the boundaries between aimags, leagues, and banners, as according to the Qing laws, the Mongol nobilities and commoners were physically bonded to their banners and forbidden to trespass upon the territories of their neighbors. The maintenance of these military infrastructures required the mobilization of a vast amount of resources, services, and means of transport across distances. Whereas the relay stations and guard posts of Inner Mongolia were supported by the supervising Manchu governor's offices, the financing of those in Khalkha fell solely upon the four aimags. Each aimag and banner was responsible for supplying soldiers, mounts, means of transport, and provisions for the devices located in their domains. One statistic shows that over four thousand Mongol households served at the one hundred and twenty relay stations of Khalkha every year, with 47,364 camels, 249,544 horses, and 527,749 sheep expropriated, commandeered, or consumed.[69] Likewise, it took a considerable number of personnel and animals and a large amount of supplies to maintain the guard posts. Four hundred soldiers were drafted annually from each aimag and tens of thousands of animals.[70]

A third political mechanism that enhanced the control of Chinese merchants was the institution of annual rotation (*nianban* 年班) that prescribed that all Mongol ruling princes (*jasag*), nobilities (*noyan*), and high lamas should attend the imperial audience at the Qing court in Beijing on the Lunar New Year in rota. The frequencies of *nianban* duty varied by region: three rotas for the jasags and nobilities of Inner Mongolia, four for those of Outer Mongolia and Qinghai, and six for the high lamas.[71] These trips entailed great financial costs, including transport expenses, tributes to the emperor, presents to bureaucrats and imperial personnel, banquets, and so on. Gifts and bribes offered to the Lifanyuan officials and *yamen* functionaries also incurred considerable expenses. Apart from the trips to Beijing, the Mongol nobilities and high lamas also made frequent pilgrimages to celebrated Buddhist sites such as the Kumbum Monastery of Kokonor (Qinghai) and Mt. Wutai of Shanxi, which proved expensive owing to the handsome offerings made to the monasteries there.

These official obligations imposed by the Manchu rule proved to be extremely burdensome on the Mongolian economy. Although no direct taxes were levied from the Mongols, they took the form of official duties required at the post stations and guard posts. According to official records, the principal Manchu taxes in cash in Khalkha amounted to 619,350 taels of silver a year. Given a total of 21,015 tax-paying households in Khalkha, the apportionment that each household received was nearly thirty taels per year.[72] Pozdneyev interviewed a local Mongolian administrator in Tüshiyetü Khan aimag who complained of the straitened conditions of his banner:

> Now we are obliged to pay the jisang (*"assembly"*) of the diet elders more than one thousand *liang* and upwards of thirteen hundred bricks of tea for the maintenance of the soldiery and to meet various official requirements. We have to send eight horses and one camel to the Kobdo government herds; we must deliver nine horses to Urga for the herd maintained for the performance of the official business of the ambans and the diet administration. People from our sumun do duty so far distant that you will find them at as many as twenty stations in Khalkha (on the Kalgan-Uliyasutai post road). We furnish altogether an entire company of soldiers who do duty under the Kyakhta [jarghuchi— *"judge"*]. We must furnish nearly one hundred thirty yurts for the guard posts, stations, and [chaghdagha—*"militiamen"*]. We must pay more than ten thousand [taels] in rent to various [khoshuuns] who perform duty in the place of these yurts. We owe sixty horses to the treasury of the Urga [khutugtu] . . . We owe Chinese merchants living in Peking, Urga, Uliyasutai, and Kyakhta . . . and various small Chinese merchants numbering more than seventy, as well as Mongols. This is exclusively for official requirements, and it is more than one hundred thousand [taels] with interest. In the various [khoshuuns] of our aimak, we owe more than ten thousand [taels]: debts which have accrued as a result of assessments and in compensation for funds spent for official needs. Now we have come to such a pass that, if they were to take the last stitch from our backs and leave us naked, we still could not meet the demands that are being made upon us.[73]

This onerous burden of taxes, duties, and debts fell upon the common populace, who, while serving at relay stations and guard posts for meager wages, were obliged to provide their own livestock, manpower, and property without compensation. They also owed taxes and corvée labor to their princes, and were made to pay the latter's annual tribute of "nine whites" to the Manchu emperor as well as other gifts and offerings on their *nianban* trips to Beijing.[74] The excessive taxation, levies, and debts eventually led to the widespread protest movement called *duguilang* (see chapter 6), which started in Inner Mongolia and soon spread to the Khalkha region.[75]

These politico-military institutions, created to sustain the imperial control over an extensive frontier spanning Inner and Outer Mongolia and today's Xinjiang and

Qinghai, proved instrumental in the expansion of Chinese merchants into these peripheral territories. By the second half of the 1700s, the Mongols became increasingly absorbed into a silver-based monetary system, as the needs of tax payment at a definite time rendered them dependent on the financial mediation of Chinese merchants. While taxes collected by the Qing government were typically denominated in silver to pay for the salaries of administrators and officers and to cover other official expenses, it had to be converted into livestock due to the shortage of silver in Mongolia. This situation necessitated the intervention of a financial institution to supply the needed silver and handle the issues arising from payments in kind such as classifying animals, providing of grazing space, and transporting animals. Beginning in the early 1800s, the Qing government appointed the firm Dashengkui as its official agent in tax farming. Later, the firm was commissioned to supply the needs of the postal relay stations and frontier guard posts, in which case payments were made in advance and were paid back by the banners in livestock afterwards.[76]

The imperial state's attitude toward the Chinese merchants' penetration into Mongolia was ambivalent at most. Whereas the Chinese merchants played an instrumental role in financing and facilitating the Manchu military expansion, the Qing government undertook a series of measures to regulate trading activities in Mongol territories. Lifanyuan-issued licenses (*yuanpiao* 院票, or *zhaopiao* 照票) were required for all Chinese merchants traveling through Mongolia to trade. These licenses specified the name and number of traders, items, and quantity of goods (with a maximum of ten men and twenty cargo loads of goods per permit), as well as the date of departure and destination. Beginning in 1720, judicial superintendents (*jarghuchi*) were appointed by the Lifanyuan to supervise Chinese merchants in major market towns like Urga and Kyakhta.[77]

At first, only a limited number of licenses were given out each year, and the traders had to travel to Beijing to obtain them in person from the Lifanyuan, which naturally encouraged illegal trading without permits. From 1735 on, the licenses were made available at the major gates of the Great Wall upon duty payment, and after 1777, at Manchu military governor's offices in Höhhot, Kalgan, or Dolonnuur. Those trading in Khalkha were required to register and exchange licenses at the office of Urga superintendent, and upon arrival in the localities, to report at the aimag and banner offices.[78] The license was to be renewed each year, as the Qing laws prescribed that all Han Chinese must return to their native place by the year's end. A series of other bans were also in effect. These included prohibiting the Chinese traders from putting up permanent buildings, staying overnight in a Mongolian *ger* (yurt), bringing families, marrying Mongolian women, or trading outside the designated area.[79] Those who failed to present valid licenses, follow designated routes, or trade at predetermined places were to be punished with two months' imprisonment, a flogging of forty lashes, and expulsion. In addition, half of the trader's merchandise would be confiscated.[80]

In practice, these measures turned out to be unviable. A large number of Chinese traders managed to enter Mongolia on expired licenses or no licenses at all, and for those who had licenses, many never arrived at their destinations in trading towns but instead deviated to the countryside where the restrictions were more relaxed and the profits greater. Consequently, the Manchu government had to rescind its previous policy in 1796 to allow trade in the banners.[81] This incapacity to curtail Chinese trade may be explained by the private interests of the officialdom and their collusion with Chinese financial interests. Whereas the sale of licenses ensured that the Manchu officials shared in the proceeds, many of them profited from the trade and banking business by accepting gifts and bribes from the merchants as well as investing directly in the firms. The fact that the Urga superintendent's post was sold for twenty thousand taels in Beijing indicated its profitability.[82] The relaxation of Qing laws and regulations thus paved the way for the economic expansion of Chinese merchants in Mongolia.

Throughout the eighteenth century, silver as the official currency circulated only among the Manchu officialdom, Mongolian upper classes, and Chinese merchants. In the lower strata of Mongol society, however, where a barter commodity economy prevailed, the standard currency was brick tea (*zhuancha* 磚茶), which was a form of compressed tea leaves and powders that were molded into blocks or "bricks" to facilitate handling and transportation. Depending on its thickness, each brick usually weighed between 1.5 and 3.25 kilograms. By far the most important import from China, brick tea was heavily consumed by the nomads of Mongolia, Tibet, and Central Asia who had developed a special taste for this drink since the Song period. Through the Ming dynasty, it remained a controlled strategic commodity under state monopoly to be used in exchange for warhorses with the nomads through official channels of tribute missions and border markets.[83] When itinerant Chinese traders first penetrated the steppe, brick tea became the ideal commodity they could use to attract the nomads and open the Mongolian market. Due to its high turnover and great demand, the tea was often utilized among the nomads as units of currency for pricing other products.[84] The most important collection and distribution center of brick tea was Kalgan. It is reported that the amount of brick tea that passed through Kalgan reached one hundred and fifty thousand to two hundred thousand packages (approximately ten million to thirteen million kilograms) each year, which were transported to Höhhot, Urga, and Kyakhta.[85]

The circulation of money in the forms of silver and brick tea gave rise to a new financial apparatus called *yinpiao zhuang* 印票莊, which was a primordial banking institution developed in the late 1700s that was licensed to practice moneylending in Mongolia. Although the Qing laws prohibited Chinese merchants from lending silver to the Mongols, the rules were bent for a small number of firms that were granted a special license called *longpiao* 龍票 ("dragon note"). This license was essentially an official permit for engaging in usurious moneylending in Mongolia.[86] The institution obtained its name from *yinpiao* 印票 ("stamped note"), which was an interest-bearing bond certificate bearing the official seal of a Mongol aimag or banner issued at the time the loan was made. It prescribed that the sons and wives of the debtor were obliged to repay any debt incurred. In case the debtor died without offspring, the debt should be repaid by the aimag or banner.[87] In reality, however, debts incurred by the jasag were transferred to his subjects who were responsible for repaying both the principal and interests through taxes and levies.[88]

The moneylending business operated in two ways. The first was through loans in cash. The aimags and banner offices often needed to borrow cash from the firms in order to fulfill their official duties of providing mounts and funds for relay stations and frontier guard posts, supplying provisions for garrison troops, and covering the expenses of Manchu administrators. Meanwhile, the necessity of raising funds for the *nianban* trip and transporting the silver through the journey also made the Mongols financially dependent on the firms, which offered loans paid in advance as well as banking services provided by their various branches along the way. In addition, their employees would accompany the Mongol jasag or high lama to the capital, cover his expenses on the way, and serve as his interpreters and personal assistants throughout his stay there. Due to the abundant resources and excellent services of the firms, the Mongols often willingly entered into debtor agreements with them.[89] However, the services were obtained at a high price. As a rule, the firms charged a monthly interest rate of 3 percent that added up to an annual rate of 36 percent. In some cases, compound interests were charged that added up to 400 percent a year.[90] The accumulative debts easily amounted to tens of thousands taels of silver a year, and by the nineteenth century, all four aimags of Khalkha were heavily in debt. For instance, the outstanding debts of the Tüshiyetü Khan aimag reached 727,000 taels in 1855 and rose to over 960,000 taels by 1884.[91] Of the one hundred and forty banners and monasteries of Khalkha, only about ten did not owe substantial debts to Dashengkui.[92] The same applied to another firm, Tianyide, which was the largest creditor in the Khobdo region.[93]

The second way that the firms profited was through the credit sale of goods. The seasonal reproduction on the grassland determined that it was often necessary that the nomads had to make purchases first and pay for them in pastoral products later. Every year, the firms would dispatch caravans loaded with tea, tobacco, cotton fabrics, silk, and other commodities to Mongolia. Instead of payment in cash, a stamped note was issued by the aimag or banner office upon receipt of the goods, which specified the amount and value in silver to be paid back by the Mongols in the form of livestock in the following year. This arrangement enabled the firms to manipulate the prices by selling products dear and buying them cheap in addition to charging a high interest rate of 3 percent per month. For example, whereas the market price for a tea brick was a little more than three *qian* of silver in Höhhot, it was sold for eight *qian* on credit in Uliasutai. Similarly, a sheep worth eight *qian* of silver on the market was procured as repayment for a debt from the nomads for no more than two *qian*. Thus, the firms managed to squeeze profits that tripled the market value of the goods; a practice known as "one sheep three fleeces" (*yi yang san pi* 一羊三皮).[94]

As we can see, the political subjugation of the Mongols to the Qing was instrumental in the monetization of the Mongolian economy and their economic dependence on Chinese merchants. Not only did the establishment of a number of military-political institutions across the steppe facilitate the transregional circulation of goods and people, but the financing of these institutions also necessitated the intervention of an external financial system, which in turn helped integrate the Mongol periphery into the silver-based market economy of China. By the first half of the nineteenth century, silver and copper had become the dominant currencies in market towns of Mongolia and were circulated among Chinese firms, Qing state agencies, and the urban populace. In contrast, bartering remained the principal form of exchange among the nomads of rural areas, where silver was used exclusively for taxation purposes.[95] The penetration of the money economy led to social stratification and a widening gap between urban and rural regions. Meanwhile, the usurious moneylending caused widespread indebtedness and impoverishment among the Mongols. It resulted in the decline of the nomadic economy and growing social disintegration.

Nevertheless, the Mongols should not be viewed as mere victims in the process of monetization. They participated actively in the trade: operating as traders, partners, and principals of trading businesses. Two Mongolian institutions—the aristocracy and monasteries—played a key role in the international trade between Russia and China. They facilitated the conduct of business, supplied pastoral products that were in demand in both markets, and more importantly, provided the political backing necessary for enforcing the trading system. Both high lamas and hereditary aristocracy took advantage of a money economy by granting permission to firms to do business in their territories and investing livestock, land, and labor in the trade. The monasteries not only rented housing and land to the Chinese and lent money for interest, but they also operated their own camel caravans and offered transport services to the firms.[96] The Mongols dwelling in market centers were typically engaged in trades related to the transportation of goods, lumbering, and salt, as well as the retail sale of meat, hides, butter, firewood, etc.[97]

MERCHANTS THAT DOMINATED MONGOLIA

The Chinese merchants trading in Mongolia can be roughly divided into three types, despite a degree of mobility among them. The top strata were wealthy trading firms that engaged in long-distance trade and banking business and were known as *tongshihang* 通事行 ("translating agencies"). Their business covered the "exterior routes" (*wailu* 外路) supplying Uliasutai and Khobdo of central and western Mongolia, the "western routes" (*xilu* 西路) extending to Xinjiang and Qinghai, and the "rear routes" (*houlu* 後路) engaging in the trade with Russia.[98] The Chinese term *tongshi* 通事 (Mo: *tünsh*) originally meant "translator," for business was usually conducted in non-Chinese languages such as Mongolian, Uyghur, and Russian. In the Mongolian context, it came to denote "partner" or "client," which indicated a special privilege granted by the Mongols to the firms in return for their banking services.[99] These merchants' familiarity with the language and customs of the nomads, coupled with their experiences as contracted suppliers during the Qing-Zunghar war, enabled them to play an intermediate role between local Mongol authorities and Manchu administrators. Such connections were both economically enriching and politically empowering.

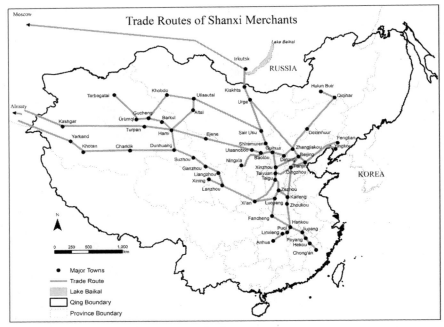

Map 2.3.　Trade Routes of Shanxi Merchants

These firms would form contracts with individual aimags and banners as guarantors and bankers, so as to meet their obligation to perform official duties in maintaining the guard posts and postal relay station, including paying the salaries of the guards and supplying them with goods. As clients of the aimags and banners, the firms were granted the privilege of monopolizing trade and finance in these territories and profited from the banking service and extending credit. They usually maintained a large number of agents, who were sent all over the region to sell goods to the Mongols in exchange for raw materials, which were collected and sent to inner China.[100]

The next type of merchant was smaller-scale sedentary merchants found in major market towns such as Urga, Höhhot, and Kalgan and monastic centers like Amurbayasqulangtu Monastery and Erdeni Juu of northern Mongolia. In addition to conducting retail business in small shops, they also undertook short excursions in the vicinity and pitched encampments near the local monasteries or headquarters of jasags. Trade was by barter exclusively. They sold all sorts of small wares such as chibouks, pipes, snuff boxes, small mirrors, rosaries, cups, toys, belts, and footwear in exchange for wool, hair, sheepskin, and felt. Over time, these merchants would lease extra housing from the monastery for warehouses and set up general stores or specialized workshops such as flourmills, oil shops, and liquor shops. These retailers lacked the funds and resources to source goods from interior China and had to depend on larger firms for the supply of merchandise. They were not allowed to participate in the lucrative moneylending, although credit sale was common. As a result, their profit margin was much smaller compared to the wealthy firms.[101]

The third strata were a large number of petty hawkers (Mo: *damnuurchin*, Ch: *huolang* 貨郎) who carried goods on shoulders to trade in periodical markets or traveled from tent to tent on donkeys or with ox carts to conduct barter trade on the steppe. Some of these traders also provided handicraft services such as making tent frames, wooden vessels, saddles and bridles, and processing animal skins. These petty traders usually departed for the grasslands every spring and returned home in late autumn after selling the livestock and other pastoral products they obtained from the nomads at nearby border markets.[102]

Large trading firms profited profusely from their connections with Manchu bureaucrats and Mongol nobilities in the role of mediators channeling the Mongols' needs to fulfill the official duties imposed by the imperial state. The three great Shanxi firms in Höhhot—Dashengkui, Yuanshengde, and Tianyide—shared a humble origin as petty suppliers during the Qing campaign of 1696 against Galdan. Dashengkui was founded by three Shanxi natives: Wang Xiangqing from Taigu county and Zhang Jie and Shi Daxue from Qixian county. The trio served as cooks and caterers for General Fiyanggu's troops stationed in Shahukou and accompanied them on the expedition to Khalkha. They would walk through the military tents with poles over their shoulders and sell an assortment of goods to the troops while sourcing livestock and meat from local herders. The three men started a partnership named Jishengtang in Shahukou that became the firm Dashengkui.[103] Tianyide was founded in the early 1700s as a partnership of three petty traders named Guo, Fan, and Ma from Shanxi. Duan Tai, another native of Qixian county, founded Yuanshengde. He began as a cameleer hired by a firm to transport provisions from Höhhot to Khobdo, and later received a share of the firm before taking over the entire firm.[104]

Once in the grassland, the merchants set out to cultivate personal relations with the local Mongol authorities by offering gifts and services to the princes and upper lamas to win their good will. Wang Xiangqing, founder of Dashengkui, was said to have cured the near-fatal illness of a daughter of a Mongol prince using remedies from Shanxi. As a token of gratitude, the prince married his daughter to Wang's second son.[105] As their business grew, the merchants also gave out financial shares of their firms in order to recruit the support of Mongol upper classes and Manchu officials. A high lama of Sayin-Noyan Khan aimag owned two out of the seven shares of Tianyide. *Beise* Delegdorji, the Manchu *amban* at Urga in the 1840s, owned stock in several Chinese firms.[106] The financial alliances with the Manchu-Mongol ruling elites were crucial to the Chinese merchants' economic dominance in Mongolia, as exemplified in the case of Dashengkui.

Among the three firms, Dashengkui was by far the largest. It remained in business for over two centuries before closing in 1929. At its prime in the nineteenth century, it had an annual turnover of ten million taels, with over seven thousand employees and thousands of camels. The capital of the firm was estimated at twenty million taels (forty million rubles in silver).[107] The most important business of Dashengkui was banking and extending credit all over northern Mongolia. Being a holder of the *longpiao* issued by the Qing court, it was among the first to establish *tongshi* or a client relationship with the Mongols by mediating financial arrangements associated with official duty payment and *nianban* trips of the princes and high lamas. Due to its connections and influence among the Mongol princes, Dashengkui managed to form client relationships in all four Khalkha aimags and in Khobdo region, whereas Tianyide's business was restricted to Sayin-Noyan Khan aimag alone.[108] Thus, Dashengkui had a near-monopoly status in these territories. Later, it was commissioned by the Qing government to collect tax in Khalkha and provide supplies to the postal relay stations and guard posts there.

The headquarters (*zonggui* 總櫃) of Dashengkui was first established in Uliasutai until they were moved to Höhhot in the mid-1800s. In order to ensure the flow of goods and credit to Khalkha, two divisions (*fenzhuang* 分莊) were set up in Uliasutai and Khobdo. Separate warehouses were built in these towns to store Chinese goods transported from Höhhot and pastoral products collected from the nomads. Linking Höhhot to Uliasutai and Khobdo was the three-thousand-kilometer-long Great Camp Road (*dayinglu* 大營路), which was parallel to but separate from the post road so as to accommodate the grazing needs of large numbers of livestock in transit. It generally took two months to reach Uliasutai from Höhhot and a few more weeks to reach Khobdo. It took an additional forty days to go to Kyakhta from Uliasutai. A third division was established in Shira Muren ("yellow river," Ch: Zhaohe 召河), a fine pasturage located eighty kilometers north of Höhhot where livestock from Khalkha were assembled and grazed before being transported to inner China. By the early 1910s, a fourth branch was set up in Hankou of Hubei province, the trading and transit port on the Yangtze River, to handle the trade of horses.[109]

Dashengkui organized long-distance caravans that traveled back and forth between Höhhot, Uliasutai, and Khobdo. The basic transport unit was called a "tent" (*fangzi* 房子), which derived its name from the cotton-cloth tent used to accommodate the traveling employees throughout the journey.[110] Each tent was made up of about two hundred camels that were organized into fourteen "chains" (Mo: *baaz*, Ch: *bazi* 把子). There were fourteen camels in each chain or line of linked camels.[111] Depending on the items transported, there were different categories of tents: cargo-tents, sheep-tents, and horse-tents. The cargo-tents usually departed from Höhhot twice a year, in the spring as well as in the late autumn. In an average year, Dashengkui would send out sixteen cargo-tents (that is, over three thousand camel loads of cargoes). Upon arriving in Uliasutai or Khobdo, the tents were then split into smaller units that set out for various local destinations along predetermined routes. Depending on the volume of cargoes, one "small tent" may consist of one, two, or three chains of camels, each led by a manager assisted by a number of employees.[112]

The Chinese commodities with the highest demand in Mongolia were brick tea, raw tobacco, cotton drills, and silk. In an average year, Dashengkui typically sold a total of four thousand boxes (i.e., 260,000 kilograms) of brick tea, one thousand *tun* 囤 (i.e. 108,000 kilograms) of raw tobacco, four thousand bolts of silk, and six thousand bolts of cotton cloth to the Khalkha region. These cargoes alone, a total value of 146,500 taels of silver, brought a net profit of 151,600 taels. The firm also carried a whole range of other products, including flour, fried millet, hard spirits, sugar and candies, cakes and pastries, medicines, ceremonial scarves, wooden vessels, copperwares, leather boots, horse gears, and hemp ropes. It is estimated that the sixteen "cargo-tents" that Dashengkui sold to Uliasutai and Khobdo every year, a total 269,045 taels worth of goods, would produce a net profit of 190,618 taels.[113] This did not include the annual interest of 36 percent charged for sale on credit. In reality, the profit margin was even greater as the firm took every means to cut expenditures on purchases and lower the prices of pastoral items procured as debt.

In the early spring and in the summer, Dashengkui would dispatch separate sheep-tents and horse-tents to collect debts in the form of livestock from the Mongols. This livestock was driven out in July and arrived at Höhhot at the end of September. Each of these tents was headed by a manager along with forty shepherds, one hundred and fifty camels, and a pack of dogs. The manager and shepherds were in charge of selecting, pricing, stamping, assembling, and transporting the animals to Dashengkui's grazing base in Shira Muren. Each sheep-tent was responsible for transporting fifteen thousand sheep, divided into a number of flocks, and each horse-tent handled fifteen hundred horses.[114] Depending on the harvest condition, Dashengkui was able to collect seven to ten sheep-tents and three to five horse tents a year, that is, between a hundred thousand and a hundred fifty thousand sheep and forty-five hundred to seventy-five hundred horses.[115] The sheep were driven for sale to Beijing and Taiyuan. A large number of horses went for wholesale on the markets of Shira Muren and Höhhot held in the seventh and tenth lunar months, and the rest were sold at annual horse fairs held in Hongdong and Changzi counties of Shanxi, Kaifeng prefecture of Henan, and Ding district of Zhili. In general, the animals were sold for no less than double the price they were obtained for in Mongolia.[116]

Several practical strategies contributed to Dashengkui's remarkable success in Mongolia. First, the firm went to great lengths to modify and improve its products in order to cater to the varying tastes and demands of their customers. The salesmen of Dashengkui had to go through a lengthy training period of ten years before their first home leave was granted. During this time, they were to spend three years each at the Uliasutai and Khobdo branches and Höhhot headquarters to familiarize themselves with the Mongolian language and social customs besides the business.[117] Their knowledge of the nomadic lifestyle and customs helped expand the scope of the business to include a whole range of products that met the everyday needs of the Mongols. For example, among the brick tea carried by Dashengkui, the "Thirty-Nine" brand was customized for the markets of Uliasutai and Khobdo, whereas the "Thirty-Six" and "Twenty-Seven" brands were primarily sold to Kalgan, Urga, and Kyakhta and the "Twenty-Four" brand to Höhhot and Baotou. Each brand, named after the number of bricks packed in each box, was specially tailored for the customary taste in the targeted region and thus gained great popularity among the

Mongols.[118] The variety of goods carried by Dashengkui also multiplied over the years, which ranged from basic necessities to a host of other utensils and luxuries. In many ways, the unprecedented flood of Chinese commodities reshaped the economic needs of the Mongols (in particular, that of the upper classes), while transforming the Mongol community in the long run.

Second, the firm organized an elaborate business network that spanned great distances as well as different types of trade-goods. Apart from various divisions, Dashengkui also invested in a number of subsidiaries (*xiaohao* 小號); each specialized in a specific line of trade such as tea, silk, banking, and livestock.[119] Among these, tea and banking were the two most important pillars that sustained its monopoly of finance and trade in Mongolia. Most of the brick tea that Dashengkui sold to Mongolia was supplied by Sanyuchuan, a Qixian-based tea firm and subsidiary of Dashengkui that sourced and wholesaled tea directly from its origin in the middle Yangtze valley of Central China. Each year, between July and December, tea pickers were hired to pluck tea leaves in the mountains in Puqi county of Hubei province and Linxiang county of Hunan province. The assembled tea was compressed into blocks in local workshops and transported from Hankou to Höhhot and Kalgan, where Sanyuchuan set up divisions. The brick tea carried by Sanyuchuan was extremely popular on the Mongolian market. During its prime, the annual sales volume was said to have exceeded ten thousand boxes (650,000 kilograms). Apart from Dashengkui, Sanyuchuan also supplied the other firms of Kyakhta, Urga, and Dolonnuur.[120]

Another important subsidiary that Dashengkui set up was Dashengchuan, a banking firm founded in the early 1800s in Qixian, home of proto-banking (*piaohao* 票號, literally "draft banks") in China. Its predecessor was a money shop called Yushengkui, one of the earliest *piaohaos* in China.[121] We mentioned earlier that the necessity to finance a series of imperial apparatuses in Mongolia gave rise to the primordial banking institutions (*piaozhuang* 票莊) that profited from usurious moneylending and credit sale in Mongolia. As a banking firm, Dashengchuan was responsible for financing the *nianban* trips of Mongol nobilities and high lamas to Beijing as well as handling monetary matters for them along the way. Meanwhile, the booming tea trade also contributed to the development of these proto-banks. The running of the tea firms demanded a large amount of working capital to cover the expenses of tea picking, storage, and transport that would not be paid back until at least a year after the tea was sold on the market. Whereas the banking firms were indispensable in supplying working capital for the tea firms, the high turnover in the tea trade helped the capital accumulation and expansion of the banking firms. By the late 1800s, Dashengchuan had opened a great number of branches in core areas of China such as Beijing, Tianjin, Shanghai, and Hankou, in frontier cities such as Kalgan, Dolonnuur, Höhhot, Baotou, and in five other locations in Manchuria.[122]

Other major subsidiaries of Dashengkui included the Tianshuntai Silk Firm that supplied silk and cotton fabrics from Shandong and Henan provinces, the Dongshengchang Supplying Firm that sourced a wide range of other Chinese commodities, and the Dehengkui Livestock Shop that wholesaled horses, sheep, and other animals.

All of these firms were based in Höhhot. In addition, Dashengkui invested in three Beijing-based sheep firms (Xieshengchang, Xieshenggong, and Xieshengyu), which were in charge of the transport and distribution of sheep to the capital.[123] By organizing wholesale and transport directly from the origin and to major markets of China, the company proposed even more. This mode of business specialization greatly facilitated the supply and distribution of goods by not only bringing about efficiency and flexibility to the logistics, but also significantly lowering the costs.

TRADE, TRANSPORTATION, AND INDUSTRIES

The Chinese commercial expansion also brought about the flourishing of various service sectors, such as transportation, food processing, and brokerage. The distribution of goods across distances relied exclusively on camel caravans. Chinese merchants usually employed Mongolian cameleers to carry goods from the fringe of China to the steppe. The monasteries often operated their own camel caravans and offered services to the firms.[124] During the mid-1700s, the Qing government began to recruit Chinese or Hui transporters to deliver grain rations to the military bases in Khalkha for a good profit. For instance, in 1754, twenty thousand *hu* 斛 (i.e. six hundred thousand kilograms) of grain was transported from Höhhot to Uliasutai at a rate of 9.8 taels per *hu*, although the grain price was between 2 and 3 taels per *hu*.[125] Natives of Qixian, Daizhou, and Youyu counties of northern Shanxi began to join the transport business during this period, along with some Hui Muslims who were recruited to transport livestock from Khalkha to Höhhot. Large firms also relied on the services provided by these commercial transporters. The Yu family of Qixian kept a herd of one thousand camels, and the Liu family kept eight hundred cattle. Both were commissioned by Dashengkui to carry goods such as tobacco and iron implements from Shanxi and Henan to Mongolia.[126] The Qing suppression of the Dungan/Hui Revolt (1862–1873) triggered a new transport boom in which Chinese settlers in Xinjiang were recruited to carry military supplies for the Qing armies. Professional transport services mushroomed in Höhhot in the late 1870s. The largest such service company was Tiandequan, which was founded by three Hu brothers from Xinjiang who owned over a thousand camels.[127]

Food industries prospered as long-distance trade and the expanding migrant population spurred the demand for food products outside the passes. Before departing for the grassland, the caravan tents needed to stock up with no less than two months' supply of food provisions and flour to sustain the journey across the Gobi Desert. Meanwhile, the booming trade attracted an influx of migrants who congregated in the expanding market towns, including merchants, artisans, and laborers. Itinerant traders had to purchase supplies of merchandise there before embarking on their excursions to the banners, and animal dealers from south of the passes would gather around the livestock markets. Large firms relied on a large number of shepherds and cameleers to raise the animals assembled in their grazing bases and on the miscellaneous services of handicraftsmen such as blacksmiths, carpenters, felt makers, curriers, and rope makers. Dashengkui, for instance, kept between two hundred to over a thousand hired hands at Shira Muren (the number fluctuated according to the season).[128] For these reasons, food processing businesses (*liuchenhang* 六陳行, "six old trades") flourished as they supplied grain, flour, oil, and liquor to merchants, artisans, and workers. Specialized workshops such as oil shops, liquor shops, and flourmills also multiplied.

The prosperous service sector accelerated the process of urbanization and settlement on the steppe. For example, Khökhe Ergi (modern Wuchuan county, Inner Mongolia), a small town north of Mt. Daqingshan, rose during the late eighteenth and early nineteenth century as an important supply center between Höhhot and Shira Muren. Its main pillar of business was food processing and transport, with its food products supplying Dashengkui primarily. Its population consisted mostly of professional transporters such as cameleers and donkey-cart drivers who hired out their services to trading firms and itinerant traders traveling between Höhhot and Shira Muren. Some of them also began to penetrate into the peripheral areas and settle down and establish shops there. Many villages situated between Khökhe Ergi and Shira Muren bear names such as Kangyoufang ("Kang's oil shop") and Xihuofang ("western kitchen"), which indicate the occupation of the earliest Chinese settlers in this area.[129]

Another common establishment found in trade centers was a commercial inn (*dian* 店), which served as a hostelry and store for itinerant merchants who conducted temporary business from inner China or other trade towns. These inns provided the traveling merchant with lodging, provisions, and a secure place for storing his goods. He may choose to sell his merchandise or commission the proprietor of the inn to sell it on his behalf free of charge. The proprietor of the inn would undertake to supply transportation for any goods sold or bought by the visiting merchant for no extra charge, and he would also serve as a guarantor in case the goods were sold on credit to local dealers. Using his local connections, these innkeepers-cum-dealers intermediated between buyers and sellers and facilitated the flow of goods and capital.[130]

The flow of trade was by no means one-directional, however. At times when supplies were running low, the nomadic Mongols would drive their animals down to the nearby market towns along with ox cart loads of pelts, skins, and other pastoral products, and exchange them for Chinese commodities. Livestock dealers and brokers (*yaji* 牙紀) thus emerged who specialized in mediating between the nomads and wholesale buyers. There were over twenty livestock dealers in Höhhot alone. Once in town, the Mongols usually entrusted their animals to a certain dealer whom they were acquainted with. For those new in town, a broker would approach them and offer help in finding dealers or wholesale buyers, with a commission collected from both the buyer and seller. Generally speaking, sheep were sold directly to the dealers, whereas a broker was required in the sale of horses.[131] Similarly, itinerant merchants doing barter trade in the banners also needed to sell the animals they obtained from the nomads before leaving Mongolia for home. The dealers often entered into agreement with them by providing funds for purchasing merchandises, and in return, their livestock had to be sold to the same dealer. For this, it was necessary for the dealers to maintain close business ties with the local money shops, so they could provide working capital for the merchants in advance.[132]

By the second half of the nineteenth century, the commercial network had further expanded to link the Mongolian steppe to the global market through Tianjin, the treaty port opened in the wake of the Second Opium War (1856–1860). The Convention of Beijing (1860) granted Russia the right to maintain a consulate at Urga and to trade directly inside Mongolia, including operating commercial caravans between Kalgan and Kyakhta. Later, a Russian commissioner was stationed halfway between Kalgan and Urga to supervise the caravans. Virtually all Russian merchants in Urga and Kalgan were engaged as commissioners in the transshipment of tea from Hankou and Fuzhou to Kyakhta.[133] Apart from Russian merchants, foreign firms from Germany, the United States, and Britain also set up offices in Höhhot and Kalgan: hiring Chinese merchants as their agents. The demand for pastoral products such as furs, sheepskins, hides, wool, and camel hair on the international market greatly boosted the trade of these raw materials in Mongolia. Dashengkui, which was engaged mainly in the wholesale of livestock, now expanded its scope of business to furs and wools, which were then sold to the foreign firms in Höhhot. The firm even established a subsidiary in Tianjin that dealt in the export of these raw materials.[134]

Thus, the incorporation of Mongolia into a global economic system helped intensify the economic dominance of Chinese merchants in Mongolia as not only traders and creditors, but also as agents of foreign capital. Over the long run, however, the competition of cheap Western imports and modern means of transportation dissolved their economic monopoly in the grassland. In addition, the shifting geopolitics of the early twentieth century made the Chinese merchants an easy target of rising Mongolian nationalism, as they were the epitome of Chinese political and economic oppression. After Mongolia proclaimed its second independence in 1924, all Chinese firms were heavily taxed and then expelled, with all their properties confiscated. Dashengkui, the trading and banking giant in Mongolia, went out of business in 1929.

CONCLUSION

This chapter has examined the process of Chinese expansion into the Mongol territories during the eighteenth and nineteenth centuries through the flow of goods, capital, and people across the Han-Mongol border. The changing connotations of *xikou* during the Ming-Qing transition show that underlying the ostensible choice between war or peace were geographical differentials that made economic exchanges between China and the northern steppe necessary. The Manchu expansion created not only an extensive frontier that spanned vast territories across the steppe but also long-lasting institutions of trade that diverged from the old arrangement of tribute and trade by allowing private merchant capital to spread along official post roads and establish trading centers on the steppe.

Spearheading the economic expansion were the merchants of Shanxi, who occupied the economic niche between inner China and the steppe. This niche allowed them to capitalize on the bilateral exchange. The case study of Dashengkui illuminates the role of the Shanxi merchants as primary intermediaries between the Mongol herders and the farmers of China, as well as between the Manchu military administration and the Mongolian elites. Their business practices resulted in flourishing markets both inside China and on the steppe, accelerated the processes of urbanization and monetization in Mongolia, and helped integrate the nomadic Mongols into the global economic system. On the other hand, they preyed on the financial dependence of the Mongolian upper classes and turned usurious moneylending into a mechanism for siphoning off the Mongol wealth. Their financial domination resulted in heavy indebtedness and the impoverishment of Mongol commoners, as well as strong anti-Chinese antagonism. This antagonism was partly responsible for the proclamation of the independence of northern Mongolia in 1911.

Just as borders like the Great Wall functioned both as obstacles to the movement of peoples and as facilitators of cross-cultural interactions, so the Shanxi merchants served as agents of the imperial order as well as cultural brokers.[135] They created entirely new social and economic amalgamations by bridging, negotiating, and mediating between groups with different cultural backgrounds (in this case, Manchu administrators, Mongol elites and commoners, and Chinese farmers and artisans) and by communicating their different needs across spaces. They themselves were not importers or "bringers of change," but the relationships they formed set off a series of developments that reshaped the socio-economic landscape of the steppe region.

NOTES

1. Dee Mack Williams discusses the negative associations with the northern frontier in Chinese perceptions of ecological identity, as reflected in terms such as *huang* 荒 (waste), *kuang* 曠 (vast), *wu* 無 (overgrown), and *ye* 野 (untamed), which carry derogatory implications of savagery, desolation, and moral deficiency. See Williams, "The Barbed Walls of China," 671–73. For the terms of kouwai/saiwai, see Millward, *Beyond the Pass*, 3–4, 153 n2.

2. For the function of walled frontier in delineating cultural and territorial space, see Lattimore, "Origins of the Great Wall of China," 530–31; Waldron, *The Great Wall of China*, 9; Williams, "The Barbed Walls of China," 669–71; Millward, *Beyond the Pass*, 3–4, 36–38.

3. For a detailed account of the Qing-Zunghar war, see Perdue, *China Marches West*.

4. Liu Zhonghe and Boyinhu, "'Xikou' bian"; Wang Laigang, "'Xikou' jianxi"; Tuimole, "Guihuacheng fei 'xikou' kao." For an overview of various connotations of *xikou*, see Liu Zhonghe, *Zouxikou lishi yanjiu*, 17–50. For a description of Kalgan, see Pozdneyev, *Mongolia and the Mongols*, volume 1, 439–57; Gilmour, *Among the Mongols*, 176–78.

5. Lattimore, "Origins of the Great Wall of China"; Waldron, *The Great Wall of China*.

6. Fletcher, "The Mongols," 15–16; Barfield, *The Perilous Frontier*, 90–91; Jagchid and Symons, *Peace, War, and Trade Along the Great Wall*; Di Cosmo, *Ancient China and Its Enemies*,

131–34. For a general discussion of the nomad-sedentary trade relations, see Khazanov, *Nomads and the Outside World*, 203–12.

7. For the tribute system as a theoretical framework, see Fairbank and Teng, "On the Ch'ing Tributary System," 135–246; Fairbank, *The Chinese World Order*. Fairbanks's framework highlights the political, diplomatic, and cultural dimension of the tribute system. For a brief introduction to the tribute system, see Hevia, *Cherishing Men From Afar*, 9–14. For discussions on the tribute system in the Ming period, see Serruys, *The Tribute System and Diplomatic Missions*, 19–28. For discussions on the tribute system within the broader context of East Asia regional order and the world economy, see Hamashita, *Kindai Chūgoku no kokusaiteki keiki*.

8. Jagchid and Symons, *Peace, War, and Trade Along the Great Wall*. It should be pointed out that the tribute relation was by no means the exclusive form of institutionalized exchange between the nomads and the Chinese. In fact, the Chinese dynasties were often forced to pay tribute to the northern nomads in exchange for peace, usually in form of royal marriage (*heqin* 和親), yearly payments (*suibi* 歲幣), and bestowal of goods and presents. In addition, border markets were occasionally opened during the Ming times as a measure of appeasing the nomads. In official Chinese records, however, all these different forms of exchange were loosely grouped under the term "tribute." See Jagchid, *Essays in Mongolian Studies*; Barfield, *The Perilous Frontiers*. For a critique of the tribute system, see Willis, "Tribute, Defensiveness, and Dependency," 225–29; Perdue, "The Tenacious Tributary System," 1007–11.

9. These included the Jurchens and Uriyangkhads of the northeast and the Central Asians of western Gansu and Hami in the northwest. See Serruys, *The Tribute System and Diplomatic Missions, 1400–1600*.

10. For more discussions on the tribute system, which was a form of state-subsidized monopoly trade covered up as rituals of symbolic subordination, see Serruys, *The Tribute System and Diplomatic Missions, 1400–1600*, 19–28; Hamashita, *Kindai Chūgoku no kokusaiteki keiki*. For discussions on the horse fair system, see Surreys, *Trade Relations: the Horse Fairs, 1400–1600*; Rossabi, *China and Inner Asia*, 80–83; Jagchid and Symons, *Peace, War, and Trade*, 81.

11. Mote, "The T'u-mu Incident of 1449"; Rossabi, "The Ming and Inner Asia," 233–35.

12. See Serruys, *The Tribute System and Diplomatic Missions*, 64–73; Rossabi, *China and Inner Asia*, 43–46; Jagchid and Symons, *Peace, War, and Trade*, 81–103. Also see Cao Yongnian, *Menggu minzu tongshi*, volume 3, 157–58.

13. See *Ming Shi* 81, shihuozhi 5; Cao Yongnian, *Menggu minzu tongshi*, volume 3, 180–82. For detailed account of the horse fairs during the Ming period, see Serruys, *Trade Relations*; Rossabi, *China and Inner Asia*, 80–83; Jagchid and Symons, *Peace, War, and Trade*, 81.

14. Liu Shiming, *Shuoping fuzhi* 2, 367. On the circumstances of constructing Pingjibu, see Zhang Weishu, "*Jianzao shahukou xinbao xiangyi*," in Liu Shiming, *Shuoping fuzhi* 5, 1426.

15. For the rise of commerce in the Ming dynasty, see Brook, *The Confusions of Pleasure*.

16. Lu Minghui and Liu Yankun, *Lümengshang*, 7–10; Rossabi, *China and Inner Asia*, 81. Later a similar system also applied to the trade of tea in Shaanxi, allowing traders contributing to grain transport to engage in the monopolized trade of tea for horses at the frontier. See Perdue, *China Marches West*, 70.

17. For instance, in 1575, the number of horses, mules, cattle, and sheep obtained from private markets of Yansui town totaled over twenty-two thousand, as compared to the 2,104 horses on official markets. See *Mingshilu* 45, WL 3/12/12.

18. See Perdue, *China Marches West*. For Galdan's invasion of Khalkha and details of the Dolonnuur Assembly, see Bawden, *The Modern History of Mongolia*, 74–80.

19. Haizhong and Lin Congjiong, eds., *Chengde fuzhi* 1, juanshou.

20. *Da Qing lichao shilu* (hereafter QSL) 151, KX 30/5/7. Translation cited from Bawden, *The Modern History of Mongolia*, 81.

21. QSL 40, SZ 5/8/20, 3.320; QSL 183, KX 36/7/14, 5.

22. Serruys, "Place Names Along China's Northern Frontier."

23. *Qinding lifanbu zeli* 32, 284–86; QHDSL 993, Lifanyuan jinling. For the regulations on *nianban*, see *Da Qing yitong zhi* 404; Sanjdorj, *Manchu Chinese Colonial Rule in Northern Mongolia*, 48. For the five routes of postal relay stations in Inner Mongolia, see Jin Feng, "Qingdai Nei Menggu wulu yizhan"; Han Rulin, "Qingdai nei menggu yizhan." For details on the Shahukou postal road, see Liu Zhonghe, "Shahukou yizhan gujin diming yanjiu."

24. See Wu Meifeng, "*Qingdai de shahukou shuiguan*," 15. For the shifting administration of Shahukou, see QSL 976, 236, 8221, 8223; QSG 125, zhi 100, shihuo 6.

25. These trading sites were Bagou (present Pingquan of Hebei), Tazigou (present Lingyuan of Liaoning), Sanzuota (present Chaoyang of Liaoning), and Ulaankhada (present Chifeng of Inner Mongolia), all located in Jehol outside Xifengkou, and Dingbian and Hengcheng (of Shaanxi), Huamachi and Pingluo (of Gansu), all situated inside the Great Wall bordering the Ordos. See Wuyunbilige et al., *Menggu minzu tongshi*, volume 4, 309.

26. For discussion on border trade along the Great Wall in the Qing period, see Qi Meiqin, "Lun qingdai changcheng biaokou maoyi," 73–86.

27. Wuyunbilige et al., *Menggu minzu tongshi*, volume 4, 156–58. For discussion of the operation of these imperial pastures and state complexes, see Bello, *Across Forest, Steppe, and Mountain*, 122–25.

28. QSL, SZ 12/11/21; Bawden, *The Modern History of Mongolia*, 62, 102; Zhukov et al., *History of the Mongolian People's Republic*, 189.

29. QSL 112, KX 22/9/15; Lu Minghui and Liu Yankun, *Lümengshang*, 32, 103. For discussion of the trade relations between the Zunghars and the Qing, see Perdue, *China Marches West*, 397–406.

30. Sanjdorj, *Manchu Chinese Colonial Rule*, 21–26; Martha Avery, *The Tea Road*; Pozdneyev, *Mongolia and the Mongols*, volume 1.

31. Pozdneyev, *Mongolia and the Mongols*, volume 1; Sanjdorj, *Manchu Chinese Colonial Rule*, 21.

32. For the economic significance of monasteries in Mongolia, see Miller, *Monasteries and Culture Change in Inner Mongolia*; Miller, "Buddhist Monastic Economy"; Pozdneyev, *Mongolia*, volume 1, 25–26.

33. For example, the Ganjuur sume of Hulunbuir had hosted one of the largest fairs in the region since 1785. The market was set at the beginning of the eighth lunar month and lasted for seven days, and coincided with annual religious assemblies and *naadam* festivals where horse riding, wrestling, and archery competitions were held. See Xiaoguang, *Ganzhuer miao*.

34. Fletcher, "Ch'ing Inner Asia c. 1800."

35. Pozdneyev, *Mongolia and the Mongols*, volume 1, 25; Avery, *The Tea Road*, 72–75. For the economic role of monasteries, see Pozdneyev, *Religion and Ritual in Society*, 31–32.

36. Pozdneyev, *Mongolia and the Mongols*, volume 1, 46–49, 77–84.

37. For the Dolonnuur Assembly, see Atwood, *Encyclopedia of Mongolia and the Mongol Empire*, 148.

38. See Jin Zhizhang and Huang Kerun, *Koubei santing zhi*, 568. Pozdneyev described the burkhan (statue of Buddha) of Maidari, the largest and highest building in Urga, was cast in a Chinese workshop in Dolonnuur. See Pozdneyev, *Mongolia and the Mongols*, volume 1, 61. On monastic workshops, see Charleux, "The Making of Mongol Buddhist Art and Architecture."

39. For details of the Baikov Embassy, see March, *Eastern Destiny*, 44–45; Demidova, "*Fyōdoru baikof shisetsu no chūgoku hōmon 1654–1658 nen.*" For genesis of diplomatic relations and early forms of caravan trade prior to 1727, see Wanner, "First Russian-Chinese Diplomatic Relations and Business Relationship 1689–1728."

40. See Parkes, "Report on the Russian Caravan Trade with China," 306–12; Sanjdorj, *Manchu Chinese Colonial Rule*, 59–60; Rossabi, *China and Inner Asia*, 124–38; Avery, *The Tea Road*, 88–90.

41. For details on the Kyakhta Treaty, see Coxe, *Account of the Russian Discoveries between Asia and America*, 306–11; Mancall, *Russia and China*, 249–55. For a general description, see Bao Muping, "Trade Centres (Maimaicheng) in Mongolia," 212.

42. For a description of Kyakhta, see Coxe, *Account of the Russian Discoveries*, 315–17; Pozdneyev, *Mongolia and the Mongols*, volume 1, 2–3. Also see Sanjdorj, *Manchu Chinese Colonial Rule*, 62; Avery, *The Tea Road*, 134–40; Bao Muping, "Trade Centres (Maimaicheng) in Mongolia," 213; Wanner, "The Russian-Chinese Trade in Kyakhta," 36–37.

43. Coxe, *Account of the Russian Discoveries*, 337–42. For discussions on imports and exports in the Sino-Mongol trade, also see Avery, *The Tea Road*; Lu and Liu, *Lümengshang*, 133; Wuyungerile, *Shiba zhi ershi shiji chu neimenggu chengzhen yanjiu*, 100–02.

44. See Lu and Liu, *Lümengshang*, 202–05; Wanner, "The Russian-Chinese Trade in Kyakhta—Its Organisation and Commodity Structure," 42–46; Wanner, "Russian-Chinese Trade in Kyakhta—Trade Development and Volume Indicators," 20.

45. Pozdneyev, *Mongolia and the Mongols*, volume 1, 444–45.

46. For the decline of the Kyakhta trade, see Wanner, "The Russian-Chinese Trade in Kyakhta—Its Organisation and Commodity Structure," 48–49; Wanner, "Russian-Chinese Trade in Kyakhta—Trade Development and Volume Indicators," 24–26. For the Sino-Russian Treaty of Tianjin, see Wang Yi and Zhang Chengqi ed., *Xianfeng tiaoyue*, 19–21.

47. Bao Muping compares the rise of maimaicheng in the Mongolian transit trade to the emergence of Chinatowns found all over the world. Both represented a distinct feature of urban development brought about by Chinese emigrants from the mid-eighteenth through mid-nineteenth century. See Bao Muping, *Mongoru ni okeru toshi kenchikushi kenkyū*, 211, 217.

48. Wuyungerile, *Shiba zhi ershi shiji chu neimenggu chengzhen yanjiu*, 19–24. For a classical analysis of the central places, see Skinner, "Marketing and Social Structure in Rural China," Part I.

49. For discussion of the various levels of market centers on the steppe, see Wuyungerile, *Shiba zhi ershi shiji chu neimenggu chengzhen yanjiu*, 92–95.

50. Gaubatz, *Beyond the Great Wall*; Hyer, "An Historical Sketch of Koke-Khota City," 56–77; Huang Li-Sheng, *You junshi zhenglue dao chengshi maoyi*. On the Chinese population and residential areas in Höhhot, also see Bao Muping, *Mongoru ni okeru toshi kenchikushi kenkyū*. On the guilds of Höhhot, see Imahori, *Chūgoku hōken shakai no kikō*.

51. Jagchid and Hyer, *Mongolia's Culture and Society*, 313.

52. The most prominent were Yekhe Juu ("Great Monastery"), one of the first monasteries ever built in Mongolia commissioned by Altan Khan in 1579, and Shireetü Juu, built in 1585

by Altan Khan's son after his death, which became the largest monastery in Höhhot. The Qing court continued to patronize Tibetan Buddhism in Mongolia, and a total of seven major monasteries and eight minor ones were built in Höhhot and its vicinity by the mid-1700s. See Rong Xiang and Rong Genglin, *Tumote yange*, 37–40, 207; Wuyungerile, *Shiba zhi ershi shiji chu neimenggu chengzhen yanjiu*, 53–55.

53. See QHDSL 976, 16861. For discussion of the Manchu Eight Banners, see Elliott, *The Manchu Way*.

54. Rong Xiang and Rong Genglin, *Tumote yange*, 44–46; Hyer, "An Historical Sketch of Koke-Khota City"; Wuyungerile, *Shiba zhi ershi shiji chu neimenggu chengzhen yanjiu*, 55–57.

55. Zhang was dispatched on a mission to negotiate the borders with the Russians, which was determined in the Treaty of Nerchinsk (1689). Joining him in the journey was Manchu ambassador Songgotu, and two Jesuit missionaries Thomas Pereira and Jean-Francois Gerbillon served as interpreters. See Zhang Penghe, *Fengshi eluosi riji*, 19–20.

56. Gerbillon, "The Travels of Father Gerbillon," 243–44.

57. See QHDSL 236, 8226. Whereas the annual tax revenue at Shahukou was around sixteen thousand taels of silver in the 1800s, that of Höhhot well exceeded twenty thousand taels, and reached 65,279 taels in 1887. See Wang Zemin, *Shahukou yu Zhongguo beibu bianjiang*, 307.

58. Suiyuan Tongzhiguan, ed., *Suiyuan tongzhigao* (hereafter SYTZG) 27.1, 564.

59. Pozdneyev, *Mongolia and the Mongols*, volume 2, 74. Bao Muping argues that it was only after the incorporation of Xinjiang into the Qing empire in 1759 that Kalgan and Hohhot began to be known as the "eastern" and "western" gateways, joined to trade routes linking Kyakhta and Ili. See Bao Muping, *Mongoru ni okeru toshi kenchikushi kenkyū*, 216.

60. Pozdneyev, *Mongolia and the Mongols*, volume 2, 137.

61. Wu Shengrong, "Woguo xibei pimao jisan zhongzhen Baotou de pimao hangye," 15, 70.

62. For the guilds of Höhhot, see Imahori, *Chūgoku hōken shakai no kikō*.

63. Flynn and Giráldez, "Born with a 'Silver Spoon,'" 206–09; Flynn and Giráldez, "Cycles of Silver: Global Economic Unity through the Mid-Eighteenth Century," 416–20. For a long-term monetary history of China, see Von Glahn, *Fountains of Fortune*.

64. Hamashita, "The Tribute System of Modern Asia," 97.

65. QHDSL 982, 16916. See Jin Feng, "Qingdai Nei Menggu wulu yizhan"; Han Rulin, "Qingdai Menggu yizhan." For a general study on the postal relay system in the Qing era, see Wuyunbilige et al., *Menggu minzu tongshi*, volume 4, 265–72; Liu Wenpeng, *Qingdai yichuan jiqi yu jiangyu xingcheng guanxi zhi yanjiu*.

66. The relay stations in northern Mongolia included sixty-one Altai military stations, fourteen Urga stations, twelve Kyakhta stations, and twenty-seven stations to frontier guard posts on the Russo-Khalkha borders and Xinjiang. The relay station system in Xinjiang comprised three routes: northern Urumqi to Ili, western Urumqi, and Tarbakhatai, with a total of forty-six relay stations. See QHDSL 982, 16913–14; *Qinding Lifanbu zeli* 31, 32. For the construction of the northern routes of postal stations in northern Mongolia and Xinjiang, see Jin Feng, "Qingdai Wai Menggu beilu yizhan," 77–102; "Qingdai xinjiang xilu juntai." For decription of post road administration, see Pozdneyev, *Mongolia and the Mongols*, volume 1, 98, 129, 135–36.

67. For the institution of guard posts and its functions, see Wuyunbilige et al., *Menggu minzu tongshi*, volume 4, 258–64; Baoyinchaoketu, *Qingdai beibu bianjiang kalun yanjiu*, 151–53.

68. QHDSL 746.

69. Nasanbaljir, *Qingchao tongzhi shiqi de yizhan yiwu.*

70. QHDSL 746.

71. QHDSL 984, 16932–39. For the annual rotation system, also see Zhao Yuntian, *Qingdai menggu zhengjiao zhidu*; Zhao Zhiheng, *Nei Menggu tongshi*, volume 3, 73.

72. Zhukov, *History of the Mongolian People's Republic* (MPR), 199; Sanjdorj, *Manchu Chinese Colonial Rule*, 50–51.

73. Pozdneyev, *Mongolia and the Mongols*, volume 1, 13, italics added by author.

74. QHDSL 980, 16896; Zhukov, *History of the MPR*, 198.

75. Serruys, "Documents from Ordos on the 'Revolutionary Circles,' Part I"; "Part II."

76. A research committee in Inner Mongolia started compiling the oral history of Dashengkui in 1960, and over the course of six years, interviewed a total of 137 people, including managers, shareholders, employees of Dashengkui and their families and offspring, as well as contemporaries who had business relations with the firm. Most of the interviewees were between sixty and eighty years of age, and eleven were over eighty. The result, published in 1984, provided a rare insider's perspective into the operation of the business giant in Mongolia. See DSK, 42, 73–78. For the scope of business of Dashengkui, also see Pozdneyev, *Mongolia and the Mongols*, volume 1, 208; Avery, *The Tea Road*, 53–68.

77. QHDSL 983, 16924. For discussion on the judicial superintendent of the Lifanyuan, see Bawden (1968); Sanjdorj, *Manchu Chinese Colonial Rule*, 35; Wanner, "The Russian-Chinese Trade in Kyakhta—Its Organisation and Commodity Structure," 18.

78. Sanjdorj, *Manchu Chinese Colonial ·Rule*, 47. The judicial superintendent was appointed by the *Lifanyuan* in the beginning of 1720s to manage the trade affairs in Urga. See Sanjdorj, *Manchu Chinese Colonial Rule*, 34–35.

79. Sanjdorj, *Manchu Chinese Colonial Rule*, 34; QHDSL 978; SYTZG 27.1, 564.

80. *Qinding lifanbu zeli*, 300.

81. Sanjdorj, *Manchu Chinese Colonial Rule*, 77–80.

82. Sanjdorj, *Manchu Chinese Colonial Rule*, 36; Chen Chongzu, *Waimenggu jinshi shi.*

83. Rossabi, *China and Inner Asia*, 78–83; Avery, *The Tea Road.*

84. For example, in Uliasutai and Khobdo, a sheep was worth two tea bricks, and a horse fourteen. Each tea brick can be exchanged for two sheepskins or two packs of raw tobacco. See Zhongguo renmin zhengzhi xieshang huiyi Nei Menggu zhizhiqu weiyuanghui wenshi ziliao weiyuanhui, ed., *Lümengshang dashengkui* (hereafter DSK), 155. Prejevalsky reported that in Urga, a sheep was worth twelve to fifteen bricks of tea, a camel 120 to 150 bricks, and a Chinese tobacco pipe two to five bricks. See Prejevalsky, *Mongolia, the Tangut Country, and the Solitudes of Northern Tibet.*

85. Pozdneyev reported that the Chinese firms of Kalgan exported seventy-three thousand packages of brick tea in 1892, including thirty thousand packages to Kyakhta, thirty thousand boxes of thick brick and fifteen thousand boxes of thin brick to Urga and northern Mongolia. It was a great slump from the figure of 180,000 packages in 1867, due to the expansion of the Russian merchants. See Pozdneyev, *Mongolia and the Mongols*, volume 1, 445–47.

86. The Dragon Note was made of a square piece of white rough paper about forty-five centimeters long, with the imperial seal of the Qing emperor printed in the center, surrounded by patterns of the dragon, on which wrote in Manchu, Mongolian, and Chinese languages a line calling for protection of life and property of the note-holder. It was first issued around 1805, at a time when the Qing government tightened its border policies. Many illegal traders

were fined and expelled, whereas those who enjoyed a close relationship with the Manchu officials were allowed to come in and reap the profit. See DSK, 81, 5.

87. DSK, 65; Lu and Liu, *Lümengshang*, 162. The Manchu government initially forbade the practice of paying private debts by the debtor's banner or sum, yet by the 1880s, it became common practice for the banners to pay off private debts in the same way as official debts. The debtors who were unable to repay the debts were punished severely, causing many of them to flee from their banners or sum. See Sanjdorj, *Manchu Chinese Colonial Rule*, 54–58.

88. For instance, the 8,660 taels of debt that the head of Jasagtu Khan aimag owed Dashengkui in 1891 was repaid by levies imposed on all twenty banners under his jurisdiction. See DSK, 68. In 1897, Lawalinqin, jasag of Sechen Khan aimag who owed the firm sixty thousand taels petitioned to have his debt repaid by his banner subjects. The head of the aimag ruled that forty thousand taels were to be repaid by his subject and the remaining twenty thousand taels needed to be repaid by himself. See Lu and Liu, *Lümengshang*, 164.

89. Lu and Liu, *Lümengshang*, 163–64.

90. Sulian kexueyuan, ed., *Menggu renmin gonghe guo tongshi*.

91. DSK, 68–73; Sanjdorj, *Manchu Chinese Colonial Rule*, 49–51, 58, 65.

92. DSK, 70.

93. Mantetsu shomubu chōsaka, ed., *Gaimo kyōwakoku*.

94. DSK, 70, 79–80, 98–99; Sanjdorj, *Manchu Chinese Colonial Rule*, 43.

95. Lu and Liu, *Lümengshang*, 165.

96. Avery, *The Tea Road*, 72–75. For the economic role of monasteries, see Pozdneyev, *Religion and Ritual in Society*, 31–32; Pozdneyev, *Mongolia*, volume 1, 25.

97. Pozdneyev, *Mongolia*, volume 1, 86, 174–75.

98. DSK, 9; SYTZG 27.1, 565; Lu and Liu, *Lümengshang*, 104–07.

99. Sanjdorj, *Manchu Chinese Colonial Rule*, 50–51.

100. Pozdneyev, *Mongolia*, volume 1, 209.

101. Pozdneyev, *Mongolia*, volume 1, 27; He Yangling, *Chasui mengmin jingji de jiepou*, 56.

102. Pozdneyev, *Mongolia*, volume 1, 65; Lu and Liu, *Lümengshang*, 45–56; Wuyungerile, *Shiba zhi ershi shiji chu neimenggu chengzhen yanjiu*, 95–96.

103. DSK, 3–7, 11–12; Lu and Liu, *Lümengshang*, 53.

104. DSK, 82.

105. DSK, 11–12; Lu and Liu, *Lümengshang*, 53.

106. DSK, 83; Sanjdorj, *Manchu Chinese Colonial Rule*, 41.

107. DSK, 3–7; Pozdneyev, *Mongolia*, volume 1, 208.

108. DSK, 81. For details on the client relationship, see Sanjdorj, *Manchu Chinese Colonial Rule*, 51–54.

109. DSK, 41–43, 104, 125. Also see Wang Zhongmin, "Dashengkui yu luotuo 'fangzi': 'dashengkui xianxiang,' Part 4," 54–56. On the operation of Dashengkui, see Bao Muping, *Mongoru ni okeru toshi kenchikushi kenkyū*, 217–21.

110. According to the Qing law, the Chinese were allowed to use only the cotton tent (*maikhan*) but not the felt one (*ger*) while traveling in the countryside outside the trading towns. See Sanjdorj, *Manchu Chinese Colonial Rule*.

111. The Chinese and Mongolian use of the word *baaz/bazi* differed in the number of camels and men included in each unit, with one *baaz* in a Mongol caravan including between forty and sixty camels. Each *baaz* was subdivided into three "fires" (Mo: *gal*), with each "fire" made up of two to four people. See Avery, *The Tea Road*, 78–79.

112. DSK, 39.

113. DSK, 98–99; Pozdneyev, *Mongolia*, volume 1, 67.

114. DSK, 102–104. Pozdneyev noted that Chinese firms sent out debt collectors to the steppe during the third lunar month and returned during the eighth, mainly collecting sheep as payment, but also taking horses, bulls, and camels. See Pozdneyev, *Mongolia*, volume 1, 452. For the operation of the tents, see ibid., 209.

115. Other firms were also engaged in the livestock trade and cattle raising. Another Höhhot-based firm, Yuanshengde, sent to China by way of Höhhot forty-five thousand sheep and five hundred camels in 1892. See Pozdneyev, *Mongolia*, volume 1, 209.

116. DSK, 102–06; Pozdneyev, *Mongolia*, volume 1, 452.

117. Pozdneyev noted Dashengkui spent thirty thousand taels for the salaries of its agents alone. See Pozdneyev, *Mongolia*, volume 1, 208.

118. The thick brick, known as *jujaghan* ("thick") to the Mongols and *ersi* 二四 ("Twenty-Four") to the Chinese, weighs 3.25 kilograms each, with twenty-four bricks filling a box. The thin brick, known as *narin* ("thin") and *sanliu* 三六 ("Thirty-Six") respectively, weighs 1.5 kilograms each, with thirty-six filling a box. See DSK, 36, 86–95; Pozdneyev, *Mongolia*, volume 1, 445.

119. These subsidiaries ran as financial autonomous enterprises with independent supplying and distributing system. The relationship between Dashengkui and its various subsidiaries were contractual rather than organizational. See DSK, 29.

120. DSK, 45.

121. A total of seventeen *piaohao* were established by Shanxi merchants prior to 1850, among which seven were located in Qixian, seven in Pingyao, and three in Taigu. See Zhang Zhengming, *Jinshang xingshuai shi.*

122. DSK, 44.

123. Among these subsidiaries, Tianshutai was the earliest, which was established in the late Jiaqing (1796–1820) and early Daoguang (1821–1851) period, and was closed in 1931. The three sheep firms were established in the 1890s. Dehengkui was established in 1919. See ibid., 46, 105–06.

124. On the camel caravans, see Lattimore, "Caravan Routes of Inner Asia: The Third 'Asian Lecture'," 497–528. Also see Avery, *The Tea Road*, 77–79.

125. See QSL 461, QL 19/4/17 (1754); 467, QL 19/6//28 (1754).

126. DSK, 97.

127. DSK, 184.

128. DSK, 127.

129. DSK, 127–28.

130. Pozdneyev, *Mongolia*, volume 1, 168–70.

131. He Yangling, *Chasui mengmin jingji de jiepou*, 64–66.

132. DSK, 145–46.

133. Pozdneyev, *Mongolia*, volume 1, 456. For Russian trade in Mongolia, also see Schlesinger, *A World Trimmed with Fur.*

134. DSK, 116–17.

135. For the concept of "cultural broker," see Eric Wolf, "Aspects of Group Relations in a Complex Society," 1075; Clifford Geertz, "The Javanese Kijaji," 228–49.

3

Beyond the Western Pass

Sojourning and Settlement across Han-Mongol Borders

In the first month we got married,	正月裡娶過門，
In the second month you went beyond the pass.	二月裡你西口外行。
Had I known you'd go beyond the pass	早知道你走西口，
I'd rather we never got married.	哪如咱們不成親。
Darling, you go beyond the western pass;	哥哥你要走西口，
Even your beloved cannot make you stay.	小妹妹也難留。
My heart grieves so, oh I cannot hold	止不住那傷心淚，
My teardrops from falling down.[1]	一道一道往下流。

This parting scene of a newlywed couple is the opening passage of "Zou Xikou," a popular folk song widely circulated in the provinces of Shanxi and Shaanxi and in the western part of Inner Mongolia since the mid-nineteenth century. It depicts a familiar scenario staged in many villages of this border region: a man leaving his native place in search of a better living outside the pass and a woman left at home awaiting his return. The folk song testifies to the massive influx of Chinese migrants from north China into the Mongol territories. The migration was locally referred to as *zou xikou* 走西口 ("going beyond the western pass") or *pao kouwai* 跑口外 ("running outside the pass"). This spontaneous trend of migration began around the end of the seventeenth century, gathered momentum in the nineteenth century, and culminated in the official campaign that opened up Mongol lands for Chinese colonization in 1902. It not only redefined the boundaries and changed the power equilibrium between the sedentary and the nomadic populations, but it also brought about far-reaching repercussions on the social, demographic, and ecological landscapes of both the origin and destination societies.

This chapter examines the processes of Chinese migration across the Han-Mongol border during the eighteenth and nineteenth centuries. It first discusses the Qing policies regarding Chinese colonization north of the Great Wall against the backdrop

101

of early Qing expansion and consolidation. Most of these policies were concentrated in the Jehol region in the vicinity of Beijing and the directly ruled "Internal Mongolia" such as the Tümed and Chakhar banners, but were later adopted in areas under the jurisdiction of autonomous jasag banners. This discussion focuses on the progression of Chinese cultivation and settlement in the Great Wall fringe region of the Ordos/Hetao, which is located inside the great bend of the Yellow River, as a case of ecologically-driven Chinese cultivation of Mongol lands that was accommodated by both Mongol elites and the Qing court. The influx of Chinese migration introduced a set of social and institutional changes to the Mongol periphery that eventually led to a more fundamental alteration of Qing policy toward the Mongols, including the creation of a centralized administrative system, the commercialization of Mongol land tenure, and the economic and social stratification of Mongolian society. Finally, this chapter provides a glimpse into the migrant life and experiences by examining folk genres that circulated in the border regions. Thus, it gives a voice to ordinary Chinese migrants and their families, who are generally overlooked by mainstream scholarship.

CHANGING QING POLICIES

Chapter 2 discussed the expansion of Chinese trade in the Mongolian steppe resulting in the incorporation of the Mongols into a silver-based market economy. Whereas lucrative trade proved a strong pull for Chinese merchants, artisans, and temporary laborers into the Mongol region, the pressure of overpopulation and frequent ecological disasters in northern China, coupled with an increased demand for supply of the Qing's military and civil administrators and their Mongol allies on the steppe, combined to push a flux of Chinese migrants beyond the Great Wall.[2] These were mostly land-poor farmers who were recruited to work in landed estates set up by the Qing court and Manchu banners or who leased land from Manchu or Mongol bannermen. Notwithstanding the unavailability of exact statistical numbers, it is estimated that the Chinese population of Inner Mongolia grew from approximately 850,000 in 1776 to 1,290,000 in 1820.[3]

Throughout most of the Qing dynasty, an official "closing off" policy (*fengjin* 封禁) was in effect to restrict Chinese migration beyond the Great Wall to preserve the imperial enclaves of the ruling Manchus and their Mongol allies. The earliest ban against the Han cultivation of Mongol pasturelands dates back to 1655.[4] Later, as migration could not be stopped effectively, the policy was modified to register the migrants through an official permit issued by the Board of Revenue, with the number of permits limited to eight hundred per year. Chinese migrants were forbidden to bring their families, marry Mongolian women, or construct permanent buildings in Mongol territories, and they were obliged to return to their native place by the end of each year.[5] The prohibition against Chinese cultivation was reaffirmed in the form of legal codes and imperial decrees during the eighteenth and nineteenth centuries, notably in *Menggu lüli* (1741), *Da Qing huidian shili* (1759), and *Lifanyuan zeli* (1815). A 1749 edict made the Mongol jasags and officials responsible for reporting all illegal cultivators on the penalty of fines. The fines were one year's salary for jasags and a combined fine of livestock, removal from office, and flogging for banner officials.[6]

The *fengjin* policy did not mean a complete closing of the gates to the north, but rather was a means to combat uncontrolled migration. This can be seen from the ebb and flow of governmental policies to foster or forbid Chinese migration. The Qing initially welcomed the movement of Chinese migrants to northern territories in order to help rebuild the economy destroyed by the Ming-Qing transitional war and to supply the Manchu and Mongol troops stationed there. In 1653, the court promulgated "Regulations on Recruitment and Reclamation in Liaodong" (*Liaodong zhaomin kaiken tiaoli* 遼東招民開墾條例) that encouraged Chinese peasants to settle in the Liao River region by offering incentives such as free seed, draft animals, and tax exemption. As their number soared, however, the policy was rescinded in 1668, and by 1681, a seven-hundred-kilometer-long Willow Palisade (*liutiaobian* 柳條邊) was erected, which was a system of ditches and embankments planted with willows intended to prevent Chinese migration into Manchuria.[7] The ban was not lifted until 1860 when Chinese settlement was encouraged as a defensive measure against Russian encroachment.

Similarly, Qing policies toward Chinese cultivation in Inner Mongolia were ambivalent and shifting, which reflected the empire's conflicting interests in the borderlands. Following the conquest of China, the Qing created an elaborate system of estates and banner lands to foster agriculture outside of the Great Wall while ensuring Manchu control over land, labor, and production in these regions. A total of 132 official or imperial estates were established in the vicinity of Beijing that were managed by the Imperial Household Department (*neiwufu* 內務府) and the Manchu Eight Banners. These estates were founded to supply grains for the imperial family, Manchu nobles, and government agencies. They were manned by Chinese bond servants, as well as tenant farmers and migrant workers recruited from northern China. Most of these estates were located in Liaodong and Jehol outside the Gubeikou and Xifengkou passes.[8]

The Qing also allocated smaller land plots to Manchu and Mongol bannermen to provide them with a livelihood. In 1670, uncultivated lands north of the Great Wall between Gubeikou and Kalgan were distributed among Manchu noblemen, banner officials, and soldiers, and Chinese migrant farmers were recruited to till these lands. By 1741, over 12,900 *qing* (86,040 ha) of these bannerlands had been put under cultivation.[9] Other Chinese migrants came to Mongolia as part of the dowry entourage of Manchu princesses. The Qing court used marriage alliances as a means of strengthening their bonds with Mongol nobilities. Qi Meiqin calculates that 364 females of the imperial clan were married to Mongol noblemen throughout the Qing dynasty, including twenty princesses, sixty-six daughters of princes of the first rank, and over two hundred other noblewomen. Accompanying them were bond servants, artisans, guards, and gardeners. Many of these Chinese entourages were allowed to cultivate land in the vicinity of their residences.[10] Also, many married local Mongol women, adopted Mongol names, and became registered as naturalized Mongols (*sui menggu* 隨蒙古).[11]

During the eighteenth century, the Qing government set up empire-wide granary and famine relief systems that extended to the Mongol territory. The Kangxi emperor particularly stressed the importance of maintaining grain holdings outside the Great Wall so as to stabilize grain prices and relieve pressure on the prefectures near the borders. Although the Mongols did practice an extensive form of ley farming, the yield was too small to meet the demand (see chapter 1). In order to promote agriculture outside the Great Wall, the emperor dispatched officials from the Lifanyuan to teach the Mongols farming techniques and provide them with free seed, draft animals, and farm tools.[12] By 1718, a grain storage system was established across the Josotu, Juu Uda, and Jerim leagues, as well as in Höhhot, with a public granary established in each banner.[13] At times of flood, drought, or famine (for instance, in 1723 and 1743), the Qing court adopted the *jiedi yangmin* or "Borrow Land to Feed People" policy that allowed disaster-stricken refugees from south of the passes to cultivate Mongol lands as a means of disaster relief.[14]

SPREAD OF CHINESE SETTLEMENTS

Through most of the eighteenth century, agriculture in Mongolia was largely concentrated in the long, narrow belt in the fringe of the Great Wall, notably the Jehol, Tümed, and Chakhar regions as well as the Ordos inside the northern bend of the Yellow River. Despite the region's topographical variety, which ranged from a dry sandy plateau in the west to the rolling grasslands in the middle and wooded mountains in the east, most of this belt was located within the four hundred millimeter annual precipitation line, which made it a semi-arid agro-pastoral ecotone suitable for both farming and animal husbandry. Parts of it were cultivated sporadically during the Qin, Han, Tang, and Ming dynasties, but most of it remained pastures for various nomadic groups. The belt is an ecologically fragile zone that is sensitive to climatic changes and human activities. Consequently, the eventual influx of Chinese migration brought severe impacts on the ecologies of this area, including deforestation, desertification, and land degradation.

Jehol (Rehe 熱河, "Hot River") was the name for the Mongol lands located directly north of Beijing outside of the Great Wall. This was a region of heavily forested mountains and steep terrains with abundant wildlife. It became the site of the Mulan Imperial Hunting Reserve, where Qing emperors from Kangxi to Jiaqing held annual Autumn Hunt rituals from 1681 to 1820. Jehol also became the site of the Chengde Imperial Summer Villa: a vast complex of palaces, gardens, and temples constructed in 1703. These lands came under the Qing rule when the ruler of Kharachin Mongols first submitted to the Manchu rule in the 1620s.[15] The territory

Map 3.1.   Frontier Belt of Chinese Colonization, Eighteenth to Twentieth Century

of Jehol in the broad sense of the term referred to the area demarcated by the Great Wall in the south, the Willow Palisade in the east, and the West Liao River (Mo: Shira Muren, Ch: Xiliao he) in the north. This region was under the jurisdiction of a Manchu military lieutenant governor (Mo: *khoshuu-yi jakirugchi said*, Ch: *dutong* 都統), who oversaw the Mongol banners of Josotu and Juu Uda leagues, the Manchu troops stationed in Chengde, as well as all affairs related to the imperial reserves, residences, temples, and estates.

The eastern part of Jehol had seen considerable farming along the Luan River valley since the early Qing period, when Chinese tenant-farmers were recruited to cultivate the official or imperial estates and the Manchu bannerlands outside of the Great Wall. They also rented plots from the Kharachin and Tümed Mongols to the north and east of the Luan.[16] The establishment of the imperial hunting reserve and summer palace also stimulated Chinese settlement by bringing thousands of officials, retainers, servants, and soldiers into the region to attend the annual court visit. This enormous entourage had to be fed and supported. Additionally, large numbers of Chinese craftsmen and cultivators came to provide labor for these extensive construction projects. Further, Jehol's proximity to the overpopulated and disaster-prone north China plain made it a popular destination for Chinese refugees in the wake of the *jiedi yangmin* policy. As the areas near the Great Wall filled up, migrants moved north into the West Liao River basin in the Juu Uda league.

To manage these migrants, maintain order, and collect taxes, the Jehol sub-prefecture was set up in 1723. It was elevated to the Chengde prefecture in 1778 and oversaw six subunits established east and north of Chengde: Pingquan, Luanping,

Jianchang (Lingyuan), Chaoyang, Fengning, and Chifeng. The territory of the Chengde prefecture and its subunits overlapped with the Kharachin and Tümed banners of Josotu league, the Ongniut, Aohan, and Naiman banners of southern Juu Uda league, and the four Chakhar Left Flank banners: Plain White, Plain Blue, Bordered Yellow, and Bordered White. The Chinese population of the Chengde prefecture grew from 557,406 in 1778 to 783,867 in 1820.[17] By 1781, the cultivated area in Chengde, Pingquan, Luanping, and Fengning reached 21,200 *qing*, producing an annual tax of twenty thousand taels of silver and a grain reserve of 165,059 *shi*.[18] The influx of Chinese farmers also led to increasing interethnic interactions. It was not uncommon for Chinese men to marry Mongol women, convert to Buddhism, adopt the Mongolian language, and register as subjects of Mongol banners or as "subordinate Mongols" (*sui menggu*). Burensain Borjigin's research shows many cases of such Mongolized Chinese who first assimilated into Mongolian society, and later reverted to Chinese society due to the influx of immigration, and then lost their Mongolian language as they and the Mongols in Jehol became agricultural.[19]

Unlike the Mongol groups of Jehol, which were Qing dependencies and enjoyed a relatively high degree of political autonomy, both the Tümed and Chakhar Mongols lost their hereditary jasags due to rebellion and were put under direct Manchu administration. The Tümed Mongols, being the appanage of Altan Khan, the ruler of the Right Wing Mongols, were considered a potential threat to the Manchu rulers given their commercial relations with the Ming and religious ties with Gelugpa Buddhism. Following their surrender to the Manchus in 1632, the Tümeds were organized into two banners, each under a non-Chinggisid Mongol military lieutenant governor, only to be abolished in 1761 and replaced by a Manchu vice lieutenant governor appointed by Beijing. After the construction of the garrison town of Suiyuan in 1739, a military governor was stationed there to command the Manchu banner troops and both Tümed banners. This governor became the highest authority in the Tümed area.[20] The Qing also compartmentalized the Tümed territory by relocating other aimags within its boundaries, including the Urads to the northwest; the Dörben Keüked, Muumingghan, and Khalkha to the north; and the Chakhar to the east.[21] As a result, the Tümeds were stripped of any territorial or economic autonomy over their lands, which made them vulnerable to the Qing court's official land expropriation and the influx of Chinese migration that would fundamentally transform the Tümed society, culture, and landscape.

The fertile Tümed plain had seen considerable agricultural development under the reign of Altan Khan. It is located north of the great bend of the Yellow River and bounded by the Great Wall on the south and the Dalan Terigün (a.k.a. Dalan Khara uul, ch: Daqingshan) mountain chain on the north. Since the 1540s, Chinese refugees, including mutinous soldiers, adherents of the White Lotus Sect, and captives from south of the Great Wall were encouraged to settle in agricultural settlements called *baishing* (Ch: *bansheng* 板升) on the plain, which supported a Chinese population of over one hundred thousand. These settlements were burned to the ground during the Manchu-Chakhar war of 1632.[22] Nevertheless, when Imperial Envoy

Zhang Penghe visited Höhhot in 1688, he saw Mongols residing in mud houses and growing wheat and millet, which showed that extensive agriculture was practiced in this area among the Mongols.[23]

With the revving up of the military campaigns against Galdan in the 1690s, and the pivotal importance of Höhhot as the headquarters of General Fiyanggû, commander of the West Route Army, the Qing court made the policy of colonizing the Tümed plain to provide supplies for these thirty thousand troops on the steppe. In 1695, the Qing enclosed the area in the valley of Yekhe Turgenghol (Daheihe) and Bagha Turgenghol (Xiaoheihe) rivers south of Höhhot to set up thirteen official estates (*liangzhuang* 糧莊 or *zhuangtoudi* 莊頭地), which covered an area of fifteen hundred *qing* (ten thousand ha).[24] Later, as a new garrison town of Suiyuan was built in 1739 in the outskirt of Höhhot, the needs of the Manchu garrison troops resulted in large-scale military colonization through state enclosure. In 1737, some 40,500 *qing* of lands were enclosed as official taxable lands (*daliang guandi* 大糧官地, or *liangdi* 糧地) and put under cultivation by recruiting migrant farmers from Shanxi and Shaanxi provinces.[25] In addition, large area of common lands (over forty-five thousand *qing* in total) were expropriated in the name of "contribution" for exclusive use by imperial postal stations, Manchu Eight Banners, Buddhist monasteries, and as private manor estate of a Manchu princess. These official estates and state-imposed enclosures, for which the Tümeds were denied the rights of land use and rent collection, added up to 85,500 *qing* and consisted of over half of the arable lands in the Tümed area.[26]

This colonization with large-scale enclosures resulted in the fragmentation of Mongol pasturelands, and it increasingly stratified Tümed society through the development of more private, commercialized land relations. The Tümed soldiers, as a quasi-militia group, were obliged to fulfill official duties, such as military conscription and corvée labor, but they received no salaries and had to provide their own horses during service. In compensation, each soldier received a land allotment called *mengdingdi* 蒙丁地 to support their families, which was set at five *qing* per soldier. These were considered communal properties to be withdrawn and reallocated in case the soldier died without offspring. As the Mongols were not skillful farmers, most of these plots were leased out to Chinese tenant farmers for rent collection. Over time, widespread private leasing, on top of a lack of enforcement to ensure equitable distribution, led to the concentration of plots in the hands of wealthy nobles, lamas, banner officials and officers, which accounted for thousands of *qing* of lands. In contrast, many hapless soldiers lost their plots due to mortgage or encroachment and were reduced to destitution.[27]

An official survey in 1742 showed the growing economic disparities among the Tümed Mongols due to Chinese cultivation. Out of 43,559 Mongol soldiers who held a total area of 60,780 *qing* of cultivated lands, 16,487 (37 percent) possessed over 42,800 *qing* (70 percent) of lands, with an average rate of 2.6 *qing* per household. In contrast, 27,072 Mongols (61 percent) held less than one *qing* per household, including 2,156 (5 percent) who held 3.34 *qing* in total (an average of 0.15

mu per household) and 2,812 (6 percent) who were completely landless.[28] The Qing court subsequently ordered a redistribution of land among the Tümeds to ensure the minimum of one *qing* per household as their habitat, known as a "household plot" (Ch: *hukoudi* 戶口地, Mo: *amijighulgha-yin aman toghatu ghajar*) or "livelihood plot" (*shengjidi* 生計地). The court also set up charity plots and used part of the revenue from the rents to supply the destitute, widowed, and childless Mongols.[29] Despite these official endeavors, however, the fragmentation and expropriation of Tümed lands irrevocably resulted in the sedentarization and impoverishment of ordinary Mongols.

By 1743, out of the total 75,048 *qing* of lands retained by the Tümeds, 60,780 *qing* (i.e. 80 percent) had been reclaimed, with only 14,268 *qing* of pasture left. The ongoing private cultivation, coupled with the official reclamation, turned the Tümed plain into a critical base of grain production outside the Great Wall. The grain supplied not only the Manchu and Mongol troops stationed there, but also the population of Shanxi and Shaanxi provinces inside the passes.[30] It is estimated that the Chinese migrant population residing on the plain reached 120,000 during this period.[31] Between 1723 and 1741, a set of centralized administrative units was established to manage affairs related to Han-Mongol lawsuits, crimes, rents, and taxes, with two vice-administrators (*lishi tongzhi* 理事同知) stationed in Höhhot and Suiyuan, and five assistant sub-prefects (*xieli tongpan* 協理通判) based in Höhhot, Qingshuihe, Togtokhu, Khoringer, and Sarachi. These were elevated to autonomous sub-prefectures in 1760 under the Guisui circuit of Shanxi province.[32] The creation of centralized units introduced a dual administrative system that allowed the bureaucrats of Shanxi to interfere in the fiscal and judicial affairs related to Chinese migrants and further encroach upon the autonomy of the Tümeds (whose autonomy had already been compromised by the Beijing-appointed military governors).

A similar fate befell the Chakhar, the personal appanage of Lighden Khan, the last Mongol Khaghan. After his son Ejei Khan surrendered to the Manchus in 1635, the Chakhar aimag was organized into a jasag banner, with other members incorporated into the Mongol Eight Banners. Following the revolt of Prince Burni in 1675, however, the Qing rescinded the Chakhar banner, abolished their hereditary nobility system, and divided the aimag into eight banners modeled after the Manchu Eight Banner system. The eight banners were placed under the direct control of a Manchu amban appointed by Beijing who reported to the lieutenant governor of Chakhar stationed in Kalgan.[33] The aimag was moved from its original pastures in southern Manchuria and resettled north of Datong and Xuanhua beyond the Great Wall. As part of "Internal Mongolia," the Chakhars were deprived of any property rights to their lands, which were at the disposal of the Qing government. A large proportion of their best pasturelands were enclosed as breeding grounds for imperial pastures or herds (Mo: *süreg*, Ch: *muqun* 牧群), which supplied military horses and dairy products for the Qing court, or they were bestowed as private pastures to members of the imperial clan and other Manchu nobility and officials. These fine pasturelands supported an unprecedented number of horses, camels, cattle, and sheep: reportedly three million heads during the Kangxi era.[34] Following the conquest of Xinjiang in 1758, however, the demands for military horses declined. Thus, many imperial pastures fell into disuse and were gradually opened for reclamation.[35]

The Qing court encouraged Chinese cultivation in the Chakhar region partly for the purposes of boosting fiscal revenue and grain reserves and partly as famine relief. Since the beginning of the eighteenth century, migrant farmers from Zhili and Shanxi provinces began to rent plots from Mongol banner officials and develop private plots in the fringe of the Great Wall. An official survey of 1724 showed that an area of 29,709 *qing* had been put under cultivation in the territory of the four Right Flank banners (Plain Yellow, Plain Red, Bordered Red, and Bordered Blue) located between Kalgan and Shahukou, with over ten thousand migrants residing in this area. In his memorial to the Lifanyuan the same year, lieutenant governor Hongsheng of Chakhar reasoned that instead of organizing official estates or expelling the migrant Chinese tenants, the best way to manage them was to set up bureaucratic units to collect taxes.[36] By 1750, a total of six subprefectures had been set up to oversee land reclamation, tax collection, granary establishment, and judicial matters in these areas. The first three were Zhangjiakou (Kalgan), Dolonnuur and Dushikou, established in 1724, 1732, and 1734, respectively, which reported to the Koubei circuit of Zhili province. The latter three were Siqi (Fengning), Fengzhen, and Ningyuan, established in 1736 and 1750, respectively, which were subordinate to the Chengde prefecture of Zhili province, and Datong and Shuoping prefectures of Shanxi province, respectively.[37] Among these, Zhangjiakou, Fengzhen, and Ningyuan oversaw the four Right Flank banners of Chakhar, whereas Dushikou, Dolonnuur, and Siqi oversaw the four Left Flank Chakhar banners. The crisscrossing of administrative boundaries testified to the increasing fiscal considerations and population pressure from north China that overtook the security concerns of the Mongolian frontier. As we will see in chapter 6, the creation of centralized administrative units caused further privatization and commercialization of Mongol lands that resulted in the official opening of Chakhar lands for Chinese reclamation in the 1880s.

The expansion of Chinese cultivation and migrants into the strategic regions of Jehol, Tümed, and Chakhar continued through the mid-eighteenth century. As we have seen, the Qing consolidation and military expansion were dependent on the allegiance of the subordinate Mongols, and land grabs in these regions through official enclosure or "voluntary" contribution were crucial to ensuring the supply of provisions and warhorses to sustain the military campaigns across the steppe. Meanwhile, overpopulation and the ecological crisis in north China pushed numerous landless farmers and refugees across the Great Wall. Their hunger for arable land, combined with the desire of Manchu and Mongol landlords for rentals, led to rampant private cultivation that necessitated centralized administration. The creation of centralized bureaucratic units, in turn, facilitated Chinese migration that soon became irrevocable by the nineteenth century. As the following sections show, this trend was not limited to "Internal Mongolia" but spread among "Out-vassal Mongolia" as well.

CHINESE CULTIVATION IN ORDOS

One of the earliest jasag regions that were put under cultivation was the Ordos/ Hetao, a plateau encircled by the great northern bend of the Yellow River on all three sides. This bend gave the plateau its Chinese name Hetao ("river bend"). After the collapse of the Yuan dynasty in 1368, the Ming had briefly occupied the area and set up military colonies in the vicinity of the Dongsheng outpost south of the Yellow River. From 1500 on, this area had been inhabited by the Ordos tümen, one of the six tümens of Right Wing Mongols, whose chief was *jinong* (the highest priest in charge of the cult of Chinggis Khan).[38] After their submission to the Manchus in 1636, the Ordos tümen was divided into six banners: the Left Flank center, front, and rear banners (a.k.a. Jiyun Wang, Jüüngar, and Dalad banners), and the Right Flank center, front, and rear banners (a.k.a. Otog, Üüshin, and Khanggin banners). The six banners comprised the Yekhe Juu or "Great Temple" league. A seventh banner, the Right Flank front end banner, also known as the Jasag banner, was added to the league in 1736.[39] Except for the Khanggin and Dalad banners along the Yellow River, all of the banners shared borders with Chinese provinces in the south and southeast. Delimiting the southern boundary of the area was a section of the Great Wall that extended over six hundred kilometers from the Guanhekou Pass of Pianguan in Shanxi to the Ningchengkou pass of Ningxia in Gansu. For simplicity's sake, I will use the term "Ordos" to refer to the area officially called the "Yekhe Juu league" in the Qing period.

During the early Qing, a buffer zone called the "Forbidden land" or "Reserve" (*jinliudi* 禁留地) demarcated the boundary between the Ordos Mongols and the Han Chinese. This zone was a forty- or fifty-*li*-wide strip on the fringe of the Great Wall in which both grazing and farming were prohibited. Trespassing from either side was prohibited by the Mongols and Chinese alike.[40] The circumstances under which the Reserve was delineated remain unclear. The term is found mostly in local gazetteers and Mongolian-language archives, but not in official documents like the Veritable Records of the Qing Emperors or the Collected Statutes and Precedents of the Qing dynasty. It is generally believed that the Reserve's demarcation is dated to the early Qing for the purpose of preventing liaisons between the Mongols and Chinese.[41] However, recent studies argue that it might date back to the practice of "burning the wilderness" (*shaohuang* 燒荒) adopted by the Ming dynasty as a defensive strategy, which involved destroying the ecosystem that the nomads depended upon. This tactic took its environmental toll including deforestation, loss of habitat, and soil erosion that resulted in a black-colored strip that lay fallow for centuries. Thus, the Reserve can be seen as a product of the sociopolitical situation shaped by the Ming-Mongol conflict that became formalized by the Qing for security purposes.[42] Either way, it was manifest that the fifty-*li* strip had been expropriated from the Mongols and put at the disposal of the Qing government.

The ban was first lifted for the Ordos Mongols, who demonstrated their allegiance in the Qing suppression of the Shaanxi insurgencies during the Revolt of the Three Feudatories (1673–1681) as well as in the Kangxi emperor's expeditions against

Galdan in the 1690s.[43] In 1682, the Mongols of the Üüshin banner were allowed to graze their cattle up to forty *li* from the Great Wall.[44] In 1697, upon request by Songrabu, jasag of the Otog banner, permission was granted for Chinese farmers to cultivate the land near the Great Wall. The Mongols were allowed to collect a tax, which was set at one *shi* of millet per *niuju* (a unit of land measurement that equals eighteen ha), plus four bales of hay that were commutable to 5.4 *qian* (ounce) of silver. No official tax was levied in these lands. The banner's right to collect taxes was revoked in 1730 and transferred to local officials for setting up granaries, but it was restored to the Mongols during the drought of 1732 as famine relief.[45] The 1697 edict marked the beginning of cultivation inside the fifty-*li* strip. By 1736, Chinese settlements north of Yulin and Shenmu of Shaanxi province had reportedly exceeded three thousand *niuju* (fifty-four thousand ha), with an annual yield of over one hundred thousand *shi* of millet.[46] The Mongols initially welcomed the arrival of Chinese farmers. As fried millet and salted milk tea had long become an essential part of their daily diet, the farmers' presence helped meet their demand for grain products, which had hitherto been obtained only from border markets.[47] In addition, the migrants brought extra revenue in silver to the jasags. In 1783, for example, the Jüüngar and Jiyun Wang (a.k.a. Wang) banners collected 3,866.44 *shi* of millet and 1,971.112 taels of silver from migrants from the Fugu county of Shaanxi province.[48]

The ever-expanding Chinese cultivation aroused the alarm of the Mongol nobility. In 1719, upon the request of Dashlabtan, jasag of the Otog banner, the Lifanyuan set up a border to delimit cultivation and protect Mongol pasturelands. The border was demarcated at thirty *li* north of the Great Wall in sandy areas and twenty *li* in sand-free areas. In 1743, as Chinese cultivators continued to push northward, a new border was delineated fifty *li* north of the Great Wall. This border was known as the "fifty-*li* Marker Border" (Mo: *Tabin-u khelkhiy-e-yin ghajar*, Ch: *wushili paijie* 五十里牌界) or the Black Border (Mo: *khara paisa*, Ch: *heijie* 黑界). It overlapped with the northern edge of the old Reserve and was marked with cairns (*oboo*) at intervals of three to five *li*. No cultivation was permitted beyond this line. Although the taxes due to the Mongols within the original thirty-*li* border remained unchanged, an additional tax of half a *shi* of millet and five *qian* of silver per *niuju* was levied for plots lying beyond that border.[49] The shifting boundaries represented a process of negotiation among Mongol herders, Chinese farmers, and the Qing government over their varying and sometimes conflicting interests. By defining a fixed boundary between nomadic and settled, the Qing rescinded its old prohibition policy and sanctioned cultivation inside the fifty-*li* strip. As it turned out, what was intended as a buffer zone was turned into a pioneer belt, and indeed, a launching board for Chinese migrants to penetrate into the heartland of the steppe. This stretch of reclaimed area has since been alienated from the control of the Mongols and incorporated into the Shaanxi province in the twentieth century.

The majority of Chinese farmers were from a string of counties and districts in the vicinity of the Great Wall, notably Fugu, Shenmu, Yulin, Huaiyuan, Jingbian, and Dingbian of northern Shaanxi; Hequ, Baode, and Pianguan of northwestern

Shanxi; and Shuozhou, Pinglu, Zuoyun, Youyu, and Shanyin of northern Shanxi. These mountainous regions suffered from insufficient arable land, because their soft, silty soil was extremely susceptible to water and wind erosion. The erosion was exacerbated by centuries of deforestation and agricultural activities, most recently in the Ming period.[50] These activities had a devastating impact upon the fragile environment and resulted in a degenerated ecosystem, recurrent natural disasters, and poor local economies. Statistics show that in the Baode department of Shanxi, drought occurred 303 times over the five-century period between 1464 and 1972 (that is, once every other year).[51] A local folk song describes the poor harvests poignantly:

In Hequ *xian* and Baode *zhou*,	河曲保德州，
The crop fails nine out of ten years.	十年九不收。
The only year when the harvest is good,	遇上一年收，
Alas, hail again falls from the sky.[52]	又把蛋蛋丢。

Whereas the harsh natural conditions rendered agriculture in these areas extremely limited and insufficient to support the local population, the proximity of the areas to the Great Wall gave the residents a unique opportunity of accessing the Mongol pasture lands beyond the wall. These border towns were heavily fortified during the Ming dynasty, and each was in charge of a series of fortresses (*bu* 堡) where garrison troops were stationed. The inhabitants were descendants of Ming soldiers relocated to the frontier from other parts of China and registered as hereditary military households (*junhu* 軍戶) bound by the Ming laws to remain in the military service. Most of the fortresses were abandoned by the early Qing.[53] They were turned into loci of temporary shelters (*huopan* 伙盤) created by migrants from the same native places who crossed the passes to enter banners with conjoined borders. These settlements were like villages of interior China, and their sizes varied from a few to a few dozen people.[54] For this reason, the cultivated strip between the Great Wall and Black Border was called *huopandi* 伙盤地 or *paijiedi* 牌界地.

The dominant mode of Chinese migration across the Great Wall was seasonal sojourning locally called *yanxing* 雁行 ("wild-goose migration").[55] As a rule, the migrants were adult males who left for the grasslands in the spring and returned in the fall or winter, so as to comply with the Qing laws that prohibited them from bringing families into Mongol territory or constructing permanent dwellings there. The migrants were forbidden to list their names under the Mongol banners and were instructed to retain household registration in their native place. As the Gazetteer of Hequ county of 1841 puts it, "Natives of Hequ are traditionally engaged in trade or farming in grasslands outside the pass. They depart in the spring and summer and return at the end of the year. Those who work diligently in trade or farming have no problem supporting their families. Because of the sterile land and poor economy in this area, thousands of local people earn a living outside the pass."[56]

Although there are no statistics about the total migrant population or area under cultivation, the local gazetteers from the eighteenth and nineteenth centuries provide a glimpse of the numbers and conditions. *Fugu xianzhi* (1783) reports that a

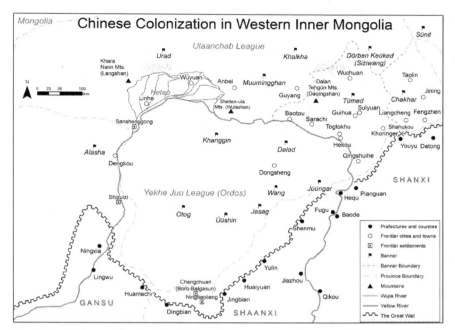

Map 3.2. Chinese Colonization in Western Inner Mongolia, c. 1900

total of 449 *huopan* shelters were established by natives of Fugu county outside its border, with 2,226 *niuju* (forty thousand ha) of land brought under reclamation. As mentioned before, this migrant workforce generated a yearly income of 3,866 taels of silver and 1,971 *shi* of millet for the Jüüngar and Wang banners.[57] *Shenmu xianzhi* (1841) records that 350 *huopan* were set up outside the pass, with 1,348.5 *niuju* of lands under cultivation.[58] Therefore, the average area under cultivation can be estimated as between four to five *niuju* per *huopan*. *Yulin Fuzhi* (1841) provides information about the population of the four counties and one department under the jurisdiction of Yulin prefecture for 1839, as well as the number of *huopan* shelters vis-à-vis villages inside the border, as shown in the following table.

Table 3.1. Population and Settlement Distribution in Yulin Prefecture, 1839

Unit	No. of Villages	No. of Huopan	Population
Shenmu xian	678	587	113,717
Fugu xian	452	441	204,357
Huaiyuan xian	796	479	89,031
Yulin xian	574	8	103,140
Jiazhou	720	0	89,988
Total	**3,220**	**1,515**	**600,233**

Source: Li Xiling, *Yulin fuzhi 6, jianzhi zhi, cunzhuang,* 16–19; 22, *shi zhi, hukou,* 1–2.

These gazetteers demonstrate that distance was a key variable that determined the distribution of settlements outside the passes. Virtually all 1,515 *huopan* were located outside the three counties of Shenmu, Fugu, and Huaiyuan adjacent to the border, whereas the number of *huopan* outside Yulin and Jiazhou located further south was almost negligible. Among these, expatriates of Shenmu and Fugu established a total of 1,028 *huopan*, which was nearly equivalent to the number of villages in their home county (1,130). Given that the average cultivated area was 4.5 *niuju* per *huopan*, by 1839, the total area brought under reclamation north of Yulin was around seven thousand *niuju*, which was more than double the figure of three thousand *niuju* in 1736. Based on the total population of 407,105 in Shenmu, Fugu, and Huaiyuan counties, the number of migrants from these counties alone can be estimated at over one hundred thousand by the first half of the 1800s.[59]

CENTRALIZED AND LOCAL CONTROL

The advance of Chinese migration complicated the administrative system in the Mongol territory. In the beginning, the Lifanyuan remained the highest governmental agency overseeing all Mongol jasagh banners. Following the reclamation of the fifty-*li* strip in 1697, the Lifanyuan appointed a judicial superintendent (Mo: *khereg shüükh tushimel*, Ch: *lishi siyuan* 理事司員) in 1708 to administer migrant-related affairs. The superintendent was headquartered in the Ningxia prefecture of Gansu province inside the border. Later, due to the expansion of Chinese settlements beyond the Shaanxi borders, another superintendent was appointed in 1722 in the Shenmu county of Shaanxi province. These positions were staffed by Manchus and Mongols exclusively and were rotated every three years. Their responsibilities included adjudicating Mongol-Han disputes in conjunction with the jasags, collecting taxes, patrolling the territory under jurisdiction once every other year, and reporting the number of registered migrants, areas under cultivation, and areas under illegitimate cultivation to the Lifanyuan.[60] Although the appointment of these officials indicated a growing encroachment of centralized control over the autonomous jasag banners, they operated under the framework intended to keep the Mongols apart from the centralized governmental system of interior China.

However, the situation began to change in the Yongzheng era with the emergence of a dual administrative system in Jehol, Tümed, and Chakhar in 1723. This dual system consisted of a set of centralized units that administered Chinese migrants and oversaw tax collection and judicial matters, which were placed under the jurisdiction of the adjacent Chinese provinces. This trend was not limited to *amban* banners under direct Manchu control, however, but also spread to autonomous jasag banners. Thus, it produced further complexities in jurisdiction. In 1743, the same year when the Black Border was redrawn, three vice-administrators were appointed to patrol the borders, verify the cultivated areas, create land and household registrations, and arbitrate disputes that might arise between Mongols and Chinese in the Ordos.

The vice-administrators were to reside in Ningxia, Shenmu, and Anbian, under the Ningxia circuit of Gansu; the Yanyusui circuit of Shaanxi; and the Yanping circuit of Shanxi, respectively.[61] After 1760, three new sub-prefects (*lishi tongpan* 理事通判) in Tümed—Sarachi, Qingshuihe, and Togtokhu—were given judicial authority over Chinese migrants in the Wang, Jüüngar, Dalad and Khanggin banners of Ordos. These sub-prefectures were subordinate to the Guisui circuit of Shanxi. The arrangement resulted in a tripartite administrative system involving representatives of the Lifanyuan, Mongol jasags, and local officials under Chinese provinces, which not only eroded the jurisdictional autonomy of the banners but also intersected them spatially among different units and provinces.[62]

The tripartite system reflected a political dilemma faced by the Qing government in its endeavor to cope with the economic needs of the land-hungry Chinese migrants and rent-hungry Mongol banners while restraining the impact of Chinese migration upon the nomadic society. To be sure, the presence of the Qing state in the Ordos remained relatively limited as compared to the more populous and centrally controlled Tümed, Jehol, and Chakhar regions. It took the form of an absentee bureaucratic administration (*yaoban* 遙辦, or *yaozhi* 遙治), as no centralized administrative unit was established in the Ordos proper, nor did the Qing seek to interfere in the local finances through tax collection. Nevertheless, the blurry boundaries between various governmental agents and their conflicting interests created numerous disputes. When coupled with the vast territories that each yamen oversaw, these disputes became a source of tension and confusion in the process of adjudication.

On the local level, starting from 1730, the Qing government adopted a *paijia* 牌甲 (Mo: *arban*, "ten men") system in *huopan* settlements that resembled the *baojia* 保甲 system of interior China, which was an institution of neighborhood guarantee based on mutual surveillance and responsibility.[63] The *paijia* was designed for the more sparsely populated territories outside the Great Wall. Each migrant community adjacent to a former fortress constituted one *jia*, which was divided into four *pai* with each *pai* consisting of a varying number of *huopan* shelters. The 350 *huopan*s north of Shenmu, for instance, were grouped into eight *jia* and thirty-two *pai*.[64] Representatives of these *paijia* units were called *zongjia* 總甲 and *paitou* 牌頭. They were held responsible for checking and reporting any law-breaking actions in addition to performing other duties like household registration, rental collection, border maintenance, and mediating between Chinese cultivators and Mongol banners.[65] During roughly the same period, the Mongol banners also appointed special administrators called *daghachin* and *darugha* to take charge of collecting rents and taxes from Chinese migrants and managing the affairs associated with them. These administrative positions were the Mongolian equivalents of *zongjia* and *paitou*, with each *daghachin* overseeing four *darugha*.[66] These new political institutions, both Chinese and Mongol, testified to the transformations taking place in the local Mongol society due to the expansion of Chinese cultivation: in particular, the growing disputes and conflicts surrounding the use of land, rentals, and debts.

DISPUTES AND CONFLICTS

Several Western explorers observed the presence of Chinese cultivation on their journeys across the Ordos, such as Huc and Gabet (1845), Przhevalski (1870), and Lesdain (1904). The French Lazarist missionaries Evariste Régis Huc and Joseph Gabet were the first Europeans to traverse the Ordos in 1845 on their journey from Beijing to Lhasa across the Mongolian steppe. While they were crossing the Khöb-chi desert of the Khanggin banner,[67] the missionaries took shelter in a cave during a stormy night. The cave turned out to be a dwelling that had been abandoned by some Chinese cultivators. Huc observed that this subterranean cave dwelling and others in the area were well laid out and constructed with elegance and solidity. They had windows on each side of the door giving light to the interior, plaster-coated walls and ceilings, furnaces, and a *kang* 炕 that was used as both a bed and cooking stove.[68] These caverns bore great resemblance to the *yaodong* 窯洞 or "house cave" structures commonly found in northern Shaanxi. Made of compacted earth and usually carved out of the side of cliffs, house caves are warm in winter and cool in summer. Thus, they are an ecological adaptation to the local climate of long severe winters and intense summer heat with minimal precipitation. In the Khöbchi desert, the natural abodes offered ideal habitation for Chinese settlers who were officially forbidden to construct permanent houses in Mongol territories. Huc reported finding about thirty of these caves. One of them was filled with millet stems and oat-straw, which showed that the settlers had deserted the area only recently.

The missionaries then encountered a Mongol herder who gave an account of his dealings with the "Kitats" or Chinese who had been turned out of the country less than two years before:

> Oh, the Kitats are sly, cheating fellows. At first, they seemed very good; but that did not last long. It is more than twenty years ago that a few of their families sought our hospi-tality; as they were poor, they got permission to cultivate some land in the vicinity, on condition that every year after harvest they should furnish some oatmeal to the [*Tayiji*] of the country. By degrees, other families arrived, who also excavated caverns wherein to dwell; and soon this defile was full of them. In the beginning, these Kitats showed a gentle, quiet character; we lived together like brothers. . . . Peace did not last long; they soon showed themselves wicked and false. Instead of being content with what had been given them, they extended their cultivation at their pleasure, and took possession of a large territory without asking any one's leave. When they were rich they would not pay the oatmeal they had agreed to pay as tribute. Every year, when we claimed the rent, we were received with insults and maledictions. But the worst thing was that these rascally Kitats turned thieves, and took possession of all the goats and sheep that lost their way in the sinuosities of the ravine.[69]

In the early 1840s, the Mongols brought the case in front of the jasag, who accord-ingly issued an order to have the migrants expelled. Yet the latter were not ready to comply without a fight:

Afterwards we learned that [the Kitats] had assembled and had resolved to disobey the orders of the king and to remain in the country, in spite of him. The first day of the eighth moon arrived, and they still occupied calmly their habitations, without making any preparation for departure. In the morning, before daybreak, all the Tartars mounted their horses, armed themselves with their lances, and drove their flocks and herds upon the cultivated lands of the Kitats, on which the crop was still standing: when the sun rose, nothing of that crop was left. All had been devoured by the animals, and trodden down. The Kitats yelled and cursed us, but the thing was done. Seeing that their position was desperate they collected, the same day, their furniture and agricultural implements, and went off to settle in the eastern parts of the [Ordos], at some distance from the Yellow River, near the Paga-Gol.[70]

The narrator, most likely a lower-level official in the local *sumun*, provided a rare Mongol perspective seldom found in Chinese sources. His testimony was informative on several aspects about the Chinese agricultural expansion in the Ordos. First of all, it indicated that by the early nineteenth century, Chinese settlement had spread from the vicinity of the Great Wall into the interior of the steppe (in this case, the Khanggin and Dalad banners in northern Ordos). The settlers in question, probably from northern Shaanxi, arrived in this unidentified locality in the Khanggin banner around 1820, and obtained permission from a local *tayiji* or nobleman to cultivate some plots in return for a share of the produce as rent. These Chinese migrants were accompanied by families, which indicated the spread of illegitimate settlement despite the Qing prohibition. In two decades' time, their community had expanded to over thirty households.

Second, we learn from the incident that relationships between the Mongols and Chinese migrants turned turbulent following the expansion of the settling community, which resulted in hostilities, lawsuits, and armed conflicts. Early settlers were usually able to cultivate good relations with the Mongols in order to win their trust. As their numbers grew, however, competition over land resources arose and disputes over rentals and debts began to sour their relationships. Judging from the Mongol's allegations against these "sly, cheating fellows" and the fact that they were "rich," it is possible that some of them were petty traders practicing credit sale while charging a high interest rate. Disputes over debts were by no means rare, as seen in a complaint filed in 1806 by a *meiren-ü janggi* ("deputy administrator") of the Jüüngar banner:

Meiren Ba-li-ge-tai reported, "While I was away from home, a group of seven Chinese, including Jin Zhenmengzi, Zhen Jingzi, Shen Mengzi, came to eat and stay at my home for a whole month. Not only did they not pay a thing for the 10 *shi* of millet they and their horses consumed, but they also took away part of the 22.5 *shi* of millet from my cellar . . . although I did owe 1,500 *qian* of silver for the goods I bought last year."[71]

The tensions between the newcomers and local inhabitants can be explained by the introduction of a money economy and the resulting indebtedness of the Mongols, whose growing taste for Chinese products and lack of financial protection rendered them easy victims of astute Han merchants. Some observers attributed such conflicts to cultural differences between the two groups, as summarized by the French traveler Count de Lesdain in 1904,

> The Mongol is in fact the prey of the Chinese, since his simplicity and his astounding idleness make him a pigeon easy to pluck. He never keeps a shop, or cultivates the ground; these occupations are too servile for him. He never works a mine, for that would bring on him the curses of the mountain genie, and in short owing to his pride, laziness, and superstition, he never obtains any advantage from the natural richness of the ground. The only occupation which he considers worthy of his lofty origin is the bearing of arms. [Beijing] pays each Mongol soldier a very small salary, which is enough for his immediate wants, and to meet any further requirements he sells his horses or his sheep to the Chinese merchants, who are constantly crossing the country in all directions.[72]

Lesdain's interpretation exemplifies the binary division between Han and Mongols and sedentary farmers and mobile herders, which reveals the ecological and cultural boundaries in determining social behaviors and practices as well as the deep-seated prejudices of each group toward the other.[73] The reality was even messier and more complex. On his trip across Mongolia in 1892, Pozdneyev notes on several occasions the fields cultivated by Mongols in the river valleys of northern Khalkha, as well as the Mongol engagement with trade and craftsmanship. Whereas the arrival of Chinese migrants in this part of Khalkha dated no earlier than the early 1880s, there is no doubt that growing encounters and interactions had resulted in overlapping economic and cultural boundaries. Some Chinese fields were entirely worked by Mongols as a means to pay off their debts.[74] Indeed, instead of cultural perceptions, direct economic interests set off the strife between the two. As their population ratio changed, the Chinese majority began to challenge the minority rule of the Mongols by the end of the nineteenth century.

Thirdly, the incident shows that when conflicts escalated, the Mongols would resort to the authority of the jasag to have the settlers expelled by force. However, these efforts were not always successful. In more populated Chinese settlements, such disputes often led to violent confrontations. In his 1834 memorial, Yande, military governor of Suiyuan, reported an incident of armed conflict in the Dalad banner. In this incident, the Mongol officials and *yamen* runners were ambushed by Chinese settlers when they set out to expel illegal settlers who reclaimed pasturelands outside the bounds of their allotments leased from the local postal-relay station. Over twenty Mongols were wounded in the conflict, including a second-class *tayiji*.[75] Chagdursereng, jasag of the Jüüngar banner, related a similar incident of violence in 1840:

> *Jakirugchi* Langrub signed the order to expel the Chinese migrants. As it got late, he and a party of fourteen people spent the night at his caverns. Early in the morning of the 16th, before daybreak, approximately seventy men headed by Chinese migrant Wang Jian besieged the caverns and attacked with sickles and wooden sticks. Sonom of the Üüshin banner and Kun-du-yun-hu and Baldan of this banner were seriously injured, and *Jakirugchi* Langrub and *Meiren-ü Janggi* Yondanjungnai were also wounded.[76]

These reports of contention and armed confrontation demonstrate that by the mid-nineteenth century Chinese migrants had proliferated to such an extent that they began to threaten the livelihood of ordinary herders and challenge the authority of jasags. In these cases, nobles and high-ranking officials were among the injured. This incident testified to the surge of Chinese migrants not only in number, but also as mobilized communities that were ready to resort to violence in defense of their economic interests. The fact that the composition of the migrant population was mainly rootless and footloose young males certainly contributed to this militant tendency.

The ethnic tensions eventually led to the 1891 Revolt in Jehol known as the Jindandao Incident, in which Han sectarians in Jianchang, Pingquan, and Chaoyang ravaged the Mongol banners, Buddhist monasteries, and Catholic churches and massacred tens of thousands of Mongols.[77] The conflict grew out of the long-standing enmity between the Han Chinese and Mongol populations of Jehol due to frictions over land taxes and other fiscal rights such as the Mongols' exclusive rights to area resources like firewood, grasses, and trees. Also, it grew out of mutual suspicion, the maltreatment that occurred between Han tenants and Mongol landowners, and the Han resentment against haughty behaviors of Mongol princes and high lamas. Most Han rebels were poor farmers mobilized through the sectarian networks of the Jindan, Zaili, and Wushengmen sects across Jehol. Although the rebellion lasted less than two months and was quenched by the end of 1891, it caused havoc and the depopulation of Mongols in Jehol. Many of them were either killed or fled to other banners. In many ways, the incident foreshadowed the shift of the Qing policy from one that was protective of Mongolian culture to one that favored Chinese migrants and the opening up of Mongol grasslands for Chinese cultivation. Further, the horror of indiscriminate slaughter contributed to the decision of the Khalkha Mongols to proclaim independence from the Qing dynasty in 1911.[78]

The impact of Chinese migration was not just limited to the economic and social aspects of Mongol society, but it also devastated the indigenous environment, both ecologically and culturally. Jehol, for example, was a region of densely forested mountains with abundant wildlife, which made it the site of the Imperial Hunting Reserve in 1682. As Chinese migrant farmers, craftsmen, merchants, and laborers began to proliferate in the region in the wake of the construction of the Imperial Summer Palace and the *jiedi yangmin* policy, land reclamation, deforestation of the mountains, degradation of grasslands, and erosion of the soil all expanded as well. When Huc and Gabet visited the area in 1845, they observed that "[a]ll the trees were grubbed up, the forests disappeared from the hills, the prairies were cleared by means of fire, and the new cultivators set busily to work in exhausting the fecundity of the soil."[79]

The advance of Chinese cultivators also forced the nomads to either retreat to remote areas of the steppe or settle down and give up their nomadic lifestyle. By the nineteenth century, both the Tümed and the Kharachin, who were among the first to adopt Chinese-style farming, had lost their native tongue and nomadic tradition altogether. The northward migration of a large number of Mongol refugees in the wake of the Jindandao Insurgence further spurred rapid agriculturalization in the northern banners.[80] In the Ordos region, although the scale of Chinese cultivation was relatively small and scattered, it nonetheless initiated a process that would accelerate in the twentieth century and bring irreversible damage to its fragile environment. The result was desertification and soil salinization.[81]

FOLK GENRES

The migrant experience was documented in a distinctive folk song genre of "mountain tunes" that circulated through oral transmission for over a century in western Inner Mongolia and northern Shanxi and Shaanxi. These folk songs are varyingly referred to as *shanqu* 山曲 in Shanxi, *xintianyou* 信天遊 in Shaanxi, and *pashange* 爬山歌 and *manhandiao* 漫瀚調 or *Meng-Han diao* 蒙漢調 in Inner Mongolia.[82] Despite their melodic and lyrical variations, the songs have much commonality in theme, structure, and style. Centering upon the everyday lives and sentiments of the migrants and their families, they typically express common themes such as love, longings, loss, and suffering, especially emotions and experiences associated with the migrating experience. As a genre originating in the multi-ethnic areas of the Han-Mongol borderlands, these folk songs fuse the singing styles of the northern Chinese with the *bogino duu* ("short song") folk ballads of the Mongols.[83] Much improvisation occurred as the songs developed, giving rise to a series of local and regional variations.

Starting from the mid-nineteenth century, a popular dramatic genre of song and dance duet called *errentai* 二人台 ("two-person stage") appeared, which incorporated the melodies of mountain-tune folk songs with the performance of a male and a female role (both played by male actors) with a developed plot.[84] The genre first gained popularity among Chinese migrant laborers and farmers in the Tümed region and then quickly spread to northern Shanxi and Shaanxi. For instance, in the Hequ and Fugu counties, performances of local *errentai* troupes can be traced to the Tongzhi era (1862–1874).[85] Later, a new musical drama called *fengjiaoxue* 風攪雪 ("wind mixing with snow") became popular in the Tümed area. This kind of drama fused Chinese and Mongolian words in performance, often with a comedic tone. It was created by a Tümed folk singer named Yun Shuangyang (1857–1928), whose many innovations and improvisations were adapted into *errentai* operas.[86] The emergence of these folk genres testifies to the interfusion of Chinese and Mongolian cultural traditions as a result of the processes of migration and border crossing, which gave rise to novel cultural forms that impacted not just the border regions, but core parts of China as well. *Errentai* opera, for instance, was included in the first list of national intangible cultural heritages in 2006.

In 1953, a group of nine researchers from the Institute of Chinese Music under the Central Conservatory of Music conducted a three-month survey trip in the

Hequ county of Shanxi with the goal of "discovering, collecting, surveying, and organizing" the folk songs prevalent in the area. They collected 545 melodies, 3,617 verses, and forty-two *errentai* operas from ten villages in Hequ. A tiny fraction of these folk songs were published in a volume entitled *Hequ minjian gequ* (1956). In the same year, Han Yanru published a selected number of songs from over one thousand *pashange* folk songs he collected in the Ordos/Hetao area over the course of two decades.[87] This repertoire provides an invaluable source of information on the everyday experiences of ordinary migrants that is rarely documented elsewhere. Incidentally, Hequ is one of the most important origins of Chinese migration during the nineteenth and twentieth centuries. It is estimated that over one hundred thousand people emigrated from Hequ to Inner Mongolia between 1875 and 1940, most of whom settled in Baotou and the Ordos/Hetao area along the Yellow River.[88] For example, in Nanshawa, a village of around 150 households, over one hundred men went outside the pass every year. Its 603 residents contributed sixty-nine melodies and 1,041 verses to the folk song collection.[89] Here, we can discern a close connection between migration and folk song transmission. The higher the migrant percentage, the more folk songs it seems to have produced. Accordingly, it is productive to examine this repertoire of folk songs to provide a glimpse into the lives and culture of migrants, as well as the changing circumstances associated with their migrant experiences.

An excerpt from the folk song "Zou Xikou" ("Going beyond the Western Pass") opened this chapter, and this song remains the best known *errentai* to this day. The earliest extant copy of the script, dated August 24, 1885, was dictated by Li You-run and recorded by Wu Shengxiang, both founding members of the Wuyuntang Wanyiban ("Five Clouds Hall Troupe") established in Tangjiahui village of Hequ in 1863.[90] There is a surprising degree of consistency between this version and a 1953 version sung by Jia Zhen of Hehui village, which is partly due to the standardization of the drama as seen from the existence of a written script and partly to its high popularity among the local audience. It is noteworthy that the form of oral transmission has made folk songs and dramas susceptible to changes of time and circumstances, which found expression in the shifting representations of "Zou Xikou" that were often temporally specific. For instance, the 1885 version began with a literary trope used in traditional drama and literature to attract the audience's attention: "In the fifth year of Xianfeng reign/A curious matter happened/The curious matter happened/In Taiyuan prefecture of Shanxi."[91] The plot was set in 1855 in the Hequ county of Taiyuan prefecture. It was about a newlywed couple: Yulian, the daughter of a well-off family, and Taichun, a man in the medical profession. No sooner had they got married in the twelfth lunar month than Taichun decided to set out for beyond the pass in the first month of the lunar New Year, as stated in the lines: "Two good friends returned from beyond the Western Pass/Inviting me to go along to Ningxia." This excerpt demonstrates that by the mid-nineteenth century, *zouxikou* had become a common practice in this part of Shanxi, involving not only the landless and deprived, but also the elite class.

In a different version of the *errentai* adapted by the Committee on Reforming Traditional Operas in Suiyuan Province in 1953, the verses read:

In the fifth year of the Xianfeng reign,	咸豐正五年，
Shanxi was hit with a year of famine.	山西遭年限。
Those with money had filled granaries;	有錢的粮滿倉，
The suffering farmers were so pitiful. . . .	受苦人真可憐 。。。
Second Cousin sent a letter saying	二姑舅捎來信，
The harvest was good outside the Western Pass.	他說西口外好收成。
I intended to go beyond the Pass,	我有心走口外，
But I feared Yulian wouldn't agree.[92]	恐怕玉蓮不依從。

Here, the lure of migration is attributed to natural disaster and the hoarding of the rich, which is absent in the original version, and the migrants are depicted exclusively as landless and famine-stricken farmers. Apart from the apparent official appropriation for political purposes,[93] the deteriorated situation of ecological degeneration, rural impoverishment, and social stratification that the *errentai* reflected were characteristic of the late nineteenth and early twentieth century. At this time, a complex set of intersecting forces, both economic and ecological, triggered the cross-border migration.

In the subsequent stanza, Yulian combed Taichun's braid of hair (a cultural indicator unique to the Qing era) and bade him farewell at the front gate. Then she offered suggestions about how to keep safe during the journey, such as taking the big roads, staying away from falling cliffs, sitting in boat cabins, lodging early and departing late, eating well-cooked food, and avoiding taking a lover. Obviously, she was not unfamiliar with the hazards and pitfalls of the road, which shows that knowledge

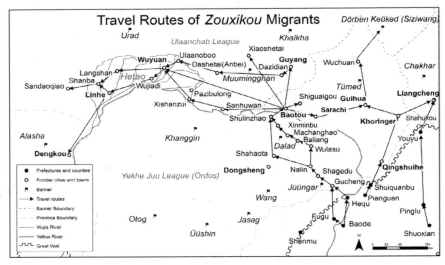

Map 3.3. Travel Routes of Han Migrants

about the journey across the Western Pass had been well circulated among locals. The idiosyncratic reference to river and boats indicates that the starting point was Hequ county along the Yellow River, which is located at the intersection of Shanxi, Shaanxi, and Inner Mongolia.[94] The section of the river between Hequ and Pianguan paralleled the Great Wall, and the series of Ming fortresses known as "waterfront passes" (*shuiguan* 水關) were later transformed into official docks (*guandu* 官渡) in the Qing period. For natives of Hequ, these docks represented a barrier that they referred to as "the Western Pass."[95]

Whereas the 1885 version of the *errentai* closes at the parting scene of the couple, the 1953 version includes a solo by Taichun that contains a day-by-day itinerary of his trip across the Western Pass.[96] It begins with familiar landmarks of Hequ—Boji Bay, the West Gate, and the Stage—where his journey began:

Toward the Boji Bay,	一溜簸箕灣，
I went down to the riverbank.	下了大河畔。
Boarding a boat outside the West Gate,	西門外上大船，
I left my beloved behind.	丟下命圪蛋。
Once the stage was passed,	一過台子焉，
Hequ county was out of sight.	瞭不見河曲縣。
Thinking of my dear Little Sister,	盤算起小妹子，
How could I leave her behind?[97]	怎扔下我毛眼眼。

Taichun then offers a road map detailing each stop he made overnight:

The first day I lodged at Gucheng,	頭天住古城，
Having walked exactly seventy *li*.	走了七十里整。
Though the distance was not great,	雖然路不遠，
I have crossed three provinces.	走了三個省。

Setting out from Hequ of Shanxi, Taichun first crossed the Yellow River to reach Mazha of the Jüüngar banner and then arrived at Gucheng of Fugu, Shaanxi. Gucheng is a village located forty *li* north of the Huangfukou Pass, inside the belt of *huopandi* south of the fifty-*li* border.[98] Therefore, it is no exaggeration that he crossed three provinces—Shanxi, Shaanxi, and Inner Mongolia—in just one day's time. From there he proceeded to traverse the Jüüngar and Dalad banners of northeast Ordos:

The second day I lodged at Nalin,	第二天住那嶺，
And ran into a Mongolian.	碰見了個蒙古人。
I had baked potato for dinner,	吃了一頓燒山藥，
And accomplished nothing.	毬也沒弄成。
The third day crossing Baliang,	第三天翻壩梁，
My eyes were filled with tears.	兩眼淚汪汪。

Thinking of my dear Little Sister,   思想起小妹子，
I felt so sad and subdued.   實是好慘心。

The fourth day at Wulasu,   第四天烏拉樹，
I found a piece of white rag.   拾了一塊破白布。
I asked a woman nearby   找一個婦女人，
To mend my torn pants.   補一補爛皮褲。

The first day at Shahaota,   第五天住在沙蒿塔，
I found a broken melon.   拾了一個破瓜把。
Picking it up to snatch a bite,   拿起來啃一口，
It was so cool and refreshing.   打涼又解乏。

Upon arrival at western Baotou,   到了西包頭，
I met with my Second Cousin.   碰見個二姑舅。
"Please bring two pieces of *khadak* silk   你給我那巧手手，
To my deft handed embroider at home."   捎上兩片哈達綢。

Staying at Shahuwan,   住在沙湖灣，
I ran into a Tartar wife.   碰見了個韃老闆。
She spoke Mongolian;   說了兩句蒙古話，
I understood not a word.   懂不得他說些啥。

Arriving at Changya Inn,   到了長牙地，
I couldn't afford to pay.   住店沒房錢。
Please Sister Changya   叫一聲長牙嫂，
Have mercy on me!   可憐一可憐。

Next, the traveler passed a set of *huopan* shelters all bearing Mongolian names: Nalin, Wulasu, Shahaota.[99] After that, he crossed Baliang, a sandy tableland and geographical landmark between the Jüüngar and Dalad banners, and arrived at Baotou (Mo: Bugutu, "place with deer") on the sixth day. The allusion to scarf silk (Mo: *khadag*), a luxurious Chinese import, hints at the flourishing cross-border trade in this frontier town north of the Yellow River. The itinerary is fairly precise, as the local saying "*kuai wu man liu, jin qi man ba*" 快五慢六/緊七慢八 ("five days if you hurry, six days if you go slow, seven days if you make haste, eight days if you take your ease") confirms that it generally took five to six days to reach Baotou from Hequ/Baode, and seven to eight days to reach it from Shenmu/Fugu.[100] Although the final destination of Taichun is not specified, the mention of Shahuwan in the Urad banner west of Baotou indicates that it was most likely Hetao in the northern bend of the Yellow River (see chapter 4). Indeed, statistics from the 1920s and 1930s show that 70 percent of the Chinese population in Hetao were natives of Hequ.[101]

This itinerary from Hequ to Baotou via the Ordos was one of the many routes across the passes. Natives of Fugu, Shenmu, Yulin, and Jingbian of Shaanxi usually entered the Ordos via the string of abandoned fortresses along the Great Wall, whereas travelers from Pinglu, Zuoyun, Youyu, and Shanyin of Shanxi typically ended up in the Tümed plain via the Shahukou Pass. An alternative route across the passes is depicted in the following rhymed monologue (*chuanhua* 串話) in a *fengjiaoxue* drama also entitled "Zou Xikou":

From home bound for beyond the pass,	從家出口外，
I arrived outside the North Tower of Togtokhu.	來到托城北閣外。
Hastening through Khara Baishing,	哈拉板升來得快，
Past Wushen, across Shangai,	走五申，過陝蓋，
From Julachin, Gongbu to Dadai.	祝拉沁公布到大岱。
From Gegen Baishing next to Khanggai,	圪旵板升挨韓蓋，
Via Gouzi Baishing and Bingzhouhai,	勾子板升兵州亥，
I sped to outside the North Gate of Höhhot.	一程趕到歸化城的北門外。
Once in the Tümed Plain,	進了土默川，
Food and clothing are not a concern.	不愁吃和穿。
The mountain is high, and rivers bend;	烏拉高，岡勒灣，
The plain of grains is vast and wide.	海海漫漫的米粮川。
Cattle are fleshy, and crops are abundant;	牛羊肥，莊稼寬，
The refugee's heart is filled with joy.[102]	逃難人見了心喜歡。

This monologue records a different migration route from northern Shanxi to Baotou via the Tümed plain, which is depicted as a vast "plain of grains" dotted with numerous *baishing* settlements juxtaposed to pasturelands. Both Togtokhu and Höhhot were cities that were the residences of Manchu civil administrators appointed to govern the Chinese migrants since the mid-1700s. Note the cheerful tone of the monologue. Unlike the mountain-tune folk songs that are often sentimental, the *fengjiaoxue* drama is more upbeat and hilarious, poking fun at certain comic situations such as those arising from cross-cultural interactions. The fusion of Mongolian and Chinese words in the performance adds to the humorous tone, as seen in the following conversation between the traveler and two Mongolian women:

Having arrived in Sanhuwan,	一走走在三湖灣，
I ran across two Tartar wives.	碰見兩個韃老板。
Understanding not a word they said,	她們說話我不懂，
I bade them good health with gestures.	比比劃劃問平安。
"Please have you a bowl of water?	"有水請給我一碗，
I must hurry on my journey."	我還著急把路趕。"
"*Tanai uge medekhui!*"	"特耐五咯免得貴,"
("I don't know your words!")	
"*Khurdun yabu*" ("Hurry up"), pointing west.	"忽爾登雅步"指向西。
I pointed at my mouth to show I'm thirsty,	手指口渴嗓子幹，
Yet she gave me a bowl of dried cheese.	她卻給了一碗酸酪丹。

The drama depicts the scene of a cross-cultural encounters between a Chinese migrant and local Mongols. The mutually incomprehensible languages they spoke led to some hilarious miscommunication. When the traveler requested water, his Mongol hostess thought he was asking for direction. When he pointed at his mouth to signal his thirst, she thought he was asking for food. A similar scenario is found in other versions of "Zou Xikou," which demonstrates mutual borrowing between the "mountain-tune" folk songs and the *fengjiaoxue* drama.[103] Indeed, these folk genres can be seen as hybrid cultural forms grown out of the processes of cross-cultural interaction and amalgamation brought by migration.

A later version of "Zou Xikou," entitled "Zou chu erliban" 走出二里半 ("Two *li* and a half away from home"), records developments in the twentieth century:

Arriving at western Baotou,	到了西包頭，
I meet my Second Cousin.	碰見二姑舅。
It is hard to get by here;	這裡難糊口，
I have to leave in tears.	忍淚還得走。
Proceeding to Wuyuan county;	上了五原縣，
Meals are given but no salary.	掙飯沒工錢。
There is no living anywhere,	到處無生路，
My heart is full of anguish.	心如滾油煎。
Out of the Jiayuguan Pass,	刮出嘉峪關，
My eyes are filled with tears.	兩眼淚不乾，
Thinking of my dear Little Sister,	思想起小妹子，
My heart is on pins and needles.	心呀心不安。

The mention of Wuyuan county suggests that this version appeared in the Republican period, as Wuyuan was first established as an autonomous sub-prefecture in 1903 and became a county in 1912. By then, waves of outmigration had caused a surfeit of labor in Inner Mongolia that forced many migrants to venture further west into new frontiers like Gansu and Xinjiang.[104] Compared with the earlier versions that depict the traveler's hardships on the road and his yearning for home, this version emphasizes his sufferings due to a depressed employment market and deteriorated economic conditions that were symptomatic of the early twentieth century.

Besides a detailed road map, the folk songs also capture the sojourner's real-life experiences and sentiments. Traveling in the context of traditional China is often associated with a sense of loss and longing due to the attachment of the traveler to his native land and a reluctance to leave (*an tu zhong qian* 安土重遷). More importantly, as mentioned previously, most migrants were single males who were forbidden to bring families into Mongolia by the Qing law. Therefore, the melancholy feelings and longings of the lonesome traveler become a constant theme of folk songs such as in the following excerpt:

Passing Gucheng, my eyes were filled with tears;	一過固城淚汪汪，
Crossing Baliang, my heart was immersed in grief.	一翻壩梁更心傷。
Three days on the road, I was far away from home;	走了三天離家遠，
Who'd pity me, the lonely drifter in a foreign land?[105]	異鄉孤人誰可憐。

At this point in the journey, the traveler journeyed exclusively on foot, covering a distance of thirty to forty kilometers every day carrying a pole, a bedroll, and a package of dry food. His daily diet was mainly millet gruel and flour pastry made of fried soybean mixed with bran. If his food supply ran low, he would have to depend on the generosities of strangers for a meal or two. He usually spent the night at kitchen lodgings equipped with a large *kang* that were used as both a bed and cooking stove. In areas where no such lodgings were available, he would sleep in the open, usually on flat surfaces near water sources, using his bedroll or simply an old sheepskin gown to keep warm.[106] The hardships on the road found expression in the following excerpt:

Here and there, I drifted along without a shelter,	東三天西兩天無處安身，
Now and then, I grabbed a bite or stayed hungry.	飢一頓飽一頓飲食不均。
Lodging on damp riverbanks, I slept on my shoes.	住河灘睡冷地脫鞋當枕，
Reeds as mat, stars as quilt, I shivered till dawn.[107]	鋪枳机蓋星宿難耐天明。

Although earlier migrants were typically engaged in trading or farming, by the late nineteenth century, commerce and land ownership became increasingly concentrated in the hands of large firms and land brokers who had cultivated relations with the Mongol upper classes. As a result, newcomers often had to start with low-paying, labor-intensive jobs, such as short-term hired hands or contracted wage laborers, and they would drift from one place to another owing to the transient nature of employment. The traveler's working conditions were depicted in the same folk song:

Up on Khanggai, I dug roots like digging my own tomb,	上杭蓋掏根子自打墓坑，
Down the stony river, I tracked boats hunching my back.	下石河拉大船駝背彎身。
Entering Hetao, I dug canals like living in a jailhouse.	進河套挖大渠自帶囚墩，
On Houshan, I plucked wheat with blistered hands.	上後山拔麥子雙手流膿。
To Houying, I pulled camels like a soldier in exile.	走後營拉駱駝自問充軍，
On Daqingshan, I carried coals breaking my back.	大青山背大炭壓斷背筋。
At Haotaliang, I herded winter sheep in icy cold,	蒿塔梁放冬羊冷寒受凍，
As plague hit, I got infected and nearly lost my life.[108]	遇傳人遭瘟病九死一生。

The string of place names in the song are localities where new migrants gathered and worked as licorice root diggers, boat trackers, canal builders, cameleers, coal miners, and shepherds. Chinese merchants also invested in the Hetao irrigation canals of Hetao (see chapter 4) and the Mt. Daqingshan coal mines by renting lands from the Mongols and recruiting migrant laborers in the construction and mining sites. Canal construction usually began in the late spring and carried on through the summer, whereas coal mines operated in the winter through summer, so as to accommodate the growing season.[109] In these cases, the accumulation of merchant capital and the ready availability of labor supplied by the influx of landless farmers and refugees from south of the passes led to growing social stratification among Chinese migrants. A small group of wealthy merchants, land brokers, and mine owners reaped profits from the cheap natural resources they obtained from the Mongols, whereas ordinary laborers were subject to exploitation and dismal working conditions.

After months of toil and strife, it was time for the sojourner to return home with the end of the fall harvest. He would either sell the cereals at the border market or barter them with Mongol herders for livestock, wools, and pelts to be sold at markets near his native place. Sometimes he could even afford to acquire a donkey or pony as a means of transport:

Rocks roll down the Mt. Daqingshan;	大青山的石頭往下拋，
I left Houtao with a crack of a whip.	大鞭子一繞離後套。
Having saved silver money for a donkey,	攢下銀錢買頭驢，
I was on my way back to Hequ on the donkey.	騎上毛驢回河曲。
The donkey's bare back was pitch black;	黑赤墨毛驢光脊梁，
Lashing the whip, I crossed the tableland.	鞭子一甩翻壩梁。
After the tableland I stopped to have a snack,	翻過了壩梁打一尖，
In a day and a night, I lodged at the dock.	一天一宿住上三道堰。
Boarding a boat to cross the Yellow River,	上了那船艙過黃河，
I sold the donkey to find myself a bride.[110]	賣了毛驢娶老婆。

Here, the list of place names captures the cheerful impatience of the traveler on his homebound journey, which contrasts with the melancholy mood of the outbound trip. The similar tone is also found in the following folk song:

Having reaped the millet after the fall harvest,	割倒糜子收倒秋，
The Brother outside the Pass was on his way back.	跑口外的哥哥往回走。
For two whole years, he traversed here and there,	前山後山二年整，
Saving enough money for his journey home.	掙下了盤纏轉回程。
A hundred miles of sands and fifty miles of water,	三百里明沙二百里水，
He joined his Little Sister from across the miles.	五百里路途卯妹妹。
Water flows a thousand miles to the sea,	水流千里歸大海，
People travel a thousand miles to return home.	人走千里蹓回來。
Feeding an extra two pints to his little black horse,	不大大的小青馬馬多餵上兩升料，
He will make a three-day journey in two days.[111]	三天的路程兩天到。

The annual migration affected not just the sojourners. Both the Qing restrictions on Chinese migration and the gender division of labor in the traditional patriarchal society determined that migration prior to the twentieth century was largely a gender-specific practice involving only the males of the family, while the women stayed at home to take care of in-laws and children while undertaking household chores. The emotional distress of the woman left behind became a common theme of folk song genres. For example,

Thinking of my beloved outside the pass,	盤算起親親跑口外，
My tears would have filled up my bosom.	淚蛋蛋流得抱一懷。
The East wind blows and the water runs west;	刮起了東風水流西，
Seeing other people, I thought of you.	看見了人家想起你。
Mountains and water stay and rocks too;	山在水在石頭在，
Everyone else was around but not you.	人家都在你不在。

You went to Houtao outside the pass,	你走口外上後套，
Leaving me behind so forlorn and lost.	你扔下了妹妹好孤少。
You went to Houshan outside the pass,	你走口外上後山，
Leaving me behind so hard to endure.	你扔下了妹妹好困難。
You went outside the pass without a family,	你走口外沒有安住家，
How should I live with so little food and fuel?[112]	你叫我少食沒燃怎介活。

In addition to emotional distress and economic difficulties, the absence of the migrant husband posed practical problems for the woman in terms of labor-intensive household chores such as cutting firewood and carrying water. The following song depicts these challenges:

You went beyond the pass, and I stayed home;	你走口外我在家，
You remained single, and I was like a widow.	你打光棍我受寡。
You hung around the shelters of Mt. Daqingshan,	你走在大青山伙房里閃，
You left your Little Sister to live in misery.	你扔下小妹妹受艱難。
Sickle in hand and rope around waist,	手拿上鐮刀腰系繩，
Who'd feel sorry if I cut wood on the cliff?	山坡上砍柴誰心疼。
Basket in hand, I dug wild lettuce for food,	手提上籃籃掏苦菜，
I had no alternative but felt so helpless.	萬般出在無其奈。
Who'd fan the stove when the fire was weak?	爐子不快誰給咱扇，
Who'd fill the jar when the water was out?	瓮子裡沒水誰給咱擔。
In bitter winter and freezing cold days,	十冬臘月數九天，
Who'd pity me when I carried water in the valley?	深溝溝擔水誰可憐？
Water on shoulder, I could hardly climb the hill.	深溝溝擔水爬不上坡，
Who else had a miserable lot such as mine?[113]	塵世上苦命人少有我。

The gender imbalance in both destination and origin societies gave rise to extra-marital relations, popularly referred to as *wei pengyou* 為朋友 ("take a lover") or *da huoji* 搭夥計 ("become partners").[114] In "Zou Xikou," the bride urges her husband: "When you cross the Western Pass/Don't you ever take a lover/If you ever take a lover/I'm afraid you'd forget about me." Such relations were typically seen between Han males and Mongol women, as shown in another excerpt: "Arriving at Shanhuhe/I met a Mongol woman/ She asked for two bran buns / And called me her sworn brother."[115] Here, *gan gege* 乾哥哥 ("sworn brother") is often used as a euphemism for a lover.

These folk genres were especially poignant in documenting the everyday experiences of migrants and their families. They capture the emotions and aspirations of the people involved in their raw vividness, and thereby give us a sense of the cultural milieu of men and women whose lives were deeply affected by the process of migration. For many families who could not produce enough to support themselves in their native places, *zouxikou* represented an alternative channel of survival, a way of life, and a destiny. It is both collective and personal. The oral transmission of these genres makes it an open project that appeals to the shared experiences and sentiments across localities, generations, and economic backgrounds, while allowing each participant to invest in their own experiences and emotions through reiteration and circulation.

CONCLUSION

This chapter examines the origins and processes of Chinese migration into Mongolian territories across the Great Wall, locally referred to as *zou xikou* or "going beyond the Western Pass." It came as a result of the multiple, sometimes contradictory, endeavors of the Qing government to cope with the challenges posed by a territorially and demographically expanding empire and its political and ecological consequences. On the one hand, the Qing court made an official policy that prohibited Chinese cultivation in Manchuria and Inner Mongolia, with important exceptions made for official enclosures, enfeoffments, and allotments that were subsequently open to Chinese cultivation. On the other hand, the pressures of overpopulation and ecological disasters pushed a large number of land-poor farmers and famine refugees from north China across the border to cultivate land in the fringe of the Great Wall. This large-scale migration brought significant ecological and social changes to the steppe.

One of the most important changes was the transplantation of centralized governmental administration from interior China to the Mongol periphery due to the rising needs of managing the rapidly expanding migrant population. It gave rise to a dual administrative framework that eventually eroded the judicial autonomy of the banners. As discussed in this chapter, overlapping jurisdictions added another source of conflict to frontier regions, on top of disputes surrounding murky land rights, unclarified boundaries, and rental payments between Chinese migrants and local Mongols. Another change brought about by the influx of Chinese migrants was the commoditization and privatization of the land regime, as communally owned Mongol lands gradually passed into private ownership. As virgin pastures were put under the plow, land use was permanently transferred to Chinese farmers, although the Mongols retained nominal ownership and the right to collect rent. This resulted in the decline of the nomadic economy, increased social stratification, and the absorption of Mongolia into the Chinese economic system.

Chinese migration across the western pass was not just a macro-history concerning broad-stroke institutional, socioeconomic, and ecological changes, but also a micro-history of various actors, both collective and individual, who interacted with the physical and social settings in which they lived and made choices and initiatives accordingly. Among these actors were farmers from northern Shanxi and Shaanxi, who in response to the ecological deficiencies at home, took advantage of their close proximity to the Great Wall and ventured into the grasslands in search of arable land and economic opportunities. Once outside the passes, many were recruited as tenant farmers at official estates or banner lands, while others obtained plots from local Mongol authorities and established scattered settlements in the fringe of the

Great Wall. Through a seasonal migratory pattern repeated on an annual basis, they recruited more fellow villagers to join them and push their settlements further northward. The lives, experiences, aspirations, and sufferings of these ordinary migrants and their families, often neglected in official narratives, are captured in vivid detail in a repertoire of folk songs and dramas, which manifest the human costs involved in the process of migration.

NOTES

1. "Zou Xikou," in Yan Zhiguo, *Xikou qingge*, 172.

2. According to Dwight Perkins, the population of the four northern provinces—Shandong, Zhili [Hebei], Shanxi, and Shaanxi—grew from 54.1 million in 1749 to 84.5 million in 1851. In contrast, there was no growth in the land under cultivation, which suggested a decline in the area of farmland per capita by approximately 35 percent. See Perkins, *Agricultural Development in China, 1368–1968*.

3. Cao Shuji, *Zhongguo renkou shi*, volume 5, 450.

4. QHDSL 166.

5. Huidian guan, eds., *Qinding daqing huidian shili "lifanyuan"* (hereafter QHDSL "Lifanyuan"), 978, 218, 221–28.

6. *Da Qing lichao shilu* (hereafter QSL), QL 14/9/12; QHDSL "Lifanyuan," 979, 230.

7. Wei Shu and Lü Yaozeng, *Shengjing tongzhi* 24; QHDSL 166; Yang Bin, *Liubian jilue* 1, 1. For discussions on reclamation in Manchuria, see Reardon-Anderson, *Reluctant Pioneers*.

8. Ji Huang et al., *Qinding huangchao wenxian tongkao* 5. For detailed discussions on the official estates in Manchuria, see Reardon-Anderson, *Reluctant Pioneers*, 27–34.

9. QHDSL 159.

10. For the marriage alliance between Manchu and Mongols, see Du Jiaji, *Qingdai manmeng lianyin yanjiu*. For a study of the entourage of Manchu princesses and daughters of the imperial clan who married Mongol nobles, see Qi Meiqin, "Gongzhu gege xiajia waifan menggu suixing renyuan shixi."

11. Zhou Tiezheng and Shen Mingshi, eds., *Chaoyang xianzhi*; Qi Meiqin, "Gongzhu gege xiajia."

12. QSL, KX 37/12/17; KX 39/8/13; Wuyunbilige et al., *Menggu minzu tongshi*, volume 4, 150–51.

13. Unlike the "Ever-normal granaries" (*changpingcang* 常平倉) of each county of Chinese provinces that were built up from combined state funds, contributions, and transferred grains along the Grand Canal, the grain reserves of "public granaries" of the Mongol banners were collected from banner subjects at a quota of millet per adult men and used as both famine relief and support of impoverished bannermen. See QHDSL 979, 236–37; Wuyunbilige et al., *Menggu minzu tongshi*, volume 4, 238–39. For discussion on the granary system of the three leagues of eastern Inner Mongolia, see Zhusa, "Youguan cangchu zhidu fangmian de jifen menggu wen dang'an wenshu." For the civilian granary system of the Qing in general, see Will and Wong, *Nourish the People*.

14. QSL, YZ 1/4/30.

15. Yilinzhen, *Nei Menggu lishi dili*, 173. For a historical account on Chengde and its symbolic efficacy to the Qing empire, see Millward et al., eds., *New Qing Imperial History*.

16. For discussion on Chinese settlements in Manchuria and eastern Inner Mongolia, see Lattimore, *The Mongols of Manchuria*; Reardon-Anderson, "Land Use and Society in Manchuria and Inner Mongolia"; Zhusa, *18–20 shiji chu dongbu neimenggu nonggeng cunluohua yanjiu*.

17. QSL, QL 43/2/15. Also see Pozdneyev, *Mongolia and the Mongols*, volume 2, 213–14. For the population figures of 1778 and 1820, see Heshen, *Rehe zhi* 91, shihuo, 5. Also see Yuan Senpo, "Saiwai chengde senlin lishi bianqian de fansi," 29.

18. See Heshen, *Rehe zhi* 91, shihuo, 1–4. There were no recorded figures for the cultivated area and grain reserves in Jianchang, Chifeng, and Chaoyang counties in *Rehe zhi*, as land rents were collected by Mongols in these areas. However, recent research using Mongolian-language archives show that cultivated area in the Kharachin right, center, and left banners alone had reached twenty-seven thousand *qing* (180,000 ha) by the mid-eighteenth century. See Zhusa, *18–20 shiji chu dongbu neimenggu nonggeng cunluohua yanjiu*, 35–64; Yi Baozhong and Zhang Liwei, "Qingdai yilai neimenggu diqu de yimin kaiken," 88–96.

19. Borjigin, "The Complex Structure of Ethnic Conflict in the Frontier," 46–50. Also see Borjigin, *Kingendai ni okeru mongoru jin nōkō sonraku shakai no keisei*.

20. Wang Yuhai points out that the two Tümed banners were initially considered part of the fifty-one jasag banners of twenty-five Inner Mongol aimags (although ruled by a non-Chinggisid lieutenant governor rather than a Chinggisid jasag), but were reduced to the status of "internal" banners like the Chakhar Eight Banners only after the abolition of both colonels of Höhhot in 1763. See Wang Yuhai, "Guihuacheng tumote erqi de neishu wenti," 237–38.

21. For a historical overview of the Tümed under the Qing, see Xiaoke, ed., *Tumote shi*, 272–330; Wurenqiqige, "Qingdai guihuacheng tumote liangyi qiquan xiaoruo wenti yanjiu," 82–84. For a description of the Tümed Mongols, including remarks on the population, customs, and manners, see Van Oost, *Notes sur le T'oemet*. It also provides an invaluable source on Chinese immigrants, agriculture, villages, and everyday life in the Tümed area.

22. Jagchid and Hyer, *Mongolia's Culture and Society*, 313; Xiaoke, *Tumote shi*, 138–39, 273.

23. Zhang Penghe, *Fengshi eluosi riji*, 14–15.

24. Each estate was overseen by a Manchu foreman (*zhuangtou* 莊頭), who was given eighteen *qing* (120 ha) of land, later increased to sixty *qing* (four hundred ha) per estate. An additional 785 *qing* of pasturelands near the Mt. Daqingshan were allocated to these estates in 1803. However, by the nineteenth century, the actual cultivated area shrank to around four hundred *qing* due to land degradation caused by flooding, desertification, salinization, and abandonment. See Zhang Erjie, "Tumote tudi wenti shihua."

25. QHDSL 119, *neiwufu tunliang*; Gao Geng'en, *Tumote qi zhi* 5, shutian ji; fushui.

26. Yilinzhen, *Nei Menggu lishi dili*, 226; Xiaoke, *Tumote shi*, 301–303.

27. Gao Geng'en, *Tumote qi zhi*, 5; Xiaoke, *Tumote shi*, 308–09, 345–47.

28. QSL 198, QL 8/8/1. For discussions on the distribution of habitats of the Tümed Mongols, see Xiaoke, *Tumote shi*, 347–49; Aramusu, "Shindai uchi mongoru ni okeru nōchi shoyu no jittai"; Tian Mi, "Qingdai guihuacheng tumote diqu de tudi kaifa yu cunluo xingcheng," 92; Liang Xiaowen, "Qingdai guihuacheng tumote hukoudi tanxi" (2018).

29. Xiaoke, *Tumote shi*, 348.

30. QSL 198, QL 8/8/1.

31. Song Naigong, *Zhongguo renkou nei menggu fence*, 49.

32. Wuyunbilige et al., *Menggu minzu tongshi*, volume 4, 239–41.

33. For an account of the Chakhar in the early Qing, see Dalizhabu, "Qingdai Chaha'er zhasake qi kao," 47–59. The eight banners were divided into two flanks (Mo: *ghar*, Ch: *yi* 翼).

The Left Flank (i.e. East Flank, Mo: *jüün ghar*, Ch: *zuoyi* 左翼) comprised of Plain Blue (Mo: *shuluun khökhe*, Ch: *zhenglan* 正藍), Bordered White (Mo: *khoboot chaghan*, Ch: *xiangbai* 鑲白), Plain White (Mo: *shuluun chaghan*, Ch: *zhengbai* 正白), and Bordered Yellow (Mo: *khoboot shira*, Ch: *xianghuang* 鑲黃) banners, and the Right Flank (i.e. West Flank, Mo: *baruun ghar*, Ch: *youyi* 右翼) Flank consisted of Plain Yellow (Mo: *shuluun shira*, Ch: *zhenghuang* 正黃), Plain Red (Mo: *shuluun ulaan*, Ch: *zhengbai* 正紅), Bordered Red (Mo: *khoboot ulaan*, Ch: *xianghuang* 鑲紅), and Bordered Blue (Mo: *khoboot khökhe*, Ch: *xianghuang* 鑲藍) banners.

34. Jin Zhizhang and Huang Kerun, eds., *Koubei santing zhi* 6, kaomu, 6.

35. Ji Huang et al., *Qinding huangchao tongdian* 3, shihuo. For an account of the cultivation in Chakhar banners and herds, see Sudebilige, "Reclamation of Pastureland in Chakhar," 33–44.

36. Jin and Huang, *Koubei santing zhi* 1, diyu, 11.

37. See Jin and Huang, *Koubei santing zhi*; Tayama, *Shin jidai ni okeru Mōko no shakai seido*; Serruys, "The Chakhar Population during the Ch'ing," 58–79.

38. *Mingshi* 327, *Dada liezhuan*. Also see Chen Yuning, "Mingdai menggu zhi ruju Hetao," 40–44. For discussion on the Ming defensive strategies in the Hetao/Ordos, see Waldron, *The Great Wall of China*, 53–164. *Jinong* was a noble title held as the most powerful institution next only to the Khan. After the subjugation of the Mongols to the Manchus, the authority of *Jinong* was greatly reduced and it was shifted to the ruling prince mainly in charge of the administrative affairs and the ceremonial affairs only secondarily. See Serruys, "*Jinong*: *Ch'ün-wang* or *Ch'in-wang*?" 199–208. Also see Hangin, "The Mongolian Titles *Jinong* and *Sigejin*," 255–66.

39. QHDSL: Lifanyuan, 963, 11–12; Zhao Chizi, *Yikezhao meng zhi*; Chen Yuning, *E'erduosi shihua*, 325.

40. Li Xiling, *Yulin fuzhi* 3, bianjie, in *Yudi zhi* 4; Wang Zhiyun, *Shenmu xianzhi* 3, jianzhi 6. Also see Serruys, "Documents from Ordos on the 'Revolutionary Circles,' Part I," 488.

41. Liang Bing, *Yikezhao meng de lidai kaiken*, 20; Qi Meiqin, "Yikezhao meng de mengdi fangken," 50; Wang Weidong, *Ronghui yu jiangou*, 54.

42. Zhang Shiming, "Qingdai 'shaohuang' kao," 87. Zhang Shuli points out that *jinliudi*, a buffer zone that was delineated in the early Qing dynasty to segregate the Mongols and Han Chinese, should be distinguished from *heijiedi*, a product of the official boundary making in 1743 to restrict Chinese cultivation and protect Mongol pasture. See Zhang Shuli, "'Jinliudi' chutan," 93. Also see Li Dahai, "Qingdai yikezhaomeng changcheng yanxian 'jinliudi,'" 43.

43. Zhao Erxun et al., eds., *Qing shi gao* (hereafter QSG) 520, liezhuan 307, fanbu.

44. Wang Zhiyun, *Shenmu xianzhi* 3, jianzhi, 7.

45. QSL, KX 36/3/1. Also see Ding Xikui, *Jingbian xianzhi gao* 4, 291–92. See Wang Zhiyun *Shenmu xianzhi* 3, jianzhi, 7. *Niuju* ("yoke-of-oxen," Mo: *anjisu*) was a measurement unit used in the newly reclaimed areas outside the Great Wall, referring to the area cultivated by one plough and a pair of farm oxen in a year's time. One niuju = 270–80 *mu* 畝 ≈ eighteen hectares (ha). *Shi* (or *dan* 石) is a grain capacity measurement unit in China. One *shi* = 2.9 bushel. See idem., 8; Ding Xikui, *Jingbian xianzhi gao* 4, yiwenzhi.

46. See Memorial of Zhu Guozheng (military commander of Yansui Circuit of Shaanxi province), in *Kangxichao hanwen zhupi zouzhe huibian*, 4/388/1. The figure reported in *Qing gaozong shilu* was between three thousand and four thousand *qing* instead of *niuju*, although the amount of annual yield remained the same. See QSL, QL 1/3/23. Here I cite the figure reported by Zhu, which seems more reliable being a first-hand record. It was probable that

niuju, being a regional unit of measurement, was unfamiliar to officials in Beijing, in comparison with *qing*, which was the standard unit of area measurement.

47. Suiyuan minzhong jiaoyuguan ed., *Suiyuan sheng fenxian diaocha gaiyao*, 185.

48. Zheng Juzhong, *Fugu xianzhi* 2, 238–41.

49. Wang Zhiyun, *Shenmu xianzhi* 3, jianzhi, 7; Ding Xikui, *Jingbian xianzhi gao*, 291–92. Also see Van Hecken, "Les Réductions catholiques du pays des Ordos," 11.

50. During the Ming period, farming was organized mainly in the form of military colonies (*juntun* 軍屯) so as to meet the needs of the troops and their families, supplemented by a number of merchant colonies (*shangtun* 商屯) organized by merchants contracted by the Ming government to transport cereals to the border granaries.

51. Chen and Yuan, "Jiusi yisheng zou xikou"; Hao Wanhu, "Zou xikou mantan," 75.

52. Hao Wanhu, "Zou xikou mantan," 75.

53. Among the 4,143 towers that dotted the 3,449-*li*-long section of the Great Wall between Shanhaiguan and Shanxi, only 661 were retained in 1647, that is, less than 20 percent. The remaining 3,482 were abandoned. See QSL 35, SZ 4/12/10, 11–12.

54. The term *huopan* was an abbreviation of *huoju panju* 伙聚盤據, "squatting together in temporary shelters." See Serruys, "Documents from Ordos on the 'Revolutionary Circles,' Part I," 488, n32. For *huopan* shelters, see Wang Weidong, "E'erduosi diqu jindai yimin yanjiu," 72–73; Yan Tianling, *Hanzu yimin yu jindai Nei Menggu shehui bianqian yanjiu*, 20–21; Wang Han, "Qingdai shanbei changcheng wai huopandi," 90–92; Hasibagen, *E'erduosi nongmu jiaocuo quyu yanjiu (1697–1945)*, 36–37.

55. Wang Jianxun, "*Chongxiu hetao sidagumiao beiji*," 44. For detailed discussion on *yanxing* activities, see Yan, *Hanzu yimin*, 134–47; Hasibagen, *E'erduosi nongmu jiaocuo quyu*, 31–34.

56. Jin Fuzeng, *Hequ xianzhi* 5.

57. Zheng Juzhong, *Fugu xianzhi* 2, 238–41. C.f. note 48.

58. Wang Zhiyun, *Shenmu xianzhi* 3, jianzhi, 8.

59. Given a sex ratio of 1:1, and the ratio of adult males between twenty to fifty years of age being 1:2 out of the male population, the adult male population was estimated as one-fourth of the total population. Hasibagen estimates the migrant population to be approximately two hundred thousand. However, this estimate is based on the presumption of equal distribution of population between *huopan* shelters and villages below the border, which seems unrealistic because of the Qing restriction. See Hasibagen, *E'erduosi nongmu jiaocuo quyu*, 84.

60. See QHDSL 976, *lifanyuan sheguan*; *Qinding Lifanbu zeli*, 5, 68–69. One of these yamens was set up in Ningxia in 1708, which oversaw migrant affairs in the Otog banner of the Ordos and Alashan special banner. The other was established in Shenmu in 1722, which was in charge of the remaining six banners of the Ordos. Similar offices were established in 1748 in Bagou, Tazigou, Sanzuota, and Ulaanhada that managed Chinese migrants in the Josutu and Juu Uda leagues. See ibid, 67. For more discussion on the offices of *lishiguan*, see Hasibagen, *E'erduosi nongmu jiaocuo quyu*, 87–100.

61. QHDSL 997, 473–74; *Qinding Lifanbu zeli* 221, 213; Li Xiling, *Yulin fuzhi* 3, jiangjie; Wang Zhiyun, *Shenmu xianzhi* 3, jianzhi, 8.

62. Gao Geng'en, *Guisui dao zhi* 5. Among the three sub-prefects, the Sarachi *yamen* was in charge of Chinese migrants in the Khanggin, Dalad, and Wang banners, whereas those in the more populated Jüüngar Banner were jointly administered by the Togtokhu and Qingshuihe yamens. See SYTZG 63, sifa.

63. *Arban* was the smallest military unit under Chinggis Khan. Over it came the *zuut* (one hundred men), *myangat* (one thousand men), and *tüm* (ten thousand men). See Sanjdorj, *Manchu Chinese Colonial Rule*, 48.

64. See Wang Zhiyun, *Shenmu xianzhi* 3, Jianzhi zhi, fu bianjie; QSG 120, zhi 95, shihuo 1.

65. *Qinding Lifanbu zeli*, 71; QHDSL 978, 220–21. Also see Zheng Juzhong, *Fugu xianzhi* 2, tianfu, 241.

66. For more details on the evolution of the institutions of *daghachin* and *darugha*, see Tamura Hideo, "*Mōkō shakai kōsei no kisō tan'i somoku*"; Hasibagen, *E'erduosi nongmu jiaocuo quyu*, 110–17.

67. Huc did not provide any precise geographical details on the part of journey. However, it is likely that they crossed the Khöbchi desert on their way, as they complained of the arid dismal country, scarcity of water, and sudden torrential rain. In the immediately following chapter Huc mentioned Dabsoun-Noor (Dabasun Nor, or "salt lake"), which is most likely the one located in the Khanggin banner. See Huc and Gabet, *Travels in Tartary, Thibet and China*, 262–64. In 1910 Pereira took the same path across the Ordos and drew a route map of this region. See Pereira, "A Journey across the Ordos," 260–64.

68. Huc and Gabet, *Travels in Tartary*, 229. *Kang* 炕 is a sort of furnace made of sun-dried mud that serves at once as heater, stove, and bed, typically found in northern China. For more description, see Huc and Gabet, *Travels in Tartary*, 11.

69. Huc and Gabet, *Travels in Tartary*, 232.

70. Huc and Gabet, *Travels in Tartary*, 232–34.

71. "The Letter from Jasag Sewangrashi Beise, head of the Ordos, to the Juridical Commissioner in dealing with Han-Mongol Affairs at Shenmu," JQ 11, 1–1, 3–7, 5–5; cited from Hasibagen, *E'erduosi nongmu jiaocuo quyu*, 52. Most of lawsuit cases were preserved in the Mongolian-language document exchanges between the banners and *yamens* of juridical commissioner/sub-prefect/councilors. The document is translated into Chinese by Hasibagen.

72. Lesdain, *From Pekin to Sikkim*, 33–34.

73. Lattimore, *The Mongols of Manchuria*, 65; Jagchid and Hyer, *Mongolia's Culture*, 316.

74. Pozdneyev, *Mongolia and the Mongols*, volume 1, 15, 37, 39–40.

75. QSG 307, fanbu 3; Yikezhao meng difang zhi biancuan weiyuanhui, ed., *Yikezhao meng zhi*, 67.

76. "The Letter from *Jasag* Chagdursereng and *tusalagchi* of the Jüüngar banner of Ordos to the Councilor at Togtokhu," DG 20/3/17, 511-1-14 (2), 184b–85a; cited from Hasibagen, *E'erduosi nongmu jiaocuo quyu*, 52–53. *Tusalagchi* is a high official secondary only to the jasag.

77. Hyer, "The Chin-Tan-Tao Movement," 105–12; Borjigin, "The Complex Structure of Ethnic Conflict in the Frontier," 41–60; McCaffrey, "From Chaos to a New Order," 528–61. For a witness report of the revolt from a Mongol perspective, see Wang Guojun, *Menggu jiwen*.

78. Hyer, "The Chin-Tan-Tao Movement"; Borjigin, "The Complex Structure of Ethnic Conflict in the Frontier," 54.

79. Huc and Gabet, *Travels in Tartary*, 4.

80. Borjigin, "The Complex Structure of Ethnic Conflict in the Frontier," 55.

81. Xiao Ruiling et al., *Mingqing Neimenggu xibu diqu kaifa yu tudi shahua*, 108.

82. Zhongyang yinyue xueyuan zhongguo yinyue yanjiusuo, ed., *Hequ minjian gequ* (hereafter HQMG); Yan Kemin, "Chilege yu pashandiao," 47; Yan Tianling, "*Zou xikou.*" On the folk songs of Zou Xikou, also see Gibbs, "Going Beyond the Western Pass," 1–31.

83. There are two major forms of Mongolian songs, *urtiin duu* ("long song") and *bogino duu* ("short song"). The former is a ritual form of expression associated with important

celebrations and ceremonies, with a long, expansive, and continuously flowing melody. The latter possesses a simple form with relatively short phrases, expressing common themes such as love, nature, suffering and loss, or the humor of a comic situation. For a description of the nomadic songs of the Mongols, see van Oost, *Au Pays des Ortos*.

84. *Errentai* was called such only in 1951, when the Suiyuan provincial government under the People's Republic of China attempted to reform and standardize popular drama and other artistic genres. Before, it was generally referred to as *wanyi'er* 玩藝兒 ["playthings"], which seems to indicate its low social status, being a popular dramatic form among the lower classes. See Yang Zhilin, "Errentai fanshen."

85. See Zhao Kuanren, "Hequ minjian liuchuan de 'errentai'"; Zhang Jinli, "Errenttai 'Zou Xikou' de yishu tese fenxi," 173.

86. Zhao Kuanren, "Hequ minjian liuchuan de 'errentai,'" 200–24; Xing Ye, "Youguan nei menggu difangxi errentai de tianye diaocha," 31–38; Liu Xianpu, "Errentai," 44–45.

87. Han Yanru, *Pashange xuan*. These selected volumes, inevitably censored and modified under the political circumstances of the early 1950s, represented the systematic efforts on the part of the central and provincial state as well as the nationalist- and revolutionary-minded intellectuals to standardize and appropriate the oral traditions so as to mobilize and control the masses. For instance, in 1951, the Suiyuan provincial government held eleven learning sessions for folk artists (Suiyuan sheng minjian yiren xuexihui 綏遠省民間藝人學習會) in Höhhot, on which the Provincial President Yang Zhilin gave the keynote speech on the "emancipation" (fanshen) of Errentai. In 1953, a Committee on Reforming Traditional Operas in Suiyuan Province (*Suiyuan sheng xiqu gaige shending weiyuanhui* 綏遠省戲曲改革審定委員會) was summoned to censor the content of traditional dramas to be staged, followed by the organization of a series of state-approved provincial and municipal troupes of *errentai* in the same year in Suiyuan as well as Shanxi and Hebei. See Hao Wanhu, "Zou xikou mantan."

88. Chen and Yuan, "*Jiusi yisheng 'zou xikou,*'" 55.

89. HQMG, 164, 244.

90. See Zhang Jinli, "Errenttai 'Zou Xikou' de yishu tese fenxi," 173.

91. "*Zou Xikou,*" in HQMG, 231.

92. This particular version was adapted by the Committee on Reforming Traditional Operas in Suiyuan Province (*Suiyuan sheng xiqu gaige shending weiyuanhui*) in 1953. See Hao Wanhu, "Zou xikou mantan."

93. Here the contrast between the rich and poor was reminiscent of the dominant political discourse of class struggle of the Chinese Communist Party. Chen also points out the discrepancies between these two versions. However, he attributes the difference to the "fabrication" of the "literary men" who recorded the oral transmission on paper. See Chen Bingrong, "Hequ: Huashuo Zou Xikou," http://hequ.xinzhou.org/2011/0927/article_2415.html.

94. The navigable section of the Yellow River is between Lanzhou of Gansu and Hequ of Shanxi via Baotou of Inner Mongolia. See Suiyuan Provincial Government ed., *Sunyuan gaikuang*, volume 2, jiaotong yu hangyun.

95. Chen and Yuan, "*Jiusi yisheng 'zou xikou,*'" 53. The two most heavily used by migrants of Hequ were the West Gate Dock (*shuixinmen dukou*) and River Bay Dock (*hewan dukou*). Migrants from Baode and Pianguan crossed the river at Shahekou and Yushuwan respectively. See Hao Wanhu, "Zou xikou mantan."

96. "*Zou chu er li ban,*" in Yan Zhiguo, *Xikou qingge*, 176–78.

97. The closest dock to the county seat of Hequ was the West Gate Dock. The Stage refers to the ancient theater state on the bank of the Yellow River, a landmark of the county seat of

Hequ. See Chen and Yuan, *"Jiusi yisheng 'zou xikou,"* 54; Guo Gai, *"Gensui 'Zou Xikou' zou Xikou."*

98. Zheng Juzhong, *Fugu xianzhi* 2, daolu, 205.

99. According to He Yangling, who surveyed the Suiyuan and Chakhar provinces in 1934, commerce in the Ordos was concentrated in Nalin and Shaheta of Jüüngar banner, with over a hundred households and a dozen shops, as well as at monasteries such as the Jüüngar Juu and Shine Juu, where temple fairs were held annually in the seventh lunar month, attracting border traders from Yulin, Shenmu, Fugu, Hequ, Huaiyuan, Jingbian, Ningxia, and Baotou. See He Yangling, *Chasui mengmin jingji de jiepou,* 72.

100. The local saying goes, *"kuai wu man liu, jin qi man ba"* 快五慢六，緊七慢八 ("five days if you hurry, six days if you go slow; seven days if you make haste, eight days if you take your ease"). See Hao Wanhu, "Zou xikou mantan," 75.

101. Wang Tao, "Hetao wuyuan xian diaocha ji"; Lin Jing, *Xibei congbian,* 55.

102. "Zou Xikou," cited from "Yun Shuangyang" in Feng Chuanyou ed., *Meili Baotou* 263. Also see Ba Jingyuan, "Tumochuan de 'Errentai' yu Lao Shuangyang," 291–93.

103. "Zou Xikou," in HQMG 234; "Zou chu er li ban," in Yan Zhiguo, *Xikou qingge,* 178.

104. During the Republican period, Shanxi migrants began to penetrate further west into Liangzhou (present Wuwei), Suzhou (present Jiuquan), Ganzhou (present Zhangye), Jiayuguan, and Dunhuang of Gansu and Hami, Guchengzi, and Dihua (present Urumqi) of Xinjiang. See Chen and Yuan, *"Jiusi yisheng 'zou xikou,"* 54.

105. HQMG, 145.

106. "An old sheepskin gown as my bedroll / Poverty pushed me outside the pass." See "Guangjing poxia paokouwai," in HQMG, 9.

107. "Zou Xikou shouku ge," in Yan Zhiguo, *Xikou qingge,* 183.

108. "Zou Xikou shouku ge," in Yan Zhiguo, *Xikou qingge,* 183.

109. He Yangling, *Chasui mengmin jingji de jiepou,* 280.

110. "Dabianzi yirao li houtao," in HQMG, 27.

111. "Ren zou qianli xue huilai," in HQMG, 26.

112. "Renjia dou zai ni buzai," in HQMG, 12.

113. "Chenshi shang kumingren shaoyou wo," in HQMG, 13.

114. Zhang Shiming discusses the various modes of sexual relations in the immigrant societies in Hetao in the twentieth century. See Zhang Shiming, "Linglei shehui kongjian."

115. "Zou chu er li ban," in Yan Zhiguo, *Xikou qingge,* 178.

4

The Rise of Land Merchants

Irrigation, Commercialization, and Local Autonomy in Hetao

The eighteenth century ushered in an era of unprecedented movement of capital and population across the Han-Mongol border as a result of the unparalleled expansion of the Qing empire, both territorially and demographically. The lucrative long-distance trade, developed in the wake of Qing military campaigns against the Zunghars and dominated by Shanxi merchants, became a tireless engine that drew heavy flows of Chinese goods into the grassland and produced a corresponding flow of livestock and pastoral products in the opposite direction. At the same time, population pressure in north China and an increasing demand for grain on the steppe combined to push Chinese migrants from Zhili, Shanxi, and Shaanxi into the pastoral regions of the Mongols: producing a belt of agricultural settlement along the Great Wall. Mercantile expansion and labor migration converged in the nineteenth century to create an economic boom in the Han-Mongol frontier of Hetao along the Yellow River. In contrast to previous migrations that were typically strategically or ecologically driven and replicated traditional modes of smallholder farming, the agricultural expansion in Hetao was planned and large-scale. In addition, it showed features that are best described as capitalist.

The development of the late imperial Chinese economy has been the focus of heated scholarly debate. Chinese historians during the Maoist period identified the expansion of commodity production and wage labor from the sixteenth century onward as "sprouts of capitalism" comparable to changes in European economies. Jing Su and Luo Lun argued that the emergence of managerial landlords in Shandong indicated a qualitative change toward a proto-capitalist economy.[1] More recently, economic historians of the "California School" such as Kenneth Pomeranz, Roy Bin Wong, and Li Bozhong, have also placed Chinese economic developments in the broader context of interregional and global economy. They argue that the Chinese economy in the high Qing period followed a pattern of growth through increasing specialization and marketization that was not inferior to its European counterparts such as England.[2] In contrast, other scholars since the 1960s have argued that despite considerable commercialization and urbanization, the Chinese economy remained bound on the path of a "high-equilibrium trap" or an "involutionary" pattern of labor use, as described by Mark Elvin and Philip Huang, which were incapable of transformative growth toward capitalism.[3] Christopher Isett aptly summarizes these two models as "Smithian" and "Malthusian-Ricardian."[4] Whereas the former stresses economic growth as the positive result of the growth of the market and the division of labor, the latter highlights the decline in labor productivity due to increasing population pressure and economic stagnation.

This chapter addresses some of the crucial issues in this debate from the perspective of China's periphery by examining the economically driven process of Chinese settlement in Hetao; the changing land use, property regimes, and labor relations it brought about; and its impact on the integration of the Han-Mongol borderland into the Chinese as well as the global economic system. In particular, I focus on a group of Chinese entrepreneurs known as land merchants (*dishang* 地商) who combined commercial capital and technical expertise in irrigation development. Within a time-span of three generations, they were able to develop a capital-intensive, market-oriented rural economy based on massive capital investment, wage labor, and commercialized agriculture. Although their endeavors were cut short by the state expropriation of the early twentieth century (more in chapter 6), they not only created a prosperous agricultural economy outside the Great Wall, but they also left behind a legacy that influenced policies of the late Qing, Republican, and PRC governments.

Depending on the political climate and ideological paradigms of the time, there are controversial opinions among historians regarding these land merchants. Japanese researchers of the 1930s and 1940s typically viewed the land merchants as "semi-feudal" and "parasitic." Anzai Kuraji refers to the land merchants as part-landlords and part-brokers mediating between Mongol banners and Chinese cultivators.[5] Marxist historian Imahori Seiji, who conducted a survey in Suiyuan in 1944, asserts that they represented a special type of landlordism in which merchant capital was drawn into parasitic landlordism that aimed at seizing high-rate feudal land taxes. Despite the form of partnership that existed between land merchants and tenant farmers, it was nonetheless "a semi-feudal Ancien Régime" that contained no "embryo of modernization" whatsoever.[6] Chinese historians of the 1980s, on the other hand, began to reassess the role of land merchants within the broader context of China's modernization. Zhang Zhihua treats them as a new type of "bourgeois entrepreneurial farmers" who not only invested large amount of capital in constructing irrigation works, but also participated in "capitalist-style commercial agricultural production" using free wage labor such as seasonal laborers: thereby departing distinctly from traditional rentier landlordism.[7] More recent studies avoid such simplistic, ideologically charged generalizations and capture the complexities and ambiguities that embedded land merchants within the broader context of social and political changes in the Mongol frontier. For example, Tetsuyama Hiroshi adopts the framework of the world-system theory and examines the land-merchant economy of Hetao as a case study of bottom-up changes in the periphery that would lead to the modernization of the Chinese agricultural economy in general.[8] Wang Jiange attributes the booming economy of Hetao to the successful ecological and social adaption to the frontier environment through irrigation development and social control.[9]

In this chapter, I offer a more nuanced assessment of land merchants as actors in their specific historical context who capitalized on the process of Chinese agricultural settlement in Mongolia as contractors, entrepreneurs, landlords, brokers, and/or wholesale merchants. I argue that these actors, operating under the unique conjunctures of historical and geopolitical conditions of a peripheral region, were able to initiate transformative changes to the Mongolian society as well as core parts of China.

THE ONE AND ONLY BEND

A set of unique natural and social conditions made Hetao a perfect locus of change. Geographically, Hetao 河套 ("river bend," a.k.a. Houtao 後套 "rear/northern bend") refers to the fertile alluvial plain lying between the old bed of the Yellow River and its present course on the northwestern section of the Ordos Plateau.[10] It is demarcated by Mt. Langshan (Khara Narin Mountains) to the north and the Yellow River to the south, and it borders Alasha banner in the west and Wulashan (Mo: Muni uul, a.k.a. the Sheiten-ula Mountains) in the east. The area was shaped during the eighteenth century by a shift of the river course. Administratively, Hetao was located at the intersection of three Mongol banners: the Dalad and Khanggin banners of the Yekhe Juu league (Ordos), and the Urad banner of the Ulaanchab league, with a total area of around ten thousand square kilometers.[11]

Like the rest of the Ordos plateau, the weather in Hetao is arid and cold, with an annual precipitation of two hundred millimeters that is mostly concentrated in the summer. Unlike the sandy soil found elsewhere in the Ordos plateau, however, the soil here is rich in alkaline contents, with an excessive sodium accumulation due to a high evaporation rate. All these factors have made irrigation indispensable for farming in this area. Fortunately, the proximity of the Yellow River made irrigated agriculture possible, in contrast to other parts of Inner Mongolia and north China where dry farming prevailed. The alluvial soil was good for planting grain and a variety of crops, such as millet, potato, and vegetables in the spring; wheat, oat, and peas in the summer; and hemp, sorghum, flax, and beans in the autumn.[12]

Compared with the areas adjacent to the Great Wall, farming in Hetao began rather late due to its geographical isolation and the capricious nature of the Yellow River. It was not until the early 1800s that a group of Chinese merchants from the nearby market town of Baotou began to penetrate the area to barter with the local Mongols. Soon the merchants began to acquire land from the Mongols and put it under irrigation. Within decades, Hetao was turned from a pastoral hinterland into one of the most prosperous agricultural zones outside the Great Wall. A local saying highlights the extraordinary prosperity of Hetao in contrast to the disaster-prone lower reaches of the Yellow River: "The Yellow River brings a hundred disasters; it enriches the one and only Bend" (*huanghe bai hai, wei fu yi tao* 黃河百害，惟富一套).[13]

A conjuncture of natural, geopolitical, and socioeconomic conditions contributed to the unprecedented agricultural boom of Hetao in the nineteenth century. First, the natural conditions of Hetao are favorable for irrigated agriculture. The flood of 1850 helped settle the Yellow River in its present course and created several natural creeks that were later developed into major irrigation canals.[14] It also enriched the soils of the area with the alluvial deposits. The irrigated land of Hetao was said to yield harvests ten times larger than those on the dry mountain lands south of the passes.[15] Although the claim may be proverbial rather than literal, it indicates the extraordinary fertility of the alluvial soil as compared to the dry land of north China. Further, the Yellow River provided cheap water transportation that linked the area to downstream markets in Baotou, Hekou, and beyond.

Second, geographical isolation and a lack of state presence also made Hetao a weak link in the traditional form of Manchu-Mongol political control, as it was largely a marshy flood zone distant from any existing political, religious, or market centers. None of the headquarters of the Mongol jasags were located within its boundary. Prior to the twentieth century, the Chinese settlers of Hetao were under the jurisdiction of a Lifanyuan commissioner based in Shenmu of Shaanxi province and a sub-prefect based in Sarachi of Tümed who answered to the administration of Shanxi province. Both officials resided outside the area. This political vacuum left ample room for the growth of a vigorous local autonomy in the region.

Third, the economic boom of Hetao was enabled by the growing commercialization of Mongolian society due to the penetration of Chinese trade. By the end of the eighteenth century, even the remotest hinterland had been exposed to a monetized economy based on silver. This was due to the economic burdens of maintaining postal relay stations and guard posts across Mongolia that could not be paid for by the available tax bases of the banners: forcing the yamens to make up their budgets with loans from "partner" (Mo: *tünsh*, Ch: *tongshi*) merchants and creating an endless cycle of debt (see chapter 2). As the interests accumulated, most banners became heavily in debt and some resorted to land mortgages to repay them. For instance, the Chanjin Canal, which was the first major irrigation project in Hetao, was developed on land that the Mongols put down as collateral. Meanwhile, the availability of private capital supplied by long-distance trade made private and corporate financing for irrigation possible. In turn, the navigable waterways lowered the transportation costs by linking Hetao to downstream market towns and thereby facilitated trade flows in and out of the area. All these factors made irrigation a high-investment, high-output enterprise that attracted many entrepreneurs.

Finally, the social turmoil and natural disasters that punctuated the final decades of the nineteenth century, paradoxically enough, proved advantageous to the economic growth in Hetao. As massive rebellions and famines threw north China into upheaval, the grassland provided a safe haven for numerous refugees, who in turn supplied abundant labor forces for the irrigation projects. For example, the ninety-*li*-long Shahe Canal was built by famine-stricken refugees from south of the passes during the drought of 1891–1892. Further, the soaring grain prices in the wake of the natural calamities encouraged cross-regional grain trade and spurred the commercialization of grain production.

So far, we have analyzed the natural and social conditions that prepared the stage for the irrigation boom of Hetao: capital drawn from the Han-Mongol trade, abundant labor forces supplied by the influx of Chinese migrants, cheap land obtained from the Mongols, water provided by the Yellow River, and the negligible presence of an intrusive state. Whereas these structural factors are indispensable in understanding the economic development and social transformation in Hetao, social actors played an equally significant role. The following section illustrates the first economic boom in Hetao during the first half of the nineteenth century and the role played by the group of Chinese entrepreneurs who invested merchant capital in irrigation systems and organized commercial agriculture.

RISE OF IRRIGATION COMMUNITIES

At the center of this agricultural boom were a group of Chinese merchants known as land merchants because of their heavy involvement in land transactions and irrigation development. Most members of this group were merchants from the adjacent provinces of Shanxi and Shaanxi, but artisans and demobilized officers from other parts of China also entered the trade, especially in the wake of the social turmoil of the 1860s and 1870s. They began by acquiring virgin land from the Mongols and investing commercial capital in irrigation works. The need to finance and maintain these irrigation systems shaped a community of common interest based on partnership and corporation. Together, they created a highly commercialized, capital-intensive, profit-oriented form of agriculture that departed from the traditional mode of production centering on small peasant family farms.

In 1904, as part of the official reclamation campaign, the imperial commissioner appointed by the Qing court, Yigu, set out to seize the assets of Chinese canal developers in Hetao, and offered them only a meager compensation. To be eligible for compensation, the owners had to provide details about the canals such as the location, dimensions, irrigable area, costs, original developer, year of construction, and transaction history. These statements, recorded in the unpublished Imperial Commissioner Supervising Reclamation Affairs of Mongol Banners (1901–1910) preserved in the Inner Mongolia Archives, offer first-hand data on the irrigation systems of Hetao and their developers.

The following statement of two Shaanxi firms, Yongshengxing and Jinyonghe, describes the circumstances surrounding the opening of Chanjindi (Mo: Chayija boro tala, in present Bayan Nuur, Inner Mongolia), which marked the inauguration of Chinese reclamation in Hetao.[16]

Yongshengxing and Jinyonghe, land merchants of Chanjin, testified as follows: In [1825], due to the silver owed our shops, the Dalad banner consulted the Lifanyuan about opening Chanjindi of Houtao as repayment, and the request was granted. At the time, the land lay in wilderness, over one hundred *li* away from the Yellow River. Our shops set out to build a small canal that extended for 170 or 180 *li* from the [Yellow] River in the south to Bulung Nuur in the northeast. We hired workers to dig the channel and dredge the bed, and it took several years and cost a fortune for water to reach the fields. The land, then covered with lush grasses, had to be cleared and weeded before farming could begin. Over the years, although the proceeds cancelled part of the debts, the banner still owed our shops a capital of fifty thousand taels of silver, interests excluded. Account books are available for verification.[17]

The statement shows how the indebtedness of the Mongol aristocracy facilitated Chinese agricultural expansion. In this case, the prince of the Dalad banner agreed to open a large block of land for cultivation in repayment of his debt. Along with the land rights, the firms also obtained water concessions. The Chanjin canal built in 1825 was one of the earliest irrigation systems developed in Hetao. The statement of another firm, Xiechenghe, provides more details on landholding and irrigation-related costs during the 1820s:

My grandfather obtained a tract of land from the Dalad banner, a total area of over twenty five hundred *qing*. From [1822] through [1824], he developed the Gangmu Creek canal, with over one hundred thousand taels of silver spent on labor costs. The intake is seven *zhang* wide and seven *chi* deep, and the end is five *zhang* wide and five *chi* deep. The entire project is between 170 and 180 *li* long. . . . It irrigates over three thousand *qing* of area, including our own land and that of others. . . . Dykes were built to protect the crops from floodwater. Each year, over ten thousand taels were spent on labor costs for repairing the dykes, and another ten thousand taels for dredging the bed. The water fee payable to Khanggin banner was convertible to two boxes of brick tea and twenty pairs of leather boots. Over the years, around eighty thousand taels of silver had been lent to the Dalad banner. Account books are available for verification.[18]

Like the two other firms, Xiechenghe acquired over twenty-five hundred *qing* (16,667 ha) of land from the Dalad banner as repayment of a loan of eighty thousand taels. It should be noted that the land was obtained through a lease rather than an outright sale, with an annual rent in cash or kind paid to the Mongol banner. In addition, a small water fee was payable in kind to the Khanggin banner, as the water route ran through its territory. These expenses were negligible, however, compared with the colossal labor expenses for the canal. They amounted to one hundred thousand taels to build the canal and another twenty thousand taels per year to maintain it. The maintenance costs were high because the heavy sediment of the Yellow River made it necessary to dredge the bed and strengthen the dykes regularly to prevent the canal from silting up and to protect the fields from floodwater.

These statements provide several facts about agricultural development in Hetao in the early nineteenth century. First, in Hetao, unlike in other peripheries, merchant entrepreneurs rather than farmers initiated the Chinese agricultural advance. From the very beginning, agriculture was part of the commercial transaction involving capital, land, and labor. Second, the endorsement of the Lifanyuan testified to a slackening of the Qing policy due to diminishing strategic concerns in the northern frontier. The Mongol elites were allowed greater freedom to ease their economic burdens and generate income out of their hereditary land, which was theoretically unalienable. Third, the natural conditions of Hetao created a high bar for irrigation development, which demanded significant capital investment in not just the initial construction but also in regular maintenance. All these factors set the merchants of Hetao apart from their kind elsewhere.

Canal building, as we have seen, was a laborious and expensive task. The colossal expenses were often beyond the means of individual firms, which made collaboration necessary. The following statement details the cooperation between two firms:

> In [1828], this firm, named Yongshenghe, acquired a tract of land from the Dalad banner. At the time, a total of fifteen hundred taels and ninety-six ounces of silver and two thousand strings of copper coins were paid to the Dalad banner. We cut a separate water route of the Gangmu Creek canal through the Khanggin territory, which cost over eight thousand taels of silver to build. Xiechenghe undertook to finish the Gangmu Creek canal from the Yongshenghe canal through the end. . . . From [1843] on, other firms concerted their efforts in dredging the canal. We own a branch canal that functions till this day.[19]

The statement testified to a form of simple partnership in irrigation development. As the Gangmu Creek canal silted up, Yongshenghe set out to cut a new intake and link it to the lower reach of the canal that was undertaken by Xiechenghe. The two firms built their sections separately, but became joint owners of the canal through a partnership, with other merchants chipping in to cover the maintenance costs after 1843. Meanwhile, individual firms began to develop private branches that extended from the trunk canal to their individual plots.

A similar form of partnership was organized in operating the Chanjin canal. Initially built by the partnership of two firms, it later passed into a multiple shareholding system. As the local gazetteer of Linhe county notes, a relatively sophisticated system of financing and organizing irrigation existed in Hetao in the first half of the nineteenth century, in which all irrigation related affairs were resolved through public discussion attended by all shareholders:

> During the Daoguang and Xianfeng periods [1821–1861], the [Chanjin] canal was jointly operated by forty-eight land merchants. The current Gongzhong Temple, built on a magnificent scale with collective funds, used to be their assembling place. At the time, the merchants rented land from Mongol banners that stretched over a large area and relied on the [Chanjin] canal for irrigation. They cooperated closely in its yearly maintenance and repair works, each contributing according to his share. No doubt a community of common interest has taken shape.[20]

As we can see, the necessity to pool resources created a densely connected yet relatively egalitarian community based on shared interests and responsibilities. The result was remarkable: during the 1850s, the Chanjin canal alone irrigated an area of between three thousand and four thousand *qing*, with an annual yield of hundreds of thousand *shi* of millet.[21]

This economic boom was cut short by the Dungan/Hui Uprising and its Qing suppression (1862–1877), which was an ethnic war instigated by a dispute between the Hui minority and Han Chinese in the northwestern provinces of Shaanxi, Gansu, Ningxia, as well as Xinjiang. The conflict caused massive carnage in the region, including an estimated death toll of eight million to twelve million people, both Hui and Han, as well as the mass emigration and decrease of Hui population in these regions. It was eventually quelled by Qing forces under General Zuo Zongtang (1812–1885) who retook Xinjiang in 1876.[22] During the suppression campaigns, the market town of Chanjin served as a supply center for the Qing troops based in Shaanxi and Gansu. The merchants were mobilized to transport military supplies and organize local militia to defend the locality against the rebels, which resulted in the neglect of irrigation works. The exaction of the army, which was garrisoned in Chanjin for three years, was followed by a rampage of "mounted bandits" (*mazei* 馬賊) in 1876 that devastated the local economy. In its aftermath, businesses were nearly wiped out, and farm estates were in ruins or deserted.[23] The economic decay was manifest in the sharp decline of the annual income of the Dalad banner, which shrank from one hundred thousand taels of silver in the 1850s to less than three thousand strings of copper coins in the 1870s.[24]

REVIVAL OF IRRIGATION ECONOMY

The end of the mid-nineteenth century crisis brought another economic boom to Hetao. The second stage, spanning from the 1870s through the turn of the century, departed from the earlier period in terms of geographical locus, organizational format, and degree of commercialization. Whereas Chinese settlement in the first stage was concentrated in the town of Chanjin in northwestern Hetao, the second stage saw a shift of economic gravity to the market town of Longxingchang (present Wuyuan county, Bayan Nuur, Inner Mongolia) in eastern Hetao. Whereas irrigation in the first stage was organized on the basis of simple partnerships (*penghuo* 朋夥), the second stage saw rapid irrigation expansion through a more inclusive shareholding (*penggu* 朋股) arrangement in which shares were offered to those who provided not just capital but also expertise and labor. Moreover, the second period was characterized by the growing commercialization of land and labor, with a greater degree of integration with the regional and global economic system.

A set of historical and social circumstances contributed to the second economic boom in Hetao. On the domestic front, massive rebellion, war, and famine had punctuated the 1860s and 1870s: first the Hui Uprising and its suppression that devastated northwest China and the adjacent Mongolian peripheries, and then the great famine of 1876–1879 that killed nine million to thirteen million people in north China.[25] Despite its adverse effects, the social turmoil brought new opportunities. The necessity to supply the Qing troops and expand fiscal revenue during the expeditions resulted in a further slackening of the ban on Chinese cultivation, especially in the previously uncultivated Khanggin banner.[26] The warfare also brought new settlers to the area, among whom were a group of demobilized officers from southern China who made fortunes during the military campaigns. Attracted by the economic opportunities in Hetao, they began to invest in irrigation works and soon rose to power in their contest for land and water. At the same time, the social unrest and natural disasters drove large waves of refugees from north China into the grasslands. In 1876, the ban against Chinese women outside the Great Wall was lifted by the Qing court: spurring the process of migration into Inner Mongolia and Manchuria. These new immigrants supplied cheap labor for the irrigation systems and farm estates of land merchants. Further, the soaring grain prices in the wake of catastrophes made cross-regional grain trade prosperous and lent great impetus to the commercial agriculture in Hetao.

On the international front, a series of unequal treaties signed between China and the Western powers in the wake of the Second Opium War (1856–1860) increasingly absorbed China and its peripheries into the global framework of capitalism and nation-states. The opening of Tianjin as a treaty port turned Mongolia into a sourcing ground for animal skins, wools, and medicinal herbs, which were in great demand in the international markets. The treaties also opened up the entire Qing-Russian frontier to trade. They allowed Russian merchants the privilege of carrying out duty-free trade across Mongolia and Xinjiang, which gave them an edge over their Chinese competitors in these regions. In Höhhot, Chinese firms suffered great loss on Bohea tea because of competition from the Russians, and the markets of cotton textiles were completely dominated by foreign products.[27] Meanwhile, the opening of the Suez Canal in 1869 and the construction of the modern railway caused the trade routes to shift, which resulted in the decline of the caravan trade over land. Foreign competition and the introduction of modern means of transportation led some Chinese firms to redirect their investment from the traditional lines of trade of tea and cotton cloth into the more profitable grain trade: thus spurring the commercialization of grain production.

With capital and labor flowing into Hetao in the 1870s, an economic surge was underway. By the early 1900s, the irrigation networks in Hetao consisted of eight major canals and around forty minor ones. The canals had a total length of 1,543 *li* (889 kilometers) and covered an irrigated area of 10,829 *qing* (approximately seventy-two thousand ha).[28] In just a few decades, Hetao became one of the most important grain-producing areas outside the Great Wall, with an estimated annual yield of over one hundred thousand tons of millet, sorghum, wheat, and oat (enough to feed half a million people).[29]

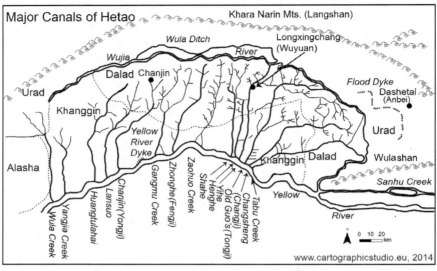

Map 4.1.   Major Canals of Hetao, c. 1908
Courtesy of Cartographic Studio, 2014

Table 4.1 contains information about the eight major canals that survived into the twentieth century. Each of these trunk canals (*ganqu* 幹渠) supplied a hierarchical system of branches (*zhiqu* 枝渠) and sub-branches (*ziqu* 子渠) that provided water to individual plots.

Table 4.1.   Eight Major Canals of Hetao, c. 1900

Canal	Year	Builder	Length (li)	Branches	Area (qing)
Gangmuhe	1822	Xiechenghe, Yongshenghe	130	12	1,000
Chanjin	1825	YYongshengxing, Jinyonghe	150	6	3,000
Old Guo	1866	Wandeyuan, Wantaigong, Shi Laohu, Guo Dayi, Guo Minxiu	102.5	27	1,500
Changsheng	1872	Hou Shuangzhu, Zheng He, Hou Yingkui, Dehengyong	109	21	1,800
Tabuhe	1875	Fan Sanxi, Xia Mingtang, Cheng Shunchang, Gao Hewa, Ji'erguqing	120	21	1,700
Yihe	1880	Wang Tongchun	115	4	1,600
Yonghe	1891	Wang Tongchun	90	10	1,100
Zhonghe	1899	Wang Tongchun	96	5	1,000

Sources: Han Meipu, *Suiyuan sheng hetao diaocha ji*; Feng Jilong, *Diaocha hetao baogao shu*; Wang Zhe, "Hetao qudao zhi kaijun yange," 123–51; Zhou Jinxi, *Suiyuan hetao zhiyao*; Chen Erdong, *Hetao guanqu shuili jianshi.*

Table 4.2 is a list of private canals confiscated by the Qing state in 1904. It includes details about the canals, such as the owner, builder, year of construction, location, length, and amount of compensation paid by the state, which was often as little as 10 percent of the original construction costs. As of 1907, a total sum of 72,175.651 taels of silver were paid to thirty-eight parties in return for the forty-four canals confiscated, with the amount each party received varying from one hundred to ten thousand taels.[30]

Table 4.2. Confiscation and Compensation of Private Canals of Hetao, 1907

Canal	Owner	Builder	Year	Length (li)	Silver (taels)
Chanjin	Yongshengxing et al.	Father	1825	150	1,000
Zhang Shuangju	Yan Changren et al.	Zhang S.J.	1843	10	1,946
Halawusu	Xiao Shirong	Grandfather	1865	35	
Ashan	Xiao Shirong	Grandfather	1867	45	2,000
Heheyuan	Zhang Shoupeng	Grandfather	1866	26	
Shi-da-gu	Zhang Shoupeng	Grandfather	1866	30	1,100
Old Guo (Si-da-gu)	Guo Minxiu	Father	1867	80	7,000
Changsheng	Hou Yingkui	Uncle	1872	109	1,400
Tiandeyu	Wei Fengshan et al.	Father	1875	40	3,000
Tumo'erdi	Li Zhenhai	Self	1875	48	3,000
Tabuhe (Wu-da-gu)	Cheng Shunchang et al.	Self	1875	120	400
Changxingtang	Chang Xiuchun	Father	1876	30	700
Caojiadi	Cao Qingzhang	Father	1878	83	
Halaga'er	Cao Qingzhang	Father	1878	75	1,200
Liusandi	Liu Buyun, etc.	Father	1878	20	1,200
Weiyangdi	Wei Fengshan	Father	1878	28	4,000
Wu-da-gu (Xiuhuatang)	Zhen Yu	Self	1878	25	1,200
Yihe	Wang Tongchun	Self	1881	115	
Yonghe	Wang Tongchun	Self	1891	90	
Henghe	Wang Tongchun	Self	1892	83	25,000
Zhonghe	Wang Tongchun	Self	1899	96	6,000
Wujiadi	Wu Huaiqing, Xiao Shirong	Father	1883	8	
Halaga'er	Wu Huaiqing, Xiao Shirong	Father	1883	25	400
Jinxiutang	Chen Jinsheng	Father	1894	30	600
Decheng	Li Fuguo et al.	Self	1894	30	2,400
Futaichang	He Ruixiong	Self	c.1890	(Old Guo br.)	(800)
Naobaohaodi	Li Dayuan	Self	c.1890	(Old Guo br.)	360
Baijiadi	Liu Zhibang	Self	c.1890	(Old Guo br.)	500
Yichenggong-Guanghetang	Shi Guangyu et al.	Self	c.1890	(Old Guo br.)	900
Wantaigong	Zheng Yingdou	Self	c.1890	(Old Guo br.)	200
Ji'ermantai	Zhu Kaidi et al.	Self	c.1890	(Old Guo br.)	300

(continued)

Table 4.2. *(Continued)*

Canal	Owner	Builder	Year	Length *(li)*	Silver *(taels)*
Yaozhanggai	Yao Deming	Grandfather	1847	(Tabuhe br.)	150
Xiamingtang	Xia Mingtang	Self	1875	(Tabuhe br.)	300
Yaojiahetou	Li Anbang	Father	1876	(Tabuhe br.)	600
Budaikouzi	Zhang Zhao	Self	c.1890	(Tabuhe br.)	600
Halatelihai	Fan Genlai	Self	c.1890	(Changsheng br.)	240
Sulongkhaiwan	Fan Sanxi	Self	c.1890	(Changsheng br.)	360
Gaojiadi	Gao Jinke	Self	c.1890	(Changsheng br.)	900
Fuhengxing-Xiaonao'er	Gao Si	Self	c.1890	(Changsheng br.)	20
Tianhechang	Qiao Tonghua	Self	c.1890	(Changsheng br.)	200
Wangcun	Wang Cun	Self	c.1890	(Changsheng br.)	100
Fuhengxing	Yang Shizhong	Self	c.1890	(Changsheng br.)	600
Shaiwusu	Chaghanbolod	Lü Pi	1902	25	200
Xiangtaiyuan	Wu Xiang	Self	1906	20	1,800
Total					**72,176**

Source: Nei Menggu dang'anguan, ed., *Qingmo nei menggu kenwu dang'an huibian*, 1421–22; Yao Xuejing, ed., *Wuyuan ting zhigao*, 12–14; He Yangling, *Chasui mengmin jingji de jiepou*, 180–86.

An analysis of the first-hand data reveals some general trends of irrigation development in Hetao. The vast majority of canals—forty-one out of forty-four—were built after the crisis of the 1860s. This number includes six out of the eight major canals. At the time of confiscation, thirty-seven canals were still owned by their builders or their first-generation descendants: showing a significant surge in irrigation development in the final decades of the nineteenth century. Compared with the earlier period, the number of single-owned canals increased distinctly, which was due partly to the proliferation of smaller-size canals and partly to the growing trend of consolidation. This can also be seen from the naming of the canals. Whereas the earlier canals were typically named after places, the newer ones usually bore the name of a single investor, be it a firm (e.g. Heheyuan), a lineage hall (e.g. Changxingtang), a family clan (e.g. Caojiadi), or a person (e.g. Old Guo). Out of the thirty-four canals that were single owned, twenty-six were minor ones or branches that were less than fifty *li* long. This may be explained by the opening of the hitherto uncultivated land of the Khanggin banner adjacent to the Yellow River, which made minor canals a more affordable option for developers. Further, the influx of Chinese settlers also made fragmentation and the subdivision of irrigation systems necessary.

Figure 4.1. Tongji Canal, Wuyuan county, Bayan Nuur, Inner Mongolia.
Photo by the author

Meanwhile, there was a countervailing tendency toward the concentration of ownership, with some owners buying out others. This can be seen from canal names such as Si-da-gu 四大股, Wu-da-gu 五大股, and Shi-da-gu 十大股 (meaning "Four/Five/Ten-big-shares"). Although the names indicated the corporate origin of these projects, they eventually became single-owned: showing a brisk tendency toward privatization and consolidation. Further, the preponderance of technology in irrigation development also played a part, which allowed technical experts to capitalize on their expertise and accumulate wealth, as seen in the case of Wang Tongchun who singlehandedly developed four major canals in Hetao.

A SHAREHOLDING SYSTEM

Although the rise of single ownership testified to a tendency of privatization in irrigation development, this was largely applicable to smaller-scale canals. Meanwhile, partnership-owned projects continued to thrive during the second period, as the scale of larger projects often made collaboration necessary. Compared with the simple partnerships in the earlier period, which were typically formed among fellow countrymen, the shareholding system of the second period was more elaborate and complex. Shares now became fully alienable. They could be split, bought, sold, and acquired through the investment of expertise, labor, or land.

The shareholding system was developed by the trading and banking firms of Shanxi merchants in the early nineteenth century, and it had gained popularity among the canal developers since the 1860s.³¹ Under this system, each shareholder obtained a certain number of shares according to his investment, which were typically expressed in 10-percent (*fen* 分) or 1-percent (*li* 釐) units. Benefits (*li* 利) and duties (*hai* 害) were distributed proportionately among shareholders. Apart from irrigating their own plots, shareholders could also sell water rights to others or rent them out for a fee. Meanwhile, they were responsible for paying their allotment of labor costs in proportion to the area of irrigable land they possessed. Like other forms of property, shares were inheritable and transferable. It was also possible to divide the shares into smaller portions, with branches developed and the owners of new sections sharing in the costs of trunk maintenance.

The shareholding system was reinforced by devices such as written agreements and the building of temples. Partnership contracts (*hehuoyue* 合夥約) established the terms of shareholding by specifying the rights and responsibilities of each partner. They were primarily private and signed in the presence of two to four middlemen who included both Chinese and Mongol representatives. The contracts helped ground economic transactions in a set of social relations and customary practices and thus facilitated the process of commercialization.³² Apart from partnership contracts, temples were sometimes erected as an inculcation of religious and symbolic bonds among shareholders. For instance, the stele inscription of the renovated Si-da-gu Temple shows that it was originally built to commemorate the partnership of the original four big shareholders.³³ Moreover, temples also provided a public space for discussing irrigation-related affairs as well as staging public rituals and festivities, and thereby embedded the economic practices in social and symbolic terms.

The following contract provides more detail on the terms of shareholding:

> The merchants residing in the vicinity of the Gangmu canal, troubled by its siltation and unable to expand it on their own, have decided to collaborate with the Dalad banner in widening and deepening the channel from the intake to the end. In terms of expenses, the banner is to take charge while the merchants contribute. Those who have money should contribute money, and those who have not should offer their land to cover the duties. From the intake to the end, wherever water is accessible, duties are applicable to the land. It is determined that each *qing* of land is considered equivalent to fifty thousand copper coins of labor costs incurred by the canal, on top of the land proceeds payable to the banner. Once the duties are paid in full, the land should be returned to its holder. Water is to flow unblocked, and allotments should be paid in proportion to the shares. The Dalad banner may freely dispose of any land without holder. Should any dispute on the canal arise, it will be taken care of by *meiren* Mantou. Lest words have no guarantee, this contract is made in witness whereof.³⁴

Here we see an example of a joint venture between Chinese merchants and the Mongol banner in irrigation development, as the shareholding system allowed the latter to acquire shares in return for the land it provided. In this case, the *meiren-ü janggi* or deputy administrator of the Dalad banner served as the guarantor and nominal head for the irrigation project and received a share in the canal, as well as the right to freely dispose of any unleased land that would potentially benefit from the project. This was by no means an isolated case. Several Mongols were listed as canal contributors during the official reclamation campaign. Among them were a Ji-er-gu-qing of the Dalad banner who was one of the five shareholders of the Tabuhe canal, and *meiren* Chaghanbolod of the Khanggin banner who offered two canals located within the boundary of his habitat to the Qing authorities.[35]

The merchants were responsible for any applicable duties incurred by the construction and future maintenance of the canal. In lieu of capital, they could offer land in payment, at a rate of fifty thousand copper coins (equivalent to twenty-five taels of silver) per *qing*. On top of that, they were to pay the rent due to the Dalad banner as usual. Once the due amount was cleared, the land would be returned to its original holder. What was involved here was in fact conditional sale of the right of use of the land: showing a higher degree of land commodification as a result of its potential increase in value with irrigation. Here we see an arrangement in which irrigation was financed by offering shares to those who provided capital, land, and political support. According to the contract, the water route must not be blocked so as to ensure equal access to water for all shareholders. At the same time, duties should be distributed according to one's respective share, in proportion to the area of irrigable land he possessed. Hence the larger the area, the greater the share of duty payment as well as the benefits brought by water.

Contracts were also used to settle disputes over water use, as seen in the following contract concerning the Si-da-gu canal:

> Wandeyuan, Demaoyong, Wantaigong, and Gongyiyuan hereby conclude the below contract as evidence. In [1870], Wandeyuan cut a canal from Tuchengzi and linked it to the old creek of the Yellow River to irrigate the land of Man-ge-su-tai. In [1873], Gongyiyuan cut a canal from the old creek of the River to irrigate the land of Ha-lin-jia-ba Monastery. No previous agreement was made regarding the amount of water to be used. In the fourth month of [1876], the matter is being settled through the mediation of middlemen, and both parties voluntarily agree that from now on, for using the shared water route, Gongyiyuan is to pay Wandeyuan six hundred strings as the water route fee and four hundred strings as the construction fee for the canal and dykes. Henceforth, all expenses incurred by the building of Tuchengzi canal as well as the repairing of the Dingtou dykes should be divided into four equal shares. Once water reaches the old creek of the River, each shareholder may cut intakes and build their own branches. Water is to flow unblocked; no dams should be made inside the canal. From now on, Gongyiyuan is allowed to use water only for irrigating its own plots; selling water rights to outsiders for a fee is prohibited. Lest dispute arises in the future, we hereby conclude a written contract as evidence.[36]

The contract shows the growing competition among canal developers due to the commodification of water. Gongyiyuan, which owned a downstream branch canal, had been selling water rights to lower-level users without the permission of upstream developers, so the upstream developers dammed up the canal in response. The scenario was common between owners of trunk and branch canals, or between upstream and downstream users of the same canal, and it often resulted in feuds and armed conflicts. Under such circumstances, shareholding provided a means to settle such disputes by offering shares for purchase and turning competitors into partners. After mediation, Gongyiyuan agreed to pay one thousand strings of cash to Wandeyuan, forfeit its right of selling water to outsiders, and help cover any future costs incurred, in exchange for a share in the Si-da-gu canal.

However, such contracts were not always binding. It often took multiple rounds of mediation, negotiation, and contract signing to settle a dispute. In this case, after the initial contract was signed in 1876, Gongyiyuan clashed again with an employee of Wandeyuan, and accordingly refused to pay the agreed sum while continuing to sell water to outsiders. To resolve their quarrels, a second contract was drawn up in 1880, which reiterated Gongyiyuan's obligation to pay its due and refrain from water selling. As a penalty, the new contract granted Wandeyuan the right to dam up the Gongyiyuan canal for ten days in the autumn, which was an open breach of the principle of equal access to water by all shareholders. It was not until after a third round of mediation in 1883 that the issue was settled, with Gongyiyuan made to pay an additional sum of 350 strings to Demaoyong and Wantaigong in exchange for Wandeyuan forfeiting its extra water rights over the Gongyiyuan canal.[37] All this showed the limitations of shareholding due to the lack of legal enforcement. The multiple contracts indicated a dynamic process of power negotiation among shareholders that was grounded in customary practices rather than in the adjudication of the court.

The shares were not acquired through financial investment alone. Shanxi merchants traditionally divided the shares in their trading and banking firms into two types: (1) "monetary" shares (*caigu* 財股) obtained through capital investment and (2) "corporeal" shares (*shengu* 身股) granted in honor of special contributions by the founders and managers. In canal building, *shengu* shares were offered to technical experts and skillful workers for the expertise and labor they provided, in lieu of most of the wages they would otherwise be owed.[38] This was because irrigation demanded not only considerable capital input, but also technical know-how, expertise, and experience. To prevent silting up and to ensure proper water flow, it was crucial to carefully choose the location of the intake, design the route, and build sluiceways to carry off surplus water. Technical details such as these were often neglected by previous builders, which resulted in not only a waste of time and resources, but also in severe flooding and even the financial ruin of the owner.

The shareholding system thus provided opportunities for upward mobility for those who possessed expertise but little capital. The most prominent example was Wang Tongchun, the self-made "King of Canals" in Hetao. At age twelve, Wang left home in Zhili for Dengkou in Alasha banner on the left bank of the Yellow River, to work in a leather workshop owned by a relative. There, he acquired hydraulic skills from observing practitioners from Ningxia. Later he was hired as overseer of the Si-da-gu canal and acquired a *shengu* share through his service. At age thirty, Wang set out to build his own canal, and in two decades, completed four major canals—Yihe, Yonghe, Henghe, and Zhonghe—and became the wealthiest land merchant in

Figure 4.2. Yihe Canal, Wuyuan county, Bayan Nuur, Inner Mongolia.
Photo by the author

Hetao.[39] Much of Wang's success was attributable to his skills as a hydraulic engineer. The stele inscription of the Si-da-gu Temple compares him to legendary figures like King Yu and Li Bing who were renowned for taming rivers and creating irrigation systems in ancient China:

> Following King Yu's example in managing the river, and imitating Li Bing's way of building canals, His Honorable Mr. Wang designed the intake with the right width and cut the ditches with suitable depth, so that there is no fear of drought in high places nor risks of flooding in lowlands. It has benefited hundreds of farming households ever since. Now two decades have elapsed without a lean year, while the old and young enjoying prosperity and peace. Although the blessing of the Heaven and Earth is depended upon, it is indeed the achievements of one person.[40]

Apart from his talent, Wang drew on his previous experiences and the expertise of others. He first acquired his skill from the canal developers of Ningxia, where irrigation may be traced back to the Eastern Han Dynasty (25–220 CE).[41] He also hired canal experts from the Daming and Shunde prefectures of Zhili to work with him during the construction of the canals. Even after his canals were confiscated, Wang continued to play a role in the state-run irrigation projects operated by the late Qing and Republican governments. After his death in 1925, the locals of Hetao worshipped him as the River God, with a temple dedicated in his memory and ritual services held on the anniversary of his death and during periods of drought or flood. His achievements attracted the attention of nationalist-minded intellectuals like the renowned historian Gu Jiegang and geographer Zhang Xiangwen, who hailed him as a paragon of frontier development and a national hero.[42]

Thus far, we have analyzed the role of land merchants as entrepreneurs investing in and organizing the irrigation works of Hetao. As we have seen, shareholding enabled an alliance of capital, expertise, labor, and land in irrigation: thereby lending a degree of efficiency and flexibility to the system. In what follows, we shall discuss the role of land merchants as landlords and land brokers, with a focus on their relations with the Mongols and with Chinese peasants and rural workers.

COMMERCIALIZATION OF LAND RELATIONS

Before we probe into the changing land relations in Hetao, it would be helpful to overview the existing land regime in the Mongol territories in general. As many previous studies have shown, there was a general trend of privatization and fragmentation of landownership across the cultivated areas of Inner Mongolia throughout the eighteenth century. The land regimes there can be divided into three main types: (1) "official lands" (*guandi* 官地) that belonged to governmental organs such as banners, postal relay stations, and official estates; (2) "private lands" (*sidi* 私地) that were granted as hereditaments to jasags, noblemen, officials, bannermen, and soldiers; and (3) "common lands" (*gongdi* 公地) accessible to all banner subjects for grazing purposes. All three types of lands had been opened to Chinese cultivation by the nineteenth century, despite great regional variations in terms of intensity and settlement patterns.[43] The advance of Chinese settlement outside the Great Wall was essentially a process of gradual displacement of land ownership from the Mongols to Chinese cultivators. This shift resulted partly from the appropriation of Mongol lands by the Qing imperial state through infrastructures such as official estates and relay stations, and partly from the widespread private cultivation with or without official sanction. In either case, the purpose was to generate more revenue out of the land, be it in the form of official land taxes or rents collected by the Mongol authorities. These developments resulted in the separation of land ownership and actual land use, so that the communal ownership (*sōyūsei* 総有制) that characterized the nomadic society gradually gave way to what Anzai Kuraji terms a "divided ownership" (*bunkatsu shoyūsei* 分割所有制) between hereditary land possession by the Mongols and actual land use by Chinese cultivators.[44] Land, in other words, was no longer the communal property accessible to all Mongol subjects, but increasingly turned into a source of fiscal revenue, and even a commodity to be sold on the market. As a result, many Mongol landowners were reduced to rentiers, while Chinese settlers became actual landholders. Meanwhile, the formation of commercialized land relations also resulted in distinct social stratification in the settler society, which gave rise to wage labor in irrigated agriculture.

The increasing commodification of land can be seen from the changing form of rental payment. The early Chinese settlers in Hetao obtained land from the Mongols for a minimal rent in kind that varied from several *sheng* to several *dou* of millet per *niuju*.[45] No land-contract fee was paid, except for gifts offered to the landlord known as "personal favors in handling the land" (*bandi renqing* 辦地人情). Over time, silver became the standard payment in land proceeds and fees, with *qing* replacing *niuju* as the standard unit of measurement. By the end of the nineteenth century, the rent charged by the Mongols had risen to four to five taels of silver per *qing*, or the equivalent amount of copper cash.[46] In addition, a one-time contract fee (*yadiyin* 押地銀) was charged at the time of land leasing, plus water fees (*shuiliyin* 水禮銀) due to the Khanggin banner, which was initially paid in the form of gifts and later converted into a standard payment of fifty taels per annum.[47] All this showed a growing degree of monetization and commercialization of the frontier society brought by Chinese migration.

The centrality of irrigation in Hetao also triggered changes in the land regime and sociotechnical arrangements. First, it gave rise to a land tenure called perpetual lease (*yongzu* 永租), which allowed the lease holder to hold and make full use of the land for an indefinite period of time on the condition of rent payment. The lease holder was also free to pawn (*dian* 典), sub-lease (*zu* 租), or transfer (*tui* 推) the land to others. Perpetual lease indicated an arrangement of conditional sale (*dianmai* 典賣), which differed from outright sale (*juemai* 絕賣) in that the landowner retained the title and right of rent collection. This practice was put in place to comply with the Qing laws that prohibited the sale of Mongol land, while protecting the long-term land use of the leaseholder.[48] In effect, the Mongol landowners became rent collectors, and their first tenants, who were usually Chinese, became de facto owners with full transfer rights. Eventually, the practice led to the erosion of the hereditary, communal landownership of the Mongols by a privatized property regime that resembled those practiced in other highly commercialized parts of China, such as Taiwan or the Pearl River Delta.[49]

Second, the combination of extensive land and irrigation gave rise to large-scale managerial farming based on capital accumulation and wage labor. What characterized the farm estates of Hetao was their extraordinary size, usually ranging from hundreds to over a thousand hectares in acreage.[50] For example, the Beiniuju estate owned by Wang Tongchun, located on the lower reach of Yihe canal, covered over one hundred *qing* of managerial farmland (*niujudi* 牛犋地) cultivated by hired hands and another one hundred *qing* that was rented out to tenants. During the harvest season, threshing alone was done by some three hundred hired hands, with bells used to coordinate their daily routines like clocking in and out and lunch breaks.[51]

The institution of perpetual lease in Hetao in some ways resembled the multiple land ownership regime found in southern China and Taiwan known as permanent tenancy (*yongdian* 永佃) or "one field, two owners" (*yi tian er zhu* 一田二主), which was characterized by the separation of the "surface field" (*tianmian* 田面) rights of the tenant from the "subsoil field" (*tiandi* 田底) rights of the landlord.[52] Both regimes were products of the increasing privatization and commodification of land, and both protected the long-term usufruct rights of the landholder. However, there were also important differences between them. First of all, the *yongzu* system caused a shift of de facto ownership (from Mongol to Chinese) as well as changes in land use (from pastoral to farming), whereas no such change was entailed under the *yongdian* regime. Further, the *yongzu* system benefited entrepreneurs engaging in large-scale land acquisition and development, whereas the *yongdian* regime favored small holders and tenant farmers by protecting their rights. Moreover, the *yongzu* system was developed through personal favors and oral agreements that were largely outside of state supervision, whereas the *yongdian* regime was secured by legal contracts under state regulation. The property regime in Hetao thus showed traits distinct from other parts of China: namely, the central role played by merchant-entrepreneurs in a frontier setting that enabled large-scale land development and the preponderance of commercial capital in agricultural production.

The land merchants used a hierarchical structure to organize irrigation and land. At the center was a number of *gongzhong* 公中, which was a central administrative unit in charge of a canal or a section, depending on the size of the canal. It was managed in ways that resembled a business firm, often with two layers of control. On the top level, a canal overseer (*qutou* 渠頭) was responsible for canal construction and water distribution, the setting up of dams, the hiring of labor, and the collecting of fees. As the estate grew, a further administrative level was put in place, with a manager to supervise all general affairs, a bookkeeper to keep accounts, a foreman responsible for handling land issues and for recruiting and managing labor, and several canal runners in charge of waterway patrols and fee collection. Depending on their performance, these individuals would receive dividends on top of their regular salary, usually in the form of land, which provided them incentives to optimize irrigation and land management.[53] Each *gongzhong* oversaw several *niuju* or smaller outlier settlements that resembled the village of China proper. Most *niuju* were much more sparsely populated than a typical Chinese village, however, as they consisted of only a few households or sometimes just one household.[54] Such a hierarchical structure proved effective in organizing a settler community centered on irrigation.

What distinguished the *gongzhong* estates from other business firms was that they not only controlled the water, land, and labor, but they also exercised a degree of judicial and policing authority in arbitrating disputes, providing security, and maintaining local order. We have mentioned that the indirect rule of the Qing government and the decline of nomadic society had created a power vacuum in this borderland, which allowed the growth of a quasi-autonomous settler society. Many land merchants organized private militias to protect their estates. They recruited demobilized soldiers and vagabonds for these militias. These militias also kept an eye on workers and employees. As He Yangling points out, "In the old days, all civil and criminal affairs associated with farmers were determined by the *gongzhong*, which functioned as a virtual government."[55] In the absence of centralized control, the *gongzhong* estates formed a mechanism of economic mobilization and political control that resembled that of the plantation economies in the Americas.[56]

As we have seen, the availability of large amounts of land acquired from the Mongols and the cheap labor supplied by land-poor farmers and refugees from north

China incentivized land merchants to organize large managerial farms using hired labor instead of dividing the land into smaller plots for leasing. In an interview in 1919, Wang Tongchun claimed to have established a total of eighteen farm estates that covered over one thousand *qing* of cultivated land, which amounted to an average size of 55 *qing* or more per estate.[57] Another source shows that Wang's estates yielded over 230,000 *shi* of millet and other cereals in an average year.[58] If these figures are accurate, he would have had an output of around 2.3 *shi* per *mu*, a figure nearly comparable to what is yielded by a piece of prime irrigated rice land in east or south China today.[59] The high returns were all the more remarkable given the arid and cold weather in Hetao and short agricultural work year—from April to September—as compared to more accommodating areas. It was likely that these estates benefited from the professional management of irrigation works and a higher use of draft animals and natural fertilizer. For instance, Wang was said to have owned thirty-one hundred cattle, seventeen hundred mules, 120,000 sheep, five hundred camels, and two hundred ox-carts and horse-drawn wagons.[60] The diversity of animals indicated the supplementing of agriculture by animal husbandry and trade, something that characterized these estates other than their sizes.

Apart from organizing managerial farming, the land merchants also leased out a significant proportion of irrigated land for rent. For example, Wang reportedly collected 170,000 taels in land rentals and water fees every year.[61] There were two types of land rentals: fixed-rate leasing (*fangzu* 放租) and sharecropping (*banzhong* 伴種). In fixed-rate leasing, the rate was determined after measuring the area where crops sprouted in the spring, and the rent usually ranged between twenty and thirty taels of silver per *qing*, payable in the autumn in cash or in kind, regardless of the actual yield. The tenants usually needed to provide their own draft animals, seed grains, and agricultural tools, and thus they functioned as semi-independent farmers. In contrast, sharecroppers owned very little or no means of production and had to depend on the landlord for supplying the seed and tools. The harvested crop was shared with the landlord according to a predetermined rate. Depending on soil quality and capital input, the rate varied from a three-seven distribution (three parts for the landlord and seven for the tenant) to a four-six or half-half distribution.[62]

Most settlers of Hetao were from the Baode department or Hequ county of Shanxi, with those from Fugu county of Shaanxi forming the next largest contingent, followed by settlers from Zhili and Henan. The settlers were divided into two hierarchical groups according to their social and economic positions: (1) merchants and peasant proprietors and (2) tenants and rural workers. These two groups were set apart by their landholding capacity and ability to gain access to irrigation. Whereas the former were landholders who leased land directly from the Mongols and invested in irrigation works, the latter either rented land from the former or sold their labor in return for wages. Their migration pattern also differed: whereas the merchants and peasant proprietors tended to reside in the area for extensive periods of time, the rural workers typically arrived in the spring, departed in the autumn, and drifted from place to place in search of well-irrigated plots, which earned them the name *paoqing* 跑青 or "green-shoots chasers."[63]

These groups of settlers were further divided into several subgroups across the social spectrum. On the top were land merchants who contracted large tracts of land from the Mongols and owned either shares of trunk canals or branch canals or both. The next level were proprietor farmers who acquired modest plots but owned no canals themselves, and therefore needed to purchase water rights from the land merchants. There was a certain degree of mobility between the two because of the capriciousness of the Yellow River, which could ruin or enrich farmers in unpredictable ways. Likewise, the tenants were also divided into two subgroups according to the different methods of rental payment: (1) fixed-lease tenants who organized farming relatively independently and (2) sharecroppers who depended on the landlord for supplying most or all means of production. At the other end of the spectrum was a group of long-term and short-term laborers who hired out their labor at irrigation sites or farm estates owned by land merchants. This group was supplied by the influx of landless farmers and refugees from south of the passes who traveled north in the wake of natural disasters. The application of wage labor, coupled with the privatization of land ownership and the growing estate economy, greatly facilitated the development of commercial agriculture in Hetao.

COMMERCIAL EXPANSION AND INTEGRATION

The economic boom in Hetao paved the way for its further commercialization and urbanization and for Hetao's integration into larger regional and global economic flows during the late nineteenth and early twentieth century. On the one hand, the rapidly expanding grain trade integrated Hetao with the market of north China through the water transportation provided by the Yellow River, which was navigable by wooden boats from Shizuizi of Ningxia to Qikou of Shanxi between April and November.[64] On the other hand, the opening of treaty ports and the construction of roads and railroad lines further integrated this borderland with the global market as a supplier of wool, pelts, and medicinal herbs.

As Chinese settlement expanded, commerce and handicrafts industry flourished. Apart from their engagements in irrigation and land management, the land merchants predominantly specialized in the long-distance trade of tea, cotton cloth, tobacco, and other Chinese products in exchange for livestock and pastoral products of the Mongols. Some were also engaged in handicrafts industries such as food processing and felt making. Commerce and agriculture often sustained each other in these enterprises: profits from commerce were invested in irrigation and land acquisition, and proceeds from the land were in turn converted into merchant capital.

Take Longxingchang, the largest trading firm in Hetao, for example. It was founded by a retired Qing officer in 1880 and acquired by Wang Tongchun in 1893. The firm sold grains, oil, pelts, medicinal herbs, and soda to Baotou and Hekou in exchange for consumer goods from China proper. It also participated in the trade of lumber and coal that were procured from Mt. Helanshan and mines near Baotou.

The firm was equipped with around two hundred iron and wooden-wheeled carts, dozens of wooden boats, and over one hundred camels, which traversed the trade routes between Mongolia and north China over land and water. It also operated a set of mills, oil presses, distilleries, and felt shops, as well as engaging in the credit sale of consumer goods.[65] The commercial success of the firm not only supplied the capital needed in Wang's irrigation endeavors, but it also gave rise to a market town that bore the same name as the firm. Located on the bank of the Yihe canal seventy *li* north of the Yellow River, the town of Longxingchang served as an important trade link between the regional market system and the hinterlands of western Inner Mongolia.

The thriving commerce of Hetao testified to the emergence of an interlinked regional economy that encompassed both sides of the Great Wall. They were bound together by extensive caravan and water transport routes. The completion of the navigable Yihe canal in 1893 not only facilitated the flow of goods within Hetao, but also connected the area with other parts of Mongolia and north China via downstream market centers like Baotou and Hekou. Two cart roads linked these river ports to overland traffic: one extending from Baotou northward to Mongolia and the other from Hekou eastward to Fengzhen and Datong of Shanxi. The rise of a grain base north of the Great Wall thus considerably reduced transport costs and enriched contractors and brokers in these market towns.

With new land brought under cultivation, cross-regional grain trade became phenomenal. Every year, between one hundred and twenty thousand and one hundred and eighty thousand tons of grains were transported from Hekou to the markets of north China. A large proportion of the grains came from Hetao. Further, a good proportion of the Hetao grains (mostly millet, sorghum, and wheat, up to thirty thousand tons a year) was transported to Mongolia via Baotou.[66] As the local gazetteer notes, "Upon harvest, the cereals are immediately transported via the Yellow River and sold to the markets of Baotou, Hequ, and Qikou. No attempts are made to store it because of the easy profits."[67] The mountainous areas of northern Shanxi and Shaanxi, in particular, had long depended on grain imports from the north China plain. This dependence was exacerbated during the frequent natural calamities that plagued north China during the late nineteenth century. Thanks to its extensive irrigation systems, Hetao continued to produce grain in years when drought and famine caused grain prices to soar across north China and many parts of Inner Mongolia. During the famine of 1891–1892, the price of coarse grains (such as maize, millet, and sorghum) in Inner Mongolia quadrupled from three hundred to twelve hundred copper coins per *dou* [i.e. sixty taels per *shi*] and the price of wheat rose from seven hundred to eighteen hundred coins per *dou* [i.e. ninety taels per *shi*].[68] The famine thus provided an opportunity for the land merchants to profit from the grain trade. In 1892, Wang Tongchun sold twenty-five thousand *shi* of grains to northern Shanxi and Shaanxi and donated ten thousand *shi* to Beijing for famine relief. In 1901, he sold twelve thousand *shi* of grains to Shanxi, six thousand *shi* to Beijing, and seven thousand *shi* to the Otog banner.[69]

Apart from the grain trade, the trade of wool and pelts also flourished. The Treaty of Tianjin (1858) opened more Chinese ports to foreign trade, while granting foreign merchants tax exemption on exports purchased inland with the exception of a single charge of 2.5 percent.[70] The treaty paved the way for the large-scale export of wool and pelts from Mongolia to the wool textile and leather industries of Europe and America. Following the opening of Tianjin in 1860, foreign firms from Germany, Great Britain, and the United States began to establish branch offices in Inner Mongolia that purchased rawhides, goatskins, and sheep and camel wools for transport to overseas markets via Tianjin. Specialized wool and pelt firms mushroomed in Baotou and Hohhot. These firms served as commission-based brokers intermediating between itinerary traders and foreign firms.[71] According to the Imperial Customs data, the export amount of wool and pelts increased forty-fold from 310,000 customs taels in 1876 to 13,370,000 taels in 1899, and despite a temporary setback in 1900 due to the Boxer Rebellion, reached 26,120,000 taels in 1905. Likewise, their ratio in the entire export of north China ports rose from 0.4 percent in 1876 to 11.5 percent in 1905, while the prices for wool and pelts shot from less than nine taels per picul in 1895 to over seventeen taels for wool and twenty-six taels for pelts in 1905.[72]

Another important export from the Ordos region (Hetao included) was medicinal herbs. In particular, the trade in licorice root (*gancao* 甘草, a.k.a. *genzi* 根子) became profitable because of its high demand in the world market. Licorice root is a wild desert plant found in many parts of Inner Mongolia, especially in the Khanggin and Dalad banners of northern Ordos, as well as in the Khalkha region. Its extracts are widely used in cough syrups and the flavoring of chewing gum, tobaccos, nonalcoholic beverages, soy sauce, etc. It is also used in medicine to help lower the body temperature and by women during childbirth.[73] The trade was monopolized by merchants from the Baode department of Shanxi, who obtained license from the jasags and hired hundreds of migrant laborers to dig up the root in the banners from the end of the fourth lunar month to the middle of the ninth lunar month. The collected root was sold to the firms at low prices and transported to Baotou and Hekou by caravan or boat.[74] Hekou was especially known for its enormous trade of licorice root. In the late 1800s, up to five million catties (three thousand tons), valued at four hundred thousand taels, were assembled in Hekou each year and shipped to Hequ and Qikou and further to Tianjin and Qizhou of Zhili (the present Anguo county of Hebei).[75]

The expanding long-distance trade gave rise to new urban centers that linked Hetao to a trading network spanning both sides of the Great Wall and reaching out to the world market through treaty ports like Tianjin. New market towns emerged in Hetao and its immediate peripheries. The most significant new town was Longxingchang, which served as a collecting and distributing center of grain and pastoral products supplied by emerging local markets in Ulaan Oboo, Xiaoshetai, and Dashetai along the caravan routes to the Urad banner as well as Mongolia.[76]

The second half of the nineteenth century also saw the rise of new regional market centers along the Yellow River. Located two hundred kilometers east of Hetao, Baotou became a major trading hub and tax port on the trade routes to Gansu,

Xinjiang, and Mongolia due to its easy accessibility to both land and water transport. Situated 150 kilometers further downstream, Hekou remained the largest distribution center of licorice root until the first half of the twentieth century. Its business waned only after the railway from Beijing to Hohhot was extended to Baotou in 1923, which provided a far more efficient means of transport than carts and boats.[77]

The emergence of Baotou and Hekou indicated a trend of urbanization characterized by a high degree of commercialization as well as mutual dependence between economic cores and their peripheries that was mediated by the market rather than by political or symbolic power. Unlike earlier frontier centers like Höhhot and Urga that were initially palatial and religious centers, these new market centers grew out of the Chinese commercial expansion relatively independently of official intervention. These were further linked to the frontiers of Mongolia, Qinghai, and Xinjiang, as well as to downstream river ports like Hequ and Qikou of Shanxi and to the treaty port of Tianjin. From those places, they reached the markets of north China and the world. The expanding trading network thus integrated the hinterlands of Mongolia into the larger regional and global economic system.

CONCLUSION

In this chapter, I examined the emergence of Hetao as a prosperous Chinese agricultural colony outside the Great Wall during the nineteenth century, which exemplified a new form of economically driven settlement that was distinguished from the earlier modes of strategically or ecologically triggered migration. The economic boom was made possible by a set of ecological, historical, and social conjunctures. First, it took place in a geographical and cultural periphery, with favorable irrigation conditions and water transport provided by the Yellow River, large amounts of land owned by the Mongols, and the negligible presence of the state that allowed ample room for a rigorous local autonomy. Second, the ongoing Chinese commercial expansion and labor migration across the Great Wall into the grasslands paved the way for the irrigation boom in Hetao by supplying the necessary capital and labor. Third, the process of commercialization was greatly accelerated during the late nineteenth century. Whereas the social turmoil and natural calamities in north China supplied a large amount of cheap labor for commercial agriculture in Hetao, the expanding trading network further integrated the region into larger regional and global economic flows.

Whereas these structural factors were indispensable in understanding the economic development and social change in Hetao, social actors played an equally significant role. At the center of the agricultural boom was the land merchants who combined capital with expertise in developing irrigation works and organizing commercial agriculture. By obtaining previously uncultivated land from the Mongols and investing in irrigation systems, the land merchants were able to significantly increase the value of water and land, which turned these resources into profit-generating assets and commodities on the market. They successfully mobilized capital, expertise, land, and labor through an innovative shareholding system characterized by a lively trade in shares, multiple levels of ownership, and cross-investment. The high returns incentivized them to expand reproduction by establishing large-scale managerial farms using hired labor and by participating in long-distance trade and handicrafts industries. These activities by the land merchants integrated the area into the larger regional and global economic system and gave rise to a capital-intensive, market-oriented mode of production centered on massive capital accumulation, commercial agriculture, and wage labor, which can be best described as capitalist.

The development of Hetao agriculture, as we have seen, departed distinctly from the small-scale household farming and low commercialization of north China and other frontier regions such as Manchuria, where Han migrants simply replicated the agrarian regime of north China.[78] Christopher Isett argues that under the Qing, any large-scale agricultural production in China was under challenge from peasant communities that used customary practices such as partible inheritance and labor intensification to break up estates and ensure the long-term pattern of small-holder family farms and "involutionary" growth. He casts this pattern as the fundamental feature of the Chinese agricultural regime.[79] Such fundamental features did not apply to Hetao, however, for a number of reasons. Unlike in Manchuria, the Han migrants in Hetao lived with Mongols in a mixed environment. They were obliged, at least initially, to adapt to different social customs in their new environment. The booming international trade with Russia gave rise to an elaborate trading network and an active market, to which the Han migrant communities had easy access. Property relations were also commercialized, with an active market for land mortgage, sub-leasing, as well as perpetual leasing. Meanwhile, the Mongol landownership and competing land use between Han farmers and Mongol herders also meant that the peasants' possession of land was not as stable and permanent as in Manchuria. Finally, the unique natural conditions of Hetao made it possible for land developers to invest capital in developing irrigation projects, which increased the value of land and allowed the organization of large managerial farms. All these developments made Hetao an exception to the rule of smallholder farms found elsewhere in China. The existence of such an exception demonstrates that there were important deviations from either the "Smithian" or "Malthusian-Ricardian" paradigms that offer an explanation of the development in parts of Europe and China. Evidently, these paradigms do not encompass the circumstances arising in a frontier setting that saw successful, if not sustainable, sprouts of agrarian capitalism.

On the other hand, there were admittedly limits as to what kinds of development these arrangements were capable of over the long run without the input of modern technology or legal frameworks. Much of the investment made by the land merchants was relatively short-term working capital—money spent to pay workers involved in the digging and dredging processes that needed to be partially repeated frequently—rather than long-term investment in physical capital with a low depreciation rate or in modern technology that could be used to improve their efficiency. It remains unclear, therefore, as to what extent this development was sustainable beyond the initial stage of frontier thrust had it not been subject to the state intervention.

Further, the lack of a modern legal system made this development vulnerable to internal disorder and external coercion, partly because the property rights of the entrepreneurs, though acknowledged in customary practices, were not protected by governmental laws whatsoever. The economy of Hetao suffered under the double pressures of an extortive military and banditry during the 1870s. Later, starting from the New Policies reform of the early twentieth century, the state-making efforts of the Qing and Republican governments, in particular the expropriation of private canals, resulted in the eclipse of land merchants as major actors on the local scene and eventually in the decline of the Hetao economy. Land merchants continued to play a role as land brokers and absentee landlords into the Republican period, yet the degree of capital investment in irrigation was nothing comparable with their investment in the nineteenth century. Many canals silted up due to poor maintenance, and by 1919, the irrigable area of Hetao shrank to less than five thousand *qing*, which was about half the irrigable area of 1907.[80] To some extent, it was almost inevitable that the Chinese state would monopolize and then expropriate any big capitalist enterprise. This intervention by the state shows that economic development did not simply concern economy but was the result of a complex set of political and social arrangements.

Nevertheless, the existence of such positive, domestically financed and organized, developments, however short-lived, counters the conventional view that the Chinese kept reproducing the same involutionary structure and were incapable of initiating change on their own. The case of Hetao provides an example of how change was made possible from the periphery where certain geographical, historical, and socio-economic contingencies met, and how a group of local actors were able to induce fundamental change that not only had an enduring impact upon the frontier society, but also facilitated China's integration into a new global system. As we will see in chapter 6, the wealth of Hetao and the fiscal weight it carried proved conducive to the Qing court's decision to open up Mongol lands for Han cultivation during the New Policies reform.

NOTES

1. Xu Dixin and Wu Chengming, *Zhongguo zibenzhuyi de mengya*, volume 1; Jing Su and Luo Lun, *Landlord and Labor in Late Imperial China*.

2. Pomeranz, *The Great Divergence*; Wong, *China Transformed*; Bozhong Li, *Agricultural Development in Jiangnan, 1620–1850*.

3. Elvin, *The Pattern of the Chinese Past*; Huang, *The Peasant Economy and Social Change in North China*. Also see Perkins, *Agricultural Development in China, 1368–1968*; Myers, *The Chinese Peasant Economy*; Chao, *Man and Land in Chinese History*; Huang, *The Peasant Family and Rural Development in the Yangzi Delta*.

4. Isett, *State, Peasant, and Merchant in Qing Manchuria*, 4.

5. Anzai, "Shinmatsu ni okeru suien no kaikon," *Mantetsu Chōsa Geppō* 18.12, 25; 19.1, 19–20.

6. Imahori, *Chūgoku no shahai kōzō*, 41–55.

7. Zhang Zhihua, "Luelun hetao dishang," 97; Chen Erdong, *Hetao guanqu shuili jianshi*, 48.

8. Tetsuyama, *Shindai nōgyō keizaishi kenkyū*.

9. Wang Jiange, "Qingmo hetao diqu de shuili zhidu yu shehui shiying," 127–56.

10. In the broad sense of the term, Hetao is used interchangeably with the Ordos or Ordos Plateau, denoting the entire bend of the Yellow River that is bounded by the Alasha (Helanshan), Khara Narin (Langshan), Muri uul (Wulashan), and Dalan Terigün (Daqingshan) Mountains on the west, north, and northeast, and the Great Wall in the south and southeast. Such a usage is found mostly in the Ming and Qing official discourses. See Xia Zhengnong, ed., *Cihai*; Chen Erdong, *Hetao guanqu shuili jianshi*, 2–5.

11. Feng Jilong, ed., *Diaocha hetao baogaoshu*, 2–4.

12. Chen Erdong, *Hetao guanqu shuili jianshi*, 1–7; "Baoxi gequ quwu qudao gaikuang," 42.

13. Feng Jilong, *Hetao xinbian*, 156.

14. Chen Erdong, *Hetao guanqu shuili jianshi*, 21–23, 49.

15. Yao Xuejing, ed., *Wuyuanting zhigao* 2, 7.

16. QSG 47, 14375.

17. *Qinming duban mengqi kenwu dachen quanzong dang'an* (hereafter KWDC), [433-106-20]. The tael (*liang* 兩) is a unit of weight measurement and the basis of silver currency in China and other East Asian countries. One tael was roughly equivalent to thirty-eight grams (1⅓ ounces).

18. KWDC, [433-106-23].

19. KWDC, [433-352-5]. The copper coin (*qian* 錢) was usually counted by strings (*diao* 吊) (i.e. one thousand coins [*wen* 文]). A string of one thousand coins was supposed to be equal in value to one tael of silver. However, its conversion rate with silver in the late 1890s in Hetao was around two thousand coins for one tael of silver.

20. Wang Wenchi, *Linhe xianzhi*, 130–33.

21. Wang Wenchi, *Linhe xianzhi*, 130–33.

22. For the Hui Muslim Rebellion, a.k.a. the Dungan Revolt, see Lipman, *Familiar Strangers*; Dillon, *China's Muslim Hui Community*, 60–70.

23. For the impact of Hui Uprising on Hetao, see QSG 47, 14371–72, 14376–77.

24. QSG 47, 14378; Suiyuan Tongzhiguan, ed., *Suiyuan tongzhigao* (hereafter SYTZG), 5, 589–90; Wang Wenchi, *Linhe xianzhi*, 131.

25. Edgerton-Tarpley, *Tears from Iron*.

26. Wang Zhe, "Hetao qudao zhi kaijun yange," 124.

27. Pozdneyev, *Mongolia and the Mongols*, volume 2, 49.

28. Zhang Zhihua, "Luelun hetao dishang," 91. The major canals were typically over fifty kilometers long, ten to sixteen meters wide, and 1.3 to two meters deep. The minor canals were usually less than twenty-five kilometers long. See Wang Zhe, "Houtao qudao zhi kaijun yange," 123–51.

29. The yield is calculated based on J. L. Buck's report of twenty-four bushels (c. 653 kg) of wheat per acre on irrigated land in north China, multiplied by the arable land of Hetao. See Buck, *Land Utilization in China*, 233. For an estimation of a similar figure, see Zhang Zhihua, "Luelun hetao dishang," 91.

30. Nei Menggu dang'anguan, ed., *Qingmo nei menggu kenwu dang'an huibian* (hereafter KWDA), 1421–22.

31. For the shareholding system of the Shanxi merchants, see Zhang Zhengming, "Qingdai jinshang de gufengzhi"; idem, *Jinshang xingshuai shi*. For partnerships among merchants elsewhere in China, see Zelin, "Capital Accumulation and Investment Strategies in Early Modern China," 79–122; Pomeranz, "'Traditional' Chinese Business Forms Revisited," 1–38.

32. For the use of contracts in late imperial China, see Cohen, "Writs of Passage in Late Imperial China," in Madeleine Zelin et al., eds., *Contract and Property in Early Modern China*, 37–93.

33. Yao Xuejing, *Wuyuanting zhigao* 2, 43–46.

34. KWDC, [433-244-9].

35. KWDC, [433-244-7]. Habitats were allocated in several Ordos banners in the 1860s, as a reward for the Mongol soldiers who contributed to the suppression of the Hui Muslim Rebellion. See Kuraji, "Mōkyō ni okeru tochi bunkatsu shoyūsei no ichi ruikei," 31–98, 53.

36. KWDC, [433-285-4].

37. KWDC, [433-285-1].

38. KWDC, [433-154-12].

39. Gu Jiegang, "Wang Tongchun kaifa hetao ji," 2–10; Wang Wenchi, *Linhe xianzhi* 2, 29; Su Xixian, "Wang Tongchun," 43–91, 57–59.

40. See Yao Xuejing, *Wuyuanting zhigao* 2, p. 45. King Yu (c. 2200–2100 BCE) was a legendary ruler in ancient China famed for introducing flood control along the Yellow River. Li Bing was an administrator and engineer renowned for the construction of the Dujiangyan Irrigation System of Sichuan in 256 BCE.

41. Chen Erdong, *Hetao guanqu shuili jianshi*, 65; Du Yasong, "Wang tongchun shilue," 30. Ningxia has the earliest irrigation systems in China. The oldest of them, Hanyan and Tanglai canals, date back to the Han and Tang dynasties. See Feng Jilong, *Diaocha hetao baogaoshu*, 157–79.

42. Gu Jiegang, "Wang Tongchun kaifa hetao ji," 10; Zhang Xiangwen, "Wang Tongchun xiaozhuan," 52–53.

43. Tayama, *Shinjidai ni okeru Mōkō no shakai seido*, 193-195, 211-232; Anzai, "Mōkyō ni okeru tochi bunkatsu shoyūsei no ichi ruikei," 32; Wang Jiange, "Qingdai mengdi de zhanyou quan, gengzhong quan yu menghan guanxi," 81-89. For the three types of Mongol land, see Yao Xiguang, "Chengfu jinghua dongsimeng menggmu tiaoyi," in *Choumeng chuyi*, 114.

44. Anzai, "Mōkyō ni okeru tochi bunkatsu shoyūsei no ichi ruikei."

45. *Niuju* (yoke-of-oxen) refers to the area cultivated by one plough in a year's time, equivalent to 270 or 280 *mu* or eighteen ha. See Ding Xikui, *Jingbian xianzhigao*, 291–92. One *dou* = ten *sheng* = 0.1 *shi*.

46. Xibei kenwu diaocha ju, ed., *Xibei kenwu diaocha huice*, 112.

47. KWDC, [433-102-2].

48. For a general discussion on the institution of perpetual lease, see Tayama, *Shin jidai ni okeru mōko no shakai seido*, 226–27.

49. Cohen, "Writs of Passage in Late Imperial China"; Siu, *Agents and Victims in South China*.

50. Yao Xuejing, *Wuyuanting zhigao* 2, 7.

51. Su Xixian, "Wang Tongchun," 83.

52. It is notable that in Taiwan, the land rights held by the tenant were called "subsoil" rather than "surface" rights as in mainland China. For a detailed illustration of the

one-field-two-masters regime in Qing Taiwan, see Wen-Kai Lin, "Land Property and Contract in Taiwan during the Qing and Japanese Colonial Period."

53. Su Xixian, "Wang Tongchun," 60, 82–83; Du Yasong, "Wang tongchun shilue," 27; Han Xiangfu, "Wo suo zhidao de wang tongchun," 98.

54. Qu Zhisheng, "Fuji er," *Yu Gong banyuekan* 4, No. 7 (1935).

55. He Yangling, *Chasui mengmin jingji de jiepou*, 127.

56. For a survey of plantation economy (rice, sugar, cotton, and tobacco) in the American South, see Follett, Beckert, Coclanis, and Hahn, *Plantation Kingdom*. For the development of sugar plantations in the Spanish Caribbean, see Ayala, *American Sugar Kingdom*.

57. Feng Jilong, *Diaocha hetao baogaoshu*, 263.

58. For the annual yield, see Wang Zhe, "Wang Tongchun xiansheng yiji"; Su Xixian, "Wang Tongchun," 60, 69; Du, "Wang tongchun shilue," 28.

59. Li Bozhong estimates that the output of a piece of prime irrigated rice land in Jiangnan was between 2.4 and 3.6 *shi* per *mu*. See Li, *Agricultural Development in Jiangnan*, 126.

60. Wang Zhe, "Wang Tongchun xiansheng yiji"; Su Xixian, "Wang Tongchun," 60, 69; Du Yasong, "Wang tongchun shilue," 28.

61. Su Xixian, "Wang Tongchun," 60.

62. Yao Xuejing, *Wuyuan tingzhigao* 2, 7; Imahori, *Chūgoku hōken shakai no kōzō*, 776–779.

63. Yao Xuejing, *Wuyuan tingzhigao* 2, 7.

64. Navigability of the Yellow River varied by season of the year and by section. It is not navigable from December through March due to freezing. The part between Lanzhou to Ningxiafu was passable only by rafts. The section between Dengkou and Hequ was navigable both ways, whereas the sections between Shizuizi and Dengkou and between Hequ and Qikou were good only for downstream traffic because of the narrow course and stony bottom. See Fan Rusen, "Minguo yilai de huanghe hangyun," 285–300.

65. Su Xixian, "Longxingchang shanghao xinshuai shimo," 36–38.

66. Zhang Rui, "Guzhen hekou," 215–19; Duan Shengwu, "Kaifa Hetao de shangque."

67. Yao Xuejing, *Wuyuan tingzhigao* 2, 2.

68. "Wuyuan diqu ziran zaihai shiliao."

69. Su Xixian, "Wang Tongchun," 67–68.

70. Wang Yi and Zhang Chengqi, eds., *Xianfeng tiaoyue*, in Shen Yunlong, ed., *Jindai zhongguo shiliao congkan xubian*, Treaty of Tianjin, Article XXVIII.

71. Wu Shengrong, "Woguo xibei pimao jisan zhongzhen Baotou de pimao hangye," in *Nei menggu gongshang shiliao* 39, 215–62.

72. Huang Yanpei and Pang Song, *Zhongguo shangzhan shibai shi*. One picul (*dan* 擔) = one hundred catties (*jin* 斤) = sixty to sixty-four kilograms.

73. Pozdneyev, *Mongolia and the Mongols*, volume 1, 36.

74. See "Zhongguo gancao zhi shuchu ji shengchan qingxing," *Zhongwai jingji zhoukan* 7, 1923. In the late nineteenth century, the price for one hundred jin (one jin/*catty* = 1.33 pounds) of licorice root was eight taels of silver. The annual output in Dalad banner alone was around 2.5 million jin, which sold for two hundred thousand taels of silver. The export of licorice root reached its peak in the 1910s and 1920s, increasing from four hundred million to fifteen hundred million piculs a year, due to reduced production in Russia and Turkey in the wake of World War I. See He Yangling, *Chasui mengmin jingji de jiepou*, 90–91. Pozdneyev noted that the transportation cost from Khalkha to Kalgan ranged from one and a half to two taels of silver per 250 jin pack. See Pozdneyev, *Mongolia*, volume 1, 36. For the trade, see SYTZG 26, 555.

75. See Zhang Rui, "Guzhen hekou," 215. The export of licorice root reached its height in the 1910s and 1920s due to World War I, which totaled from four hundred million to fifteen hundred million piculs a year for four hundred thousand to two million taels of silver. See He Yangling, *Chasui mengmin jingji de jiepou*, 90–91.

76. Su Xixian, "Wang Tongchun," 56.

77. Wu Shengrong, "Woguo xibei pimao jisan zhongzhen Baotou de pimao hangye," 216.

78. James Reardon-Anderson sees Han settlement of Manchuria as essentially a process of "China's expansion northward" that facilitated no change in terms of economic innovation or cultural adaptation. See Reardon-Anderson, *Reluctant Pioneers*. Similarly, Christopher Isett argues that Han peasants' possession of land in Manchuria allowed them to avoid specialization for market and to allocate their resources to intensify their labor input or extend arable area, thereby reinforcing the smallholding farms rather than introducing structural changes in improving labor productivity. See Isett, *State, Peasant, and Merchant*, 10–14.

79. Isett, *State, Peasant, and Merchant*, 299–303.

80. Feng Jilong, *Diaocha hetao baogaoshu*, 5.

5

Cultivation for Salvation

Missionaries, Migrants, and Catholic Expansion

The second half of the nineteenth century saw the conjuncture of two unprecedented trends of expansion: (1) agrarian Chinese pushing forward the frontier of settlement into Inner Mongolia, and (2) Western powers forcing their way into China through gunboats and unequal treaties. At the forefront of the Western expansion were Catholic missionaries. The Sino-French Convention of Beijing in 1860 allowed them to enter not only the Chinese interior, but also the Mongolian frontier beyond the Great Wall, where they rented or purchased land, constructed churches, and propagated Roman Catholicism.

In charge of the missionary work in Inner Mongolia was a Belgian Catholic order named the Congregation of the Immaculate Heart of Mary. These missionaries developed an evangelical strategy centered on land acquisition by converting Mongol pasturelands into farmlands. The convergence of these missionary activities with Chinese colonization turned out to be remarkably successful in attracting converts, who were mostly land-poor migrants from north China. Meanwhile, the aggressive expansion of the Catholic Church caused endless disputes with the local Mongol and non-Christian Chinese communities. The tension between the groups transformed this borderland into a hotbed of confrontation that culminated in the anti-Christian violence during the Boxer Rebellion of 1900. It also resulted in growing penetration of the Qing state in Mongolia that exerted its power in the full-scale reclamation of Mongol pasturelands.

This chapter examines the Catholic missionary encounters in the Ordos region of Inner Mongolia within the context of Chinese colonization and Western imperialist expansion. I argue that although the framework of imperialism and colonialism is indispensable in understanding the Catholic presence in the Mongolian frontier, it nonetheless should be treated as a complex and entwined process of social and cultural interactions that transcends such dichotomies as East and West, Mongol and

Chinese, colonizer and colonized, or center and periphery. A focus on the Catholic missionaries and those who encountered them enables us to see the layers of global, imperial, transregional, and local forces that were at play, whether in coordination or in contestation, in reshaping Inner Mongolia as a frontier space.

EARLY ENCOUNTERS

The interactions between Christianity and China over the past millennium have testified to the changing pattern of cultural contact between the East and West. During the sixteenth century, geographical discoveries opened new trade routes to the East: replacing the ancient Silk Road over land. The string of trading posts established by the Portuguese along the coastlines of Asia greatly facilitated the missionary activities of the Catholic Church in these regions. Catholicism was first introduced to China through Franciscan and Dominican missionaries sent to the Mongol court at Karakorum during the thirteenth century. The overseas expansion of the Church, however, no longer crossed paths with the Mongols. By the time the Jesuit mission led by Matteo Ricci entered China via Macau in 1582, the steppe had become a remote hinterland for the seaborne travelers. The barrier was both geographical and doctrinal. In 1578, four years prior to the Jesuits' arrival, Altan Khan of Tümed received Sonam Gyatso, head of the Gelugpa School, in Kokonor and bestowed the title of Dalai Lama on him. This event marked the conversion of Mongolia to Tibetan Buddhism.[1]

Equipped by their scientific knowledge and diplomatic skills, the Jesuits played an instrumental role in the empire-making project of the Kangxi emperor. The new technologies of weaponry, treaties, and map-making they introduced facilitated the military and territorial expansion of the Manchus and helped define the boundaries of the new empire. The hundreds of cannons casted by Ferdinand Verbiest for the Imperial Army were far superior to any previous Chinese weapons and contributed to the suppression of the Three Feudatories rebellion (1673–1681) and the conquest of Taiwan in 1683.[2] Thomas Pereira and Jean-François Gerbillon served twice as interpreters at the border negotiations between the Qing and Russia that led to the conclusion of the Treaty of Nerchinsk in 1689.[3] Between 1688 and 1698, Gerbillon made eight journeys into Mongolia and Manchuria and acquired much geographical and ethnographical information on these regions. Another pioneering project undertaken by the missionaries was the geographical surveying and mapping of the Qing empire that produced the Kangxi Atlas (*Huangyu quanlan tu* 皇輿全覽圖) in 1718, which was the first imperial atlas based on Western cartographic techniques.[4] The expeditions by the Jesuits were scientific rather than evangelical. At this point, Mongolia remained an unchartered frontier rather than a target of religious propagation.

As recompense for the services rendered by the Jesuits in the areas of astronomy, diplomacy, and gun manufacture, the Kangxi emperor issued an edict of tolerance in 1692 granting them freedom to preach Christianity in China. The mission in China flourished, and the number of converts had reached a total of three hundred thousand by 1724.[5] The Jesuits also succeeded in sowing the seed of Christianity beyond the Great Wall: targeting the Manchu garrison troops stationed along Gubei-kou and Zhangjiakou. The first known Catholic convert beyond the passes was a Chinese bannerman named Zhang Genzong, who settled in 1646 in a small village called Xiwanzi (presently Chongli county, Hebei province), about forty kilometers northeast of Kalgan. He was believed to be baptized around 1700. By 1726, over one hundred Catholics resided in Xiwanzi, and a small oratory had been built.[6]

The Jesuits' success was cut short, however, by a century-long dispute within the Catholic Church over the Chinese practices of ancestor veneration and Confucian rituals. This led to the decree of Pope Clement XI condemning the Chinese rites in 1715 and the subsequent ban of Christian missions by the Kangxi emperor in 1721. The Yongzheng emperor further denounced Christianity as heterodoxy in 1724 and ordered the expulsion of all foreign missionaries to Macao. Thus, persecution of the missionaries ensued throughout the eighteenth and first half of the nineteenth century.[7]

The persecution provided a unique opportunity for Christianity to take root outside the Great Wall. The Jesuit order was dissolved in 1783, and a French order named Congregation of the Mission (a.k.a. Lazarists or Vincentians, C: Qianshihui 遣使會) took its place. Unlike the Jesuits who targeted the ruling elites and gentry classes in large urban centers, the Lazarists organized missions among the common people, especially the poor and underprivileged in the countryside. This strategy was crucial for the survival of the mission through the persecution, which was most severe in the urban areas. Upon the closing and confiscation of the Beitang church in Beijing in 1827, a Chinese priest in charge of the mission named Matthew Xue fled the capital and arrived at Xiwanzi in 1829. The remote village outside the pass provided a safe haven for Catholic refugees and clandestine priests from Beijing and Zhili. By 1835, when the Lazarist missionary Joseph-Martian Mouly secretly arrived in Xiwanzi from Macau, he was greeted by a community of over six hundred native Catholics.[8]

Scattered religious communities also appeared across the northern fringe of the Great Wall. Ningtiaoliang (in Jingbian county, Shaanxi province) of southern Ordos and Daqiangpan (in Liangcheng county, Inner Mongolia) of southwestern Chakhar were established by Catholic fugitives from Shaanxi and Shanxi around 1750.[9] In central Chakhar, refugees from Zhili settled in a small village named Huangyuwa (in Xinghe county, Inner Mongolia) at the foot of Mt. Daqingshan around 1820. In Jehol, a number of Catholic communities appeared during the late 1700s and early 1800s that were comprised of fugitives from Zhili and Shandong.[10] By 1835, there were around two thousand Catholics residing beyond the Great Wall.[11]

The dispersion of Christianity outside the passes largely coincided with the flow of Chinese migration into the Mongol periphery. It was by no accident that all these communities were located on the frontier belt between Jehol and Ordos, which was brought under cultivation over the course of the eighteenth century. For these Catholic migrants, the grassland provided not only arable lands and a better living, but also a sanctuary free from governmental persecution. In this sense, the Chinese agricultural expansion had paved the way for the spread of Catholicism outside the passes. When international and domestic circumstances began to change during the second half of the nineteenth century, these seeds of Christianity were ready to break ground and burst into blossom.

WINDS OF CHANGE

The 1840s saw renewed missionary initiatives in China, which were made possible by the drastic changes in the political situation in China and Europe. Following the defeat in the first Opium War (1839–1842), China was forced to open her doors to foreign powers through a series of unequal treaties. The Treaty of Nanjing (1842) first established the principle of extraterritoriality for the British while opening five treaty ports for foreign trade. The same privileges were extended to France through the Treaty of Whampoa (1844), which allowed missionaries to settle and erect churches at the treaty ports. These treaties provided a legal basis for the Catholic Church's expansion in China. In February 1846, the Daoguang emperor (r. 1821–1850) issued an edict revoking the proscription of Christianity and promising the restitution of all church properties confiscated since the Kangxi era.[12] The Lazarists returned to the China scene on the eve of all these changes. The small village of Xiwanzi outside the passes became the headquarters of an independent vicariate apostolic of Mongolia in 1840, which bordered Manchuria in the east and the Great Wall in the south. In the west, it was bounded by the vicariate of Shanxi under the administration of the Franciscans, yet the boundary was not clearly demarcated.[13]

At first, the Lazarists endeavored to spread the Gospel among the Mongols. Joseph Gabet succeeded in converting two novice lamas, and with their help, translated Christian doctrines and prayers into classical Mongolian. In 1844, he and Evariste-Regis Huc embarked on a journey across Mongolia to Tibet, guided by Samdad-chiemba, who was a former lama of ethnic Mongour origin from Qinghai, with the hope of winning over the lamas and using their influences to convert ordinary Mongols. The plan was unsuccessful due to the deep-rooted Buddhist beliefs of the nomads, and the missionaries were expelled from Lhasa to Canton in 1846.[14] Nonetheless, Gabet and Huc's account of this remarkable journey, *Travels in Tartary, Thibet and China, 1844–1846*, achieved immense success in Europe after its publication in 1850. Their vivid portrayal of the lives and people of the remote steppe captured their readers' imaginations and became an important source of inspiration for the future generations of Scheut missionaries from Belgium and Netherlands. As previously mentioned, these were Roman Catholic missionaries belonging to the Congregation of the Immaculate Heart of Mary or CICM (*Congregatio Immaculati Cordis Mariae*, Ch: *shengmu shengxin hui* 聖母聖心會) and were known as Scheutists after the Brussels suburb in which the congregation originated.

The fruitless endeavors among the Mongols forced the Lazarists to focus on their Chinese converts, most of whom were illiterate farmers from north China. At first, the missionary activities were restricted to the eastern Chakhar and Jehol regions. It was not until 1849 that the Lazarists took over the converts of southwestern Chakhar and Tümed plain from the Franciscans of Shanxi. Several new missions were organized that centered on the existing Catholic communities in these areas.[15] In terms of proselytizing method, the Lazarists focused on the training of native priests and catechists, who would make annual visits to the communities.[16] Attention was also paid to public works such as schools, orphanages, and famine relief. The first girls' school was founded in Xiwanzi in 1836, which was the earliest in all of China. The nurseries of Xiwanzi and Ershisanhao, established in 1862, were also the earliest Christian orphanages in the country. By the early 1860s, the practices of foot binding and child brides had been abolished among native converts even though they were still widely practiced in China proper and among Chinese migrants of Mongolia.[17] Thanks to the pioneering efforts of these missionaries, the remote Mongol periphery was turned into a forefront of Western civilization and social reforms that rivaled the coastal treaty ports in many ways.

The Lazarists encountered many difficulties in their missionary work. Official persecution persisted, so traveling priests and catechists had to disguise themselves as itinerant merchants to avoid official attention. Missionaries and converts were harassed, arrested, imprisoned, and banished. Meanwhile, disputes with non-Christians over tributes to temple festivals and other communal activities, coupled with the local officials' inability to handle them evenhandedly, forced the native Christians to move to remote mountainous areas.[18] Moreover, the geographical span of the vicariate hampered the mission given the sheer size of its administrative area and dispersion of Christian communities. When the Scheutists succeeded the Lazarists in 1865, there were 8,666 converts in the vicariate of Mongolia, who inhabited a vast region between Chaoyang (in the present Liaoning province) and Höhhot.[19]

The Scheut missionaries arrived at the threshold of a new era of evangelization. The second Opium War (1856–1860) opened the interior of China to foreign influences as never before. The Treaty of Tianjin (1858) granted the Western powers the right to station legations in Beijing, while allowing foreigners to travel in the interior of China. Article XIII of the Sino-French Treaty further asserted the right of Christians and missionaries to practice Christianity in the interior of China.[20] Moreover, the Chinese text of Article VI of the Convention of Beijing (1860) included a clause that permitted the missionaries to "rent and purchase land in all the Provinces, and to erect buildings thereon at pleasure."[21] It is generally believed that the clause was fraudulently inserted by the French priest undertaking translation, as it was not found in the original French version of the Convention.[22] Despite its questionable legality, the French legation managed to secure the follow-up Berthemy Convention (1865) and Gérard addition (1895), which reaffirmed the missionaries' rights to acquire land at will in the interior of China.[23]

As a result of these treaties, France established a protectorate over all Catholic missions in China, regardless of nationality, as well as the right to mediate the restitution of confiscated properties by communicating directly with the newly established Zongli Yamen (abbr. for *Zongli geguo shiwu yamen* or "Office in Charge of Affairs of All Nations") on behalf of native Christians. From 1861 on, France began to provide passports to all Catholic missionaries under her protection. The French protectorate greatly enhanced the prestige of the Catholic Church, which, coupled with the principle of extraterritoriality, gave the missionaries a "semi-official" status in dealing with local officials. It thus enabled them to protect the native converts and intervene in local politics and justice, as seen in the numerous disputes and lawsuits with the non-Christians that were known as "religious cases" (*jiao'an* 教案).[24]

Meanwhile, disagreement arose between the French and Qing authorities over the implementation of the treaties outside the Great Wall. Whereas the treaties guaranteed the missionaries the right to preach in the interior of China, opinions were divided regarding the connotation of the "interior" (*neidi* 內地). The French referred to it as the opposite of the "treaty ports," whereas in the Chinese context, the term was used interchangeably with the eighteen provinces of China proper vis-à-vis the Qing frontiers of Manchuria, Mongolia, and Tibet, which were considered off-bounds to the missionaries. In 1861, concerning a religious case in Fengzhen, the French interpreter Eugéne de Méritens asked the Zongli Yamen, "Since [Xikouwai] was not part of Mongolia, why was the treaty of our country not posted there?"[25] Obviously the French tried to distinguish the areas outside the western pass, which was inhabited by Chinese migrants administrated by rotational Qing officials, from the rest of Mongolia.

The Zongli Yamen, however, was reluctant to make such a distinction. After all, religious patronage had been an important tool used by the Qing to control the Tibetans and Mongols. It was one thing to make administrative fine-tuning to accommodate the growing Chinese population in Mongol territories, but it was quite another to integrate these territories into China proper on legal terms, which meant a fundamental change of its old policy of "divide and rule." In its reply dispatch, the officials suggested that the French consider not sending the notices because "the Mongols have long since believed in Tibetan Buddhism, and their territories were autonomously ruled by princes of the first and second ranks;" hence they "may not comply" to the French request.[26] As we will see in the following sections, the different interpretations of boundaries between the Chinese interior and Mongolia often turned out to be a source of dispute between the missionaries and local officials in the Han-Mongol borderlands outside the passes.

The Sino-French Convention inaugurated a new epoch of missionary enterprise, and the number of foreign missions sent to China proliferated. Among them was the Congregation of the Immaculate Heart of Mary, a Belgian order founded in 1862 that was dedicated to founding an orphanage in China for abandoned infants. Most of its members were young seminarians from Belgium and Holland, many of humble origins, who were as inspired by Huc and Gabet's best-selling account, *Travels in*

Tartary, Thibet and China, 1844–1846, as they were invigorated by the signing of the Convention. Rather than serving in narrow country parishes at home, they dreamed of an adventurous mission to the remote, exotic steppe.[27] In 1864, the congregation was entrusted by Rome with the Mongolian mission, with its founder Théophile Verbiest appointed as provicar apostolic (administrator of the vicariate apostolic). On December 6, 1865, Verbiest arrived at Xiwanzi with his three companions. They were to take over the eastern and central districts from the Lazarists, and after 1866, the western district as well.

In the initial years of transition, the Scheut fathers faced many challenges, including the cultural barrier, shortage of personnel and funds, and widespread drought, famine, and disease. Therefore, the focus of the mission remained one of nurturing existing Catholic communities rather than attempting new conversions.[28] Nonetheless, inspired by the ever-growing number of Chinese migrants pushing steadily into the grasslands, the missionaries soon recognized the importance of land for providing for the converts and sustaining the mission. Their opportunity came in 1870, when the Scheutists acquired large tracts of Chakhar pastureland through the hard-won Fengzhen case, thanks to the intervention of the French legation and the Zongli Yamen.

THE FENGZHEN CASE[29]

The religious case arose from the dispute over the plots of Huangyuwa at the foot of Mt. Daqingshan, under the jurisdiction of the Plain Yellow banner of Chakhar Right Flank and Fengzhen sub-prefecture under the Datong prefecture of Shanxi province. Some Catholic refugees from Zhili province began to move into this area around 1820, and by 1861, their community had expanded to seventy households and three hundred converts in four villages.[30] The Catholics rented hillside plots from a Mongol bannerman named Chengqi who inherited the lands as rewards granted to his ancestors for their military merits.[31] A dispute arose in 1859, as the owner demanded an increase of rent and successfully extracted 203 taels of silver from the Catholics by threat of force. In 1861, the case was brought to the French minister in Beijing, who notified the Zongli Yamen. Thanks to the foreign intervention, the Catholics were allowed to continue cultivating the plots, and the extorted silver was returned. Nonetheless, local officials refused to issue title deeds for these plots and ignored the missionaries' request for a land survey to determine their boundaries. Due to their delays and evasions, the dispute remained unsettled.[32]

Before probing into details of the Fengzhen case, it might be useful to first understand the changing land use and land ownership in the Chakhar region. The lands of Chakhar consisted of three main types. The first kind was private endowments of Manchu and Mongol princes and nobility, which were inheritable and accounted for 40 percent of the entire Chakhar lands. The second type was official pastures, including common pastures of the eight banners of Chakhar and breeding grounds for the imperial herds administered by the Court of Military Stud (*taipusi* 太僕寺) and Imperial Household Department (*neiwufu* 內務府). The third kind was "incense lands" (*xianghuodi* 香火地) that were the properties of Buddhist monasteries. Following the Qing conquest of Xinjiang in 1758, many official pastures fell into disuse as the demand for warhorses drastically shrank. The *taipusi* pastures were the first to open to cultivation, followed by the private pastures after 1771. Only in common pastures of the eight banners and monasteries was the ban in place, despite growing Chinese encroachment in these areas.[33]

We have mentioned earlier that Chinese migrants from Shanxi, Zhili, and Shaanxi began to advance into the grasslands in the eighteenth century. As their number expanded, escalating disputes arose between the Chinese migrants and the Mongol communities over competitive land use and murky land ownership. The influx of Chinese cultivators increasingly turned Mongol land from an inheritable estate and open grazing space into a tradable commodity on the market.

The Fengzhen case began as a dispute over ownership of the plots cultivated by the Catholic community between landlord Chengqi and a certain commander of a nearby banner company named Dagdanlosol. The official investigation confirmed that the plots were indeed situated within Chengqi's private pastures, although the actually borders remained undefined.[34] As one investigating official observed in 1872:

> The pastures outside the passes produced nothing but animals. In the past, although the lands were roughly marked with four bounds (*sizhi* 四至), there was no restriction on accessing them for nomadic usage. Prior to their opening for cultivation, the lands were treated as common properties with no specific ownership. Even Mongol officials and offspring of princes were unable to determine the boundaries of their lands. Therefore, it was not unusual that a piece of land was tilled for decades before its owner and the officials were even aware of it, so that it became as good as permanent property of the settlers. Once exposed to changing hands and disputes among younger generations, it became the source of endless feuds and conflicts.[35]

Apart from forces of commercialization, the role of Mongol and Manchu officials, clerks, and yamen runners in condoning and even encouraging rampant illegitimate cultivation cannot be overlooked. Many colluded with Chinese land brokers in selling common pastures. In this case, Dagdanlosol, the said commander, had cut deals with both the Catholics and non-Christian cultivators regarding the land sale.[36] Given the number of official personnel profiting from illegitimate cultivation, it was no wonder that they had little incentive to conduct land surveys or register plots for official taxation. For example, when a land survey was ordered, the missionaries accused the sub-prefect of Fengzhen of being directly involved in selling common pasturelands to Chinese settlers and attempting to bribe the Catholics into falsely claiming more plots than they cultivated.[37]

In 1869, the French minister Lucien de Rochechouart pressured the Zongli Yamen to settle the case as well as several other pending cases throughout the country.[38] The joint investigation by the local officials of Datong, Fengzhen, and Chakhar decided that landlord Chengqi was to forfeit his ownership of the plots permanently, a total of over three hundred *qing* of area, to the Catholics. A land survey ensued the next spring, and border ditches were dug under official supervision. In three more years, the plots became eligible for official taxation (*shengke* 升科), with a land tax of 0.014 tael of silver per *mu* applied.[39]

Thanks to the intervention of the French minister, the Catholics were able to secure their lands once and for all. Compared with the verdict of 1861 in which the Catholics were merely permitted to till these plots, the verdict of 1869 gave them actual ownership of the land, which was sanctioned by the Qing state through official survey, licensing, and taxation. This victory was substantial, given the context of over a century of governmental persecution against Christians as well as prohibition on illegitimate Chinese cultivation in Mongol territories. In both cases, the cultivators' claim to the property were insecure and liable to forfeiture. The French intervention not only confirmed the Catholics' right of land use, but it also secured them the right to purchase and own Mongol land, which was hitherto denied to all Chinese cultivators. Thus, what started as a dispute between two owners laying claims to the same piece of land ended in the expropriation of the rightful owner. Over the long term, this would become one of the cracks that eventually led to the crumbling of the Mongol property regime that the Qing had endeavored to preserve.

The verdict of 1869 was not the end of the story. New complexities soon arose, due to controversy over ownership of the Catholic plots. The missionary Remi Verlinden asserted that the title deeds should be issued to the Church in compensation for the confiscated church properties since the Jiaqing era (1796–1820). Besides, the Church had spent twenty-five hundred taels of silver on litigation over the years. However, the local officials insisted on issuing the deeds to individual converts. They argued that this was a matter of "national polity" (*guoti* 國體), for it was stipulated in the treaties that foreigners were not allowed to possess Chinese land. For them, it was one thing to grant lands to converts who were Chinese subjects; but it was another to hand them over to the foreign Church, especially in strategic frontier regions such as Chakhar. For the same reason, the local officials refused to comply with Verlinden's request for land deeds for two other tracts of land that the converts purchased. Instead, the officials accused the missionaries of being greedy and fickle. The real reason for this accusation, as revealed by the prefect of Datong in his report to the governor of Shanxi, was that these tracts were several times the size of the said Catholic plots, and three coal pits were located within their bounds.[40] In a resource-rich province like Shanxi, it is not surprising that local officials would jealously guard mineral resources against possible foreign encroachment. The French minister traveled to Fengzhen and debated in person with the local officials, but to no avail. Beijing was behind Shanxi on this matter and urged the missionaries to refrain from interfering in the local affairs.[41] In the end, a tacit compromise was reached in 1872. Title deeds were issued to individual converts who then handed them over to the Catholic Church.[42]

Meanwhile, violence broke out on the local scene. In May 1871, the converts complained to the local official about being attacked by a mob of over two hundred men from nearby villages. Several converts were wounded. A joint court of Shanxi, Zhili, and Chakhar was summoned. The dispute centered on a tract of land granted to the Catholics, which the villagers claimed to have leased from Dagdanlosol in 1863. After the plot was assigned to the Catholics, the villagers attempted to redeem it by cutting a deal with two underlings of the commander, who then pocketed the money without delivering the land as promised. The investigating officials convicted the two underlings of fraud and ordered that the money be restored to the villagers and the converts retain the land.[43] Although it favored the converts and the Church, the arbitration barely scratched the surface of the problem of leasing one plot to more than one tenant.

The conflict was renewed a year later. In May 1872, Verlinden reported another incident of violence associated with the same villagers, in which a missionary named Alfons Devos was severely injured and thrown into a cesspit with his hands and feet tied up.[44] The dispute again concerned the problematic boundaries of the Catholic plots. The villagers accused the converts of bribing Dagdanlosol, who oversaw the digging of border ditches in 1870, into misappropriating a tract of land that they had cultivated for decades.[45] The said plot belonged to the taxable croplands (*shengke liangdi* 升科糧地) sanctioned by the Qing state, which were presumably part of the official pastures put under cultivation since the early nineteenth century. Verlinden contended that Dagdanlosol had assigned the plot to compensate the Church for the two other tracts of pasturelands that the Catholics purchased but were denied by local officials.[46] Interestingly, both the Catholics and non-Christians blamed Dagdanlosol for secretly making deals with the other side, which was probably the case.

The joint court, headed by officials of Zhili province, was sympathetic to the villagers' appeals. Without the plots, they reasoned, hundreds of households would be deprived of their livelihoods, which would lead to more disturbances.[47] The governor-general of Zhili, Li Hongzhang (1823–1901), a leading reformist official in the 1860s, was in favor of cultivating Mongol pastures to combat foreign influences. Compared with their more conservative counterparts in Shanxi province, the local officials of Zhili demonstrated a degree of flexibility and a readiness to compromise in order to settle the disputes, although the verdict of 1872 was not to be reversed. In the end, another compromise was arranged in which an uncultivated tract within the nearby croplands was assigned to the villagers in compensation for their loss.[48]

Thus, the decade-long Fengzhen case finally drew to a close, with the Church obtaining the de facto ownership of three hundred *qing* (two thousand ha) of lands in the heartland of Chakhar. The missionaries resold the plots to Catholic converts for three thousand taels of silver and used the money to establish a new mission in Xiyingzi (a.k.a Nanhaoqian, present Shangyi county, Hebei province), which became a crucial Catholic settlement in central Inner Mongolia.[49] The land acquisition not only enhanced the Church's prestige, but also facilitated its expansion into the western part of Inner Mongolia. As Verlinden and Devos later undertook the exploratory mission in the Ordos and Alasha regions, their negotiating experience with the Mongols, Chinese settlers, and local officials in Fengzhen certainly helped their adventure into these new territories. They also introduced a new evangelizing strategy through land acquisition that differed from the earlier method focusing on catechizing and preaching.

Meanwhile, the Fengzhen case brought about significant repercussions in the Qing policy regarding the Mongol frontier. Being the first religious case centering on land disputes outside the passes, it represented an urge to enforce state regulation in standardizing land survey, boundary demarcation, and tax registration to combat pervasive illegitimate cultivation controlled by local agents such as Chinese land brokers and Mongol and Manchu officials and personnel. By necessitating the intervention of the Zongli Yamen in settling local disputes, the foreign presence effectively facilitated state penetration into the frontier society.

Further, the Church's craving for lands led to a reassessment of the time-honored "closing off" policy in Mongolia. The Fengzhen case triggered a vigorous debate in 1871 among provincial officials in responding to the foreign encroachment on the Mongol frontier. To prevent the infringement of the Church, both authorities of Shanxi and Chakhar, in accordance with the Zongli Yamen, were in favor of enforcing the ban in pasturelands not yet opened up. In contrast, Governor-general Li Hongzhang of Zhili pointed out that underlying the rampant illegal reclamation were the issue of the decline of the pastoral economy and the poverty of Mongol herders, and he proposed opening up Mongol pasturelands for Chinese cultivation as a means to curtail foreign influence while providing livelihood for the Mongols.[50] The discrepancy reflected the parting of ways between the conservative and reformist factions of the imperial court. Although Li had to back up from his position due to opposition from Shanxi and Chakhar, his proposal was a prelude to the reversal of Qing policies in Chakhar.[51] By 1879, uncultivated pastures of the Chakhar Left Flank had been officially put under plow, followed by the creation of the Reclamation Bureau of Fengzhen and Ningyuan in the Chakhar Right Flank in 1882. These reversals of Qing policy served as precursors to the full-scale reclamation of Mongol pastures in 1902.[52]

MISSIONS TO THE WEST

The new settlement of Xiyingzi, situated on the caravan route from Höhhot to Beijing, became a pivotal base for the Catholic Church's westward expansion. A European-style church, funded by the proceeds of the land sale of Fengzhen, was built in 1872, with the hope of attracting the attention of Mongol princes, pilgrims, and caravans on their journey to the capital.[53] Sure enough, it impressed two jasags who were passing by—Gungsangjürmid of the Alasha banner and Janagardi of the

Jüüngar banner of Ordos—to the extent that they invited the missionaries to visit their headquarters in early 1873.[54]

A sequence of events in the 1860s and 1870s had made the Ordos an ideal place for missionary expansion. It was a main battlefield during the Dungan/Hui Uprising and its subsequent Qing suppression (1862–1877), which left the entire region in ruin.[55] The Otog banner lost over half of its population, and the Khanggin and Üüshin banners also suffered great casualties, with livestock looted by Hui rebels or commandeered by the Qing troops. The rebels ravaged Ningtiaoliang, the Chinese market town in southern Ordos, and nearly wiped out its population through slaughter or suicide. The combat left many monasteries demolished and lamas dispersed.[56] The brutal warfare was followed by the great famine of 1876 through 1879 that swept across the provinces of Shanxi, Henan, Shandong, Zhili, and Shaanxi. The famine was caused by severe drought and back-to-back harvest failures, which resulted in the demise of nine million to thirteen million people. Over one-third of Shanxi's population perished, and in some counties, the population loss was as high as 80 percent.[57] The death toll was also high in northern Shaanxi, which had already suffered serious population loss during the Hui Rebellion. The catastrophe left the official granary system in havoc, which was a system that had been vital in providing emergency relief.[58] The presence of a destitute populace devastated by war and famine, coupled with weakened religious adversaries, provided a unique opportunity for the expansion of the Catholic Church, as it offered much needed relief to refugees and helped restore morale and social order.

In February 1874, Verlinden and Devos undertook an expedition from Xiyingzi to the Ordos and reached the headquarters of Janagardi in the Jüüngar banner, where they received a warm welcome. In April, the missionaries crossed the plain of Boro-Balgasun ("gray city," in the present Otog Front banner of Ordos municipality, Inner Mongolia). Lying north of the Great Wall, the plain got its Chinese name, Chengchuan, from a ruined walled city of Youzhou dating back to the ninth century. Unknown to the Scheutists, a small Catholic community had thrived since 1750 in Ningtiaoliang, the nearby Chinese market town. The Friars Minors used to visit them from Xi'an before the invasion of the Hui rebels, which reduced the Catholic community from two hundred members to forty members. In July 1874, at the site of a ruined farm estate in Boro-Balgasun, the Scheutists established the first Ordos mission and a fortified settlement.[59]

The initial target was to convert the Mongols. The missionaries learned Mongolian and adapted to their customs by wearing fur-lined robes, drinking milk tea, living in felt tents, and going about on horseback. They succeeded in converting several Mongol households by offering them livestock and free medicine. In 1875, the missionaries obtained permission from the authorities of the Otog banner to cultivate a tract of land east of Boro-Balgasun, where they settled a number of destitute Mongol herders along with some Chinese households from northern Shaanxi who were registered as naturalized Mongols. They were provided with livestock, agricultural tools, and seed-grains.[60] Later, with the help of Samdanjamba, a lama-turned convert originally from Qinghai who accompanied Huc and Gabet on their journey, the missionaries successfully converted several local lamas and a group of migrant Mongols from Qinghai.[61]

During the great famine, the Catholic missionaries' relief work attracted many Mongol and Chinese converts, whose number reached one hundred households at one point but dropped sharply afterwards. Meanwhile, there were many aban-doned children on the streets of Ningtiaoliang due to the famine. The missionaries took these orphans in and arranged to have them raised by childless Mongols. By 1880, the number of converts in Boro-Balgasun had increased to forty households, comprised of a mixed group of uprooted migrants from other parts of the Ordos as well as Chakhar, Alasha, and Qinghai. Therefore, the Mongols of Boro-Balgasun were called *alag* ("mixed-blooded") Mongols.[62] This unique intersection of ethnic groups and cultures, combined with the conjuncture of human and natural disas-ters, contributed to the survival of the Mongol mission in the southern Ordos. It remains to this day the single surviving Catholic mission among the Mongols of Inner Mongolia.[63]

Figure 5.1. Catholic Church of Chengchuan (Boro-Balgasun), Otog Front Banner, Or-dos, Inner Mongolia. The church was first constructed in 1882 and destroyed in 1900. It was rebuilt in 1906 and again demolished in 1966. The church was rebuilt at its current location in 1988.
Photo by the author

Figure 5.2. Msgr. Giuseppe Ma Zhongmu Tegüsbilig (1919–2020) of Chengchuan Church, 2005. Bishop Ma was the only bishop of Mongolian ethnicity.
Photo by the author

Elsewhere across the Ordos and Alasha regions, the Scheutists' presence drew such strong opposition that they were either unable to obtain any foothold or their missions were destroyed and the converts dispersed.[64] In contrast, missions created among Chinese migrants such as in Ajirma (1875) of the Jüüngar banner, Sandaohe (1876) of the Alasha banner, and Ligangbu (1880) and Xiayingzi (1881) of Ningxia all survived.[65] As the Scheutists soon came to realize, the Mongols' entrenched belief in Gelugpa Buddhism and the jasag system created an unsurpassable barrier for their missionary activities. The fierce Mongol resistance forced them to shift attention to Chinese migrants, whose status as uprooted refugees made them more susceptible to conversion.

While en route to the court of the Prince of Alasha, the Scheutist missionaries crossed the fertile plain of Sandaohe (in the present Dengkou county, Inner Mongolia) on the left bank of the Yellow River. This well-irrigated area was first opened to cultivation in the early 1700s. Vegetable fields were planted for a Manchu princess who married the Prince of Alasha.[66] By the 1820s, over 1,190 *qing* (approximately eight thousand ha) of pastures had been brought under cultivation. Trade and commerce flourished in the area due to its location on the trade route between Baotou and Ningxia and its easy access to river transportation, so that the area was dotted with Chinese shops and farm estates owned by merchants from Shanxi and Shaanxi.

Figure 5.3.   Sanshenggong Catholic Church, Dengkou county, Bayan Nuur, Inner Mongolia. The gothic church was completed in 1893. Its inscription, *"wanyou zhenyuan"* (The origin of the universe), and couplets hung on the columns that read *"wushi wuzhong zhenzhuzai, xuanren xuanyi daquanheng"* (Ever existing king forever and ever; Savior of charity, God of power), were written by the Kangxi Emperor for the North Church of Beijing in 1693.
Photo by the author

Most of these, however, were destroyed during the Hui revolt, with only four hundred *qing* of cultivated lands left by the mid-1870s.[67] In 1876, Devos purchased two abandoned farm estates in Sandaohe through a Hui merchant. By 1880, more farm estates and shops had been acquired and the Catholic settlements rapidly expanded. These enclaves generally bore the old name of previous Chinese shops such as Jinhengxi, Hongshengyi, and Sanshenggong, which were reminiscent of the prosperity of the region before the 1860s. During the great famine, the Sandaohe mission provided a sanctuary for hundreds of converts, who moved there from the famine-stricken areas of northeastern Ordos (Ajirma) and southwestern Chakhar (Daihai plain).[68]

This movement of people attracted official attention. In 1878, local officials of Ningxia notified the governor-general of Shaanxi-Gansu, Zuo Zongtang, of the Catholic settlement and of missionaries who were purchasing food provisions in the market town inside the passes. Later that year, Zuo dispatched two subordinates to check the foreigners' passports. Their report provides first-hand observations of the Catholic settlements and the daily life of the converts:

Anyone who would willingly follow their teachings, whether male or female, young or old, would be accepted, with their names and number of family members registered. Each of them is provided daily food ration, as long as they chant prayers. There were about three hundred followers in total, who have resided here for the past [three] years. Not counting women and children, there were around a hundred adult men . . . Every morning, between 3 and 5 o'clock, all assemble to chant prayers. After daybreak, men cultivate the fields, children study, and women sew. At night, they gather to pray once more. The houses that they reside include old structures and new buildings. Each follower is given 1.5 *dou* of millet and 1 *jin* of rapeseed oil every month. Children under the age of six receive 2.5 *ge* of millet every day, and those under the age of three receive none. All due taxes and levies on the lands they cultivate are paid . . . When inspecting their residences, we saw various farming equipment, but not many cattle, horses, or sheep.[69]

As the officials observed, new converts were provided with land, food rations, draft animals, farming implements, and seed grains, which were to be paid back in kind to the Church after the fall harvest. Usually 30 percent of the harvest was required to be paid back. In turn, the Church was responsible for paying all state taxes and duties incurred.[70] This approach proved attractive to new converts, especially during the famine. As one missionary put it, "Two particular circumstances were conducive to the development of agricultural colonies: the availability of cheap arable land after the Hui uprising and the crossing of the Great Wall by many land-poor farmers and victims of natural calamities."[71] By the early 1880s, a string of Catholic villages were flourishing on the left bank of the Yellow River.

The CICM historian Joseph van Hecken compares the Scheut missions of southwest Mongolia to the Jesuit reductions of Paraguay.[72] The settlements organized by the Jesuits among indigenous people of Latin America during the seventeenth and eighteenth centuries provided a remarkable precedent for the Scheut missions. The Scheutists, like the Jesuits, organized self-sufficient colonies in a predominantly nomadic frontier region. They assumed the roles of community manager, magistrate, and educator while organizing public works and self-defense militias against bandits and other hostile invaders. Their Catholic villages, like the Jesuit reductions or settlements for indigenous people, achieved a high degree of autonomy and considerable economic success. Even the layout was similar: both communities were centered on the church and surrounded by the residences of converts.

Unlike previous Catholic communities outside the passes that were shaped by the spontaneous migration of converts, the new settlements were the result of calculated moves to attract new converts through land acquisition, the transplantation of converts, and the use of famine relief. Later, these strategies were applied to expanding Catholic mission work in the Ordos. In the southern Ordos, the missionaries turned their attention to famine-stricken Chinese refugees assembling in the Black Border lands (the fifty-*li* Marker Border). Most of these refugees came from northern Shaanxi. Although the Mongol mission of Boro-Balgasun was created in 1875, severe friction between Mongol herders and Chinese farmers obliged the Scheutists to maintain two separate mission stations. In 1878, Jan-Baptist Steenackers rented fifty *qing* of cultivated land inside the Black Border from Chinese merchants and established the Chinese mission station of Xiaoqiaopan (in the present Jingbian county, Shaanxi province).[73]

In the northeastern Ordos, the barren, poorly irrigated land and impoverished converts made the Ajirma mission difficult to sustain. In 1880, the Chinese priest Lu Dianying sub-leased a tract of land near the Yellow River and built a new mission called Ershisiqingdi (in the present Tümed Right banner, Inner Mongolia). It was located in the heavily disputed area between the Dalad and Tümed banners following a shift in the course of the Yellow River in 1863. Finally, the two banners accepted the mediation of the Lifanyuan that divided the area into ten parts, with the Tümed banner obtaining six and the Dalad banner obtaining four. The Ershisiqingdi mission was situated in the six-part territory (*liuchengdi* 六成地) that belonged to the Tümed banner. Its name, meaning "Twenty-four *qing* of land," was derived from a rough estimation of its area carried out by a ride on horseback, as the Mongols would typically do. The actual acreage, officially measured in 1887, was well over one hundred *qing*.[74]

In 1883, the vicariate of Mongolia was divided into three independent vicariates: central, east, and southwest. By then, the Scheutist missionaries had established three bases in the far-west Ordos and Alasha regions: two Chinese missions along the Yellow River (Sandaohe, Ershisiqingdi) and a mixed Mongol-Han mission on the edge of the Great Wall (Boro-Balgasun, Xiaoqiaopan), with around fifteen hundred converts.[75] All three missions had seen considerable Chinese cultivation prior to the arrival of the Europeans, which led to the growing privatization and commercialization of Mongol lands. As a result, land was increasingly alienated from the pastoral usage of the Mongols and turned into a commodity on the market controlled by a group of Chinese or Hui land brokers. Most lands acquired by the Church, often through the mediation of these land brokers, were not uncultivated pasturelands but plots already under plow by Chinese migrants. In the Black Border lands along the Great Wall where the only Mongol mission, Boro-Balgasun, was located, the Mongols had long been exposed to Chinese-style agriculture and had adapted to a semi-nomadic and semi-settled lifestyle. In this sense, Chinese migration had paved the way for missionary enterprises in the Mongol territories and provided potential converts for their expansion.

The crisscrossing boundaries existed not just between grazing and farming, but also among multiple forms of political and symbolic control. As the following table shows, the ecclesiastical boundaries defined by Rome did not coincide with any of the Mongol, Chinese, or Manchu administrative boundaries. This discrepancy between the boundaries added yet another layer of complexity to the intricacy created by ongoing Chinese migration.

The boundaries of the southwest Mongolia vicariate were especially complicated. Most of the territories it encompassed were ruled by semi-autonomous Mongol jasags, whereas the Chinese migrants were administered by sub-prefectures under adjacent Gansu, Shanxi, and Shaanxi provinces, along with the Lifanyuan

Table 5.1. Ecclesial and Administrative Boundaries of Central-Western Inner Mongolia

Ecclesial			Mongol Admin		Han Civil Admin		Lifanyuan Admin
Vicariate	District	Mission	Banner	League	ting	Province	
Central	Xiwanzi	Xiwanzi	–	–	Zhangjiakou	Zhili	Chakhar DT*
Central	Fengzhen	Xiyingzi	Chakhar PY	–	Zhangjiakou	Zhili	Chakhar DT
Central		Ershisanhao	Chakhar PY	–	Fengzhen	Shanxi	Chakhar DT
Central		Daihai plain	Chakhar PY	–	Ningyuan	Shanxi	Chakhar DT
Central	Höhhot	Höhhot	–	–	Höhhot	Shanxi	Suiyuan JJ
Central	Höhhot	Houba	Dörben Kheükhed	Ulaan/chab	Höhhot	Shanxi	Suiyuan JJ
Southwest	Ershisi-qingdi	Hejiao	Muumingghan	Ulaan/chab	Sarachi	Shanxi	Suiyuan JJ
Southwest	Ershisi-qingdi	Ershisi/qingdi	Tümed R	–	Sarachi	Shanxi	Suiyuan JJ
Southwest	Ershisi-qingdi	Balagai	Tümed R		Sarachi	Shanxi	Suiyuan JJ
Southwest	Ershisi-qingdi	Chengkui-haizi	Jüüngar	Ordos	Togtokhu	Shanxi	Shenmu SY
Southwest	Ershisi-qingdi	Xiaonao'er	Dalad	Ordos	Sarachi	Shanxi	Shenmu SY
Southwest	Sandaohe	Olan Bohereg	Dalad	Ordos	Sarachi	Shanxi	Shenmu SY
Southwest	Ningtiao-liang	Bagha Shibar	Üüshin	Ordos	Anbian	Shaanxi	Shenmu SY
Southwest	Ningtiao-liang	Boro-Balgasun	Otog	Ordos	Anbian	Shaanxi	Ningxia SY
Southwest	Ningtiao-liang	Xiaoqiaopan	Otog	Ordos	Anbian	Shaanxi	Ningxia SY
Southwest	Sandaohe	Sansheng/gong	Alasha	–	Ningxia	Gansu	Ningxia SY
Southwest	Sandaohe	Xiayingzi	–		Pingluo	Gansu	Ningxia SY

Sources: Chang Fei, *Tianzhujiao suiyuan jiaoqu chuanjiao jianshi*; Taveirne, *Han-Mongol Encounters and Missionary Endeavors*; Verhelst, "Th. Verbist and CICM Pioneers," in Ku Weiying ed., *Saiwai chuanjiao shi*, 125–280; Lievens, "The Spread of the CICM Mission in the Apostolic Vicariate of Central Mongolia (1865–1911): A General Overview," in Walle, *The History of the Relations Between the Low Countries and China in the Qing Era (1644–1911)*, 301–24.
*DT = *dutong* (lieutenant-governor), JJ = *jiangjun* (military governor), SY = *lishi siyuan* (superintendent).

superintendents based at Shenmu and Ningxia. The incongruity of administrative and ecclesiastical boundaries was indicative of the multilayered identities of this borderland under transition, where various forces competed for power and control. The power dynamics at play and the ambiguity and fluidity of boundaries turned out to be advantageous to the spread of the foreign doctrine. As we have seen, the Catholic missions were often situated on geographic or ethnic frontier zones, or on border areas between two adjacent banners, as compared to Mongolia proper or Chinese market towns. Geographical isolation helped shelter the missionaries and converts from the intervention of Manchu and Mongol authorities and from the influences of Buddhist monasteries and Chinese gentry elites.

RESISTANCE AND CONFRONTATION

Despite their success among land-poor Chinese migrants, the Scheutists met strong opposition from other social groups in western Inner Mongolia. The deep-seated religious belief and decentralized jasag system of the Mongols caused difficulties for their missionary activities. Other than the Mongol nobles and lamas, Manchu and Chinese local officials, Chinese merchants, and gentry elites also jealously guarded their political and commercial privileges against possible foreign infringement. The resistance that the missionaries encountered in the Höhhot and Ordos regions departed distinctly from the resistance they met in the Chakhar region, and therefore, it merits separate discussion.

In Höhhot, the buzzing market town and political and religious center outside the passes, the Manchu government represented a major obstacle for the missionary activities. Even with the withdrawal of the imperial proscription against Christianity in 1846, official persecution of native priests and converts persisted into the 1860s.[76] In 1873, the Scheutists purchased a vacant property outside the town for a procuring base to supply necessities for missions in the Ordos and beyond. Yet the sub-prefect of Höhhot nullified the transaction, imprisoned the seller, and posted placards prohibiting Han Chinese to trade with missionaries except for the purpose of supplying provisions.[77] The same ban was applicable to a Belgian merchant named Paul Splingaerd, who arrived in Höhhot from Kalgan and cofounded a trading firm.[78] The French and German legations protested to the Zongli Yamen about the breach of treaties.

In response to the ensued official investigation, the local officials produced two public petitions opposing foreign religion and trade. The first petition came from local Tümed Mongols and lamas, who were devout Buddhist adherents. They expressed concerns about the spread of foreign doctrine that conflicted with their own beliefs and customs, and argued that the presence of foreigners would only stir up thugs and bandits and give them pretenses to trick or agitate people and cause troubles. The second petition, signed by 841 registered Chinese and Hui firms, emphasized the detrimental impact of foreign trade upon the local economy. It cited the demise of Chinese trade in Kalgan due to foreign competition. Over one hundred firms were forced out of business, particularly those dealing in tea and cotton fabrics. The same fate befell several other trading towns on the route to Xinjiang and Mongolia. Therefore, the merchants petitioned against the presence of foreign traders in the town of Höhhot.[79]

The concerns of these groups were real and legitimate. During the 1860s, a series of unequal treaties opened the northern frontier of the Qing empire to Russian influences and granted favorable terms to Russian merchants. In addition to duty-free trade throughout Mongolia, the merchants received tax reduction and exemption along the trade route from Kyakhta to Tianjin via Kalgan.[80] Later, duty-free trade was extended to Xinjiang, whereas trade routes from interior China to Xinjiang were cut off for over a decade during the Hui Rebellion.[81] The Russians' treaty privileges, along with their cheap, machinery-manufactured products, shattered the commercial dominance of the Shanxi firms in these regions. In the 1850s, Russian firms based in Tianjin and Kalgan started to source tea directly from its origin by establishing factories in Hankou, Fuzhou, and Jiujiang, and their products took over a good proportion of markets in Mongolia and Xinjiang. The Russian scholar Pozdneyev reported that in 1893, dozens of Chinese tea firms in Höhhot had gone bankrupt because of Russian competition. He also reported that foreign textiles had completely dominated the market of Höhhot.[82]

Figure 5.4.   Catholic Church of Höhhot, Inner Mongolia. The Romanesque church was completed in 1924.
Photo by the author

After the Zongli Yamen intervened, the case ended in the concession of local officials in 1875, and a chapel was built on the site of the disputed property.[83] Antagonism against the Church remained strong among local officials and gentry elites, and thus a sizeable Catholic community never developed in Höhhot.[84] The Scheutists' proselytizing efforts in other trading centers such as Dingyuanying (in Alasha banner) and Baotou also met with little success.[85] However, it was in the banners where they encountered the fiercest opposition from the Mongol nobility and clergy. Among these, the dispute with the Üüshin banner from the 1870s to 1890s was noteworthy, which demonstrated the decline of the nomadic order under the double impact of Chinese migration and foreign aggression.

In 1876, Verlinden established a small mission in Wulong in the Üüshin banner. The foreign settlement incited hostility from local nobles and lamas, where several incidents occurred in which the converts were beaten and their horses stolen. The banner officials turned deaf ears toward the missionaries' protests. In 1878, the missionaries filed a complaint to the Zongli Yamen against the jasag of the Üüshin banner and incumbent governor of the Yekhe Juu league.[86] Meanwhile, another incident of a more serious nature occurred. A group of Mongols led by a Üüshin noble burned down the Wulong mission and dispersed the converts. It turned out that they were also responsible for a previous disturbance in the adjacent Otog banner, in which over one hundred Üüshin Mongols looted the converts and occupied a tract of land granted to the mission by the jasag of the Otog banner.[87]

Following a joint official investigation, the jasag agreed to punish a lama, a *janggi*, and several others for stealing horses from the mission compound, but he denied all allegations about looting and burning of the church or harassment of converts. The feud reportedly arose from an incident in 1876 in which Steenackers shot and killed the dog of a Mongol noble named Damrinjab as it attacked his horse. The enraged noble had the missionary tied up, his beard plucked, and his Mongol companion badly beaten.[88] Steenackers was further accused of being heterodox for not abiding by the treaties and the king's rule (*wanghua* 王化). In the end, the Lifanyuan dismissed the case as a trifling matter of no particular importance.[89] Thus the dispute ended up in the demise of the Wulong mission. It was one of the rare occasions in which the intervention of the French legation and Qing high authority failed to overturn the decision made on the local level, due to the autonomy of Mongol jasags over their domain backed by Lifanyuan officials keen to preserve the existing social and political order.[90]

Patrick Taveirne attributes this missionary failure to the "inexperience of missionaries and subsequent harassment of Mongol converts by local authorities and lamas, the apparent indifference of the Chinggisid and Lamaist nobles to the tenets of the Catholic teaching, and the lack of financial resources."[91] Although his argument offers insight into the unsuccessful proselytizing endeavors among the Mongols in general, there were deeper institutional and cultural motives underlying the Mongol hostility against the foreign mission. First, harassments against Mongol converts need to be viewed against the feudal-like rule of jasags and high lamas, which prescribed that commoners (*albatu*, "persons with duty") and serfs (*shabinar*, "disciples") were personally bonded to their masters through duties such as military services, corvée labor, and taxes, and they were unable to legally depart from the banner they were born into or the monastery to which they belonged.[92] From the perspective of the Mongols, the Christian doctrines, especially the absolute loyalty to God and egalitarianism they promoted, were subversive to the secular and ecclesiastic order of Mongol society by eroding the base of rule of the nobility and high lamas. Second, the entrenched belief of Tibetan Buddhism and strong attachment to the Chinggisid cult posed a major obstacle to the spread of Christianity among the Mongols. As mentioned in chapter 1, the Manchu court had long fostered Gelugpa Buddhism as a form of sociopolitical control in Mongolia. At its peak in the late Qing era, there were 243 monasteries in the Ordos, with approximately twenty thousand resident lamas. Considering the total population numbered around eighty thousand, lamas comprised over half of the adult male population.[93] Besides

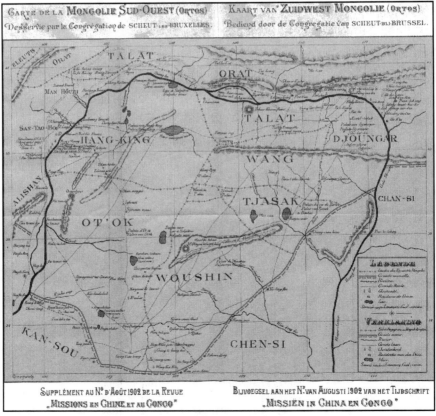

Figure 5.5.   C.I.C.M. map of southwest Mongolia (Ordos) vicariate, 1902.
Courtesy of Staatsbibliothek zu Berlin – Preussischer Kulturbesitz, Orientalabteilung

the Buddhist institution, the ancestor cult of Chinggis Khan also held strong in the Ordos, which was the locus of the Eight White Tents, the Mausoleum and sacred shrine of the great Khan.[94]

Although structural factors may have explained the Mongols' immunity to the Catholic teaching, it often took some specific conjuncture to turn clashes of cultural ideas into physical violence. As the Üüshin case shows, part of the Mongol antagonism was derived from their grudges against the growing Chinese encroachment of Mongol pastures. Although the circumstances surrounding the establishment of Wulong mission remained unclear, it can be conjectured that the land was not acquired with the consent of the jasag, whom the missionaries described as "long detesting Catholicism."[95] It was likely that it was subleased from some Chinese migrants from Jiazhou of Shaanxi who inhabited the area.[96] The missionaries used the land to settle famine-stricken Chinese converts from northern Shaanxi, as they had done in the Otog banner. It was therefore probable that the Chinese infringement of Mongol pastures ignited the violence that led to the demise of the Wulong mission.[97]

EXPANSION AND CONFLICTS

Starting from the 1880s, circumstances in the international arena became more favorable for the Church's expansion. With the end of the Sino-French War (1884–1885), Beijing was not in a hurry to resume diplomatic disputes over missionary affairs. The subsequent agreements concluded between French legations and the Zongli Yamen granted the Catholic Church greater liberty in acquiring land and properties in the Chinese interior. Although the Berthemy Convention (1865) stipulated that local authorities should be notified before the completion of any transaction, the Gérard addition (1895) made it clear that no such authorization was necessary.[98]

By 1892, the vicariate of southwest Mongolia was divided into three ecclesiastical districts: Sandaohe, Ershisiqingdi, and Ningtiaoliang. Each district had experienced considerable expansion in the previous decade through the acquisition of Mongol lands for settling Chinese converts. Table 5.2 lists the missions and approximate acreage of land acquired in southwest Mongolia prior to 1900 (the names of main churches with resident priests are marked in bold).

The table shows that twenty out of the thirty missions of southwest Mongolia were formed between 1885 and 1900, and that 1,052 *qing* out of the total 1,426.5 *qing* of lands (i.e., over two-thirds) were acquired during this period. The number of converts grew threefold from 1,657 in 1885 to 5,680 in 1900.[99] Thus, Catholic communities flourished in the well-irrigated areas of Sandaohe and Ershisiqingdi, which were both located in the vicinity of the Yellow River. In contrast, the expansion in southwest Ordos near the Great Wall was relatively limited due to the inadequate land resources, the underdevelopment of the land market, and the absence of a full-fledged land merchant class there. Nevertheless, the missionaries managed to

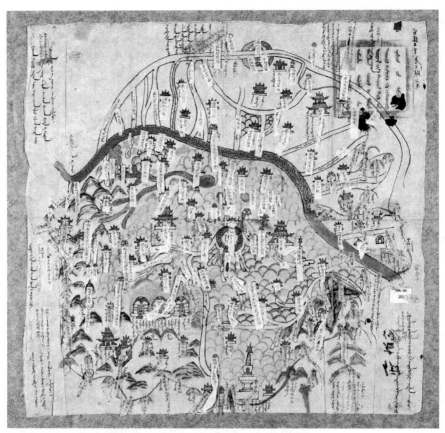

Figure 5.6.   Manuscript map of Ordos, 1911.
Courtesy of Staatsbibliothek zu Berlin—Preussischer Kulturbesitz, Orientabteilung, Manuskriptkarte SBB-IIIE

establish two footholds in the pastoral areas of the Otog and Üüshin banners, albeit not without struggles, which we shall recount later in this chapter.

Besides land acquisition, natural disasters also contributed to the expansion of the Church in southwest Mongolia. As one Scheutist put it, "famine is a good harvest for God."[100] The famine of 1891–1892 brought waves of conversion, and seven new mission stations were established near Ershisiqingdi. The depressed land prices made land acquisition easier. In some cases, entire villages were converted.[101] During the severe drought of 1899–1900, the district saw such a surge of converts that Bishop Ferdinand Hamer decided to move the headquarters there from Sandaohe in the spring of 1900. As many of the converts were attracted by the material benefits offered by the Church, they were often contemptuously referred to as "millet

Table 5.2.   Missions and Land Acquisition of Congregatio Immaculati Cordis Mariae (CICM) in Southwest Mongolia, 1874–1898

District	Year	Mission	Location	Acreage (qing)	Total (qing)
Sandaohe	1876	Dongtang	Alasha	60	
	1877	Shengmutang	Alasha	–	
	1878	Jiudi	Alasha	–	
	1879	Xingshengyang	Alasha	50	
	1880	**Sanshenggong**	Alasha	–	
	1894	Nanliangtai	Alasha	60	
	1894	Tianxingquan	Alasha	–	
	1880	Ligangbu	Pingluo	32	
	1881	**Xiayingzi**	Pingluo	82.5	
	1885	Yulongyong	Dalad	50	
	1890	**Dafagong**	Dalad	120	454.5
Ershisiqingdi	1887	**Xiaonao'er**	Dalad	360	
	1891	Dalamayaozi	Dalad	–	
	1891	Gaoshangyaozi	Dalad	–	
	1892	**Yinjiangyaozi**	Dalad	60	
	1892	Danao'er	Dalad	–	
	1891	**Chengkuihaizi**	Jüüngar	40	
	1899	Jiangjunyaozi	Jüüngar	40	
	1880	**Ershisiqingdi**	Tümed	100	
	1894	Balagai	Tümed	120	
	1897	Gangfangyingzi	Tümed	20	
	1898	Daifuyingzi	Tümed	–	
	1899	Rensanyaozi	Tümed	20	
	1893	Hejiao	Muumingghan	12	772
Ningtiaoliang	1874	**Boro-Balgasun**	Otog	50	
	1878	**Xiaoqiaopan**	Otog	?	
	1890	Ningdiliangzi	Otog	50	
	1895	Dayangwan	Otog	100	
	1895	Köber	Otog	?	
	1898	Bagha Shibar	Üüshin	–	200+
Total (qing)					**1,426.5**

Source: Carlo Van Melckebeke, *Bianjiang gongjiao shehui shiye*; Chang Fei, *Tianzhujiao suiyuan jiaoqu chuanjiao jianshi*; "*Hetao jiaoqu chuanjiao yange*," 233–56; *Jiaowu jiao'an dang*, ser. 7, vol. 2, 1116.

Christians" (*mizi jiaoyou* 糜子教友) for their lack of spiritual faith. As a folk song goes, "Why are you joining the church? I do it for two strings of cash. Why are you saying the prayers? I do it for three pecks of millet."[102] Others joined the Church for protection and financial security, especially those entangled in litigations or feuds or who had incurred bad debts.[103]

The missionary approach in southwest Mongolia was more than a proselytizing strategy: it represented a response to the economic and social turmoil of the latter half of the nineteenth century. The economic disintegration of north China in the wake of massive rebellions and famines had pushed waves of landless farmers into the grasslands at a scale and intensity unseen in previous periods. Under such circumstances, the Church helped maintain local order, as traditional means of control were breaking down or were significantly weakened. It accomplished this by providing sanctuary, livelihood, and education to an uprooted, destitute, and often-unruly population.

Meanwhile, despite the many benefits to the society provided by the missions, the Scheutist tactic based on land acquisition, which was pursued at the expense of Mongol interests, ignited more clashes. As recent research in Mongolian archival sources shows, the increasing number of religious cases in the Ordos during the 1890s were predominantly caused by land disputes, which reflected the significant changes occurring in Mongol society during this time (notably, the ever-increasing encroachment of Mongol land rights and the erosion of the autonomy of the banners).[104] The religious case in the Dalad banner of the northern Ordos served as a good example of these land-related disputes. Between 1885 and 1892, the missionaries acquired 590 *qing* of well-irrigated lands from the Dalad banner—by far the largest amount among the Ordos banners—via Chinese land brokers settling near the Yellow River, with seven missions established. By the mid-1890s, the number of Chinese converts residing in the Dalad banner reached thirteen hundred and comprised over one-third of the entire Catholic population in southwest Mongolia, which was 3,631 in 1896.[105] However, this expansion of the Church was not achieved without bitter struggles. The land of Xiaonao'er (Mo: Bagha Nuur), a total of 360 *qing* in acreage, was acquired in 1884 from a Chinese merchant who owed the Church five hundred taels of silver. Resenting the loss of grazing land, a group of Mongols led by a noble attacked the mission and dispersed the converts, but they had to compensate for the damage under pressure of the Church.[106] Later, the banner officials brought the issue to the attention of Manchu officials in Suiyuan and Sarachi. They demanded that the merchant be punished and the foreigners expelled. The Qing officials indicated their disapproval of the unauthorized transaction, but they did not take any measures to convict the transgressor or stop the encroachment.[107] Due to the official nonintervention, the relationship between the Church and the Dalad banner deteriorated rapidly. During the Boxer Uprising of 1900, the Dalad banner was the first banner to respond, and it also caused the greatest damage to the Church during the upheavals.

Besides riding on the wave of Chinese migration, the missionaries were also involved in entanglements concerning land disputes and local feuds of the Mongols, as manifest in the long-standing dispute between the neighboring Üüshin and Otog banners in which they served as conciliator (see chapter 6). The mission of Boro-Balgasun was located in the contested territory near the border of the two banners that the Üüshin banner had obtained from the Otog banner and subsequently sold a part of it to the Scheutist missionaries. Later, as part of the indemnity paid to the Church for damages caused in the Boxer Uprising, the Otog banner deliberately ceded the disputed land to the Church in the hope that the latter would take its side to secure its investment.[108]

Another incident of conflict concerned the new mission of Bagha Shibar in the Üüshin banner in 1898. A Üüshin noble and a lama who had feuds with another noble sought asylum at the church of Boro-Balgasun in the Otog banner. The noble converted and offered to sell the Church a tract of land with an area of about seven hundred square kilometers (10,500 *qing*) for twenty thousand taels of silver.[109] The deal aroused opposition from fifty households of nobles and commoners in the neighborhood, who submitted a petition to the jasag of the Üüshin banner against the sale of common grazing land to foreigners. The banner authority dispatched troops to Boro-Balgasun to arrest the two men, because it was against the Mongol law for any subject or lama to leave their own domain without official authorization. The missionaries refused to comply: claiming that the said men had converted to Christianity. A crowd of two hundred Mongols confronted the missionaries, beat them up, and expelled them from the banner.[110]

The official arbitration rejected the Church's acquisition of pastureland, as rumors were spread by suspicious Mongols. In this way, the Church was denied the land, but it was allowed to keep the house properties it purchased.[111] An agreement reached between the church of Boro-Balgasun and the Üüshin banner stipulated that, although the banner was obliged to protect the church and its Mongol converts, the missionaries were to refrain from obstructing the apprehension of any criminals taking refuge in the church. It also stated that the sale of Mongol land was prohibited by Qing laws and the banner officials should be notified beforehand of any transaction of Mongol properties.[112] This arbitration indicated an official endeavor to strike a balance between the French and Mongol interests.

As Sudebilige points out, the religious cases in the Ordos were illustrative of the institutional dilemma that the Mongol banners found themselves in under the dual challenges posed by Chinese migration and Western imperialist expansion.[113] A series of pervasive crises since the 1860s—massive rebellions, wars, famines—began to reshape the Qing court's conceptualization of the Mongol periphery and the ways in which it interacted with Western missionaries and Chinese settlers. The once-invincible Mongol cavalry was defeated and nearly wiped out by the Anglo-French forces in Beijing in 1860. The Ordos Mongols were unable to protect their own home from the ravage of Hui rebels, whose suppression had to rely on the Xiang Army led by General Zuo Zongtang. Meanwhile, the trend of Chinese settlement became irreversible as population pressure and devastating famines pushed unprecedented waves of refugees into the Han-Mongol borderlands.[114] Although the Mongols and conservative Manchu officials still sought to resist this trend, leading reformists such as Li Hongzhang, Zhang Zhidong, and Hu Pinzhi began to advocate Chinese cultivation in Inner Mongolia to raise funds for the New Army and for border consolidation.[115] Although these proposals were not accepted by the court, they nevertheless suggested a major cognitive shift away from the old imperial model toward that of a "modern" Chinese nation-state. As chapter 6 will show, this cognitive shift would lead to structural changes in the Qing policy toward the Mongol frontier.

The Catholic missionaries arrived in the Ordos and its peripheries at this historical conjuncture of the Chinese expansion into the Mongol periphery and the simultaneous expansion of Western-style modernization into a non-Western world. They promoted a different property regime from the communal land ownership of the Mongols, as well as a free market economy that steadily converted Mongolian grasslands into farmlands. At the same time, they advocated a modern political system of nation-states that overrode and eroded the decentralized authority of Mongol jasags and monasteries. For the Europeans, the feudal-like social system of the Mongols was archaic and anachronistic. Seen from the Mongol perspective, however, all these were not just foreign but also heterodoxy. They had everything to lose in this mix of Sinification and Westernization. Not only were their pastures shrinking, but their autonomy was being encroached upon by an increasingly Sinicized Qing state, which explained the wide opposition against the Church among all Mongol social classes: nobility and commoners, lay and clergy.

The Church's expansion also led to a conflict of interests with the Chinese migrants already inhabiting the region. For instance, the land merchants of Hetao had successfully resisted the Church's penetration until the early 1900s.[116] Elsewhere, clashes frequently broke out between the Church and non-Christian migrants, with whom they competed for land, water, and power. In 1895, the Scheutists filed a complaint to the French legation and the Governor of Shanxi about two incidents occurring in southwest Mongolia. The first involved the abduction of a missionary by a group of Chinese settlers in Olan Bohereg of the Dalad banner.[117] The abductors were related to a Shaanxi merchant family named Yang, from whom the church subleased a plot in 1885. The land depended on an irrigation canal Yang developed, which went obsolete after his death. Yang's elder son offered to reduce the rent from 180 to eighty taels per year, in exchange for an advance of five years' proceeds that would enable him to return his father's remains to his native place. A dispute arose when Yang's widow, who was the stepmother of the son, refused to honor the arrangement. The family property was divided after Yang's death and the plot in question belonged to the stepmother. She then pressed the missionary for the original sum of rent, and when rejected, had him kidnapped and extorted a ransom of 508 taels.[118] Previously, the two parties also quarreled over the use of the irrigation canal, leading to a clash in 1891 in which a group of henchmen hired by Widow Yang broke into the church and caused much damage.[119]

The second dispute concerned 120 *qing* of Mongol land in Balagai of the Tümed banner that the missionaries rented from seventeen Mongol households through the mediation of a Chinese settler named Qin in 1894. However, a settler named Guo accused the Church of trespassing. He claimed that his family had subleased the plot for three generations. The local official of Sarachi ruled that the Church was to retain the land while paying Guo a sum of cash in compensation. A disgruntled Guo brought the case to the office of the Manchu vice lieutenant governor overseeing the Tümed Mongols of Höhhot. The vice governor overturned the previous verdict on the grounds that the Qing law prohibited the sale of habitats granted to Tümed Mongols as a means of livelihood, and he ruled that the land was to be withdrawn from the Church with their money returned.[120] The missionaries then appealed to Beijing and Shanxi. Another round of official investigation revealed that the dispute was over competing rental terms negotiated between the Mongol landowner and different sublessees. Although Guo claimed to have paid forty strings of cash a year to the Mongols, the latter contested that they had received only 13.6 strings each year. By contrast, the Church paid two hundred strings per year in rent plus a land price of fifteen hundred strings to Qin, the original tenant. The favorable terms led the Mongol land owner to terminate contract with Guo and conclude the deal with the Church.[121] Nevertheless, the officials in charge of the case insisted that the land, being inalienable from the Mongols, should be withdrawn with the money, a total of 2,050 strings of cash, returned to the Church.[122] Finally, after a third round of arbitration authorized by the Zongli Yamen, the Church was allowed to retain the land until the sum was paid back. This was unlikely to happen, as both the Mongols and Qin's family pleaded a lack of means to repay the money. In turn, Guo had to relinquish the land and pledge to never cause trouble for the Church again.[123] Similarly, Widow Yang lost her title to the land of Olan Bohereg. As a result, the Church was able to pay rentals directly to the Dalad banner without mediation and share the use of the irrigation canal with the Yang family.[124]

These religious cases testify to a number of changes taking place in the Mongol periphery toward the end of the nineteenth century. Both cases took place in the well-irrigated valleys of the Yellow River, which had seen considerable development in the agricultural and commercial sectors due to the influx of Chinese settlers. Prior to the arrival of the missionaries, a process of privatization and commercialization was underway in both the habitats of Tümed Mongols and common pastures of the Ordos. Emerging as a strong competitor on the local land market, the Church benefited from the process and accelerated it by jacking up the market price. Most land merchants were no match for the Church in terms of financial prowess and flexibility. Apart from land purchase, the Church also acquired land from conditional land sales. It was common for people to borrow loans against properties when urgent needs arose, such as returning a family member's remains to his/her native place. The Church's financial power and generous loan terms made it a welcome alternative to the money shops established by Shanxi merchants that charged exorbitant interests.[125] In cases where debtors were unable to repay the loan, their land went to the Church.

The expansion of the Church thus led to growing frictions with local interest groups among Chinese settlers, against whom it had to compete for resources such as land and water. In Ningxia and Hetao, the missionaries clashed with Hui and Han Chinese land-merchants and canal-developers over the use of irrigation canals.[126] For instance, the case of Olan Bohereg partly arose from the feud between the Church and the Yang family over the access to irrigation. Depending on the availability of irrigation, the land proceeds fluctuated between 180 and eighty taels a year. Other triggers of disputes included undefined property rights, unclearly demarcated boundaries, and arbitrary practices in land transaction—such as rental payments and the exchange of land deeds—leading to competing claims to the same land by multiple parties. Such problems were especially common in areas newly brought under cultivation.[127] The lack of long-term commitments and good faith in the mobile migrant society further contributed to difficulties in enforcing contracts and rental payments. When a tenant failed to pay rent for some reason, the Mongol owners would lease out the plot to another party. This practice easily gave rise to disputes and religious cases when the Church was involved.[128]

These cases suggested the Qing state was losing grip under the dual challenge of Chinese migration and Western aggression, as shown in the growing tendency of local militarization in the frontier society.[129] The Fengzhen case in the 1870s in which one missionary nearly lost his life already displayed an inclination toward the use of physical force. The Olan Bohereg case further demonstrated signs of organized violence, as the abduction of the missionary was obviously premeditated. The key figure in the incident was a henchman hired by Widow Yang named Ran Si, whom the missionaries referred to as an "infamous local bully."[130] This tendency of militarization was especially prominent in Hetao, where it was common for land merchants to hire martial art practitioners or local thugs to defend their farm estates and irrigation privileges against competitors or to organize a private militia to enforce taxation and adjudication.[131]

Moreover, the official vacillation toward land acquisition by the Church was symptomatic of the Qing government's failure to devise a coherent strategy to cope with the many internal and external crises it faced at the turn of the twentieth century. The indecisiveness was notable in the Balagai case, in which local officials diverged in their responses toward the changing situations. Whereas some endeavored to come to terms with the change by striking a compromise among various interest groups, others pretended that the old Manchu-Mongol order was intact and that the steppe remained a horse-breeding ground for a conquest elite. This indecisiveness mirrored the divergence between the reformist and conservative factions of the Qing court, which was partly responsible for the spread of Boxer violence in north China and Inner Mongolia.

In the end, the Church emerged triumphantly from these local disputes, which represented a victory for Western capitalism and for an imperialism delivered through gunboat and the treaty system. The series of humiliating impositions that the Qing suffered on the international scene were easily translated into concessions and compromises on the local front. Thanks to active French intervention, the end result of many religious cases departed distinctly from their original verdicts on the local level. Therefore, the triumph of the Church was achieved often at the expense of local interests of the Mongols and non-Christian settlers, as well as those of the Qing sovereignty and judicial autonomy.

BOXER UPRISING

The escalating violence at the local level soon led to a major crisis in the capital and across northern China. The Boxer uprising, first emerging in northwest Shandong in 1898 as a local response to imperialist expansion and missionary evangelism, spread into Zhili, Beijing, and Tianjin by early 1900. As the Boxers began to gather in Beijing and Tianjin in June under the banner of "Support Qing and destroy the foreign" (*fuqing mieyang* 扶清滅洋), the conservative faction of the imperial court decided to ally with the Boxers in confronting the foreign pressures. On June 21, the empress dowager declared war on eleven foreign powers, and the Boxers were enlisted as official militia in fighting the foreigners along with the imperial troops.[132]

The movement spilled across the Great Wall into the Mongol periphery. Groups of Boxers appeared in Kalgan in late May and in the Tümed area by June. The first Boxer practitioner in this area was a muleteer from Shanxi, who established an altar in the town of Togtokhu in late June and recruited over two hundred followers in a few days. The movement soon spread into Sarachi and Höhhot, where placards were posted on main streets, stipulating that all people must perform cleansing rituals, prostrate themselves on the ground facing northeast, and identify Christian homes.[133] As the Boxers set out to attack missionary compounds and extirpate Christians across the Tümed plain, the fortified settlement of Ershisiqingdi became a primary target. It was the vicariate headquarters and was sheltering over a thousand converts from nearby villages who had taken asylum there since late June.[134]

An earlier incident in May provided a fuse for anti-Christian hostility. In a bloody feud over land disputes in the Jüüngar banner, a Chinese family of nine were killed. The culprits were identified as Catholic converts, including a catechist and a lay leader of Ershisiqingdi. The missionaries reportedly refused to turn the accused over to local authorities, thereby igniting public rage against the Church.[135] On July 3, Yuxian, newly appointed Governor of Shanxi, brought the case to the Grand Council in Beijing, and the latter replied that he should do as he saw fit to suppress the Christians if they continued to reject orders from local authorities.[136]

The situation deteriorated quickly. On July 6, Bishop Ferdinand Hamer received a message from Janagardi, jasag of the Jüüngar banner, informing him of impending danger and suggesting that they take refuge in Sandaohe in the Alasha banner. Hamer ordered all six missionaries to depart for Sandaohe immediately, but he chose to stay behind with the converts in Ershisiqingdi. On July 19, assisted by two hundred Qing troops and the local forces of Togtokhu and Sarachi, thousands of Boxers besieged the village. At dawn on July 20, the church fell, followed by the massacre of some nine hundred Catholics. Bishop Hamer was captured and taken to Togtokhu where he was tortured and burned to death on July 24.[137] The Boxers plundered the nearby Catholic villages and burned churches and homes to the ground.[138]

The violence spread to territories under the jurisdiction of Mongol jasags. The Church in the Dalad banner suffered heavy casualties at the hands of Mongol troops. On July 24, the Mongols breached the church of Xiaonao'er and demolished several

Catholic settlements. A Chinese priest and about one hundred converts perished, many of whom were refugees from Ershisiqingdi. On July 30, the Mongol cavalry attacked Olan Bohereg and killed 150 converts.[139] Joining in the attack was the private militia of Chinese land merchants including Wang Tongchun, Guo Minxiu, and Widow Yang, who had had feuds with the Church.[140] Slain by the Mongol soldiers were also five Protestant missionaries from the United States and Sweden and their families.[141]

In southern Ordos, a Boxer leader from Shanxi had established himself in Ningtiaoliang since late May and had recruited over two hundred followers. The local officials of Shaanxi imprisoned the leader and suppressed the movement. The area remained relatively quiet through July, thus allowing time for the missionaries to reinforce self-defense forces in Xiaoqiaopan. A stockade had been constructed there earlier to guard against attack from Hui rebels, which made the church a stronghold for the fourteen missionaries (nine Scheutists and five Franciscans from Shanxi) and over three hundred Catholics taking refugee there.[142] The Boxer attacks began on August 7, 1900. They targeted mainly the Catholic settlements within the Black Border lands, whereas the Mongols of the Otog and Üüshin banners organized vigilante forces called *duguilang* ("circles," Ch: *duguilong* 獨貴龍) to burn down churches in Boro-Balgasun, Köber, and Bagha Shibar and destroy the homes of Mongol converts. The siege of Xiaoqiaopan lasted for fifty-two days from August 9 through September 29. During this period, hundreds of Boxers, assisted by some two hundred *duguilang* forces and three hundred cavalrymen from the banners, launched a series of attacks. The Catholics managed to overpower them with better weapons and tactics.[143] In the end, local officials of Shaanxi disbanded the Boxers and persuaded the Mongol troops to retreat. The church of Xiaoqiaopan remained intact, with a relatively small Christian casualty of one missionary and eleven converts, as compared to the over two hundred Boxers and ten Mongol soldiers killed in the battles.[144]

Compared with heavy casualties in Tümed and Ordos, the damage in the Alasha banner was minimal. A Mongol official promised to protect the Catholics of Sandaohe as long as they renounced the faith, which most did. On August 18, fifteen missionaries, including the six who had escaped from Ershisiqingdi, were expelled to Urga and returned to Belgium via Kyakhta.[145] The church of Sanshenggong was converted into a Buddhist monastery, and three other chapels in the areas were torn down. No priest or convert was harmed in the region.[146]

In Central Mongolia vicariate, the western section that overlaps with Shanxi suffered the severest damage. In Togtokhu and Khoringer, over four hundred converts were slaughtered in the undefended Catholic villages, most of which had been established only shortly before 1900.[147] In Dörben Kheükhed (Ch: Siziwang), a banner of the Ulaanchab league, three Scheut missionaries, thirteen Protestant priests and their families, and more than a thousand Catholics gathered in the chapels of Tiegedangou and Wo'ertugou to organize self-defense. On August 22, hundreds of Qing troops breached the churches, assisted by three hundred Boxers and 105 Mongol cavalrymen. Over six hundred Catholics and sixteen foreigners were burned alive.[148]

Ironically, the massacre occurred just two days after an imperial edict was issued warning the General of Suiyuan against using force.[149] By then, the Allied forces had occupied Beijing, ending the fifty-five-day siege of foreign legations.

In the Chakhar region, combat was largely restricted between the Church and Boxers, with little involvement of Qing troops. The missionaries organized an effective defense against the often poorly armed Boxers. The church of Xiwanzi, which sheltered thousands of Catholics from the nearby areas and other parts of Zhili, gained the reputation of being impregnable thanks to the military expertise of Arthur Wittamer, a visiting officer of the Belgian Army. In Fengzhen, the church compounds of Xiyingzi and Ershisanhao withstood several Boxer attacks, whereas a number of smaller villages were ruined. The local officials of Fengzhen arranged for the missionaries to return to Europe via northern Mongolia, and so none of them was hurt.[150] The two missionaries of the Daihai plain of Ningyuan were less fortunate. Although they resisted the attacks by the Boxers and Qing troops for over a month, they were lured to Höhhot by an invitation from the circuit intendent of Guisui and killed on the way by the Boxers.[151]

Table 5.3 shows the damages caused by the Boxer violence in Inner Mongolia as recorded in official documents. Compared to areas bordering Gansu, Shaanxi, and Zhili provinces, those adjacent to Shanxi suffered by far the severest damages, which caused the loss of over two thousand Catholic lives. In addition, some sixteen hundred women and children from Sarachi alone were sold by human traffickers to Hui households of Ningxia. The remaining twenty thousand survivors were deprived of

Table 5.3. Human and Property Damages in Southwest and Central Mongolia, 1900

Vicariate	Province	Banner	Division	Death Toll		Damage		
				Missy.	Convert	Church	Chapel	Home
Southwest	Shaanxi	Otog, Üüshin Jasag	Shenmu	1	11	4	–	621
Southwest	Gansu	Alasha	Ningxia	–	–	–	3	–
Southwest	Shanxi	Tümed R Dalad	Sarachi	11	1,000+	7	5	592
Southwest Central	Shanxi	Jüüngar Tümed L	Togtokhu	–	345	2	2	2,066
Central	Shanxi	Tümed L	Khoringer	–	?	2	3	?
Central	Shanxi	Tümed L Dörben Kheükhed	Guihua	18	972	3	15	2,557
Central	Shanxi	Chakhar	Ningyuan	–	11	2	1	171
Central	Zhili	Chakhar	Fengzhen	–	60+	2	5	?
Central	Zhili	Chakhar	Zhangjiakou	–	10+	–	2	?
Total				**30**	**2,470**	**22**	**36**	**7,600+**

Sources: *Jiaowu jiao'an dang*, ser. 7, volume 1, 511–18, 529; *Qingmo jiao'an*, volume 3, 604; *Suiyuan tongzhigao*, 580–84.

their homes and livelihood.[152] The havoc caused to the Church of Inner Mongolia was next to that of Shanxi province, where 191 missionaries and families and over six thousand Christians were murdered. Moreover, 225 churches and over twenty-two thousand homes were destroyed.[153]

Several factors contributed to the eruption of anti-Christian violence outside the passes. First, ecological and demographical links had made the border regions of Inner Mongolia a homogenous extension of the rural communities of northern China. The severe drought sweeping across Shandong and Zhili in 1899–1900 likewise devastated the Xikouwai region (Tümed and western Chakhar), and created a hungry and restless population easily lured by the Boxer practice and ideology. Further, the Boxer movement in Inner Mongolia followed the same pattern of dispersion as that of Chinese migration. As most migrants in Xikouwai and Chakhar regions were natives of Shanxi and Zhili, to some extent the uproars in these areas can be seen as the repercussion of Boxer violence in these provinces.

Despite its exogenous origin, however, the anti-Christian violence in Inner Mongolia was primarily an endogenous phenomenon. Unlike other parts of north China, the Boxers were only partially responsible for the atrocities against Christians in these regions. In the Ordos, Mongol troops played a major role in attacking the church compounds. This was due to the loyalist stance of the Mongols as long-term allies of the Qing court, which was in stark contrast to the high Chinese officials in southeastern provinces who entered into a neutrality pact with the foreign powers so as to protect their provinces from the Boxer catastrophe. The Mongols' deep-seated grievances toward Chinese colonization also played a role. Most violence took place in the territories of Tümed and Ordos and in the Ulaanchab league, which witnessed rapid Church expansion in previous decades. In southern Ordos, the land-acquiring Church became a main target of the *duguilang* movement of the Mongols.[154] Thus, the disturbance in the Mongol territories departed distinctly from those in China proper, where violence was largely fueled by a set of distinctive rituals and cultural practices as well as resentment against foreign privileges.

Further, the severity of damages that occurred in any specific area hinged upon the personal choice of the Qing officials overseeing that area to either encourage or suppress the anti-Christian violence. For example, the Military General of Suiyuan, Yongde, sent Qing troops to besiege Ershisiqingdi and Houba and caused the death of seventeen missionaries and over fifteen hundred converts. In contrast, Governor Duanfang of Shaanxi put an end to the siege of Xiaoqiaopan by disbanding the Boxers and persuading the Mongol troops to disperse. The local officials' attitudes toward the missionaries also varied. Whereas the Guisui circuit intendent lured the missionaries of Ningyuan to their doom in Höhhot, the local officials of Alasha and Fengzhen arranged for missionaries to escape to northern Mongolia, thus sparing them harm.

On the other hand, the action taken by the Qing officials depended on their capacity to mobilize military forces. In Suiyuan, the Manchu Banner troops and Datong New Army that ravaged the churches were under Yongde's direct command.[155] In Chakhar, however, the attempt to attack Xiwanzi failed because the Manchu banner troops based in Kalgan were relocated to Beijing, and the Koubei circuit official refused to send the New Army stationed at Xuanhua.[156] Distance was another factor that affected the official decision. Whereas all three devastated churches were located within a one-hundred-kilometer radius of Höhhot, the marginal location of Fengzhen and Alasha made it difficult for the Qing troops to reach across distances.

BOXER INDEMNITIES

In the wake of the Boxer Protocol of 1901, which imposed a colossal sum of 450 million taels of silver as indemnity upon the Qing government, punishment was meted out to individual officials, provinces, and banners that inflicted harm on the Church and Christians.[157] Shanxi agreed to pay an indemnity of 2,680,000 taels of silver to the foreign missions, including 650,000 paid to the vicariate of Central Mongolia and two hundred thousand taels to the vicariate of southwest Mongolia.[158] Leading the negotiations was the newly appointed governor of Shanxi, Cen Chunxuan. His collaboration with the Church in offering relief to tens of thousands of homeless Christians and recovering the Catholic women and children from Ningxia made the negotiation process relatively smooth.[159]

Meanwhile, negotiations for the Mongol indemnities were especially complicated. Some banners, like the Dörben Kheükhed and Alasha, refused to discuss compensation matters with the Church. Others were unable to deliver the payment after the amount was fixed. There were rumors about plotted Mongol attacks on the churches—some presumably circulated by suspicious converts and missionaries seeking to enhance their bargaining power—and the missionaries threatened military intervention by the international troops in Beijing.[160] The inexperience of the Mongols placed them in a disadvantageous position in negotiating the indemnities. In the end, the banners were obliged to pay a daunting 598,000 taels to the Church: nearly threefold the amount paid by Shanxi (two hundred thousand taels).

Not surprisingly, such a large amount of silver was beyond the capacity of the Mongols. As loans from adjacent provinces and land proceeds from Chinese settlers were exhausted, the banners had to resort to land cession for payment. The Dalad banner was forced to cede 4,816 *qing* of irrigated lands along the Yellow River, among which 2,161 *qing* went directly to the Church. Another 2,655 *qing* went to the Qing government in exchange for the advance of payment to the Church.[161] The Dörben Kheükhed and Otog banners yielded 3,666.66 and twenty-six hundred *qing* each. It should be noted that the prices varied in accordance to land quality and the availability of irrigation.[162]

The Boxer indemnities thus led to the cession of 11,502.66 *qing* (seventy-six thousand ha) of land from the Mongol banners, with two-thirds going to the Church and one-third to the Qing state. The Church was able to secure the long-coveted lands near its bases in Olan Bohereg, Boro-Balgasun, Sanshenggong, and Houba. Furthermore, the peace agreement signed in June 1901 formally granted the Church

Table 5.4. Mongol Indemnities, 1901–1902

Banner	Indemnity (taels)	Form of Payment		
		Land to the Church (qing)	Land to Qing State (qing)	Loans, etc. (taels)
Dalad	370,000	2,161 = 147,800 taels (2,095 [1,400 net land] in Olan Bohereg; 76 in Danao'er)	2,655 = 137,450 taels (1,235 in Sichengdi; 1,420 in Changshengqudi)	66,300 (loan from Shanxi); 10,000 *shi* of grains (borrowed from Guisui circuit) = 11,550 taels; Land proceeds = 4,733 taels; Livestock = 590 taels
Otog	84,000	2,600 (Boro-Balgasun, Xiaoqianpan)	–	–
Üüshin	45,500	–	Yekhe Nuur alkaline lake	59,500 (loan from Shaanxi)
Jasag	14,000	–		
Jüüngar	27,000	–	300 (Hetaochuan)	
Alasha	57,500	120 = 30,000 taels (Sanshenggong, Monohai, etc)	–	10,000 (loan from Gansu); Land proceeds = 17,500 taels
Dörben Kheükhed	110,000	2,833.33 = 85,000 taels	833.33 = 25,000 taels	–
Tümed	1,500	–	–	Cash
Total	**709,500**	**7,714.33**	**3,788.33**	**164,173**

Sources: *Qingmo jiao'an*, volume 3, 111, 411–12, 702–04, 728–31, 735–37, 1012; "Hetao jiaoqu chuanjiao yange," in *Bayannao'er shiliao*," 241.

the right to possess land in Mongol territories, as well as the right for Mongol subjects to practice Christianity without being harassed. Therefore, the agreement provided a legal basis for the sale of land and evangelism in Mongol regions.[163]

Meanwhile, the Mongol indemnities greatly facilitated official reclamation of land in Inner Mongolia. In 1901, Cen Chunxuan's proposal of reclaiming Mongolian pastures for raising funds for the central government was approved, and a high-ranking Manchu official named Yigu was appointed imperial commissioner to supervise reclamation in the Yekhe Juu and Ulaanchab leagues. More about this will be discussed in chapter 6. Here, it suffices to say that the Mongols' financial predicament provided a perfect opportunity for the central state to introduce the new policy. In several banners, Yigu offered to advance the balance due in exchange for handing over thirty-eight hundred *qing* of Mongol lands to the Qing state. In this sense, the Church's expansion had accelerated Chinese colonization in the Mongol periphery not only through active promotion of Chinese settlement, but also through their function as a catalyst to the large-scale colonization sponsored by the central state.

The subsequent decades saw unprecedented missionary expansion in Inner Mongolia. The steady acquisition of Mongol lands had made the Catholic Church a major player in conducting land redistribution and social reforms in the frontier. As new centralized administrative units were created, Rome readjusted the ecclesial boundaries in Mongolia to align with the Chinese administrative boundaries. In 1922, the three vicariates of Inner Mongolia were reorganized into four Chinese vicariates apostolic: Jehol (east Mongolia), Chakhar (central Mongolia), Suiyuan, and Ningxia (southwest Mongolia). In 1940, two new vicariates, Chifeng and Jining, were divided from those of Jehol and Chakhar, so that there were altogether six full-fledged vicariates in the Mongol region with a total of 212,000 converts (virtually all of whom were Han Chinese).[164]

CONCLUSION

This chapter examines the Roman Catholic missionary enterprise within the larger context of the changing social dynamics of the Han-Mongol frontier during the second half of the nineteenth century. Tracing the initiatives of these religious enterprises, the foreign influence that they wielded, and the responses of local peoples has allowed us to observe two intertwining and mutually reinforcing processes within the steppe: the ecologically driven Chinese migration into the grasslands and the imperialist expansion of the West into a non-Western world. Rather than focusing on such essentialized notions such as the nation or ethnic group, it has proven more fruitful to conceptualize the frontier as a multiplicity of overlapping and intersecting identities: geographical, ecological, linguistic, ethnocultural, ecclesiastic, and administrative. As we have seen throughout this book, the emergence of new patterns of settlement within Inner Mongolia are not best conceptualized as a clash of different civilizations. Instead, as this overview of religious settlement illustrates, groups and identities emerged through processes of negotiation that were contingent upon specific historical circumstances.

The Scheut missionaries were particularly adept at negotiating the circumstances that they encountered and turning them to their benefit. Their advance into Mongolia was punctuated by events in the international arena as well as within the Qing empire itself. Although their motivation was predominantly spiritual, a number of tactical moves that they employed resulted in the radical transformation of the Han-Mongol frontier. The pervasive crises that the Qing faced in the 1870s—massive rebellion, war, famine—provided a unique opportunity for the missionaries to penetrate the Mongol periphery that had been previously sealed off to them. There, they learned to negotiate and manipulate a complex landscape, adjusted their target of conversion from the Mongols to Chinese migrants, and adopted an apostolic strategy of acquiring Mongol lands to attract Chinese converts. During the process, they became entangled in conflicting local interests that often crossed national, ethnic, and regional boundaries. The mounting tensions culminated in the eruption of violence during the Boxer Uprising that resulted in significant loss of human lives and properties. Yet, paradoxically, it ushered in an unprecedented development of the Church in Inner Mongolia during the first half of the twentieth century, thanks to the large indemnities in the form of the Mongol lands it received.

Like their Jesuit predecessors in Latin America, the Scheut missionaries of Mongolia can be understood in light of the expansion of the West into the non-Western world, with the purpose of Christianizing and "civilizing" the indigenous population. Nonetheless, the political, socioeconomic, and ethnocultural circumstances in nineteenth-century Inner Mongolia were more complicated than in seventeenth- and eighteenth-century Latin America, where relationships between the metropole and colony were relatively clearly defined. Whereas the Jesuits were mainly entangled in the political struggles between the church and state (as well as between different colonial states) in the new world, the Scheutists faced an intricate landscape that had been exposed to multiple influences of Tibetan Buddhism, Manchu supremacy, and Chinese trade and migration before the missionary encounter.

Over the long term, the impact of the missionaries went far beyond merely reshaping the cultural norms of the region. In addition to preaching theological beliefs, the Church played a central role in "civilizing" the frontier region by undertaking public works and social reforms in the fields of relief, education, and medicine, which proved beneficial to a local population afflicted with chronic natural disasters and plague epidemics.[165] The pioneering works of missionary scholars contributed significantly to the studies of Mongolian language, history, and culture.[166] All these achievements can be viewed as the code of "taming the natives" against the backdrop of the process of Westernization by which China was incorporated into the new world order of capitalism and nation-state system. The observations and practices of the missionaries certainly contributed to the body of knowledge needed for Western expansion and domination.

Alongside their Westernizing endeavors, by promoting agricultural colonization and accelerating land commercialization, the Roman Catholic missionaries also helped shatter the existing property regime of the Mongols. This had the effect of inviting a higher degree of state intervention and penetration that ended up in the official reclamation of Mongol pasturelands and the decline of the Mongol banner system. Eventually, it would lead to the formation of a top-down state and the integration of Inner Mongolia into a centralizing and homogenizing Chinese nation-state in the early twentieth century. In this sense, the missionaries, who were often labeled as the agents of Western imperialism, turned out to be instrumental to the nationalizing process that would eventually incorporate the Mongol frontier into an ethnically Chinese national state. Thereby, the missionaries facilitated what Owen Lattimore terms a "secondary" imperialism that was modeled after and developed as a counter to the primary imperialism of the West.[167]

NOTES

1. John of Plano Carpini (O.F.M.) and William of Rubruck (O.F.M.) arrived at Karakorum in 1246 and 1253. See Geng Sheng and He Gaoji, trans. *Bolang jiabin Menggu xingji, Lubuluke Dongxingi*. For the meeting of Sonam Gyatso and Altan Khan, see *Erdeni tunumal neretü sudur orusiba*, ca. 1607, translated by Elverskog, *The Jewel Translucent Sūtra*; Sechen, *Erdeni-yin Tobči/ Precious Summary.*

2. Hoang, *Zhengjiao fengbao*, volume 2, 82–85.

3. Gerbillon, "The Travels of Father Gerbillon," 214–356.

4. On the relations between cartography and empire making, see Perdue, "Boundaries, Maps, and Movement," 263–86; Millward, "'Coming onto the Map,'" 61–98; Hostetler, *Qing Colonial Enterprise*; Sun Zhe, *Kang yong qian shiqi yutu huizhi yu jiangyu xingcheng yanjiu.*

5. See *Feng Bingzheng xinjian*, 341.

6. Rondelez, *Xiwan shengjiao yuanliu*, 11–13.

7. Latourette, *A History of Christian Missions in China*, 46–77; Ku Wei-ying, *Saiwai chuanjiao shi*, 17.

8. Ku Wei-ying, *Saiwai chuanjiao shi*, 95–123; 17–20.

9. These communities were headed by local lay leaders called *huizhang* 會長 and occasionally visited by the Franciscan friars from Xi'an. See Chang Fei, *Tianzhujiao suiyuan jiaoqu chuanjiao jianzhi*, 11–12.

10. Larger Catholic communities in Jehol included Heishui plain, Bieliegou (both in today's Chifeng, IMAR), and Songshuzuizi (in Chaoyang, Liaoning province). For the missionary endeavors of the Lazarist in Jehol, see Huc and and Gabet, *Travels in Tartary, Thibet and China.*

11. Ku Wei-ying, *Saiwai chuanjiao shi*, 23.

12. Wenqing et al., eds., *Chouban yiwu shimo* 73.

13. A vicariate apostolic is a Roman Catholic missionary district under a titular bishop (vicar apostolic; *zongzuo daimu* 宗座代牧) having jurisdiction in missionary regions where dioceses (*jiaoqu* 教區) have not yet been established. See Chang Fei, *Tianzhujiao suiyuan jiaoqu*, 11; Ku, *Saiwai chuanjiao shi*, 26–27.

14. Huc and Gabet, *Travels in Tartary, Thibet and China.*

15. These included Ershisanhao near Huangyuwa (in Xinghe), Daihai plain near Daqiangpan (in Liangcheng), Sanhecun (in Höhhot), and Houba (in Dörben Kheükhed banner, Ulaanchab league). See Chang Fei, *Tianzhujiao suiyuan jiaoqu,* 11–12.

16. The seminary of Xiwanzi, founded in 1829, remained a crucial part of the mission. A smaller seminary was also built in Xiaodonggou. All seminaries were to join the mission afterwards. Training sessions were organized for catechists during the winter, usually lasting three months. See Ku Wei-ying, *Saiwai chuanjiao shi,* 28–29, 41.

17. Ku Wei-ying, *Saiwai chuanjiao shi,* 37–38; Chang Fei, *Tianzhujiao suiyuan jiaoqu,* 13.

18. Chang Fei, *Tianzhujiao suiyuan jiaoqu,* 15.

19. Verhelst, "Th. Verbiest and CICM Pioneers," in Ku, *Saiwai chuanjiao shi,* 144.

20. Hertslet, *Treaties, &c., between Great Britain and China,* volume 1, 274.

21. Hertslet, *Treaties, &c., between Great Britain and China,* volume 1, 289. For the Chinese version, see Wang Yi and Zhang Chengqi, eds., *Xianfeng tiaoyue,* in Shen Yunlong ed., *Jindai zhongguo shiliao congkan xubian,* volume 8, 7.

22. Cole, "Origins of the French Protectorate over Catholic Missions in China," 488; Cohen, *China and Christianity.*

23. Hertslet, *Treaties, &c., between Great Britain and China,* volume 1, 320–21.

24. Esherick, *The Origins of the Boxer Uprising,* 83.

25. Zhongyang yanjiuyuan jindaishi yanjiusuo, ed., *Jiaowu jiao'an dang* (hereafter JWJAD), ser. 1, volume 2, 692.

26. JWJAD, ser. 1, volume 1, 3.

27. Taveirne, *Han-Mongol Encounters and Missionary Endeavors,* 196.

28. Ku Wei-ying, *Saiwai chuanjiao shi,* 47–53, 143–48, 161.

29. For studies on the Fengzhen case, see Taveirne, "The Religious Case of Fengzhen District," 369–416; Zhang Yu, "*Wanqing shiqi shengmu shengxin hui zai nei menggu,*" 36–47.

30. JWJAD, ser. 1, volume 2, 692, 696, 700–01; ser. 3, volume 1, 438; Chang Fei, *Tianzhujiao suiyuan jiaoqu,* 13.

31. Chengqi's ancestor, Dambakhashkha, was a Mongol chief who pledged allegiance in 1696 and was appointed *janggin* ("commander") of a *sumun* ("company"). His son, Bandi, received another tract of six hundred *qing* of pasture in reward for his military merits as commander of the campaigns against the mountain peoples of Jinchuan in 1747 and Zunghars in 1755. See JWJAD, ser. 1, volume 2, 694. A company (Ma: *niru,* Mo: *sumun,* Ch: *zuoling* 佐領) consisted of three hundred men. For the Manchu Eight Banner system, see Elliot, *The Manchu Way,* 58.

32. JWJAD, ser. 1, volume 2, 694–99, 704–05, 708–10; ser. 2, volume 1, 447.

33. According to Wulan, there were altogether thirty-five private pastures in Chakhar in the nineteenth century. See Wulan, "*Cong chaha'er fangken zhangcheng kan chaha'er kenwu,*" 193–94. For the cultivation of the *taipusi* and private pastures, see Gao Geng'en, *Guisui dao zhi* 18.

34. JWJAD, ser. 1, volume 2, 692, 699, 706.

35. JWJAD, ser. 3, volume 1, 259.

36. JWJAD, ser. 2, volume 1, 421; ser. 3, volume 1, 433.

37. JWJAD, ser. 1, volume 2, 700.

38. JWJAD, ser. 2, volume 1, 446. Besides the case in Fengzhen, the French minister also demanded the closure of the religious cases in Youyang of Sichuan and Zunyi of Guizhou, as well as other pending cases in Hubei, Shanxi, Henan, and Guangdong provinces. See JWJAD, ser. 2, volume 1, 454.

39. JWJAD, ser. 2, volume 1, 454–56; ser. 3, volume 1, 421, 449–53.

40. JWJAD, ser. 2, volume 1, 421; ser. 3, volume 1, 432–34, 438–39.

41. JWJAD, ser. 3, volume 1, 439–41.

42. JWJAD, ser. 3, volume 1, 258, 450–51.

43. JWJAD, ser. 3, volume 1, 429–31.

44. JWJAD, ser. 3, volume 1, 244.

45. JWJAD, ser. 3, volume 1, 253–54.

46. JWJAD, ser. 3, volume 1, 258. The investigating officials rebutted Verlinden's claim about the compensated land because it was not officially approved. Dagdanlosol, however, argued that although he did strike a deal with the converts about the surplus lands of Yushuwa, it did not work out because the missionaries said the land was too barren. See JWJAD., 258, 260.

47. JWJAD, ser. 3, volume 1, 254, 259.

48. JWJAD, ser. 3, volume 1, 266.

49. Ku Wei-ying, *Saiwai chuanjiao shi*, 53, 161; Taveirne, "The Religious Case of Feng-zhen District," 405.

50. JWJAD, ser. 3, volume 1, 422–28, 443–49, 457.

51. Elehebu, military governor of Chakhar, explicitly rejected the idea of reclamation in preference of prohibition. Bao Yuansheng, governor of Shanxi, also sided with Elehebu. See JWJAD, ser. 3, volume 1, 457, 460.

52. Wang Yanping, "*Qingmo chaha'er baqi mengdi de fangken*," 210.

53. Ku Wei-ying, *Saiwai chuanjiao shi*, 53, 161; Taveirne, "The Religious Case of Feng-zhen District," 405. Even Pozdneyev who visited Nanhaoqian in 1893 was impressed by the "extraordinary magnificence and striking beauty" of the church, especially seen among the surrounding low mud houses of the Chinese. See Pozdneyev, *Mongolia*, volume 2.

54. Chang Fei, *Tianzhujiao suiyuan jiaoqu*, 16. For the imperial attendance in Beijing, see QSL 347, TZ 11/12/30.

55. For the Dungan/Hui Revolt and its Qing suppression, see Lipman, *Familiar Strangers*, 103–66.

56. QSG 48; Nei Menggu daxue menggu xue yanjiu zhongxin, ed., *Zhunge'er qi zhasake Yamen dang'an yibian*, volume 3, 829; Sude, "*Shaangan huimin qiyi qijian de yikezhaomeng.*"

57. Edgerton-Tarpley, *Tears from Iron*.

58. Ding Xikui, *Jingbian xianzhigao*, 109, 315–17.

59. Chang Fei, *Tianzhujiao suiyuan jiaoqu*, 16; Taveirne, *Han-Mongol Encounters*, 231–35.

60. Hao Chongli, *E'erduosi geming laoqu xubian*, 6.

61. Huc and Gabet spell his name as Samdadchiemba. See Huc and Gabet, *Travels in Tartary, Thibet and China*. According to my interview with Msgr. Giuseppe Ma Zhongmu 馬仲牧 (Mongolian name: Tegüsbilig, 1919–2020), the first and only Mongol bishop, on August 13, 2005, the twelve households of Qinghai Mongols had been converted before moving to Boro-Balgasun. Because of the prestige they enjoyed among the local Mongols, the Mongolian dialect of Boro-Balgasun became completely assimilated to the dialect of Qinghai. Also see Hao Chongli, *E'erduosi geming laoqu xubian*, 6. However, it remained unclear whether there had been Mongol Catholics residing in Qinghai prior to 1879, when Qinghai was assigned by Rome to the newly established vicariate of Gansu.

62. JWJAD, ser. 4, volume 1, 304–05. Msgr. Ma asserted that the Mongols at the time were in urgent need of "changing blood," due to the widespread sexually transmitted diseases that left many Mongols childless. See the author's interview with Msgr. Ma on August 13, 2005.

63. In 2004, there are 4,491 Catholics residing in Otog Front banner, including 2,091 Mongols and 2,400 Han Chinese. http://www.etkqq.gov.cn/SmallClass.asp?typeid=20&BigC lassID=47&SmallClassID=260. Since the 1990s, the Scheutists and other Catholics are present in the Republic of Mongolia.

64. Taveirne, *Han-Mongol Encounters*, 238–39.

65. Chang Fei, *Tianzhujiao suiyuan jiaoqu*, 16–17; Taveirne, *Han-Mongol Encounters*, 236–37, 245–47; Van Hecken, *Les réductions catholiques du pays des Ordos*.

66. Taobuxin, "*Nei menggu de 'xiao Beijing' – Dingyuanying*," 140.

67. Taveirne, *Han-Mongol Encounters*, 240–41, 340.

68. Liu Jingshan, "Hetao jiaoqu chuanjiao jianshi"; "*Hetao jiaoqu chuanjiao yange*," 236; Taveirne, *Han-Mongol Encounters*, 241.

69. JWJAD, ser. 3, volume 3, 1897–98. The local official mistook the year when the Scheutists first arrived for 1871, and stated accordingly that they had resided there for eight years, which is incorrect.

70. Chang Fei, *Tianzhujiao suiyuan jiaoqu*, 4.

71. Steenackers, "Aperçu sur le Vicariat de la Mongolie Sud–Ouest (Ortos)," 353–58; Taveirne, *Han-Mongol Encounters*, 240.

72. Van Hecken, *Les réductions catholiques du pays des Ordos*; Van Hecken, "Les réductions catholiques du pays des Alasha," 29–144. For the Jesuit reductions, see Huonder, "Reductions of Paraguay."

73. Van Oost, *Min Yuqing zhuan*, 39–40, 74; Chang Fei, *Tianzhujiao suiyuan jiaoqu*, 16–17; Taveirne, *Han-Mongol Encounters*, 244–45, 351–52.

74. Chang Fei, *Tianzhujiao suiyuan jiaoqu*, 22. For the division of the territory, see QSL 206, GX 11/4/2.

75. Chang Fei, *Tianzhujiao suiyuan jiaoqu*, 17–18; Taveirne, *Han-Mongol Encounters*, 253; Ku Wei-ying, *Saiwai chuanjiao shi*, 163; Lievens, "The Spread of the CICM Mission in Central Mongolia," 308–10.

76. Chang Fei, *Tianzhujiao suiyuan jiaoqu*, 12.

77. JWJAD, ser. 3, no. 1, 463–64; Chang Fei, *Tianzhujiao suiyuan jiaoqu*, 57.

78. Paul Splingaerd (林輔臣 1842–1906) arrived in China in 1865 as a lay helper for the Scheut mission. Between 1881 and 1896, he served as the customs inspector at the far west treaty port of Suzhou (present Jiuquan) of Gansu province. He later helped the Scheutist missionaries during the Boxer indemnity negotiations. See Megowan, *The Belgian Mandarin*, 75; Taveirne, *Han-Mongol Encounters*, 227.

79. JWJAD, ser. 3, no. 1, 464–66, 470–71.

80. Wang Yi and Zhang Chengqi, *Xianfeng tiaoyue*, volume 1, 19–21.

81. Wang and Zhang, *Xianfeng tiaoyue*, volume 5, 15–21; Lu Minghui and Liu Yankun, *Lümengshang*, 224.

82. Pozdneyev, *Mongolia*, volume 2, 92–97. For foreign impact on trade in Mongolia, see Lu and Liu, *Lümengshang*, 221–27.

83. JWJAD, ser. 3, volume 1, 467–69.

84. Chang Fei, *Tianzhujiao suiyuan jiaoqu*, 57; Taveirne, *Han-Mongol Encounters*, 228–29.

85. Chang Fei, *Tianzhujiao suiyuan jiaoqu*, 18; Taveirne, *Han-Mongol Encounters*, 391–92.

86. JWJAD, ser. 3, volume 1, 510–11.

87. JWJAD, ser. 3, volume 1, 514–15.

88. JWJAD, ser. 4, volume 1, 304–06, 310. According to the witness report of Haljatai, grandfather of Msgr. Ma Zhongmu and companion of Steenackers, the nobleman Damrinjab

accused the missionary of killing his seventh son and companion at night—he had six sons who kept him company during the day—and demanded a thousand taels of silver as compensation. He even preserved the dog's body in salt. Haljatai was brutally beaten and forced to stay overnight in the open in freezing winter night, and lost one big toe to frostbite. See the author's interview with Msgr. Ma Zhongmu, August 13, 2005. Also see Taveirne, *Han-Mongol Encounters*, 239.

89. JWJAD, ser. 4, volume 1, 311.

90. In the end, however, in the wake of the Boxer Protocol in 1901, the banner was forced to pay an indemnity of thirty-five hundred taels of silver for these early offenses. See YHTDX, 1186–88. According to Msgr. Ma, besides the indemnities in silver, the mission also received other compensation for the humility—for each beard hair Steenackers lost, the Üüshin banner had to repay a tree. The timbers were used for the construction of the new church of Boro-Balgasun in 1900. See the author's interview with Msgr. Ma Zhongmu, August 13, 2005.

91. Taveirne, *Han-Mongol Encounters*, 256.

92. Jagchid and Hyer, *Mongolia's Culture and Society*, 274–92.

93. Liang Bing, "*Lamajiao zai e'erduosi de chuanbo ji yingxiang*," 10. Tibetan Buddhism was also held responsible for the sharp decline of the Mongol population due to its principle of celibacy and widespread diseases. The population of the Ordos dropped sharply from around two hundred thousand in the early Qing to less than ninety thousand in the Republican period.

94. For the cult of Chinggis Khan, see Bold, "The Death and Burial of Chinggis Khaan," 95–115; Yang Haiying, *Chinggisu haan saishi*.

95. JWJAD, ser. 3, volume 1, 510.

96. JWJAD, ser. 4, volume 1, 304.

97. Taveirne, *Han-Mongol Encounters*, 236.

98. Hertslet, *Treaties, &c., between Great Britain and China*, 320–21.

99. For the figure of 1885, see Taveirne, *Han-Mongol Encounters*, 637–38. For the figure of 1900, see Li Di, *Quanfei huojiaoji*, 318.

100. Taveirne, *Han-Mongol Encounters*, 345.

101. The entire villages of Dalamayaozi and Gaoshangyaozi were converted in 1891. See Chang Fei, *Tianzhujiao suiyuan jiaoqu*, 34, 46.

102. Dai Xueji, "*Xifang zhiminzhe zai hetao eerduosi dengdi de zuie huodong*."

103. For instance, Lu Ying, a wealthy farmer of the village of Rensanyaozi, was tired of the endless harassment of hungry crowds demanding relief and offered his house properties to the Church in 1899. Miao Guozhen of Miaoliuquanzi donated his lands to the Church in order to avoid persecution by his enemies. See Chang Fei, *Tianzhujiao suiyuan jiaoqu*, 31, 46.

104. Sudebilige, "Tianzhujiao yu qingchao jinken mudi zhengce de feichi," 143–55; Meirong, "Gengzi nian yikezhaomeng dalateqi jiao'an xintan," 156–62.

105. See *Missions en Chine et au Congo*, 86; Chang Fei, *Tianzhujiao suiyuan jiaoqu*, 19; Taveirne, *Han-Mongol Encounters*, 637.

106. Sudebilige, ed., *Jüüngar khoshuun no jasag yamon no dangan* (hereafter JKJYD), volume 65, 250; Meirong, "Gengzi nian yikezhaomeng dalateqi jiao'an xintan," 158.

107. JKJYD, volume 71, 56–60; volume 77, 291–92; Sudebilige, "Tianzhujiao yu qingchao jinken mudi," 150; Meirong, "Gengzi nian yikezhaomeng dalateqi jiao'an xintan," 158–59.

108. For the land dispute, see Van Hecken, "Une dispute entre deux bannières mongoles," 276–305; Serruys, "A Question of Land and Landmarks between the Banners Otog and Üüsin (Ordos)," 215–37. For an analysis of the letters regarding the dispute, see Elverskog, *Our Great Qing*, 127–133.

109. Yang Haiying ed., *Guowai kanxing de E'erduosi menggu zu wenshi ziliao,* 1–2.

110. JKJYD, volume 80, 186–89, 220, 313, 430–33; Sudebilige, "Tianzhujiao yu qingchao jinken mudi," 151–53.

111. JWJAD, ser. 6, no. 3, 738.

112. JKJYD, volume 80, 471; Sudebilige, "Tianzhujiao yu qingchao jinken mudi," 153.

113. Sudebilige, "Tianzhujiao yu qingchao jinken mudi,"154–55.

114. The Qing ban against Chinese migration into Manchuria and Taiwan was officially lifted in 1860 and 1875, and by 1878, the ban against Chinese women outside the passes as well.

115. Zhang Zhidong, *Zhang wenxianggong quanji,* volume 2.

116. SYTZG, volume 7, *juan* 58, 543.

117. JWJAD, ser. 5, no. 2, 398, 400.

118. JWJAD, ser. 6, no. 1, 536–37, 591.

119. JWJAD, ser. 6, no. 1, 589–90.

120. JWJAD, ser. 6, no. 1, 595–97. For the habitats of Tümed Mongols, see Editorial Committee of Tümed Left Banner, ed., *Tumote zhi.*

121. JWJAD, ser. 6, no. 1, 597–98.

122. JWJAD, ser. 6, no. 1, 599.

123. JWJAD, ser. 6, no. 1, 657–58, 733.

124. JWJAD, ser. 6, no. 1, 662, 726–28.

125. In the case of Olan Bohereg, among the 508 taels of silver extorted from the Church by Widow Yang, four hundred taels were withdrawn from two shops named Qingfengquan and Rendetang. Presumably, these were local money shops that functioned as primordial banks. See JWJAD, ser. 6, no. 1, 535.

126. In 1880, the missionaries of Ligangbu was involved in a dispute with local Hui Muslims over the use of an irrigation canal near Pingluo, which led them to develop their own irrigation canal in Xiayingzi. See Liu Jingshan, "Hetao jiaoqu chuanjiao jianshi," 1–2; Taveirne, *Han-Mongol Encounters,* 246–47.

127. Buoye, "Litigation, Legitimacy, and Lethal Violence," in Zelin et al., eds., *Contract and Property in Early Modern China.*

128. Zhu Jinfu, ed., *Qingmo jiao'an,* volume 3, 515.

129. Kuhn, *Rebellion and Its Enemies in Late Imperial China.*

130. JWJAD, ser. 6, no. 1, 590, 592.

131. Su Xixian, "Wang Tongchun," 61–66; Wang Zhe, "Wang Tongchun xiansheng yiji."

132. Esherick, *The Origins of the Boxer Uprising;* Cohen, *History in Three Keys;* Bickers and Tiedemann, eds., *The Boxers, China, and the World.*

133. SYTZG, volume 7, 584; Chang Fei, *Tianzhujiao suiyuan jiaoqu,* 21.

134. Chang Fei, *Tianzhujiao suiyuan jiaoqu,* 23.

135. Zhu Jinfu, *Qingmo jiao'an,* volume 3, 516.

136. Guojia dang'anju mingqing dang'anguan, ed., *Yihetuan dang'an shiliao* (hereafter YHTDA), 225, 229; Chang Fei, *Tianzhujiao suiyuan jiaoqu,* 23–24; Mi Chenfeng, "Cong Ershisiqingdi jiao'an riqi de fengqi kan jiaohui shiliao de juxian."

137. Li Di, *Quanfei huojiaoji,* 322; Ku Wei-ying, *Saiwai chuanjiao shi,* 204; Chang Fei, *Tianzhujiao suiyuan jiaoqu,* 20, 24; YHTDA, 437–39.

138. Li Di, *Quanfei huojiaoji,* 330; Chang Fei, *Tianzhujiao suiyuan jiaoqu,* 50; SYTZG, volume 7, 581–84.

139. JKJYD, volume 82, 605; Sharula and Sude, "1900 nian Nei Menggu xibu de mengqi jiao'an," 511; Meirong, "Gengzi nian yikezhaomeng dalateqi jiao'an xintan," 161. According to the Mongol archives, around three hundred Catholics perished in Dalad banner. The missionaries, however, accused the Dalad troops of killing eight hundred people. Yet the number was reduced to 150 when it came to the negotiation of indemnities in 1901. See Zhu Jinfu, *Qingmo jiao'an*, volume 3, 123.

140. JWJAD, ser. 7, no. 1, 241.

141. SYTZG, volume 60, 581.

142. JWJAD, ser. 6, no. 3, 1881; Van Oost, *Min Yuqing zhuan*, 62; Li Di, *Quanfei huojiaoji*.

143. The Boxers were using largely spears, swords, and some old muskets. The Mongol cannon fire also failed to break through the earth rampart of the church. In contrast, the Catholics were equipped with twenty-five rifles and four thousand bullets. On several occasions, the missionaries and Catholics organized effective counterattacks so as to collect firewood and harvest crops outside the stockade, while shooting tens of Boxers and Mongol soldiers along the way. See Van Oost, *Min Yuqing zhuan*, 62; Li Di, *Quanfei huojiaoji*; Hao Chongli, *E'erduosi geming laoqu xubian*, 7.

144. Van Oost, *Min Yuqing zhuan*, 62–71; JWJAD, ser. 7, no. 1, 413, 416; Zhu Jinfu, *Qingmo jiao'an*, volume 3, 105.

145. Some of the former Catholics were converted to Chinese folk religion that venerated Guandi and other gods. See JWJAD, ser. 7, no. 1, 1107, 1113.

146. Van Oost, 72; JWJAD, ser. 7, no. 1, 1107; Li Di, *Quanfei huojiaoji*, 324; YHTDX, 1633.

147. Li Di, *Quanfei huojiaoji*, 302; SYTZG, volume 7, 581–84.

148. Li Di, *Quanfei huojiaoji*, 301–02; SYTZG, volume 7, 582–84; YHTDA, 659–60; YHTDX, 1417–22.

149. YHTDA, 489.

150. The Boxers burned down the undefended Catholic villages of Gaojiayingzi and Wuhao near Kalgan, and Shabo'er and Old Huangyangtan of Fengzhen, in which over seventy Catholics were killed. See Li Di, *Quanfei huojiaoji*, 300–01; SYTZG, volume 7, 582; YHTDX, 1721.

151. YHTDX, 1166–67; SYTZG, volume 7, 582.

152. Zhu Jinfu, *Qingmo jiao'an*, volume 3, 604; SYTZG, 587.

153. JWJAD, ser. 7, volume 1, 495–510; Zhu Jinfu, *Qingmo jiao'an*, volume 3, 546.

154. *Duguilang* ("circles") was a form of Round Robin that articulated popular grievances against higher authorities through petitions and lawsuits. See C. R. Bawden, *The Modern History of Mongolia* (New York, 1968), 176; Serruys, "Documents from Ordos on the 'Revolutionary Circles,' Part I," 482–507.

155. Zhongguo diyi lishi dang'an guan bianjibu, ed., *Yihetuan dang'an shiliao xubian* (hereafter YHTDX), 659.

156. JWJAD, ser. 7, volume 1, 107.

157. Among the high officials, Yongde died before the sentence was pronounced, and Zheng Wenqin of Guisui circuit completed suicide after being sentenced to death. Local officials of Höhhot, Khoringer, Togtokhu, and Ningyuan were dismissed and banished, and military officers in charge of the Qing troops were also punished. Among the Mongol princes, the *jasag* of Dalad banner was removed from office and deprived of noble rank, and the jasag

of Alasha banner and governor of the Yekhe Juu league were reprimanded. See JWJAD, ser. 7, volume 1, 453; Zhu Jinfu, *Qingmo jiao'an*, volume 3, 51.

158. This included 930,000 taels to the Italian Franciscan Friars of northern Shanxi, 550,000 taels to the Dutch Franciscan Friars of southern Shanxi, two hundred thousand taels to the Scheut mission of southwest Mongolia, 650,000 taels to the Scheut mission of Central Mongolia, and 350,000 taels to the seven Protestant missions. An additional 1,460,000 taels of silver were assigned to the missions of Shanxi from the general indemnity. See Zhu Jinfu, *Qingmo jiao'an*, volume 3, 174, 363; YHTDX, 1715.

159. For relief in the seven sub-prefectures of Shanxi province, see JWJAD, ser. 7, volume 1, 455; for relief in southern Ordos, see JWJAD, ser. 7, volume 3, 1074–76. For the retrieval of women and children, see SYTZG, volume 7, 585–87; YHTDX, 1171, 1445.

160. JWJAD, ser. 7, volume 1, 396, 408, 413–14, 424–26, 439, 1116–18.

161. Zhu Jinfu, *Qingmo jiao'an*, volume 3, 728–31.

162. Yigu, *Suiyuan zouyi*; Zhu Jinfu, *Qingmo jiao'an*, volume 3, 737.

163. For the agreement between the Church and Otog, Üüshin, and Jasag banners, see YHTDX, 1166–90; Zhu Jinfu, *Qingmo jiao'an*, volume 3, 111–5. For discussions on the impact of the agreement on the propagation of Christianity in Mongol territories as well as the quasi-feudal social system of the Mongols, see Sudebilige, "Tianzhujiao yu qingchao jinken mudi," 154.

164. Van Melckebeke, *Bianjiang gongjiao shehui shiye*, 4.

165. For instance, the Belgian missionary Joseph Rutten (1874–1950) developed a vaccine in 1931 that successfully controlled the epidemic typhus fever, which was the most common epidemic disease in northern China, having claimed over one hundred Scheut missionaries' lives. See Van Melckebeke, *Bianjiang gongjiao shehui shiye*.

166. For instance, Antoine Mostaert (1881–1971) was a prominent Mongolist who pioneered the studies of Mongolian phonology and history, as well as folklore and ethnography of the Ordos Mongols. See Sagaster, ed., *Antoine Mostaert (1881–1971)*. Józef Van Oost (1877–1939) was dedicated to collecting Mongolian folklore and proverbs. See Heylen, *Chronique du Toumet–Ortos*. The anthropologist and ethnographer Louis Schram (1883–1971) is the author of the classic study, *The Mongours of the Kansu–Tibetan Frontier*, first published in 1954.

167. Lattimore, *Inner Asian Frontiers of China*.

6

Moving People to Strengthen the Border

Official Reclamation and State Building

In 1901, following the Boxer Uprising that ended in the Qing's humiliating defeat by the Allied Forces, the court instigated a series of institutional and political reforms known as the New Policies (Ch: *xinzheng* 新政, Mo: *Shine Jasag*). Modeled after the Meiji reforms of Japan, the New Policies aimed at transforming the Qing empire into a modern nation-state.[1] In an effort to guard the nation from the imminent threat of the partition at the hands of Western imperialist powers, the Qing drastically changed its frontier policy from an isolationist policy that restricted Chinese cultivation and settlement in the non-Han peripheries to one that actively promoted "moving people to strengthen the border" (*yimin shibian* 移民實邊). In 1902, Yigu, a high-ranking Manchu official, was appointed as imperial commissioner to oversee land reclamation in the Mongols banners. The purpose of the land reclamation was to mobilize new fiscal resources to finance the reform programs and to counter foreign influences on the northern frontiers.[2]

The previous chapters discussed how population pressures in China proper and market expansion resulted in changing economic practices and a changing property regime in the Mongol society: notably the shift of communally owned banner land toward more privatized land holding. The pervasive private cultivation, with the connivance of Mongol nobles and officials, provided opportunities for local actors such as Chinese land brokers and Catholic missionaries to thrive. Meanwhile, the competition over land and water gave rise to growing tensions and conflicts between different social groups. Land disputes, above all else, accounted for numerous disputes involving Catholic missionaries in Inner Mongolia that culminated in the eruption of violence during the Boxer Uprising of 1900. Under such circumstances, opening the Mongol lands for reclamation became an attractive option for the Qing state, not only to expand revenue so as to finance its modernizing programs, but also to reinforce state control in order to combat foreign influences and curtail local autonomy.

In many ways, the late Qing official colonization not only reshaped the political, ethnic, and ecological landscape of the Han-Mongol borderlands, but it also had a profound impact upon the territorial, geopolitical, and cultural constitution of twentieth-century China. However, this subject remains understudied, especially in English-language literature.[3] Japanese researchers of the Southern Manchuria Railway Company carried out in-depth, comprehensive studies on the subject in the 1930s. Anzai Kuraji's detailed and regional specific account on the late Qing reclamation in Suiyuan remains a benchmark study on the subject to this day.[4] However, although his analysis tends to be more descriptive than critical, Anzai betrays a linear, progressive view of history in seeing the replacement of the nomadic economy by Chinese cultivation as both inevitable and necessary within the broad context of Western capitalism supplanting "decadent feudalism" in China in general and Mongolia in particular. The opinions of Chinese historians are overwhelmingly negative. The official reclamation of Mongol lands is widely criticized as "predatory" and "reactionary" for the extraction and expropriation involved, which resulted in intensified social and ethnic conflicts as well as long-term environmental degradation.[5] Part of the reason is that the late Qing government is often portrayed as the villain in orthodox Marxist-Leninist narratives, as being either incapable of carrying out real reforms that benefited all peoples or unwilling to do so. Partly, it also reflects the Maoist rhetoric of opposition against "Han Chauvinism" in favor of "class struggle" in ethnic studies since the 1950s. Although such critiques have some validity, many of their arguments suffer from generalization and oversimplification. Consequently, they do not pay sufficient attention to specific historical contexts and regional differences.

This chapter provides a layered and nuanced account of the late Qing reclamation campaign as a historical event by examining the encounters, interactions, and conflicts between an aggressively modernizing state and the existing political, economic, and social structures in the Mongol frontier. Instead of a clear-cut process of expropriation and victimization, I argue that the actual processes of official reclamation and state expansion involved multiple levels of negotiations and mutual accommodations among different social actors. This chapter begins with a brief overview of the late nineteenth-century reformist discourses concerning colonization and frontier consolidation. Next, it examines how the new policy was implemented through a set of new institutions such as land reclamation bureaus and corporations. Focusing on the Chakhar and Ordos, I analyze how Yigu and his subordinates varied their approaches and strategies according to different circumstances and how the Mongols responded to the state initiatives. In particular, I examine the interactions among Qing officials, Mongol jasags, and Chinese land merchants through the process of opening up irrigated lands in Hetao by expropriating Mongol lands and nationalizing the private-owned irrigation systems. Finally, I discuss how land reclamation facilitated the administrative incorporation of the heterogeneous periphery into the centralized framework of a nation-state.

"MANAGING THE FRONTIER"

Two major challenges that the Qing faced at the turn of the twentieth century accounted for this policy reversal toward the Mongols: (1) an exacerbated financial crisis and (2) an imminent national security predicament. On the one hand, the Qing government was in desperate need of expanding its fiscal base to cover its colossal war indemnities and to finance its military, educational, and administrative reform programs. On the international front, the scramble of the Great Powers for concessions threatened to carve China up into various "spheres of influences." In particular, the occupation of Manchuria by Russia in the wake of the Boxer Uprising and the rivalry between Russia and Japan in Manchuria posed a grave menace to the empire's frontier security and territorial integrity. Under such circumstances, the new policies represented a desperate attempt to survive by modernizing the empire and centralizing control in the frontier.

Meanwhile, the grave internal and external crises that punctuated the second half of the nineteenth century had rendered the Mongol troops ineffective in matters of national defense. The defeat of the Mongol cavalry led by Prince Sengge Rinchen (1811–1865) during the British and French invasion of Beijing and the subsequent death of the prince in a campaign against the Nian Rebellion (1853–1868) reveal that the Mongols, once formidable allies of the Qing dynasty, could no longer protect the empire from its many new challenges.[6] The rise of regional militia forces organized by Han officials and funded by local gentry in the wake of the Taiping Rebellion (1850–1864) and the Dungan/Hui Uprising (1862–1877) further weakened Mongol influence over the military, so that they were increasingly viewed as a weak link in national defense. All of these situations showed the feebleness of the old Manchu-Mongol alliance in sustaining the empire through its many new challenges, foreign or domestic.

The changing perception of the Mongols was exemplified in the memorial to the throne by Cen Chunxuan, governor of Shanxi, on June 6, 1901 regarding reclaiming the Mongol land. Cen began by praising the military feats of the dynasty in opening up new territories and using the Mongols as a screen to guard the northern frontier. He went on to point out the imminent plight caused by the decline of the Mongols, whose poorly trained troops and primitive weaponry had left the vast frontier "empty as an unpeopled land" in the face of Russia's strength.[7] In a separate memorial on disciplining the Mongols for anti-Christian incidences, Cen again blamed the Mongols for their reckless actions during the Boxer rebellion: "Now the Mongols are mired in poverty and weakness—how should they be expected to contend against the foreigners? . . . Eventually, they are sure to be humiliated by defeat and bring disaster to our nation."[8] Obviously, for Cen, not only were the Mongols incapable of guarding the frontier, but their poverty and weakness had made them a burden and an obstacle to the nation in its quest for wealth and power.

Cen was by no means the only official who advocated opening up Mongol lands for cultivation. Starting from the 1870s, "managing the frontier" (*choubian* 籌邊)

had become a pivotal concern for reform-minded officials like Li Hongzhang, then governor-general of Zhili. Li proposed that Chinese settlers be permitted to cultivate surplus Mongol pastures in Chakhar as a means to curtail foreign infringement while providing for the impoverished herders.[9] Similarly, Zhang Zhidong, governor of Shanxi in 1881–1884, called for institutional reform (*gaizhi* 改制) in the Chakhar and Tümed areas by legalizing Chinese migration, granting household registration, and conducting land surveys.[10] Both proposals targeted "Internal Mongolia" under direct Manchu command rather than "Outer-vassal Mongolia" ruled by semi-autonomous jasags. Nonetheless, they foreshadowed the changing Qing policies in favor of Chinese colonization and direct rule in the Mongol periphery. Apparently, the Han officials and policymakers deemed it justifiable to seize Mongol lands and assimilate the Mongol people for their "own good." Indeed, the Mongols' peripheral position in the money economy introduced by the Qing and its Chinese financiers made them an easy target of blame for their own economic plight.

Apart from its strategic function, Cen also noted the fiscal role of the frontier as a potential source of revenue. Particularly, the Hetao plain was known for its fertile soil and irrigation advantages. The former governor of Shanxi, Gangyi, reported in the 1850s that Chinese cultivation generated one hundred thousand taels of annual proceeds to the Dalad banner. The lieutenant governor of Chokhar, Shaoqi, who arbitrated in the land dispute between the Dalad and Tümed banners in 1885, testified that the contested land brought a yearly income of one hundred thousand taels to the banners. Like his predecessor, Cen suggested these revenues could be utilized to train Mongol troops.[11] He went on to cite the precedents of the Russians, Americans, and British when they developed Manchuria, San Francisco, and Melbourne. In all these cases, he reasoned, not only were desolate frontiers turned into fertile settlements and populous cities, but they also generated enough revenue to benefit the entire nation. Unlike these projects that started from scratch, the Mongol frontier enjoyed the advantage of a well-built irrigation system and a ready pool of settlers. Thus, success could be anticipated. Cen's proposal exemplified a major cognitive shift among Qing high officials, most of whom were Han Chinese, concerning the non-Han frontier, which was conceptualized not just as a locus of strategic defense, but as an untapped wealth of resources to be exploited and a vacant space to be filled. The precedents of the Western powers spurred their aspirations for the Qing's own colonizing and civilizing project in the frontier.

On the other hand, Cen's proposal grew out of more immediate concerns. Ever since his appointment as governor of Shanxi in March 1901, he had faced a drained treasury in the province.[12] The Boxer upheavals of the previous year incurred an indemnity of 3,130,000 taels imposed on the provincial coffers on top of its share of nine hundred thousand taels of national indemnity.[13] For these reasons, Cen proposed to open the Mongol lands in the Yekhe Juu and Ulaanchab leagues bordering Shanxi province for cultivation, to raise funds and "strengthen the border." He predicted that it would bring up to two million taels for the imperial treasury:

The total area of the banners [of the Yekhe Juu and Ulaanchab leagues] adds up to over 3,000 or 4,000 *li* in circumference. With only three or four tenth put to cultivation, we will have hundreds of thousands *qing* of farmlands. In 1899, former military governor of Heilongjiang, Enze, petitioned for opening the lands of the Jalaid banner. Given half of the land fees, it will bring an income of four to five hundred thousand taels. With even half of the Ordos and nearby banners opened, it will bring revenue three or four times that sum.[14]

The precedent Cen cited here occurred in Manchuria, where the official ban against Chinese cultivation had been partially lifted since 1860. It created a flux of over three hundred thousand migrants from Shandong and Zhili each year into the previously undeveloped frontiers to work on horse farms, hunting reserves, and general waste-lands.[15] In 1896, Russia secured a concession from the Qing government to build the Chinese Eastern Railway through Manchuria. As the proposed railroad was to run through the territories of the Jalaid, Ghorlos Rear, and Dörbed banners of the Jerim league, military governor of Heilongjiang Enze petitioned the court to reclaim Mongol pasturelands in these banners to counter Russian influences and increase fiscal revenue. The proposal was approved in 1900.[16]

By the 1880s, booming agriculture in Hetao had attracted the attention of Qing military and civilian officials. In 1886, Changgeng, commander of the garrison city of Bayandai (Huining) in Ili, memorialized the court on military colonization in Chanjin of Hetao, where the Qing troops suppressing the Hui Rebellion were stationed for three years. Gangyi, governor of Shanxi, even penned a detailed plan on setting up military (*juntun* 軍屯) and merchant colonies (*shangtun* 商屯) in Chanjin through expropriating private irrigation canals and organizing military and civil administration.[17] These proposals represented initial attempts to incorporate part of the Mongol territory into centralized administration via expropriation and military colonization.

Later, a deepened financial crisis made the officials shift to a more comprehensive colonizing policy. In 1897, Huang Siyong, director of Imperial Hanlin Academy, petitioned the court on full-scale reclamation in the two western leagues: Yekhe Juu and Ulaanchab. It was endorsed by Hu Pinzhi, who was then the governor of Shanxi.[18] These proposals targeted "Outer-vassal Mongolia" overseen by the Lifanyuan, rather than "Internal Mongolia" under direct Qing rule or special grain-producing areas like Hetao. Although these proposals were rejected by the court citing strong Mongol opposition, they indicated a growing consensus among Qing officialdom on the inevitability and urgency of abolishing the existing Manchu-Mongol ruling system in favor of an aggressively modernizing and centralizing state. Note that advocates of official reclamation were predominantly Han Chinese officials who felt little sympathy toward the old Manchu-Mongol political order in the first place. Four of them served as the governor of Shanxi: Zhang Zhidong (1881–84), Gangyi (1885–89), Hu Pinzhi (1895–99), and Cen Chunxuan (1901–02), which illuminates the financial preponderance of the Xikouwai region to Shanxi province due to the immigrants it absorbed and revenue it generated.

IMPERIAL COMMISSIONER

On January 5, 1902, the Qing court endorsed Cen's proposal and appointed Yigu (1853–1926), deputy minister of war, as the imperial commissioner to supervise land reclamation in the thirteen banners of the Yekhe Juu (Ordos) and Ulaanchab leagues and the Chakhar region. The purpose, as the imperial edict stated, was to "substantialize frontier reserves and benefit the livelihood of Chinese and banner people." The imperial commissioner would be in charge of formulating a concrete plan of opening up the Mongol lands, setting up rules and regulations, and mediating between the Qing court and Mongol jasags in coordination with the military and civilian governors of border regions and provinces.[19]

Yigu's first task was to enlist the cooperation of the Mongol jasags. In his decree to the Mongols and Chinese, he assured them that the purpose of the campaign was to "exploit the productivity of land and extend solicitude to the Mongol people, in order to secure the borders externally and eliminate potential dangers internally,"[20] rather than to deprive the Mongols of their lands and the merchants of their properties. He then listed two causes of this change of policy. First, the old *fengjin* policy had resulted in the underdevelopment of agriculture, so that fertile lands lay wasted and left the people impoverished. Second, the rampant illegitimate cultivation had caused social instability, as widespread arbitrariness and violence in land transactions reduced the society to lawlessness. Yigu stated that without the state-issued land deeds, "people cannot settle down and the lands cannot be turned into permanent properties."[21] Therefore, the goal of official reclamation was to turn poverty and weakness into wealth and power, so that the Mongols could have resources to provide for their people and train their troops. He ensured them favorable revenue-sharing terms, including the remittance of half of the land-contract fees and all annual taxes to the banners and the allocation of vocational plots (*suiquedi* 隨缺地) to Mongol personnel and soldiers.[22]

Yigu's arguments echoed the agriculturalist and statist ideologies that he shared with many contemporaries, which asserted the superiority of agrarianism over nomadism, and centralized forms of government over decentralized ones. Nevertheless, his concerns regarding the absence of the state in a frontier setting were legitimate. In his joint memorial with Governor Cen on May 6, Yigu listed several potential dangers that needed to be eliminated in order to implement the new policy. First, many Mongol nobles and officials profited from illegal reclamation and arbitrary practices in land transaction, which was the underlying reason why they opposed official reclamation. Second, the existing settlers feared that their plots would be revoked and given to new cultivators. Because many of them kept private militias, they needed to be pacified to avoid local disturbances. Third, the spread of Catholic villages across Inner Mongolia represented another source of instability, because any land dispute case could become elevated into missionary cases and jeopardize diplomatic relations with the Western powers.[23]

Unsurprisingly, the new policy aroused strong protest from jasags from both leagues. They submitted petitions opposing the policy to the military governor of Suiyuan. Their objections were based on three grounds. First, the lands of Inner and Outer Mongolia were bestowed by the Kangxi emperor to the Mongol vassals as a hereditary habitat, so that they could carry on their pastoral life in perpetuity. It would be against the will of the sacred lord to open these lands for cultivation. Second, pastureland was indispensable to sustaining the nomadic economy and culture. The Mongols depended on grazing animals to maintain their livelihood; support their nobles, lamas, and soldiers; and fulfill military and imperial duties. Once their pastures were reclaimed, the people would be left destitute and homeless. Third, cohabitation with the Chinese would jeopardize rather than benefit the Mongols, for it would bring endless trouble and disputes. One petition insisted that it was unheard of that Mongols should mix with the Chinese to till the land, just as wild monkeys never share homes with domestic fowls. Therefore, the Mongols entreated the court to revoke the policy.[24]

Here, the princes used the rhetoric of allegiance to the Kangxi emperor to address their more immediate concern: the fear of compromising their hereditary rights over their lands. Needless to say, the Mongol nobles were not strangers to cultivation in their realms or to engaging in monetary transactions with Shanxi merchants. However, it was one thing to lease land to pay off debts or to gain extra revenue, as in this case, the yamen retained jurisdiction over the land. It was another thing to give up their banner lands altogether as taxable land to the Qing authorities. For average Mongols, the danger was more concrete: the possibility of losing their habitat and pastures, which formed the foundation of their way of life. There were other considerations, too. In a petition presented to Yigu by a *duguilang* (a popular resistance movement) of the Üüshin banner, the signees spoke of defending their "temples and shrines, flags and objects of veneration, graves and human remains venerated from early days," so that "the dead be left undisturbed and the living may keep habitat and pastures in peace."[25] Indeed, what the average Mongols fought to defend was their home, their cultural heritage, and their right to make a living.

Thus, Yigu's campaign came to a deadlock in both leagues, as the governors (*chuulghan darugha*) of both leagues refused to answer his call to convene in Suiyuan. In turn, Yigu blamed this lack of compliance on the selfish motives of those who profited from illegal cultivation.[26] Meanwhile, he was aware of the political stake that the new policy entailed, as manifested in a secret memorial he presented to the throne in September 1902:

> Had there been more delays, it would necessarily firm up [the Mongols'] heart in ignoring [the imperial orders] and make future endeavors even more difficult. Consequently, not only would we lose economic rights (*liquan* 利權) and administrative authority (*shiquan* 事權), but it would also enhance the difficulty of retrieving the right of reining the outer vassals (*yufan* 馭藩).[27]

Here Yigu made it clear that the ultimate goal of the campaign was to "retrieve the right of reining the outer vassals," by revoking the relative economic and administrative autonomy that the Mongols had so far. Endorsing Yigu's concerns, the Qing court issued a second imperial edict on September 21 admonishing the governors of both leagues and urging them to comply with the imperial commissioner's order immediately. As reinforcement, Yigu was given the title of minister of the Lifanyuan, and he was later appointed military governor of Suiyuan.[28] Thus, he was granted the highest administrative and military authority over the banners, including the capacity of deploying the Qing troops should the need arise.

As the official campaign came to a gridlock, Yigu shifted his attention to the Chakhar banners under direct Manchu rule. As mentioned in chapter 5, most of the pastures in Chakhar had fallen into disuse after the mid-eighteenth century and were open to illegitimate cultivation. A group of land brokers (*huzong* 戶總) mediated the transaction and contracted large tracts of land from the Mongols. They then subleased smaller plots to individual cultivators. Many of them maintained private militias to guard their interests. Feuds and armed conflicts were common due to unclear property rights, overlapping boundaries, and arbitrary practices in land transactions, as exemplified by the Fengzhen missionary case (see chapter 5). Since 1882, attempts had been made to impose state regulation in standardizing the survey, sale, and registration of Chakhar lands, with offices of the Land Reclamation Bureau (*yahuangju* 押荒局) set up in Fengzhen and Ningyuan to register cultivated lands for taxation and to collect the arrears of land payments.[29] All these actions came to little avail, with only some three thousand *qing* registered (less than 20 percent of the entire cultivated area in Chakhar Right Flank).[30]

This time around, Yigu was determined to use Chakhar to crack open the western leagues. He restructured the Land Reclamation Bureau and set up two branches in Fengzhen and Kalgan to oversee reclamation in the two flanks that were under the jurisdiction of Shanxi and Zhili provinces, respectively. The Bureau then set out to enforce cadastral surveys and boundary demarcations.[31] Each banner was required to map the *sumuns* or sub-units within their boundary, with a clear indication of cultivated and uncultivated areas.[32] A thirty-two-*li*-long boundary from north to south was demarcated between the Right and Left Flanks, which also defined the extended border line between Zhili and Shanxi provinces outside the passes.[33] Measures were taken to enforce the payment of land fees and annual taxes. A one-time land contract fee (*yahuangyin* 押荒銀), at a flat rate of three *qian* per *mu*, was due three months after completion of the land survey. Upon payment of the fees, title deeds were to be issued, with all previous contracts and agreements nullified.[34] Those who failed to pay the due sum by the posted dates risked having their rights revoked and given to others. For plots already under cultivation, an annual tax of 1.8 *fen* per *mu* was applied starting from the following year after the payment of fees, whereas the previously uncultivated lands were subject to taxation (*shengke* 升科) in three years after they were put under cultivation.[35]

Yigu's reclamation campaign in Chakhar turned out to be a sweeping success. By the end of 1904, over forty-four thousand *qing* (approximately three hundred thousand ha) of land had been surveyed: generating seven hundred thousand taels of land fees and an annual tax of fifty thousand taels.[36] The campaign also eliminated the pervasive influences of Chinese land brokers by confiscating their lands, disbanding their militias, and abolishing all private headquarters that handled land transactions. Part of its success can be explained by Yigu's joint role as imperial commissioner and military governor of Suiyuan, with several camps of infantry and cavalry troops garrisoned in Datong and Fengzhen at his disposal. The concentrated political and military power helped facilitate the implementation of the new policy. On several occasions, the troops were deployed to suppress the defiant Mongols or local strongmen engaging in armed resistance.[37] Moreover, unlike the previous endeavors that targeted illegitimate cultivation, Yigu's reclamation campaign was far more comprehensive. By imposing a standardized procedure of land survey, registration, and taxation, it aimed at retrieving the Mongol lands for official taxation as well as incorporating the Mongol periphery into China's centralized administrative system.

Another factor that contributed to the campaign's success in Chakhar was the absence of hereditary jasag rule in the region. Although the banners and nobility were entitled to land allocations, these land grants were considered a grace or favor bestowed by the Qing emperor that could be revoked at any time in the name of "contribution" (*baoxiao* 報效) or "return" (*fenghuan* 奉還).[38] The official reclamation campaign turned out to be one such occasion, in which ownership of land in the area was transferred from individual Mongol banners, herds, and nobles to the Qing state. Granted, measures were taken to provide for their livelihood through the allocation of habitats and common pastures as well as limited monetary compensation. For each *mu* of land under cultivation, the banners and herds were given a modest share of four *fen* out of the three *qian* (i.e. 13 percent) of land-contract fees, which amounted to 192,000 taels in total. Nobles were allowed to keep the four *li* of surcharge, which was about 17,500 taels per year.[39] Each Mongol functionary and soldier was granted a vocational allotment, which they were free to cultivate or rent out but prohibited to sell. Depending on the military and official ranks, the land allotments varied from sixty to eight hundred *mu* per person. Meanwhile, an area of between 180 to 240 *qing* of common pasture in each banner was designated for grazing purposes, and cultivation was prohibited on these lands.[40] As a result of the new policy, the Mongols lost not only access to vast pasturelands, but they were also denied the rights to possess land.

DIVIDE AND RECLAIM

Compared to the ease with which official reclamation proceeded in Chakhar, Yigu had to fight an uphill battle in the western leagues. After a second imperial edict was issued in September 1902, both governors of the Yekhe Juu and Ulaanchab leagues called for an assembly of constituent banners to voice unanimous opposition to the reclamation project. A petition signed by all thirteen jasags was submitted to the Lifanyuan in November.[41] To implement the new policy, Yigu needed to break the Mongols' confederation. He picked four targets: Khanggin and Dalad banners of the Ordos, and Western Urad and Dörben Kheükhed (Siziwang) banners of Ulaanchab. He then dispatched official envoys and recruited Mongolian-speaking Chinese merchants and high lamas as lobbyists. These were chosen partly because Hetao, the primary target of the campaign, was located within the boundaries of many of these banners and partly because the jasags of the Khanggin and Dörben Kheükhed banners also served as incumbent governors of the two leagues. The compliance of these governors was critical for the campaign.[42]

Yigu tasted victory first in the Dalad banner. The banner was in a financial predicament because of the massive Boxer indemnity of 370,000 taels of silver it owed, and it had to resort to ceding 2,161 *qing* of well-irrigated lands to the Church (see chapter 5). Its jasag, Tümenbayar, was on the brink of being stripped of rank for the violence during the rebellion, and therefore had no bargaining leverage against the Qing authorities. Yigu successfully extracted an agreement from Tümenbayar to open up his domain for cultivation, in exchange for an advance payment of the remaining sum to the Church. Apart from the 2,655 *qing* of well-irrigated land, Yigu also secured concessions to build irrigation works in the Dalad banner, with all irrigable lands in the vicinity of the canals opened to cultivation. As result, the banner lost over forty-eight hundred *qing* (thirty-two thousand *ha*) of its best land as "indemnity lands to the Church" (*peijiaodi* 賠教地), as well as its rights to collect tax under the terms of perpetual lease (*yongzu* 永租).[43]

Yigu soon encountered open opposition from the jasag of the Khanggin banner, Arbinbayar, who was also the incumbent governor of the Yekhe Juu league. The prince refused to comply with Yigu's request to hand over the Khanggai area of Hetao for official reclamation and reproached other jasags for their compromises. He insisted that no action be taken before a formal response from the Lifanyuan was received.[44] His defiance created problems for Yigu, for the reclamation campaign hinged on securing the Khanggai land where all irrigation canals were linked to the Yellow River. He had already made plans to seize all the assets of Chinese land developers just for that purpose. Moreover, the prince's noncompliance set a poor example for other jasags. As punishment, Yigu engineered the removal of Arbinbayar from his position of league governor. It was a tactical move, for he knew from experience the value of titles and ranks to Mongol nobles. Previously, the two princes of the Dalad and Dörben Kheükhed had consented to pay Boxer indemnity on pain of losing their ranks.[45]

Yigu's strategy was effective. Arbinbayar backed down and consented to open up the Khanggai lands (a total of four thousand *qing*) for official cultivation. The land reclamation was arranged as an open sale (*fangken* 放墾) rather than a perpetual lease, which effectively transferred the land ownership from the Khanggin banner to the Qing state.[46] Further, Arbinbayar agreed to "contribute" half of the annual taxes due to the banner in addition to a "donation" of thirty thousand taels to Beijing and Suiyuan. He was eventually reinstated to his position as league governor only after Yigu's dismissal in 1908.[47]

The other Ordos princes followed Arbinbayar's example and agreed to the plowing of their lands and to "contribute" 20 percent of annual taxes to Beijing.[48] The jasag of the Üüshin banner and deputy league governor sought Yigu's favor by offering his entire domain for cultivation. The prince of the Jasag banner was the only jasag who answered Yigu's summon to Baotou in person. Both princes were subsequently nominated as the new governor and deputy governor of the league. In October 1904, in honor of the empress dowager's seventieth birthday, the duo jointly offered a tract of over one thousand *qing* along their borders for official cultivation, which was called "Longevity Land" (*zhugudi* 祝嘏地, or *wanshoudi* 萬壽地). Along with the land, they offered all the taxes it generated to be contributed to the imperial treasury. In return, both princes received a promotion in rank.[49]

Obviously, the official campaign provided opportunity for some nobles to enhance their personal prestige by collaborating with the state. In other cases, there were underlying reasons behind their actions other than personal gains. For instance, the Wang banner was the first to open its territory to cadastral survey and open land sale in May 1904. Within two years, over half of its realm was surveyed and released: adding up to 9,639 *qing*. This was done on condition that the western section of the banner be enclosed for habitats and pastures. Disputes ensued as the Chinese migrants refused to vacate the area, which resulted in a two-year feud. Only after Yigu intervened by sending troops from Suiyuan was the enclosure completed. The incident soured the banner's relationship with the local officials of the adjacent Shenmu sub-prefecture who oversaw the Chinese migrants of southeast Ordos. In 1905, upon the creation of a new Wuyuan sub-prefecture in northwest Ordos, both jasags of the Wang and Jasag banners petitioned Yigu to sever ties with Shenmu under Shaanxi province and be affiliated with Wuyuan under Shanxi province instead.[50]

The case was illustrative of the grim situation in banners that adjoined Chinese provinces. All lands reported by the Üüshin, Jasag, and Wang banners were located inside the Black Border near the Great Wall, which had been open to Chinese cultivation since the end of the seventeenth century (see chapter 3). Even though an *oboo*-marked border (*paijie* 牌界, Mo: *paisa* "paizi") was set up in 1749 to curtail farming, much of the banner land had been put under cultivation by the Chinese beyond the border. In the Wang banner, the jasag ordered the remaining banner land to be distributed among his subjects in a move to check the process. However, this only led to more encroachment, as the Mongols simply let the Chinese till the land for them for a fee.[51] At the same time, the arid climate and sandy soils in this area, combined with the common practice of land abandonment, resulted in land degradation and desertification. The deteriorating environment and low productivity led to tax evasion and the infringement of pasturelands among the Chinese migrants.[52] The partiality of Shenmu officials only exacerbated the situation.[53] Under such circumstances, the official reclamation campaign may be seen as empowering to some Mongol authorities in terms of countering the influences of Chinese migrants and officials alike through the enforcement of land surveys, boundary demarcations, and official taxation. In addition, the land prices and taxes, to be divided between the Qing state and the banners, provided the latter with a relatively stable source of revenue.

In comparison, the opening up of the Jüüngar banner was the most turbulent. Like the Dalad banner, the Jüüngar banner owed twenty-nine thousand taels of Boxer indemnity to the Catholic Church, which enabled Yigu to enforce his new policy. At first, it was decided that the banner should cede three hundred *qing* in the Khangkha (Hetaochuan) area north of the Yellow River directly to the Church. However, violent resistance from local Mongols and Chinese alike prompted Yigu to rearrange the plan, so that the Qing government paid the indemnity on behalf of the banner in return for the latter to open up its banner land for cultivation.[54] The plan for opening up the Khangkha area was soon shelved because the land was reportedly barren. Instead, Yigu demanded the Black Border lands bordering the Wang banner to be opened. After much procrastination, its jasag reluctantly opened the area for plowing. In June 1905, three branch offices of the Reclamation Administration were established within the Black Border. They were headed by Yue Zhonglin, the newly appointed administrator of Dongsheng sub-prefecture under Shanxi province who also oversaw the Wang banner branch office.[55]

The official presence sparked conflicts between local Mongols and Chinese settlers along the border between the Jüüngar and Wang banners. A group of armed, mounted Mongols, led by two nobles of the Wang banner and two *janggi* officers of the Jüüngar banner, attacked the settlers in newly cultivated areas, seized their animals and cereals, and obstructed them from registering their land at the branch offices. The mob also harassed the office functionaries and captured, robbed, and tortured them. It targeted especially the Mongols who had collaborated with the Qing authorities in conducting land surveys and sales.[56] The mastermind behind all these disturbances was believed to be a noble and senior *tusalagchi* named Dampil, who happened to be the most influential political figure in the Jüüngar banner.[57] In May 1905, Yigu petitioned the Lifanyuan to admonish Dampil and strip him of the hat sphere that marked his rank on the grounds that the noble repeatedly ignored his summons to Höhhot.[58]

Dampil's defiance, as it turned out, was not completely based on adherence to the nomadic lifestyle. The Black Border lands of the Jüüngar banner had been plowed since the 1870s as a means of providing famine relief, and Dampil himself was in charge of leasing the land to Chinese settlers and collecting taxes. In his memorial to the throne, Yigu reported that over one thousand *shi* of millet were stored at an oil mill in Shilata that was allegedly owned by Dampil, as well as at his residence.[59] He further accused the noble of surreptitiously opening up banner lands and embezzling taxes for years, deceiving the jasag, and suppressing the commoners. However, Mongolian sources showed that the opening up of the Black Border lands was sanctioned by the Lifanyuan and the oil mill allegedly owned by Dampil was used as a common granary of the banner.[60]

The situation in the Jüüngar banner soon deteriorated. In June, Yue Zhonglin arrived with a squad of Qing troops in the Black Border lands and began to evict the Mongols and Chinese settlers forcefully: causing one death and injuring two others.[61] Yue and his troops encountered persistent resistance from local Mongols who joined the insurgents of the Wang and Jüüngar banners in revolting against the Qing authority.[62] On August 24, a group of armed Mongols, vowing to expel outside intruders and recover all lands from Chinese settlers, attacked the Shilata branch office of the Reclamation Administration, burned its documents and books, and forced Yue and his subordinates to flee to Hequ in Shanxi across the Yellow River.[63]

An enraged Yigu immediately dispatched Qing troops from Suiyuan, Baotou, and Datong to suppress the rebellion. He accused Dampil of instigating the entire affair. The troops attacked Dampil's residence, which was believed to be a main stronghold of the insurgents, and burned it to the ground. When Dampil and some followers fled, they were listed as wanted across the two western leagues. Eventually, after a month's pursuit, the troops captured the fugitive and about thirty adherents near the Yellow River. The seventy-five-year-old noble was convicted of plotting rebellion against the Qing and executed in Suiyuan in 1906. Dampil's death cleared the obstacles to official reclamation in the Jüüngar banner. Nevertheless, Yigu's hasty decision to convict Dampil on the grounds of insufficient evidence eventually led to his downfall in 1908.

The resistance movement soon spread to other banners. In the Üüshin banner, in reaction to its prince's promise to offer the entire banner territory for official cultivation, local Mongols organized twelve *duguilangs* ("circles"), which was a form of Round Robin that articulated popular grievances against higher authorities through petitions and lawsuits.[64] These vigilante groups, comprised of low-ranking and impoverished nobles, lamas, and commoners, took it upon themselves to defend their livelihoods from the mass land sale connived by the banner authorities, Qing state, and Chinese land brokers. In 1905, they set out to remove landmarks on the borders of neighboring banners and petitioned Yigu to allow them to keep their pastures. They even approached Bishop Alfons Bermijn of the Catholic Church about interceding on their behalf.[65] In the end, Yigu refrained from sending troops to suppress the opposition. Thus no land was surveyed during his tenure. It was only after the newly reinstated league governor Arbinbayar dissolved these *duguilangs* in 1909 that the Üüshin lands were finally opened for cultivation. Nonetheless, cultivation was restricted to the Black Border and Longevity lands (an area of nearly two thousand *qing*). In the Khanggin banner, popular resistance forced Yigu to set a limit of four thousand *qing* in the cultivated area, so that the Mongols were able to keep part of their habitat and pastures.

In all these cases, Yigu invoked the time-honored imperial strategy of "carrot and stick" (*en wei bing shi* 恩威並施, "combination of benevolence and severity") in dealing with the Mongol vassals.[66] Meanwhile, he readily adjusted his measures to different situations in the locality. One of his methods involved taking advantage of financial woes or local frictions. One by one, the jasags were persuaded, lured, or coerced into subjecting to the new policy. The success of his approach testifies to the weakness of the banners in defending the Mongolian property and interests against an expansive central state and gave rise to widespread popular discontent in the form of *duguilang*. Their discontent was most often directed against jasags, banner officials, and functionaries. Again, it should be noted that most lands opened up had already been under cultivation, such as the Black Border lands near the Great Wall and the Hetao area along the Yellow River, and thus were not virgin pasturelands. As shown in the conflicts in the Jüüngar banner, what was at stake was the abrogation of the Mongols' hereditary rights to the land, particularly their right to collect taxes from Chinese settlers. Therefore, the central issue here was not the competing usage of the land between farmers and herders, but rather the massive expropriation of Mongol land by the Qing government and Chinese land speculators as well as the appropriation of land-generated income by the amban offices supervising the banners.

INSTITUTION BUILDING

Yigu's new policy was implemented through a set of new institutions that superseded the existing administrative system of indirect rule through the Lifanyuan. The first institution was the Reclamation Administration (*kenwu zongju* 墾務總局, hereafter "the Administration") set up in Suiyuan in 1902 to handle all reclamation-related affairs such as liaison with the Mongol banners, land surveys, sales, taxation, the demarcation of boundaries, the collection of fees, and the issue of land deeds.[67] It functioned in many ways as the precursor of the centralized administrative units in the Mongol territory. Initially, it comprised two administrative sections: an Eastern section that covered the two flanks of Chakhar, and a Western section that oversaw the Yekhe Juu and Ulaanchab leagues, with three branch offices set up in Fengzhen, Kalgan, and Baotou. Following the closure of the campaign in Chakhar in 1905, the Administration was moved to Baotou (hereafter Baotou Bureau), with Yao Xuejing, magistrate of Wuyuan sub-prefecture, appointed as its director.[68]

By 1907, a total of fifteen branch offices had been established to handle reclamation-related affairs in the localities. In addition to the banner lands of Chakhar and the western leagues, the official pastures of Suiyuan's Eight Banners and the lands belonging to the twelve postal relay stations outside Shahukou were also brought under plow. Measures were also taken to survey and register the cultivated lands of the Tümed banners.[69] These activities showed that Yigu's campaign was a systematic attempt to eliminate differences between official lands (such as the Eight Banner pastures and relay station lands), semi-official lands (such as the enfeoffment of Manchu and Mongol nobles in Chakhar and Tümed soldiers' habitats), and Mongol lands owned by banners and monasteries (such as the common pastures of the Yekhe Juu and Ulaanchab leagues), by subjecting them to standardized surveys and taxation.

The new institution was expensive to maintain. The Administration and branch offices were generally composed of a staff numbering seventy to one hundred persons or more.[70] For instance, the Baotou office had 104 employees, whose salaries alone cost nineteen hundred taels per month, without taking into account subsidies given to them for working onsite in the localities. Extra salaries and subsidies were paid to the Mongol personnel and local officials who participated in land survey and tax collection. Between 1902 and 1908, the executive costs of the Administration amounted to 652,467 taels in total, including 471,257 taels in the Eastern section and 181,210 in the Western section.[71] All expenditures were paid for by revenues from the sale of Mongol lands. In Chakhar, one-third of the land fees was used to cover executive expenses. In the Ordos, the administrative appropriation was set at 20 percent of the land fees and later raised to 30 percent.[72]

The primary tasks of the Administration were surveying and receiving the lands (*kanshou* 勘收) and measuring and releasing them for sale (*zhangfang* 丈放). Upon receiving the stamped documents from the jasag's office declaring the lands suitable for cultivation, the Administration would dispatch functionaries to measure and evaluate the lands in person. The standard unit of measurement was *gong* 弓. One *gong* was equivalent to 1.667 meters and 240 square *gong* were equivalent to one *mu* (667 square meters).[73] The survey was typically undertaken by three or four measurers using a hemp rope with a length of forty *gong* and two marking flags. Upon the completion of measuring one plot, its location, four boundaries, and area were reported to the Administration along with a sketched map.[74]

Before a plot could be measured and released, the Administration needed to determine its ownership and settle all disputes and lawsuits. As mentioned in chapter 5, the Mongol territories were notorious for murky property rights and ambiguous boundaries that easily gave rise to entangled disputes. Although lawsuits were generally arbitrated at the sub-prefecture yamens, the verdict reached was often overturned at the locality. In such cases, a rehearing was necessary. The large distances between the yamen and the localities added to the difficulties. Therefore, one of the main tasks of the Administration was to adjudicate lawsuits caused by land disputes, which was facilitated by the dispersion of branch offices and their functionaries into the localities. For example, in the Chakhar Right Flank, the Fengzhen and Ningyuan bureaus received hundreds of complaints. Of these grievances, 80 percent were settled within a year.[75]

In surveying the land, the Administration adopted a standard that prioritized its utility for farming by taking into account only net arable land (*jingdi* 淨地) and leaving out rivers, canals, roads, tamarisk bushes, and sandy and saline areas. Such areas were classified as nonproductive "wasteland." This practice gave rise to many disputes with local Mongols, who considered all lands to be part of a continuous topographical landscape. Take the "indemnity lands" of the Dalad banner, for example. When the banner agreed to cede the two thousand *qing* of Sichengdi ("four-part-territory") as an indemnity payment owed to the Church, it was measured only as 1,225 *qing* based on the official standard. As a result, the banner was forced to cede another 1,420 *qing*, called Sichengbudi ("supplement to Sichengdi"), to meet the required amount. By adopting the new standard, the Administration was able to extract an extra 645 *qing* of land in addition to the agreed amount, despite strong protests from the Mongols.[76]

Upon the completion of land surveys and evaluations, the Administration negotiated specific terms of land rates and taxes with each banner. A flat rate of land-contract fees and annual tax was applied in Chakhar, whereas in the western leagues, the rates were more diversified according to soil conditions and the availability of irrigation. The fees were due within three months after the completion of the land survey. Upon payment of the fees, the cultivator would receive a title deed from the Administration, and the plot would be registered for taxation. All previously signed contracts and agreements were thereby nullified.

By demarcating fixed boundaries and enforcing land surveys, licensing, and taxation, the Administration established the Qing state as the exclusive authority in sanctioning land transactions in Mongol territories. It abrogated the hereditary rights previously held by the Mongols over their land and outlawed the private bureaus set up by Chinese land brokers. Thus, it established private property rights in the Mongol territories and incorporated the decentralized periphery into the bureaucratic control of the Qing state.

Another new institution set up by Yigu was the Reclamation Corporation (*kenwu gongsi* 墾務公司, hereafter the Corporation), which was jointly managed by the government and private sectors under the rubric of "joint official-merchant enterprises" (*guanshang heban* 官商合辦) that emerged in China in the 1880s and 1890s. The rubric became widely adopted in large-scale business enterprises for the purposes of soliciting investment and promoting railway construction, mining, industries, and in this case, the colonization of Mongol land.[77] The idea of the corporation was proposed by Cao Runtang, a Höhhot-based merchant from Taigu county of Shanxi province, who later served as director of the Western Route Corporation founded in Höhhot in late 1902. Its eastern counterpart, the Eastern Route Corporation, was set up in Kalgan in early 1903. Both corporations had an initial capital of 120,000 taels, drawn equally from governmental and private funds, which was divided into twelve hundred shares, with each share worth one hundred taels. This format allowed Qing bureaucrats, functionaries, Chinese merchants, and Mongol nobles to invest private money in the corporations and become shareholders.[78] Due to its emphasis on state supervision and control, the format easily produced clientelism, cronyism, and corruption, thus allowing the investing individuals to profit from the land sale at the expense of average Mongols.

Operated under the Administration, the Corporation mainly handled land transactions and payments by mediating between the Administration and individual cultivators. Once the measurement and pricing of the lands were completed, the Corporation would acquire large tracts directly from the Administration by paying

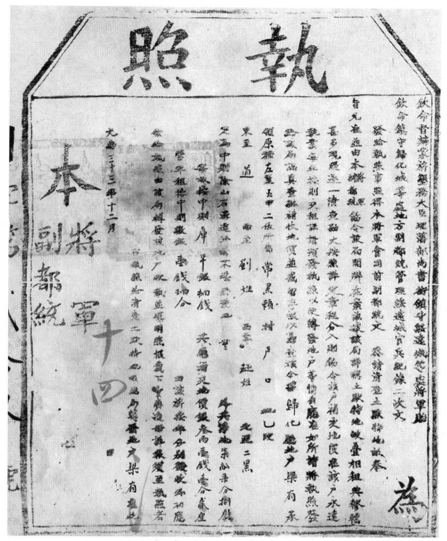

Figure 6.1. A land deed issued by the military governor of Suiyuan Yigu and vice lieutenant governor of Höhhot Wenzhehun, 1907.
Beijing Taihe Jiacheng Auction Co. Ltd

a lump sum of land-contract fees, and then it would either sell the plots or rent them out to individual cultivators with a surcharge. In this sense, it functioned as a licensed broker that monopolized land sales through the same method as the private land brokers it replaced.[79] However, not all lands were handled by the Corporation, as it sought only lands of superior quality that promised better returns. Out of the total of 44,600 *qing* of land measured and released in Chakhar, 25,854 *qing* (i.e. less than 60 percent) were sold through the Eastern Route Corporation. Likewise, the Western Route Corporation handled only 12,665 *qing* (i.e. 40 percent) out of the entire 30,600 *qing* of land released in the western leagues, most of which were fertile irrigated lands of Hetao.[80]

Land sale proved a lucrative business. In Chakhar, while the land-contract fee was set at a fixed rate of thirty taels per *qing*, the price set by the Corporation usually went up to eighty taels per *qing*. According to the Charter of the Corporation, 20 percent of the profits were to be paid as bonuses to Administration employees, another 20 percent was to be saved as accumulative funds, and the remaining was to be distributed among all shareholders. Before its closing in 1905, the Eastern Route Corporation claimed a net profit of 291,800 taels, with 60,980 taels (20 percent) paid to the governmental shares (*guangu* 官股), 73,383 taels (25 percent) paid to the merchant shares (*shanggu* 商股), and another sixty thousand taels (20 percent) sent to the Qing court as donations (*baoxiaoyin* 報效銀).[81] In this way, the Qing state received over 120,000 taels in net profit from the Eastern Route Corporation, apart from regular land-contract fees and annual taxes due to the Administration. These profits were used to fund the New Policies reform programs in the cities of Beijing and Suiyuan: two-thirds were handed to Military Training Offices (*lianbing chu* 練兵處) for training New Armies and purchasing firearms and the remaining was invested in the Western Route Corporation.[82]

The situation surrounding the Western Route Corporation was more complicated. Chronologically, it was divided into two stages, with the first stage lasting from 1902 to January 1906 and the second stage from February 1906 to May 1908. The first stage of the Corporation had a capital of 120,000 taels drawn equally from the Shanxi governmental and merchant funds.[83] The initial purpose was to raise funds by selling the 2,645 *qing* of irrigated lands in Hetao that the Dalad banner had handed to the Administration in lieu of Boxer indemnity owed to the Church. These lands were acquired at a rate of about fifty taels per *qing* and sold at an average rate of ninety-one taels per *qing*: bringing a profit of 105,300 taels to the Corporation.[84]

Apart from land brokerage, the Corporation also functioned as a major sponsor of irrigation works in Hetao. It spent over three hundred thousand taels on new construction projects and compensating private canal owners.[85] Due to its financial capacity, the Corporation also served as a banking institution that provided loans to various organizations and individuals. Over the years, it lent out over 140,000 taels to official organizations such as the Suiyuan Monetary Bureau and various branch offices under the Baotou Bureau, as well as Mongol banners and Chinese merchants. Occasionally, it interfered in the local grain market by making large purchases. In 1907, for instance, when a good harvest in Hetao depressed the grain price, the Corporation spent 47,164 taels purchasing grains from local farmers to stabilize markets.[86]

In 1905, Yigu decided to settle the accounts of the first-stage Corporation by paying back all capital and interest. As he explained in his memorial, the reason for doing this was to "increase official shares and reduce merchant shares, so that the state can get the bulk of profits from irrigation."[87] The reorganization of the Corporation thus provided an opportunity for the Qing government to squeeze out the private investors and monopolize the profits. The first-stage Corporation closed with a net profit of 140,000 taels. With nearly half of the amount deducted as bonuses, funds, and donations, the remaining profit was distributed among shareholders, with the Shanxi government receiving 42,180 taels and the merchants receiving 32,240 taels. However, the Corporation was able to declare a profit only because its outstanding debts of over 245,000 taels, which were mostly irrigation expenses, were transferred to its successor.[88]

The second-stage Corporation, lasting from early 1906 until May 1908, had an initial capital of four hundred thousand taels. Yao Xuejing, director of the Baotou Bureau and administrator of Wuyuan sub-prefecture, served as its director. It was divided into two sections: a Reclamation Department (*renkenchu* 認墾處) that handled land sale, and an Irrigation Department (*qulichu* 渠利處) that operated the irrigation works of Hetao. The Reclamation Department had a capital stock of 280,000 taels. Most of this stock was drawn from non-official sources through the open sale of the four thousand *qing* of well-irrigated Khanggai land in the Khanggin banner in 1906, which the department acquired at a rate of seventy taels per *qing*. As of 1908, 2,357 *qing* had been sold for an average price of 93.5 taels per *qing*. The Corporation also handled over twenty-three hundred *qing* of the Urad banner lands in a similar fashion. In contrast, the Irrigation Department depended preponderantly on official funds, because irrigation building, as Yigu had envisioned it, was a long-term, high-risk, high-yield investment and therefore should remain under government control. Among its 120,000 taels of initial capital, ninety thousand taels (75 percent) were drawn from governmental funds and only thirty thousand taels from the private sector. In addition, it borrowed around 253,000 taels from the provincial coffers and from private money shops. In May 1908, the Corporation was dissolved with over 630,000 taels in deficit.[89]

The closing of the second-stage Corporation occurred in the aftermath of Yigu's impeachment in 1908. One of the main charges against him was the embezzlement of official funds. According to Grand Councilor Lu Chuanlin (1836–1910), who led the investigation, most of the claimed "merchant shares" turned out to be owned by functionaries of the Administration and Yigu's associates in Suiyuan who used public offices for self-profiting. As a result, "lands offered by the [Mongol] vassals were embezzled, while Chinese cultivators had to pay a higher tax due to the Corporation's extraction; both Mongols and Chinese suffered great loss, while the State remained impecunious."[90] Although not all accusations against Yigu were verified, it is clear that the lucrative land sale created opportunities for amban officials and their subordinates to seize land from the Mongols, and to a large extent, from Han proprietors as well, while appropriating land fees and taxes for their own benefits. However, such a massive expropriation of Mongol and Han wealth was not inflicted by certain corrupted individuals as projected by official documentations, but they were systematically administered during the New Policies through apparatuses like the Administration and the Corporation under the name of "revitalizing Mongolian affairs" (*zhenxing mengwu* 振興蒙務) and "opening up profit resources" (*kaijun liyuan* 開濬利源).[91]

REVENUE COLLECTION

By early 1906, official reclamation had been accomplished in all six Ordos banners (except in the Üüshin banner, where *duguilang* resistance held off state-imposed land surveys until 1908) and in the Yekhe Juu Monastery (Wang-un Juu, located in the Wang banner). Except the Dalad banner, all banners forfeited the ownership of the lands put under terms of open sale, which were transferred to Chinese settlers and subject to official taxation. The revenues thus generated were split equally between the Qing state and the banners, which explains why most banners settled for open sale.

The only exception was the land called Yongzudi ("land on perpetual lease") of the Dalad banner, which was rented out under the terms of perpetual lease so that the banner retained land ownership. However, the banner had to accept unfavorable terms in rental distribution, with the state retaining 56 percent and the banner only 24 percent. The remaining 20 percent was deducted as irrigation funds for investment in constructing and maintaining the canals. The chief reason the Dalad banner retained the ownership of Yongzudi was because these lands, being far-flung from the Yellow River, were dependent on irrigation and therefore defied standardized measurement. Depending on the availability of irrigation, the cultivated area fluctuated year by year from fifteen hundred to over three thousand *qing*. Thus, instead of settling on a fixed land fee and tax rate, the Administration would send functionaries to measure the areas of green shoots (*qingmiao* 青苗) in late summer and early autumn each year, in the same way as the Mongol tax-collectors and Han land merchants had done in the past.[92]

Tables 6.1 through 6.3 provide an overview of land charges applicable in all the Ordos banners, as well as the proportion of the revenue distribution to the Administration, the Qing state, and the respective banner.

The reclaimed Mongol lands were subject to a variety of charges, including a one-time land-contract fee (*huangjia* 荒價, ranging from ten to seventy taels per *qing*) or, in some cases, a land fee (*dijia* 地價, ranging from sixty to 110 taels per *qing*) with a surcharge due to the Corporation. There was also an annual rental fee (*suizu* 歲租, ranging from one to 2.2 taels per *qing*), and in the case of irrigated lands, a fixed canal tax (*quzu* 渠租, set at 4.5 taels per *qing*). The only exception was Yongzudi of the Dalad banner, where a combined canal and land rental fee (*qudizu* 渠地租) was charged.[93]

The rates of land-contract fees and annual taxes varied according to the banner, locality, and time period. Depending on the soil condition, the lands were divided

Table 6.1. Land Fees/Rents Due from Ordos, as of 1911

Banner	Type	Rate (tael/qing)					Area (qing)	Fee/Rent (tael)	Proportion (%)		
		I	II	III	IV	V			Admin	State	Banner
Dalad	Sichengdi	110	90	80	70	60	1,225.22	100,447*	–	–	–
	Sichengbudi	100	95	90	85	–	1,420.00	135,234*	–	–	–
Khanggin	Yongzudi	40	30	25	–	20	2,000.00	409,867 (eight-year total)	20	56	24
	Qudi (Yongzu)	–	–	26	–	20	(1,527.94)	36,015	20	40	40
	Irrigated land	100	95	90	85	80	2,357.25	220,471			
		90	85	80	75	70	482.25	36,817			
	Dry land	50	40	30	20	10	1,178.53	47,983			
	Short Rent	35	–	27	–	20	(1,178.53)	145,740	100	–	–
Wang		30	–	20	–	10	9,638.94	108,219	30	35	35
Jasag	B. Boundary	30	–	20	–	10	1,608.00	20,407	30	35	35
	Longevity						575.35	6,016	30	70	–
Üüshin	B. Boundary	30	–	20	–	10	1,452.50	18,820	30	35	35
	Longevity						535.77	5,540	30	70	–
Jüüngar		60	–	40	–	20	1,588.25	60,339	30	35	35
Otog		40	–	30	20	10	201.93	4,954	30	35	35
Wangai	East section	40	–	30	20	10	1,267.12	26,840	50	–	50
Juu	West section	30	–	20	–	10	150.59	1,661			
Total (tael)							25,681.70	1,385,370 (1,149,689)	377,509 (33%)	448,587 (39%)	323,591 (28%)

Source: Gan Pengyun, *Diaocha guisui kenwu baogaoshu*.
* The land fees (235,681 taels) generated by Sichengdi and Sichengbudi were collected exclusively by Sichengdi and Sichengbudi were collected exclusively by the Corporation, as repayment of the 137,065 taels of Boxer indemnity advanced to the Church. However, the annual taxes thus generated were due to Shanxi province.

Table 6.2. Annual Land Taxes Due from Ordos, as of 1911

Banner	Category	Rate (tael/qing)				Area (qing)	Tax (tael)	Proportion (%)		
		I/II	III	IV	V			Locality	State	Banner
Dalad	Sichengdi	1.4	1.4	–	1.3	1,225.22	1,676	–	100	–
	Sichengbudi*	2.2	1.8	–	1.4	1,420.00	2,812			
Khan-ggin	Irrigated land*	2.2	2.0	–	1.4	2,839.50	5,163	20	30	40
	Dry land	1.6	1.2	–	1.0	1,178.53	1,663		10 (Admin)	
Wang	B. Boundary	1.4	1.0	–	0.6	9,638.94	6,350	20	20	60
Jasag	B. Boundary	1.6	1.2	–	1.0	1,608.00	1,373	20	20	60
	Longevity					575.35	310	–	100	–
Üüshin	B. Boundary	1.6	1.2	–	1.0	1,452.50	1,546	18	10 (Admin)	72
	Longevity					535.77	541	–	100	–
Jüüngar		2.0	1.6	1.2	1.0	1,588.25	2,359	20	–	80
Otog		2.0	1.6	1.2	1.0	201.93	280	20	–	80
Wang-un Juu	East section	2.0	1.6	1.2	1.0	1,267.12	1,702	10	18	9 (Wang banner) 63
	West section	1.6	1.2	–	1.0	150.59	154			
Total						23,681.70	25,929	3,901.5 (15%)	10,102.7 (39%)	11,924.84 (46%)

Sources: Gan Pengyun, *Diaocha guisui kenwu baogaoshu*; Yigu, *Mengken xugong*.

* In the irrigated area of Dalad and Khanggin banners, a separate irrigation tax of 4.5 taels per *qing* was charged every year. It produced an annual income of 17,860 taels in 1905 to 1907, which was used as funds for repairing the irrigation works. See Nei Menggu dang'anguan, ed., *Qingmo nei menggu kenwu dang'an huibian*, 1295.

Table 6.3. Land Released and Revenues in Inner Mongolia, as of 1911

Location	Type	Area (qing)	Land Fees (tael)	Annual Taxes (tael)
Chakhar RF		25,390.50	1,047,989	35,547
Chakhar LF	Banner lands	19,956.01	728,965	26,172
Yekhe Juu league		23,681.70	793,823	25,929
Ulaanchab league		7,380.29	330,562	7,837
Shahukou relay stations		11,729.97	285,640	–
Suiyuan Eight Banner Pastures	Official lands	2,493.55	29,532	–
Tümed	Livelihood lands	9,985.61	222,136	–
Total		**100,617.63**	**3,438,648**	**95,485**

Sources: Gan Pengyun, *Diaocha guisui kenwu baogaoshu*; Yigu, *Mengken xugong*; Baoyu, "Qingmo suiyuan kenwu," in *Nei menggu shizhi ziliao xuanbian* 1.2.

into a variety of grades ranging from Grade I of superior quality (*shangdi* 上地) to Grade V of inferior quality (*xiadi* 下地), with charges differing accordingly. For instance, the rates for the sandy lands of the Wang, Jasag, and Üüshin banners were between ten to thirty taels per *qing*, which were much lower than that of the irrigated lands of the Dalad and Khanggin banners, which were set at between sixty to 110 taels. The situation in the Khanggin banner was particularly complicated. Prior to 1906, its irrigated lands were held in perpetual lease, with cultivators paying a combined irrigation fee and land tax of 23.6 taels. Since June 1906, when the banner opened up the lands for open sale, a total of four thousand *qing* were released to the Corporation at a fixed rate of seventy taels per *qing*, which then sold the land use right to cultivators with a surcharge of between ten to thirty taels. Up until 1908, 2,357 *qing* were sold for an average price of 93.5 *taels* per *qing*. After that, 482 *qing* were sold by Yigu's successor, Xinqin, at a reduced price of seventy-six *taels* per *qing*. The remaining 1,178 *qing* were sold in 1911 as dry land (*handi* 旱地) for a price of forty *taels* per *qing*. Before these dry lands was measured and sold, however, they were leased out to cultivators on a short term basis, with a rental fee of twenty-seven taels per *qing* charged.[94] All these demonstrate a high degree of flexibility in the policymaking of the Administration according to the geographical and economic conditions of different localities.

By 1911, a total of 25,681.70 *qing* of Mongol lands had been opened for reclamation in the Ordos, in which 23,681.70 *qing* (92 percent) was subject to state taxation. The sale generated a total income of 1,385,370 taels in land fees, along with an annual tax of 43,789 taels (including land and irrigation taxes). All these revenues (except the canal tax) were to be divided proportionally among the Qing state, Mongol banners, and the Administration. There were exceptions, however. The Sichengdi and Sichengbudi of the Dalad banner, being Boxer indemnity lands, were ceded permanently from the banner. Thus, the Mongols were not able to enjoy any benefit from these lands, as all the land fees were collected exclusively by the Corporation and all the annual taxes went to the Qing state. Similarly, all the revenues generated by the Wanshoudi or Longevity Land of the Üüshin and Jasag banners went to the imperial coffers, as these lands were presented by their jasags to the empress dowager in 1904.[95]

As Yigu indicated, the primary purpose of the official reclamation campaign was to turn the enfeoffment (*fentu* 分土) of dependent vassals (*fanfeng* 藩封) into official lands for tax collection, so that these vassal territories could be incorporated into the national territory (*bantu* 版圖) along with the Chinese provinces.[96] His goal was partly achieved. By 1911, a total of 100,618 *qing* (670,000 ha) of Mongol lands had been measured and released with official title deeds issued in western Inner Mongolia, including 45,346 *qing* in the Chakhar region, 31,062 *qing* in the Yekhe Juu and Ulaanchab leagues, 9,985 *qing* in the Tümed banners, and 14,223 *qing* of official lands owned by the Shahukou relay stations and Suiyuan Eight Banners.[97] Together they generated a total land fee of 3,438,648 taels and an annual land tax of 95,485 taels. Most of these were accomplished during the six-year tenure of Yigu as imperial commissioner.

NATIONALIZING IRRIGATION

Another major task undertaken by Yigu and his subordinates was to nationalize the irrigation system, which went hand-in-hand with the official survey and sale of Mongol lands in Hetao. Chapter 4 mentioned that irrigation was indispensable to cultivation in the arid and alkaline environment of Hetao. By the end of the nineteenth century, an elaborate irrigation system had been developed there, which was funded by Chinese land merchants who functioned simultaneously as land brokers, entrepreneurs, and managerial landlords. These private canals became easy targets for an aggressively centralizing Qing state. Unlike the Mongols who were shielded, however nominally, by their hereditary rights over their lands, there was no legal protection for the properties of Chinese settlers. Having secured the concessions of irrigation rights from the Dalad banner in 1903, Yigu set out to expropriate the private canals owned by Chinese proprietors, who were offered no more than 10 percent of the assessed original costs in compensation. By the end of 1907, all eight major canals and dozens of minor ones had been expropriated, with some seventy-two thousand taels paid to a total of thirty-eight individual and group owners. Among these, thirty-one thousand taels went to Wang Tongchun.[98]

Following the changing hands of canals, the maintenance obligations were shifted to the Administration in order to ensure their proper functioning and supply the water necessary for tilling the Hetao lands. Construction work began in 1903 at the sites of Changji (formerly Changsheng) and Yongji (formerly Chanjin) canals, with thousands of workers hired to dredge the beds, strengthen the embankments, expand the intakes, and develop new branch channels. Later, expansion projects were carried out in other major canals such as Fengji (formerly Zhonghe), Gangmu, and Tongji (formerly Old

Guo), Yihe, and Shahe (formerly Yonghe). Besides expanding existing irrigation works, the Administration also undertook several new projects, including a seventy-*li*-long Lansuo canal in the Khanggin banner, a new intake of Changji canal with a length of thirty *li*, and an earthen dam in the Urad banner with a length of thirty *li* that protected the farmlands from flash floods from Muni uul (Wulashan).

In charge of the irrigation works were a total of eleven branch offices (*qugong fenju* 渠工分局) under the Administration, which were responsible for surveying and mapping the canals, overseeing construction projects, and ensuring the proper functioning of the canals.[99] A number of labor contractors (*qutou* 渠頭) were appointed, who were responsible for recruiting laborers and supervising construction work. The laborers' wages were calculated by the number of earth cubes (*tufang* 土方) removed. Depending on the methods used in removing the earth, the wages ranged from 0.7 to 1.4 *qian* per earth cube, or higher during the late summer and autumn when labor was in short supply. Payments were often made in kind rather than in cash, and the commodities used for payment included millet, cotton cloth, brick tea, and tobacco.[100]

Upon the completion of the construction work, the branch offices developed a set of charters, which provided guidelines for regulating irrigation works and coordinating water use in areas under their supervision. These charters helped with standardizing practices and popularizing technical know-hows such as the differentiation of five types of irrigation water (spring, hot, summer, autumn, and winter) and their corresponding farming seasons and suitable crops.[101] In distributing water, the principle of "benefit sharing" (*shuili junzhan* 水利均霑) was adopted. That is to say, water should flow without hindrance (*pingkou liushui* 平口流水) and be accessed by all land users equally. Illegal blocking of the canal and the theft of water through the construction of sluice gates or earthen dams in trunk canals were prohibited on pain of heavy fines ranging from twenty to fifty taels per *qing*. Only when the water levels were low did it become necessary to build sluices and schedule rotational irrigation (*lunjiaofa* 輪澆法).[102] The aim was to balance water use among cultivators to ensure equal access to all.

By 1905, the entire irrigable area in Hetao had allegedly reached ten thousand *qing*. It was bringing in an income of about three hundred thousand to four hundred thousand taels in the form of land and canal fees. Yigu, who inspected Hetao twice in 1905 and 1907, knew only too well the vital importance of irrigation to cultivation in the region. As he repeatedly stressed, "[The land of] Hetao is thoroughly dependent on irrigation as its lifeline, so that no irrigation literally means no land." He thus envisioned an ambitious plan to thoroughly expand the existing irrigation system, so that "the silted channels should be dredged, the shallow ones deepened, the short ones lengthened, and branches added to the trunks."[103] He dispatched subordinates to survey the seven-hundred-*li*-long old bed of the Yellow River (Wujia River), and a proposal was made regarding dredging its upper reaches and using it as a sluiceway for other major canals to facilitate drainage and transport in the area.[104]

Attempts were also made to modernize agricultural production by adopting Western machinery and technologies. For instance, in 1905, the Administration purchased eleven plowing, sowing, and reaping machines valued at a total of 1,321 taels from Europe through a Tianjin-based German firm called H. Mandl & Co (*Xinyi yanghang*).[105] The proposal on dredging the Wujia River also included the use of mechanical excavators and adoption of the Western sand-washing technology to wash away silts.[106] Yigu was convinced that once accomplished, the project would bring tens of thousands of additional *qing* under cultivation and produce several times more revenue for the state. To fund the expensive project, Yigu proposed retaining the state's share of revenue from selling the lands of the Ordos. Using the railway as an example, he reasoned that it was most efficient to use profit generated from existing canals to fund new ones, and that the long-term benefit of irrigation would surpass any temporary profit brought to the imperial treasury. The proposal was approved by the court.[107] However, this project and all other irrigation projects were suspended following Yigu's dismissal from office in 1908 and the subsequent closing down of the Administration.

In May 1908, Yigu was impeached by Wenzhehun, vice lieutenant governor of Höhhot and a former colleague at the Administration, for "jeopardizing the frontier, making profits through trickery, and causing resentment among the Mongols."[108] The subsequent investigation led by Lu Chuanlin and Shaoying resulted in the double charges of "greed" and "cruelty": the embezzlement of official funds through the Corporation and the execution of Dampil based on false charges. Although the first charge was never verified, Yigu was sentenced to exile in Xinjiang in 1910, and several of his subordinates were also convicted.[109] With Yigu's dismissal, official reclamation in the western leagues was largely suspended and all bureaus and corporations were shut down (except the Baotou Bureau that oversaw the irrigation works of Hetao). Yigu's successor, Xinqin, picked up whatever was left unfinished during Yigu's tenure, including surveying and selling the lands of the Üüshin banner and several banners of the Ulaanchab league, but no large-scale land reclamation was attempted in the remaining days of the Qing dynasty.

During Yigu's six-year tenure, the Administration spent a total of 488,274 taels on maintaining and expanding the irrigation works of Hetao, including 385,794 taels on construction labor, 72,078 taels on compensating the private land developers, and 30,401 taels on the subsidies and transport costs of the troops and employees.[110] Therefore, not only was the entire governmental share of land revenue from the Ordos, a total of 448,588 taels, invested in the irrigation systems, but there was a deficit of around forty thousand taels. This provides an idea of the scale of official investment during this period. The result of the nationalization policy can hardly be called successful. The irrigable acreage of the Yongzudi initially increased from 2,006 *qing* in 1905 to 3,122 *qing* in 1907, but then dropped to 1,566 *qing* in 1909.[111] Obviously, the levels of capital and labor input in irrigation were extremely pertinent to the cultivable area, and hence, the revenue collection in Hetao. The decrease may be explained by official negligence and the lack of investment following Yigu's demotion in 1908. The situation deteriorated even further during the Republican period when many canals silted up and the irrigated areas shrunk to a mere one-third of the figure of 1907.[112] As we can see, the state expropriation of the irrigated lands of Hetao turned out to be a sheer disaster, and a costly one, too. Unlike enterprises of the private sectors, these irrigation projects suffered from the general failings of state-run enterprises, such as the lack of rational decision making based on market factors, the lack of initiative and efficiency, and conflicting incentives of the leadership as both managers and bureaucrats.[113]

CENTRALIZING STATE

On the heels of the settlers followed the state-building process in the decentralized periphery. In 1902, Zhao Erfeng, acting governor of Shanxi, memorialized the court to expand the centralized administrative system in the Mongol territories to manage the growing Chinese migrant population there.[114] A series of sub-prefectures were set up in 1903—Xinghe, Taolin, Wuyuan, and Wuchuan—to administer Chinese settlers in the Chakhar Right Flank and two western leagues. All these sub-prefectures reported to the Höhhot circuit of Shanxi province. Later, in 1907, a separate Dongsheng sub-prefecture was set up to govern those living in the Wang, Jasag, and Jüüngar banners, which had previously been under the jurisdiction of Shenmu of Shaanxi and Togtokhu of Shanxi, respectively.[115]

Chapter 1 states that during the Yongzheng and Qianlong reigns, a total of eighteen bureaucratic units had been established outside the Great Wall: six each in Jehol, Chakhar, and Tümed areas (see table 1.2). The new establishments in 1903, however, differed from their predecessors in significant ways. Whereas the previous units were installed in territories of "Internal Mongolia" under direct Manchu rule, the new ones were built in areas that had previously been off bounds to centralized control. It demonstrated an unprecedented level of state penetration into the areas ruled by autonomous Mongol jasags. Moreover, the challenges they faced were also different. The local officials in the newly settled areas were appointed as magistrates with judicial titles, which meant that their priorities were revenue collection rather than judicial administration. Apart from traditional duties such as collecting land taxes, arbitrating lawsuits, and instituting the *baojia* system at the village level, they were also responsible for implementing New Policies programs such as organizing new armies, police forces, schools, prisons, post and telegram services, and mapmaking. In Inner Mongolia, such programs were predominantly funded by the revenue brought by official land sale.[116]

Meanwhile, there was growing pressure to incorporate the non-Han peripheries into China's provincial system. Statecraft scholars such as Gong Zizhen and Wei Yuan first advocated Chinese colonization and the establishment of a Chinese-style province in Xinjiang in the 1820s as a means of stabilizing the frontier and easing population pressures in China proper. General Zuo Zongtang, who reconquered Xinjiang from the Hui rebels in 1877, made the same argument for the purposes of saving costs and consolidating Qing control. Eventually, in 1884, Xinjiang was incorporated as a province into the Qing empire. This development marked a major departure from the previous Qing policy of "rule by customs" in non-Han frontiers.[117]

A similar transformation took place in Manchuria, which saw an unprecedented influx of Chinese population since the 1860s. With the opening up of the Josotu, Juu Uda, and Jerim leagues for official reclamation, a total of five sub-prefectures, three prefectures, two districts, and thirteen counties were set up from 1902 to 1910 to govern the rapidly increasing number of Chinese settlers in the Mongol territories (see table 1.2). Further, the completion of the Russian-controlled Chinese Eastern Railway in 1903 and the subsequent Russo-Japanese War of 1904–1905 turned Manchuria into a battleground for imperialist aspirations between the two powers. To counter the foreign influences, in 1907, the Qing court replaced the existing military governments of Fengtian, Jilin, and Heilongjiang with three new provinces, each administered by a civil governor, with a governor-general appointed to oversee affairs in these three provinces.[118]

Likewise, the issue of establishing direct rule in Mongolia was brought up on the agenda of the Qing court. In 1905, Yao Xiguang (1857–?), deputy Military Administrative Commissioner of Military Training Department, presented a detailed proposal on abolishing the banner and league system of the Mongols and replacing it with China's provincial system.[119] Another minor official named Zuo Shaozuo proposed to set up two provinces, Jehol and Suiyuan, to unify administrative authorities in managing the Mongol frontier.[120] Zuo's view was shared by Cen Chunxuan, governor-general of Liangguang, who memorialized the court in 1907 to reform the indirect rule over the Mongols by revving up the reclamation of pasturelands and setting up three provinces in Inner Mongolia: Jehol, Chakhar, and Suiyuan.[121]

In assessing their options regarding provincialization, the Qing court solicited opinions from *amban* officials and military governors. Their views were polarized along regional lines. The administrators of Inner Mongolia, including the military governors of Jehol, Chakhar, and Suiyuan, the vice lieutenant governor of Höhhot, and the governor of Heilongjiang, all concurred regarding significance of reclamation and direct rule in managing the frontiers and strengthening border defense. In contrast, those who served key positions in Outer Mongolia, such as the military governor of Uliasutai, the counselor minister of Khobdo and Uliasutai, and the minister superintendent of Urga and Khobdo, opposed the plan because of difficulties in financing and promoting reclamation among nomads. In the end, the proposals were shelved.[122] It was not until after the fall of the Qing dynasty that the three Special Regions (*tebie qu* 特別區) of Jehol, Chakhar, and Suiyuan were established in 1914 and turned into full-fledged provinces in 1928.

Among these proposals, Yao Xiguang's *Choumeng chuyi* 籌蒙芻議 ("Preliminary suggestions on managing Mongolia") offered a systematic approach of colonizing Mongolia and integrating it into the centralized framework of the Chinese state. It consists of a set of proposals presented to the Military Training Department (*lianbing chu* 練兵處) in 1905 after he undertook an investigation in Jehol. Yao's scheme represented a radical way of conceptualizing the frontier based on the Western discourses of sovereignty and modernization as well as colonial practices of the Western powers. Therefore, it deserves careful examination.[123]

Economically, Yao advocated modernizing Mongolian economy through agricultural colonization, financial reform, and industrialization. Unlike the current methods of revenue extraction centering on areas already under cultivation, Yao promoted the opening up of virgin pastureland by soliciting capital investment from well-off regions such as the lower Yangtze delta, Canton, and Southeast Asia and by organizing corporations and large plantations similar to those of America. Drawing from precedents in America and Australia, Yao emphasized the success of capitalists in developing new frontiers, which surpassed that of laborers.[124] The state's obligation, he argued, was to make laws protecting properties and taxation rather than interfering in the transactions and extracting land fees. The key was to guarantee profits to both the Mongols and the Chinese settlers so that the lands could be opened up with little resistance.[125] This, of course, was a typical cant of conquest that naturalized colonization and rationalized official expropriation at the expense of the interests of Mongol herders. As for the fiscal revenue of the state, Yao advocated putting the prime quality Üjümchin salt under state monopoly and using the revenue to form state banks.[126] He proposed to establish investment and saving banks and use them as a foundation to promote industries like manufacturing, railways, and mining in Mongolia. Reforming the financial system, he reasoned, was critical to promoting the local economy, financing New Policies programs, and countering Russian and Japanese influences.[127]

Administratively, Yao proposed to replace indirect rule of the Mongols with direct rule by the central state by establishing five provinces there: the Eastern and Western provinces of Inner Mongolia, and the Eastern, Western, and Northern provinces of Outer Mongolia. In Inner Mongolia, all cultivated areas should be absorbed into the centralized bureaucratic system of districts and counties under a civil governor who oversaw both Chinese and Mongols affairs. Imitating the administrative systems in the West and Japan, a hierarchical system of townships, towns, and villages should be set up to facilitate the vertical penetration of state power down into the rural areas and to curb the political and economic leverage of clerks and yamen runners.[128] In the untilled areas of Inner Mongolia, an Agricultural Administration Section (*nong-zhengsi* 農政司) should be established to promote colonization, which was modeled after Japan's Hokkaido Development Agency (Ch: *tuozhishi* 拓殖使, J: *kaitakushi* 開拓使). In Outer Mongolia, military settlements should be organized under the supervision of a Military Colonization Section (*tunken si* 屯墾司), similar to the Seventh Division of Imperial Japanese Army in Hokkaido.[129]

Politically, Yao advocated replacing the autonomous rule of jasags with the sovereignty of the nation-state. His argument was based on the dichotomy between *fengjian* 封建 (enfeoffment system) and *junxian* 郡縣 (prefecture and county system), which were two key concepts in the Confucian political discourse.[130] According to Yao and many contemporaries, these terms best captured the distinction between political systems in Mongolia and China proper. He argued,

In my humble opinion, *fengjian* and *junxian* cannot coexist. The *fengjian* system was particularly ill-suited to today's world, as division weakens a nation's strength. Unless united, there is no way to defend the nation against foreign aggression, or for it to last long. Thus, there will be no effective government without replacing the *fengjian* with the *junxian* system. In order to convert fully to the *junxian* system, it is necessary to revoke the power of the jasags over the land and the people. . . . Today, our strong neighbors press on us on the eastern and northern borders. Without uniting the dispersed and undisciplined Mongols, and joining their forces to build a virtual Great Wall made of men, there is no way to protect the imperial capital and strengthen our frontier.

Here Yao asserted that the goal of the New Policies reform in Mongolia was to abolish the decentralized rule of jasags and nationalize the Mongol land. He further compared the jasags with the Japanese daimyos during the Meiji Restoration:

In Japan, the Restoration would not have been achieved had the lands of daimyos not been retrieved. Today, there is no way to strengthen our nation without retrieving the Mongol land and people. The daimyos of Japan shared weal and woe with the nation, while continuing to enjoy their titles and salaries. Our relations with the Mongols should be no different. . . . It is thus essential to adjust one's policy according to the changing situation, rather than stick to the laws of the old times. The *fengjian* system proved auspicious at the beginning of our dynasty, thus self-rule was allowed of the Mongols. Today, however, unification is to our advantage, so it is necessary to retrieve sovereignty from them.[131]

Citing the example of Japan, Yao reframed the Confucian debate between *fengjian* and *junxian* within the modern nation-state context by linking *fengjian* to the idea of self-rule, and *junxian* to that of national sovereignty. Thereby, he justified the territorial and political claims of the nation-state over its ethnic frontier.

Culturally, Yao advocated supplanting nomadism with agrarianism, which he deemed to be both inevitable and desirable, as seen in the example of the Russian colonization of Siberia:

Nowadays, with all nations closely linked to one another, there is no way for the nomadic lifestyle to sustain. Such [a] trend can be seen from the rapid colonization of Siberia. It is likely that in less than fifty years, nomadism would disappear completely from the earth. It is therefore better to adjust early, so as to provide for the Mongols' livelihood. Further, the nomadic culture values aggression and mobility, yet has shallow roots. It may be useful for claiming hegemony among tribes, yet it cannot be relied upon for building a nation. For two thousand years since the Han dynasty, this vast area spanning tens of thousands of *li* has seen the rise and fall of numerous racial groups (*zhongzu* 種族) that competed against one another, yet the landscape remains wild and desolate with very little advancement (*jinbu* 進步). That nomadism cannot be relied upon for livelihood is manifest. When we speak of managing Mongolia, it is apparent that a livelihood that values openness is more favorable than one of isolation.[132]

Yao's views bear the distinct influence of the discourses of Social Darwinism, which portrayed nomadism as primitive, backward, and therefore unfit to survive in the modern world. They also reflect the Sino-centric narratives of Confucian Cultural-ism that emphasized the superiority of agrarianism over nomadism, cultured *hua* over barbarian *yi*. In either case, nomadism was regarded as a barrier that must be overcome for China to transform itself into a modern nation-state. What Yao intended was no different from what the Japanese colonizers did to the Ainu of Hok-kaido: that is, colonization and cultural assimilation to the effect of the extinction of the natives and their cultures. Ultimately, what Yao envisioned was a Mongolia free of the Mongols.

In sum, Yao advocated a process of radically integrating the Mongol periphery through agricultural colonization, political centralization, and cultural assimilation. Specifically, in order to defend the empire against foreign encroachments, he argued that the Qing needed to transform itself into a colonizing power by imitating other powers in the world and establishing a centralizing, homogenizing framework of the nation-state that eliminates the differences between China proper and the non-Han peripheries. Although Yao's proposal on the all-encompassing incorporation of Mon-golia was not endorsed by the Qing court due to its radicalness and impracticability, his viewpoints continue to find reverberation in the statist discourses on frontier colonization and nationalization through the Republican and People's Republic of China periods.

Whereas no provinces materialized in Mongolia during the remaining span of the dynasty, more reforms were underway. In 1906, the Lifanyuan, the agency in charge of all non-Han dependencies, was reorganized into the Ministry of Dependencies (Lifanbu 理藩部), with a Survey and an Editorial Bureau set up to organize surveys and compile information on the frontier.[133] In 1910, the Qing abrogated all old statutes prohibiting the Chinese cultivation of Mongol lands, intermarriage between the Mongols and Han Chinese, and the adoption of Chinese names by the Mongols. This decision paved the way for the full-fledged colonization and cultural assimila-tion of Inner Mongolia.[134]

CONCLUSION

This chapter examines the late Qing campaign of opening up Mongol lands for Chi-nese reclamation led by Imperial Commissioner Yigu as a precursor of the wholesale colonization and political integration of this borderland into the Chinese nation-state. On the one hand, Yigu's campaign can be seen as an overall success on the practical and institutional levels. First, over 670,000 hectares of Mongol lands were measured, mapped, and categorized for official sale and taxation. The reclamation of the lands generated over 3,400,000 taels in land-contract fees and over ninety-five thousand taels of annual taxes. In this sense, the original goals of raising funds to finance the reform programs and to repay the Boxer indemnities were largely met.

Second, by enforcing cadastral surveys and standardizing land transactions, Yigu's campaign demarcated boundaries, clarified property rights, and mitigated land-related disputes. Third, in the wake of the reclamation campaign, centralized bureaucratic units proliferated in Mongol territories ruled by jasags. These units paved the way for the administrative incorporation of Inner Mongolia into the provincial system of China during the Republican period. Lastly, given the scale and complexity of the issues involved, it was remarkable that the campaign proceeded largely without the use of force or without sparking widespread armed resistance (except the *duguilang* insurgences in southern Ordos). This success was partly due to Yigu's skills in tempering his efforts to adjust to various local situations. The nationalization of the irrigation system of Hetao also went smoothly through a functional compensation and hybrid funding system. Nevertheless, the campaign garnered antagonism in the localities for extorting money from the Mongols and Chinese migrants alike and for Yigu's highhandedness in suppressing Mongol resistance, which eventually led to his downfall and the demise of his campaign.

On the other hand, the reclamation campaign also brought about far-reaching impacts upon the Mongol periphery. It opened the floodgate of Chinese colonization that would transform the political, social, and cultural landscape of Inner Mongolia, and eventually destroy the physical environment that the nomads depended upon for their livelihood. The state's sanctioning of the sale of Mongol banner lands abrogated the hereditary land rights of the Mongols and their ability to tax Chinese settlers. Whereas some members of the Mongol nobility profited from the land sales through collusion with Qing officials and Chinese land brokers, the majority of the herdsmen as well as lower-level nobles, officials, and lamas faced a dismal fate of displacement and acculturation. Many settled down and became farmers, while others were forced to move to remote mountains or deserts. Still others took up arms to defend their lands against state dispossession, as seen from the *duguilang* movement in the Üüshin banner of Ordos and a host of Mongolian uprisings in the Ghorlos and Khorchin banners of the Jerim league. These uprisings culminated in the unsuccessful bid by some Inner Mongolian princes to join the independence movement of the Khalkhas in 1912.[135] Meanwhile, waves of Chinese migration also took an environmental toll by disrupting the delicate ecological equilibrium in the grasslands and causing land degradation and desertification.

Furthermore, the campaign greatly facilitated the administrative, economic, and cultural integration of the Mongols into the Chinese nation-state. In 1914, three "special administrative zones" of Suiyuan, Chakhar, and Jehol were created on the Mongol territories, which were elevated to provinces in 1928. This decision effectively wiped Inner Mongolia off of China's map. This administrative colonization was underpinned by a discourse that upheld the notion of a unitary, homogenizing Chinese nation that included all non-Han ethnicities, and one that prioritized agrarianism over pastoralism as a higher stage in the development of civilization. According to this discourse, the Mongol system was considered backward and anachronistic due to its extensive use of land and its decentralized organization of power. It thus justified land-grabbing, systematic exploitation, and the acculturation of ethnic Mongols under the pretext of development that persisted throughout the Republican and People's Republic of China periods. Clearly ideology and economic agendas coalesced to displace a people in a process best described as internal colonialization, as in many ways, it reproduced the political and economic inequalities of a colonial setting.[136]

NOTES

1. Reynolds, *China, 1989–1912*. For a general introduction of the New Policy reforms, also see Chuzo, "Political and Institutional Reforms, 1901–1911," 375–415.

2. For a general study of the New Policies in Mongolia, see Lan, "China's 'New Administration' in Mongolia," 39–58. Also see Atwood, *Young Mongols and Vigilantes in Inner Mongolia's Interregnum Decades*, 42–47, 55–66; Taveirne, *Han–Mongol Encounters and Missionary Endeavors*, 331–39; Reardon-Anderson, *Reluctant Pioneers*, 78–84. Important works in Chinese include Zhao Yuntian, *Qingmo xinzheng yanjiu*; and Sudebilige, *Wanqing zhengfu dui Xinjiang, Menggu he Xizang zhengce yanjiu*. For the New Policies in other ethnic frontiers, see Xiuyu Wang, *China's Last Imperial Frontier*.

3. Meihua Lan provides an excellent albeit brief summary of the New Policies reform in Mongolia. See Lan, "China's 'New Administration' in Mongolia," 39–58. Also see Taveirne, *Han–Mongol Encounters*.

4. Anzai, "Shinmatsu ni okeru suien no kaikon."

5. Huang Shijian, "Lun qingmo qingzhengfu dui nei menggu de 'yimin shibian' zhengce," 65–77; Xing Yichen, "Luelun qingmo menggu diqu de 'xinzheng,'" 37–42; Lu Minghui, "Qingmo 'yimin shibian' dui menggu shehui de yingxiang," 55–60; Wang Binming, "Shi 'fangken mengdi' haishi 'yimin shibian,'" 189–97; Liu Haiyuan, ed., *Nei menggu kenwu yanjiu*; Qi Meiqin, "Yikezhao meng de mengdi kaiken."

6. For the biography of Sengge Rinchen, see T'eng, "Sêng-ko-lin-ch'in," 632–34.

7. Cen Chunxuan, "Wei ken kai jinbian mengdi tunken yi xufanshu er miyinhuan zhe" GX 27/4/20, in KWDA, 1.

8. YHTDX, 1064.

9. JWJAD, ser. 3, volume 1, 422–28.

10. Zhang Zhidong, "Chouyi qiting gaizhi shiyi zhe" (1883); "Kouwai geting biancha huji wu'ai menggu youmu shu" (1884), in *Zhang wenxiang gong quanji*, zouyi 6, 684–85; 8, 798.

11. Gangyi, "Chouyi taowai chanjin dengchu tuntian shiyi shu," in Sheng Kang, ed., *Huangchao jingshi wen xubian* 39, huzheng 11, tunken. Also see Zhu Shoupeng, ed., *Guangxu chao donghua lu*, volume 2, 2164–65. For the division of the territory between the Dalad and Tümed banners, see QSL 206, GX 11/4/2. C.f. chapter 5, n74.

12. Cen Chunxuan's memorial GX 27/11/26, in Xiehua shuju ed., *Guangxu yuzhe huicun*.

13. Zhu Jinfu, *Qingmo jiao'an*, volume 3, 174, 363; YHTDX, 1715. For Cen's other memorials on the financial difficulties, see YHTD, 1151, 1341. For Zhao Erxun's correspondence with Yigu, see KWDC, 47.

14. Cen's memorial GX 27/11/26, in Xiehua shuju ed., *Guangxu yuzhe huicun*.

15. Reardon-Anderson, *Reluctant Pioneers*, 72–83.

16. Actual reclamation in these regions did not commence until 1902, as the process was interrupted by the outbreak of the Boxer Rebellion and subsequent Russian occupation of Manchuria. See QSL 457, 5.

17. Gangyi, "Chouyi jinsheng kouwai tunken qingxing shu," in Ge Shijun ed., *Huangchao jinshi wen xubian* 66, bingzheng 5, tunxiang 2; QSL 232, GX 12/9/1.

18. QSL 404, GX 23/4/9 (1897); 406, GX 23/6/15; 415, GX 24/2/7. For Hu Pingzhi's memorial, see "Tunken jinbian zhe," in Shen Tongsheng, *Guangxu zhengyao* 33.

19. QSL 506, 10; Yigu, *Kenwu zouyi*, 13.

20. Yigu, "Banli kenwu shiyu menghan you," GX 28/3/19, in KWDA, 25–26. Also see Baoyu, ed., "Mengqi kenwu dang'an shiliao xuanbian," 34–35.

21. Ibid.

22. Ibid.

23. Yigu, "Zou wei huichou kanban mengqi kenwu dagai qingxing zhe," GX 28/3/29, in Yigu, *Kenwu zouyi*, 20–21.

24. "Yimeng mengzhang a'erbinbaya'er wei tingzhi guantian zhi zuo zhi suiyuan jiangjun chengwen," GX 28/6/26; "Wulanchabu meng mengzhang lingwangnuo'erbu deng wei kenqing tingzhi meng nei liuqi tunken shi chengwen," GX 28/8/17, in Baoyu, "Mengqi kenwu dang'an shiliao xuanbian," 37–40.

25. Serruys, "Documents from Ordos on the 'Revolutionary Circles,' Part I," 490.

26. Yigu, "Zou wei mengfan yan bu zun diao ken en chixia lifanyuan yanchi xun fu guisui yibian choushang kenli mian wu shiji zhe," GX 28/8/8; "Zou wei yikezhaomeng hangjinqi ge qian yuan lai cheng jiuyi qing jiang shenmingdayi shouxian zundiao zhi mengzhang zhasake ken'en jiajiang yi zhao jili zhe," GX 29/4/7, in Yigu, *Kenwu zouyi*, 41–43, 89–90.

27. Yigu, *Kenwu zouyi*, 45–46.

28. Yigu, *Kenwu zouyi*, 53, 55; Baoyu, "Mengqi kenwu dang'an," 40.

29. JWJAD, ser. 3, volume 1, 422–28. The payments included a land-contract fee of two *qian* per *mu*, an annual tax of 1.4 *fen* per *mu*, plus a surcharge of four *li* per *mu* to be collected by Mongol nobles or local sub-prefectures, depending on the previous ownership of the land. See Yigu, GX 28/6/11, in Yigu, *Kenwu zouyi*, 31.

30. Yigu, *Kenwu zouyi*, 29, 47; Anzai, "Shinmatsu ni okeru suien no kaikon," 31.

31. Yigu, fupian [Appendix], GX 28/6/23, in Yigu, *Kenwu zouyi*, 39.

32. Yigu, *Kenwu zouyi*, 31.

33. Yigu, "Zou wei huitong kanding zhi jin jiezhi yi xi zhengduan er zi fengshou zhe," GX 28/9/11, in Yigu, *Kenwu zouyi*, 57.

34. Yigu, *Kenwu zouyi*, 31–35.

35. The tax rate included 1.4 *fen* per *mu* of main tax (*zhengke* 正課) and four *li* of surcharge. Although the Mongol nobles who "contributed" their private pastures to the Qing state were allowed to keep the surcharge as private rent, it was renamed "additional rent" (*lingzu* 另租) to stress the state ownership.

36. Two-thirds of land revenue was fed into the state treasury, with the central government receiving 40 percent and provincial governments 27 percent. The remaining one-third was used to cover the administrative expenses, with 20 percent to be collected by the Bureau and 13 percent by the Mongol banners. See Wulan, "*Cong chaha'er fangken zhangcheng kan chaha'er kenwu*," 205.

37. Yigu, "Zou wei chaha'er youyi kenwu chengxiao guoban jinchen qianhou banfa ji geyuan chuli qingxing zhe fupian," GX 29/8/2, in Yigu, *Kenwu zouyi*, 125–26; Anzai, "Shinmatsu ni okeru suien no kaikon," 26–27.

38. Anzai, "Shinmatsu ni okeru suien no kaikon," 30.

39. It should be noted that among the 192,000 taels of land-contract fees, over eighty-two thousand taels were either misappropriated by the Administration or "contributed" to the Qing state, so that the actual sum received by the banners and herds was just 110,000 taels. See Wulan, "Cong chaha'er fangken zhangcheng kan chaha'er kenwu," 202–03.

40. Yigu, *Kenwu zouyi*, 127–31; Anzai, "Shinmatsu ni okeru suien no kaikon," 34–35.

41. "Mengzhang A'erbinbaya'er wei huitong shangyi kaiken shiyi zha zhunge'er beizi Shanjimidubu deng wen," GX 28/9/24, in JKJYD, volume 3, 264 (1204); "Fumengzhang Chakedu'erseleng, junwang qi xieli taiji burenji'ergala deng wei zuzhi kaiban guanken cheng mengzhang A'erbinbaya'er wen," GX 28/11/1, in JKJYD, volume 3, 305 (1210–11).

42. Yigu, "Zou wei yikezhaomeng hangjinqi ge qian yuan lai cheng jiuyi qing jiang shenmingdayi shouxian zundiao zhi mengzhang zhasake ken'en jiajiang yi zhao jiquan zhe," GX 29/4/7, in Yigu, *Kenwu zouyi*, 89–92.

43. Yigu, "Zou wei xushu dalateqi peijiao dimu luxu fangken jin jiang xianhou banli bing zhuoni zhengzu shengke qingxing zhe," GX 29/12/7; "Zou wei banli choushu dalateqi peidi youbi mengiao bingyi xiangxu jin chenming xianhou chouban qingxing ji zhuo bao zaishi chuli shuyuan yishi jiangli zhe," GX 30/9/12; "Zou wei chenbao xian ban kenwu qingxing bing fu chaha'er huichou zuoyi banfa qicheng riqi zhe," GX 28/11/8, in ibid., 193–96, 263–66, 67.

44. "Mengzhang A'erbinbaya'er wei chahe youwu qian guan baoke shi zha zhunge'er beizi Shanjimidubu deng wen," GX 29/7/9; "Mengzhang A'erbinbaya'er wei chaming geqi shifou qianguan zhijiao dimu yishi zha zhunge'er qi beizi Shanjimidubu deng wen," in JKJYD, 212–13 (1230–31), 276–77 (1233–35).

45. Yigu, "Zou wei michen yikezhaomeng mengzhang kang bu zunban chedong quanju qingzhi kaiqu mengzhang zhi ren lingxing jianshu yishi zhenshe er fu shiji zhe," GX 29/11/6, in Yigu, *Kenwu zouyi*, 155–61. For the Qing bestowal of titles and ranks, see the chapter on "ornamentalism" in Elverskog, *Our Great Qing*, 68–73.

46. Yigu, "Zou wei yikezhaomeng hangjinqi baoken mengdi yuan zhao gechu yilü gaishou yahuang zhe" GX 31/2/4, in Yigu, *Kenwu zouyi*, 323–25.

47. Yigu, "Zou wei hangjinqi di gaizheng yahuang yu an nian baoxiao suizu yiban wai you fu baoxiao jukuan yuken enshi yi zhao jiquan zhe," GX 31/9/8, in Yigu, *Kenwu zouyi*, 365–67.

48. Yigu, *Kenwu zouyi*, 366.

49. Prince Chakhdurseleng of Üüshin, originally a prince of third rank (*beise* 貝子), was given the title of prince of second rank (*jiyunwang* 郡王), and Prince Shagdurjab of Jasag, originally a duke of second rank (Mo: *ulus-tur tusalakhu güng*, Ch: *fuguogong* 輔國公), was raised to the rank of the duke of first rank (Mo: *ulus-un tushiye güng*, Ch: *zhenguogong* 鎮國公). Yigu, "Zou wei mengfan xiandi zhugu baoxiao qingyin juqing daichen zhe" GX 30/9/7, in Yigu, *Kenwu zouyi*, 259–61.

50. Yigu, "Zou wei yikezhaomeng junwang zhasake liangqi di you jinbian kaipi mengzhong rending jun yuan jiujin gui wuyuan tingzhi juqing zouchen zhe," GX 31/3/9, in Yigu, *Kenwu zouyi*, 337–41.

51. Serruys, "Documents from Ordos on the 'Revolutionary Circles,' Part I," 485.

52. The jasag of Wang banner, for example, complained of difficulties of collecting taxes since the Jiaqing era (1796–1820) due to evasion and frequent land ownership transference. See KWDA, 494.

53. JKJYD, volume 3.

54. "Zhunge'erqi wei gaiqi huang hei renzhong jun buyuan kaiken huanghe an'bian tudi shi cheng mengzhang wen," GX 29/8/21; "Suiyuancheng jiangjun shangzou peijiaodi shiyi bing jiang suofeng shangyu chaolu zhuanxing zhunge'erqi zhasake beizi shanjimidubu wen," GX 30/7/16, JKJYD, volume 3, GX 29, 248–51; GX 30, 155–56.

55. Yigu, "Zou wei zhunga'erqi kenwu fujing kaiban mengyuan juzhong kangzu gongqiang jusuo jushi zouqing yancheng zhe," GX 31/9/8, in Yigu, *Kenwu zouyi*, 359.

56. "Suiyuancheng jiangjun wei qina kangken menggu chuokedureng dengren shi zha zhunge'erqi beizi wen," GX 30/9/23; "Kenwu dachen suiyuancheng jiangjun wei qina chuokedureng deng kangken renyuan shi zha zhunge'erqi beizi shanjimidubu wen," GX 30/12/6; "Bangban mengwu wei qina zhunge'erqi chuokedureng junwangqi maobatu deng shi zha zhunge'erqi beizi shanjimidubu deng wen," GX 31/7, JKJYD, volume 3, 148–53, 183–84, 257–59.

57. *Tusalagchi* is a high official secondary only to the *jasag*. Dampil had served long under the former *jasag* and league governor Janagardi (r. 1852–1901), and as acting jasag during the interim before Janagardi's brother, sixty-two-year-old Shanjimidub, succeeded the position in 1902. The new jasag, being a lama returning to laity, was rarely involved in worldly affairs, thus leaving the banner administration entirely in the hands of Dampil.

58. "Kenwu dachen suiyuancheng jiangjun wei zhijiao heijiedi shi zha zhunge'erqi zhasake beizi shanjimidubu wen," GX 31/4/12; "Kenwu dachen suiyuancheng jiangjun wei chilling lai Baotou wenzui shi zha zhunge'erqi xieli taiyi danpi'er wen," GX 31/4/23, JKJYD, volume 3, 63–65, 118–19.

59. Yigu, *Kenwu zouyi*, 360.

60. "Suiyuancheng jiangjun wei pai danpi'er lai sui mianshang kenwu shiyi zha zhunge'er beizi wen huizhi," GX 31/11/18; "Kenwu dachen Suiyuancheng jiangjun wei danpi'er suoyou chuliang yiban zhun you zhunge'erqi yamen chucang yibei zainian zhenji menggu shi zha zhunge'er beizi shanjimudubu wen," GX 32/2/29, in JKJYD, volume 3, GX 31, 253–54; GX 32, 57–58.

61. "Zhunge'erqi wei wuyuanting guanbing xiang menggu renjia kaihuo bing qiangsha minren Yang Mayao zhi zi deng shi zi fuguxian yamen wen," GX 31/4/23; GX 31/8/21, JKJYD, volume 3, 65–67, 170–72.

62. "Bangban mengwu wei qina yu mengkenjiya yitong kangken zhi junwangqi taiji maobatu deng shi zha zhunge'erqi beizi shanjimidubu wen," GX 31/7/25, JKJYD, volume 3, 150–53.

63. Yigu, "Zou wei zhunga'erqi kenwu fujing kaiban mengyuan juzhong kangzu gongqiang jusuo jushi zouqing yancheng zhe," GX 31/9/8, in Yigu, *Kenwu zouyi*, 359–62.

64. The term *duguilang* or "circles" was derived from the circular manner in which the members signed their names, which was meant to conceal the identities of the ringleaders. Meetings were oftentimes held at various monasteries. See Bawden, *The Modern History of Mongolia*, 176; Serruys, "Documents from Ordos on the 'Revolutionary Circles,' Part I," 483. For a detailed account of the duguilang movement in Ordos, see Atwood, *Young Mongols and Vigilantes in Inner Mongolia's Interregnum Decades*, 198–227.

65. Serruys, "Documents from Ordos on the 'Revolutionary Circles,' Part I," 483–84.

66. Yigu, *Kenwu zouyi*, 91, 111.

67. Yigu, "Zhawei kenwu geju chaishi yuan ming zhachi zongju shouzhiju zunzhao you," GX28/4/24, KWDA, 71.

68. Baoyu, "*Qingmo suiyuan kenwu*," 33–35, 59–61.

69. Baoyu, "*Qingmo suiyuan kenwu*," 34–35.

70. The constitution of each bureau was similar. The top layer included directors, deputy directors, deputy assistant secretaries, and controllers. The second tier consisted of functionaries such as chief drafters, accountants, adjudicators, auditors, measurers, irrigation overseers, cultivation promoters, surveyors, inspectors, suppliers, translators, and clerks. Most of these positions were filled by probationary officials or reserve candidates of Shanxi and Zhili provinces. The remaining tier were other personnel such as factotums, interpreters, copyists, messengers, errand runners, and guards. See Yigu, "Jin jiang sheli ge juchu xianhou riqi ji yuansi shuchai fuyi rending eshu shanju qingdan gongcheng yulan," in Yigu, *Kenwu zouyi*, 177–81.

71. KWDA, "Yigu qingong," 1258, 1265–67. For the salaries and subsidies, see Yigu, *Kenwu zouyi*, 183–87.

72. KWDA, 295–97; Yigu, "Fupian," GX 32/4/24, in Yigu, *Kenwu zouyi*, 435–37.

73. The *mu* standard varied from place to place. In Chakhar, one *mu* was equivalent to 360 *gong* (one thousand square meters), rather than 240 *gong*, which was adopted as the official standard in China proper since 1581. This was owing to the coexistence of large and small *mu* (*da xiao mu* 大小畝) in rural China. The large *mu* remained prevalent in the Mongol periphery, probably owing to the abundance of cultivable lands there. The small *mu* standard was adopted in 1885, when the Liuchengdi ("six-part-territory") of Tümed banner was opened to official reclamation, which set a precedent for subsequent reclamation in the western leagues. The adoption of the small *mu* standard thus can be seen as part of the official endeavors to integrate the Mongol periphery into the Chinese framework. See "Kenwu zongju xiangfu salaqi ting chaming zhangfang liucheng guandi gai gong yong shan shuce you," GX 28/10/24, KWDA, 206. For land measurement in late imperial China, see Kang Chao, *Zhongguo chuantong nongcun de diquan fenpei*, 44.

74. "*Ximeng zhangliang chuchai zhangcheng*," KWDA, 206–07.

75. Yigu, *Kenwu zouyi*, 120, 371–72.

76. Yigu, *Kenwu zouyi*, 193–96, 263–65; KWDA, 1033–34.

77. Yigu, *Kenwu zouyi*, 299; KWDA, 1025–26, 1050–53; Gan Pengyun, *Diaocha guisui kenwu baogaoshu* (Shahukou, 1916), 382. On the format of *guanshang heban*, see Chan, *Merchants, Mandarins, and Modern Enterprise in Late Ch'ing China*, 85–106.

78. KWDA, 1023–27; Yigu, *Kenwu zouyi*, 49, 226.

79. Wang Yanping, "*Qingmo chaha'er baqi mengdi de fangken*," 216–18.

80. Gan Pengyun, *Diaocha guisui kenwu baogaoshu*, 383.

81. Yigu, *Kenwu zouyi*, 226–27; KWDA, 1026–27.

82. Yigu, *Kenwu zouyi*, 237–38; KWDA 1028–29.

83. KWDA, 1024–25; Yigu, *Kenwu zouyi*, 47–49, 263–65.

84. KWDA, 1054, 1059.

85. KWDA, 1053–55, 1068, 1268.

86. KWDA, 1062.

87. Yigu, "Zou wei tongchou houtao qudi quanju qiyi dajia xiuzhi tuiguang liyuan yigui jiuyuan zhe," in KWDA, 1303.

88. KWDA, 1053–58.

89. KWDA, 1055–60.

90. Lu Chuanlin and Shaoyin, "Zou wei chaming kenwu dachen beican gekuan jin fenbie qingzhong jushi luchen bing baojian xianyuan banli shanhou shiyi yi sui mengfan er shou shixiao zhe," in Yigu, *Mengken xugong*, 8–9.

91. Jin Yufu, *Da Qing xuantong zhengji* 41, XT 2/8/16.

92. Gan Pengyun, *Diaocha guisui kenwu*, 300–05.

93. Yigu, "Zou wei lükan Hangjin qi kendi nijiang yuanding zuzhang lüejia biantong yiqi yidi zhiyi zhe," in Yigu, *Kenwu zouyi*, 346; Gan Pengyun, *Diaocha guisui kenwu*, 302.

94. Gan Pengyun, *Diaocha guisui kenwu*, 306–13.

95. Gan Pengyun, *Diaocha guisui kenwu*, 300–28.

96. Yigu, *Kenwu zouyi*, 324.

97. The circumstances in Tümed banner were somewhat different. These lands were long under Chinese cultivation, because the Tümed Mongol soldiers received no salary payment from the Qing and habitats allocated to each household provided a main source of income for them. For this reason, these lands were officially measured, evaluated, but not released. The Chinese cultivators were allowed to keep their plots upon paying a land fee (which ranged from ten to 160 taels per qing) in arrears, whereas an annual tax was to be collected by the state and then given to the Mongol landowners as land rents. See Gan Pengyun, *Diaocha guisui kenwu*, 353–64.

98. KWDA, 1059, 1421–22.

99. KWDA, 1342–44. The eleven branches were merged into seven in 1908, five in 1910, and dissolved in 1912.

100. One earth cube refers to the volume of one square *zhang* by one *chi*, which is roughly equivalent to three cubic meters. The usual methods used in removing earth were by shoveling (*diugong* 丢工), carrying (*beigong* 背工), or half carrying and half shoveling (*banbei bandiu* 半背半丢), and the labor charges varied accordingly. See KWDA, 1372, 1395, 1402, 1412.

101. "Longxingchang fenju zhangcheng," in KWDA, 1329.

102. Depending on the area of green shoots, usually each *qing* of land were allowed one or two hours of watering time. In the case of Yongji canal, each of its five branch channels irrigated an area of between five hundred and six hundred qing, which was divided into twelve "numbers" (*hao* 號), with a sluice gate built at each "number" to control the water flow. It generally took forty or fifty days and nights to complete one round. It was thus important to set up a timetable for each number of each branch. See KWDA, 1328–30.

103. Yigu, "Zou wei tongchou houtao qudi quanju qiyi dajia xiuzhi tuiguang liyuan yigui jiuyuan zhe," in KWDA, 1302–05.

104. In 1905, Yuan Kai, deputy director of the Baotou Bureau, surveyed the Wujia River along the southern foot of Mt. Langshan from Alasha to Urad banner, and came up with a proposal of dredging, embanking, and expanding the old riverbed, so as to provide irrigation and facilitate grain transport in the Urad area. See KWDA, 1319–21.

105. KWDA, 280, 282–83.

106. KWDA, 1320.

107. KWDA, 1302–05, 1318–19.

108. Lu Chuanlin and Shaoying, "Zou wei chaming kenwu dachen beican gekuan jin fenbie qingzhong jushi luchen bing baojian xianyuan banli shanhou shiyi yisui mengfan er shou shixiao zhe," in Yigu (1974c), 1–24.

109. Ibid.

110. "Yao Xuejing qingong," KWDA, 1288–90. According to the Investigation Bureau, the actual expenditure was 443,898 taels, including 353,359 on construction labor and subsidies, 72,325 on compensating the land-merchants, and 18,213 on the garrison troops. See KWDA, 1364–65. According to Gan Pengyun, the total expenditure was 543,011 taels. See Gan (1916), 387.

111. Gan Pengyun, *Diaocha guisui kenwu*, 303.

112. Feng Jilong, ed., *Diaocha hetao baogaoshu*, 5.

113. For instance, misconduct of Li Degong, deputy assistant secretary of the Yongji branch office, resulted in damage of the Yongji canal by water, causing a loss of thirty thousand taels. Widespread silting was another problem that afflicted many construction projects, due to negligence and corruption of the officials. See KWDA, 1446–47, 1469–71.

114. Zhao Erxun, "Tongchou benji zhe," in Zhongguo diyi lishi dang'anguan bianjibu, ed., *Guangxuchao zhupi zouzhe*, volume 33, 19.

115. Wu Tingbin, "Zou wei linyuan weishu jinbian fenshe geting bing chenming yingban shiyi shandan juzou yi shou suibian qimin zhi xiao zhe," in KWDA, 1489–94.

116. In 1884, Zhang Zhidong memorialized the court on changing the titles of judicial sub-prefects in the seven sub-prefectures of Xikouwai into administrative magistrates with judicial title, so as to legalize Han settlement and facilitate revenue collection. See Zhang Zhidong, "Kouwai geting biancha huji wu'ai menggu youmu shu," in Ge Shijun, *Huangchao jingshi wen xu bian*, 32.

117. Gong Zizhen, "Xiyu zhi xingsheng yi," in *Gong Zizhen quanji*, 105–12; Weiyuan, *Shengwu ji* 4, 10; Zuo Zongtang, "Zunzhi tongchou quanju zhe," "Fuchen xingjiang qingxing zhe," in *Zuo wenxianggong quanji*, volumes 50 and 53. For detailed accounts on the Qing incorporation of Xinjiang, see Newby, *The Empire and the Khanate*; Millward, *Eurasian Crossroads*.

118. Wuyungerile, "Qingmo nei menggu de difang jianzhi yu chouhua jiansheng 'shibian'"; Zhao Yuntian, "Qingmo xinzheng qijian de 'choumeng gaizhi'"; Reardon-Anderson, *Reluctant Pioneers*.

119. Yao Xiguang, "Shibian tiaoyi," in Yao Xiguang, *Choumeng chuyi*, 78–79.

120. Zuo Shaozuo, "Qian jishizhong Zuo Shaozuo zou xibei bianbei zhongyao ni sheli xingsheng zhe," in Zhu Qiqian, ed., *Dongsansheng mengwu gongdu huibian*.

121. Cen Chunxuan, "Tongchou xibei quanju zhuoni biantong banfa zhe," in Sichuan sheng minzu yanjiusuo, ed., *Qingmo chuandian bianwu dang'an shiliao* , 921–26.

122. Wuyungerile, "Qingmo nei menggu de difang jianzhi"; Zhao Yuntian, "Qingmo xinzheng qijian de 'choumeng gaizhi'"; Zhang Qixiong, "Qingting dui zhengfu guanyuan menggu choubian lunshu de jueze," 34–53.

123. Yao served under He Ruzhang, first ambassador to Japan, in 1878. Later he was appointed as assistant staff of Li Hongzhang and Zhang Zhidong, and was dispatched by the latter to Japan in 1898 for investigating the education system. He twice inspected the four eastern Mongol leagues (Josotu, Juu Uda, Jerim, Shilingol) in 1905 and presented a series of proposals on managing the Mongols to Tieliang (1863–1939), minister of Military Training Office. See Shu Xilong, "Yao Xiguang shengping jiqi chengjiu chutan."

124. Yao Xiguang, "Shibian tiaoyi," in *Choumeng chuyi*, 56; "Chengfu jinghua dong simeng menggu tiaoyi," in *Choumeng chuyi*, 113.

125. Yao Xiguang, "Shibian tiaoyi," 55.

126. Üjümchin salt, acclaimed for its prime quality, is produced in the Eji dabsu noor (salt lake) along the border of the Üjümchin and Khauchit banners of the Shilin Gol league. Traditionally, it was taxed by the jasags of both banners. For the production and taxation of Üjümchin salt, see Pozdneyev, *Mongolia and the Mongols*, volume 2, 489–91.

127. Yao Xiguang, "Chafu dongbu nei menggu qingxing shuotie," in *Choumeng chuyi*, 17–28; "Chengfu jinghua dongsimeng menggu tiaoyi," in *Choumeng chuyi*, 117–27.

128. Yao Xiguang, *Choumeng chuyi*, 61–62.

129. Yao Xiguang, *Choumeng chuyi*, 79. For the Japanese conquest of Ainu, see Takakura, *The Ainu of Northern Japan*; Walker, *The Conquest of Ainu Lands*.

130. For debates on *fengjian* and *junxian*, see Duara, *Rescuing History from the Nation*, 152–60.

131. Yao Xiguang, *Choumeng chuyi*, 58–59.

132. Yao Xiguang, *Choumeng chuyi*, 53.

133. "Fu lifanbu zou choubei fanshu xianzheng yingban shiyi fenbie jihuan zeyao jinxing zhe," in Shangwu yinshuguan bianyisuo, ed., *Da Qing xuantong xin faling*.

134. Jin Yufu, ed., *Da Qing xuantong zhengji*, volume 41.

135. Underdown, "Banditry and Revolutionary Movement," 109–16.

136. Bulag, "Inner Mongolia: The Dialectics of Colonization and Ethnicity Building," 87.

Conclusion

This book examines the historical processes of Chinese migration and settlement in Inner Mongolia as a crucial part of the formation of modern China as a territorial, centralizing nation-state. It reconstructs the social, economic, cultural, and administrative history of this region at a time of unprecedented Chinese expansion into non-Han regions and China's absorption into the global frameworks of capitalism and nationalism. The parallel processes gave rise to new economic practices, property regimes, and political configurations that paved the way for the administrative integration of the Mongol periphery into the Chinese state. This study approaches these historical conjunctures from a peripheral perspective and addresses issues central to our understanding of early modern and modern China, including Qing empire-building, commercialization, market-oriented business practices, transregional interconnections and trading networks, Western imperialism, and China's modern transition from empire to nation. The book shows that these processes of transformation were much more open-ended and multilayered than has been suggested by such dichotomies as East and West, Chinese and Mongol, colonizer and colonized, traditional and modern.

The borderland here is understood as a multiplicity of overlapping, crisscrossing boundaries—geographical, ecological, ethnic, cultural, religious, administrative, and legal—that porously separated the steppe from the sown, the Mongol from the Chinese, and the nomadic from the sedentary. In this borderland, the decentralized rule of Mongol princes met the centralized bureaucracy of Chinese provinces, and Shamanism and Tibetan Buddhism intersected with Chinese syncretism. The boundaries were by no means as secure and stable as they appeared, but were drawn and redrawn through a series of intertwining historical, cultural, and political processes, which gave depth to the existing geographical and social structures in both societies. This study is an inquiry into the processes by which these boundaries were redrawn and new layers added; the borders were penetrated, negotiated, and contested; and the frontier societies, cultures, and communities were transformed and incorporated into modern nations (although this incorporation was not without contestation, active resistance, and human and ecological consequences). It further explores how domestic factors such as population pressure and ecological crises interacted with the global forces of trade, capitalism, imperialism, and religion to fundamentally alter the frontier society.

This book argues that a set of macro-historical forces transformed the nomadic society well before it was subject to the processes of modernization and national integration introduced by the West. First, under the surface of social transformation were the deep currents of human-environment interactions—climate change, population growth, natural disasters, shifting river courses—that provided the primordial driving force for human migration. The warm climate in the eighteenth century provided favorable conditions for the advance of agricultural activities on the steppe.[1] Meanwhile, the population of China more than doubled from the late seventeenth through the mid-nineteenth century: escalating from around 150 million to over four hundred million. This population expansion was partly due to the introduction of New World food crops and partly due to prolonged peace under the Qing rule.[2] The population surge triggered ecologic and social ramifications such as land shortage, deforestation, environmental degradation, and growing rural poverty. It generated a long-term push of Chinese emigrants from the core regions of China into marginal areas such as the highlands of southwest China and the sparsely populated borderlands such as Taiwan, Manchuria, and Inner Mongolia. Although the Chinese migrant population absorbed by Inner Mongolia was insignificant in number compared to that in regions with more favorable agricultural conditions, the incomers nonetheless overwhelmed the indigenous ecology and inhabitants. This event can be considered the initial steps in the full-scale Chinese colonization of the Mongol borderlands in the name of development. The longer-term process not only decisively altered the demographic profile of the region, but it also caused the marginalization of the Mongols and their nomadic culture and long-term ecological consequences, such as land degradation and desertification.

The second macro-historical forces was a series of political and socioeconomic changes during the eighteenth century that fundamentally altered the power equilibrium between steppe and sown and provided a further impetus for interregional migration. The Qing military expansion created a vast multi-ethnic empire that doubled the size of its predecessor. Whereas this resulted in new, expanded capacities to the Manchu empire, it also brought about multiple challenges in ruling a diverse collection of peoples with distinct identities. The Qing managed their extensive frontiers in ways that departed from previous Chinese dynasties. Their methods included forming military alliances with the eastern Mongols, compartmentalizing them through a territorial banner and league system, establishing indirect rule through co-opting the Mongol elites, patronizing Gelugpa Buddhism, and maintaining a segregation policy between the Mongols and Han Chinese. These policies helped ensure that the Mongol vassals felt a personal allegiance toward the Qing emperor. They also eliminated potential threats to the empire from the steppe by preventing the formation of intertribal confederacies. Meanwhile, interactions between the

Qing and Russian empires through treaties and trade helped integrate the nomadic society into the Chinese market economy as well as into global trade flows. Finally, the necessity of maintaining and financing the imperial enterprises subjugated the Mongol elites to the financial control of Chinese merchants.

The third and final sweeping macro-historical force charted by this book were the internal and external crises the Qing dynasty faced in the nineteenth century that induced unprecedented Chinese emigration into the Mongol peripheries. On the domestic level, pressures of population growth and ecological deterioration caused land shortage, rural impoverishment, and the decline of bureaucratic efficiency. It resulted in a series of devastating rebellions, wars, and famine that plagued the Qing dynasty during the second half of the nineteenth century. The social turmoil in the wake of the Dungan Revolt and its Qing suppression followed by the Great Famine of 1876–1879 triggered waves of refugees from north China into the grasslands. On the international front, Western imperialist powers deployed gunboat diplomacy to force the Qing dynasty to open its door to foreign trade and influences. Meanwhile, the adoption of Western technology, institutions, and statecraft also provided the broad configurations of structural changes that facilitated China's incorporation into the global system of capitalism and nation-states. In Inner Mongolia, this was accomplished through internal Chinese colonization in ways that resembled the imperialist expansion of the West in the non-Western world.

Within this broader set of ecological, political, and social developments, the book focuses on a series of intertwining processes of Chinese expansion that took place in Inner Mongolia from the eighteenth to early twentieth centuries. The ways in which this expansion transformed both the frontier and Chinese society are explored. The first process examined was the penetration of Chinese trade and commerce. As shown in chapter 2, the Shanxi merchants played a central role as contracted suppliers for the Qing troops during the military campaigns against the Zunghars, while mediating the financial needs of Manchu and Mongol ruling elites. This long-distance trade generated a cluster of frontier market centers and an extensive trading network linking the Mongol periphery to core parts of China. By the end of the eighteenth century, even the remotest corners of Mongolia had been exposed to a monetized economy dominated by the Shanxi merchants. Further, the installation of a set of imperial apparatuses served to incorporate the nomadic society into the silver-based economy of China as well as the global market system. These imperial apparatuses included the postal relay station and frontier guard post system, the *nianban* system for Mongol aristocracy and high lamas to attend imperial audience in Beijing, and the opening of Sino-Russian trade at Kiakhta. The financial burden to maintain these institutions, coupled with the growing taste for Chinese luxuries among the upper classes, made the Mongol elites easy prey for Chinese commercial control. The two processes of Chinese commercial penetration and Qing imperial expansion combined to provoke widespread indebtedness, impoverishment, and social stratification in Mongolia. Here, the relations between commerce and borderland were multilayered. Whereas state policies and strategic concerns set the preconditions and context for Chinese commercial expansion, it was the long-term movement of goods, capital, and people that transformed Mongol society through regional and global integration.

Alongside the expansion of trade, this book investigates the practices of land reclamation and settlement in Inner Mongolia. Beginning in the late seventeenth and early eighteenth century, a flux of Chinese farmers from northern China began to cultivate the edges of the grassland, either as tenants recruited to work in the official or imperial estates along the Great Wall or as famine-stricken refugees accommodated by the *jiedi yangmin* policy. As shown in chapter 3, the advance of Chinese cultivation brought about major changes in economic practices, property regimes, and cultural identities in frontier society. One significant change was the growing tendency toward commodification and privatization of land, as the communally owned Mongol banner lands gradually passed into private ownership. Whereas the Mongols retained the right to collect rental fees, actual land-use was permanently shifted to Chinese migrants, who were free to mortgage, sublease, and transfer the plots to others. Chapter 4 provides a case study of new property regimes and socio-technological arrangements developed by Chinese land merchants, who combined merchant capital, land resources, and technical expertise to develop an elaborate irrigation system in Hetao along the Yellow River. These endeavors exemplified a form of agrarian capitalism based on massive capital investment, wage labor, and commercialized agricultural production.

Another development was the transplantation of a centralized administrative system to the Mongol regions. This change in local government eventually eroded the decentralized rule of the Mongol aristocracy. Concurrent with such institutional changes, cross-cultural encounters and exchanges gave rise to the intermingling of cultural practices. As many early Chinese migrants adopted Mongolian names, married Mongol women, and became naturalized Mongols, their Mongol neighbors began to switch to a semi-pastoral and semi-agricultural lifestyle. This mixing of peoples with different cultures and religions naturally sparked frictions and misunderstandings, which, coupled with ever-mounting clashes of economic interests associated with land, turned the borderland into a hotbed of ethnic conflicts. The ethnic violence during the Jindandao Incident of 1891 in Jehol, which ended in the massacre of tens of thousands of Mongols, was rooted in such cultural biases and economic conflicts.[3]

In examining cross-cultural encounters, this book has taken an in-depth look at the expansion of religion and its role in facilitating Chinese settlement in the Mongol periphery. The dominant religion of the Mongols was Gelugpa Buddhism. As Joseph Fletcher aptly points out, the monasteries greatly aided the penetration of Chinese trade by providing marketplaces, shelters, and storage space for the merchants. The Buddhist lamas also acted in their capacity as landlords to mediate land transactions and as business partners and shareholders by investing in the Chinese firms.[4] This study adds to Fletcher's assessment by tracing the expansion of the Roman Catholic Church on the back of Western imperialism and the ways in which it gave impetus to Chinese colonization and social transformation in Inner Mongolia. The impact of

Catholic proselytizing was manifold. On the one hand, Roman Catholic missionaries became a crucial force in organizing settler communities, providing emergency relief and sponsoring social reforms in a frontier society plagued by rebellions, famine, and poverty. On the other hand, the missionaries' heavy-handed meddling in local land disputes necessitated intervention from the foreign legation and the central government in Beijing: thereby eroding the autonomy of Mongol banners and facilitating the penetration of a centralizing state.

These social dynamics—driven by ecological, strategic, commercial, religious, and imperialist forces—culminated in the final process of official reclamation and top-down state formation in the Mongol periphery. In 1902, the Qing court reversed its century-old protective policy toward the Mongols in favor of one that actively promoted Chinese migration and settlement in order to strengthen the frontier. By opening up Mongol banner lands for Chinese cultivation and subjecting them to state taxation, the Qing revoked the hereditary rights of Mongol princes to these lands, and hence opened the floodgate to the full-scale colonization of Inner Mongolia under the Republican and PRC regimes. What was at stake was not just the shift from a pastoral to agricultural use of land, but more importantly, the integration of the heterogenous Mongol periphery into a globalized capitalist economy and centralizing nation-state framework. This process entailed incremental changes that stripped the region of its distinctive political status, destroyed the privileges of Mongol nobility, and replaced the barter economy of nomadic pastoralism with a marketized agrarian regime.

To conclude, Inner Mongolia during the Qing period was caught in the historical conjuncture of two separate processes that converged in the second half of the nineteenth century: (1) the demographic and economic expansion of the Han Chinese into non-Han peripheries, and (2) the aggressive advance of the West into the non-Western world. The former took the shape of a spontaneous movement of population and capital, whereas the latter was exemplified by a treaty system imposed through gunboat diplomacy. Despite the apparent parallelism between these processes, the inner logic they followed was different. The former process was made possible by forces of empire building and commercialization that resulted in the redistribution of priorities and resources between the imperial core and its periphery. The latter process grew out of the global expansion of capitalism and nation-states that imposed the hegemony of Western modernity.

All these developments point to a central argument of this book: the centrality of the periphery. Contrary to the usual assumption that the border regions were little more than passive recipients of civilizing and colonizing impetuses emanating from the center, they played a critical role in China's modern transition from a multi-ethnic empire to a centralizing and homogenizing nation-state. Starting in the eighteenth century, the peripheral regions absorbed the surplus population from within the Great Wall and offered an extensive market for an array of Chinese products that greatly spurred frontier commercialism. The hybrid cultural setting of the borderlands also gave rise to economic innovations, as demonstrated by the irrigation communities of Hetao and the Catholic villages that were established across Inner Mongolia. As it turned out, the most peripheral areas of the Qing empire were actually contact zones between the Qing economy and the global economy in the same way as the treaty ports of Shanghai and Guangdong. Here, we can observe crucial transformations occurring at the weakest link of the imperial system. Some of the economic, cultural, and administrative experimentations initiated in these areas, such as the proto-bank system of Shanxi merchants and the girls' school and orphanage of Xiwanzi, were later introduced in core regions of the empire and had a significant impact on their historical development.

From the late Qing through the Republican and PRC periods, the periphery again played a crucial role in the historical and spatial imaginaries of modern China, as it was the outermost stretch of land rather than the core that defined the nation as a sovereign territorial unit. Indeed, the inclusion of Inner Mongolia in the Chinese "geo-body" plays a pivotal, though often understated, role in the self-perception of China today as a "unitary multinational state" (*tongyi de duominzu guojia* 統一的多民族國家).[5] The hardening of China's national boundaries against foreign countries, which was essential to the constitution of China as a sovereign, territorial nation-state, was accompanied by the intentional softening and even removal of the existing boundaries between the core regions of China and its heterogeneous peripheries.

Of course, the process of Chinese migration and settlement in Inner Mongolia did not stop with the fall of the Qing Dynasty in 1912. Quite the contrary, it gathered momentum during the Republican and PRC periods owing to advances in modern technologies and new forms of mass mobilization. The railway between Beijing and Kalgan, completed in 1909, was extended to Höhhot in 1921 and further to Baotou in 1923 and greatly accelerated the migration process. Compared with the earlier migration, which was largely spontaneous and initiated from the bottom up, the migration of the twentieth century was typically organized from the top down by the provincial state, the military, or another semi-official organization. For instance, between 1925 and 1934, the warlords Feng Yuxiang, Yan Xishan, and Fu Zuoyi organized military colonization in Baotou and Hetao by recruiting settlers from north China as well as central provinces such as Hunan, Anhui, and Jiangsu. Around the same time, a number of semi-official and private settlement organizations based in Shandong, Hunan, and Hebei also mushroomed, with the aim of extending the Rural Reconstruction Movement (*xiangcun jianshe yundong* 鄉村建設運動) initiated by Y. C. James Yen and Liang Shuming to the frontier regions. They organized cooperatives, popularized education, and strengthened village autonomy for the purpose of revitalizing the Chinese village and strengthening the frontier.[6] State-organized colonization reached an apex during the PRC period, which saw two major waves of Chinese emigration into Inner Mongolia as well as into other peripheries like Xinjiang and Heilongjiang, through large-scale campaigns of "support frontier construction" (*zhiyuan bianjiang jianshe* 支援邊疆建設) during the 1950s and the organization of "Production and Construction Corps" (*shengchan jianshe bingtuan* 生產建設兵團) during the Cultural Revolution (1966–1976). By

2010, the Chinese population in Inner Mongolia had reached 19.6 million, which was quadruple the number in 1947.[7]

Such dramatic population movement and top-down state formation necessarily brought about profound and far-reaching political, cultural, and environmental repercussions on the Mongol periphery. Whereas the Khalkhas of northern Mongolia proclaimed independence upon the fall of the Qing in 1911, Inner Mongolia remained a contested space of competing national claims among China, Japan, Mongolia, and Soviet Russia.[8] Its eastern part was incorporated into Khinggan province under the Japanese puppet state of Manchukuo, whereas its western part was torn between an array of clashing political forces. These forces included the Chinese Nationalist (Guomingdang, hereafter GMD) government, which endeavored to assimilate the ethnic Mongols into a culturally unified China; the Mongol ethnic nationalists, who sought support from the GMD, Japan, and the Soviet Union, respectively, in their autonomous pursuits; and Mongol Communists, who collaborated with the Chinese Communist Party. After the defeat of Japan in 1945, followed by the outbreak of civil war (1946–1950) in China, the Mongol Communists led by Ulanhu (1907–1988) established the Inner Mongolia Autonomous Government in 1947, which was incorporated as an autonomous region into the PRC in 1949.

The PRC government has continued the policy of large-scale Chinese migration and state-sponsored development schemes in Inner Mongolia since the late Qing period and carried these initiatives forward with a forcefulness and efficiency as never seen before. The most recent of such strategies is the Go-West campaign launched in 1999 aimed at developing the nation's vast but previously underdeveloped interior and western regions.[9] Over the past two decades, Inner Mongolia has experienced accelerated economic growth, rapid industrialization, and increasing urbanization due to its abundant natural resources.[10] However, decades of unrestrained reclamation and mining activities have had a devastating impact on the delicate ecology of the steppe. These activities have caused desertification, drought, land degradation, and environmental deterioration, which are chiefly responsible for the recurring sandstorms that hit northern China and other parts of East Asia every spring. All these developments await future research to understand how the processes of migration and frontier-making transform the frontier in a modern setting: in particular, the Mongol initiatives caught amid the competing forms of modernity in East Asia.

NOTES

1. For an illustration of the pattern of climate changes in China, see Zhu Kezhen, "Zhongguo jin wuqian nian lai qihou bianqian de chubu yanjiu," 168–89; Li, "Changes in Climate, Land, and Human Efforts: The Production of Wet–Field Rice in Jiangnan during the Ming and Qing Dynasties," in Mark Elvin and Liu Ts'ui-jung, eds., *Sediments of Time: Environment and Society in Chinese History*, 447–86. For the impact of climate change on the movement of frontier between pastoralism and farming, see De Vries, "Measuring the Impact of Climate on History: The Search for Appropriate Methodologies," 599–630.

2. For discussions on the relationship between China's demographical expansion and migration, see E. Eastman, *Family, Fields, and Ancestors*.

3. Hyer, "The Chin-Tan-Tao Movement," 105–12; Borjigin, "The Complex Structure of Ethnic Conflict in the Frontier," 41–60.

4. Fletcher, "Ch'ing Inner Asia c. 1800," 56.

5. See the *Constitution of the People's Republic of China* adopted at the Fifth Session of the Fifth CPC National Congress, December 1982. The term "geo-body" refers to a set of values, discourses, and practices associated with the territory of a nation. See Winichakul, *Siam Mapped*.

6. Yan Tianling, *Hanzu yimin yu jindai Nei Menggu shehui bianqian yanjiu*, 46–56. For Yen and Liang's thoughts on Rural Reconstruction Movement, see Keehn, *Y.C. James Yen's Thought on Mass Education and Rural Reconstruction*; Alitto, *The Last Confucian*, esp. chapters IX, X, XI.

7. Nei Menggu zizhiqu tongjiju, *Nei menggu zizhiqu 2010 nian diliuci quanguo renkou pucha zhuyao shuju gongbao*, 2011.

8. Xiaoyuan Liu presents a detailed account of the political and diplomatic history of the Mongolia Independence movement against the background of rising Chinese nationalism, Mongolian nationalism, and superpower politics in Asia that involved Russia, Japan, and the United States. See Liu, *Reins of Liberation*. For the entangled history of Inner Mongolia in the early twentieth century, also see Atwood, *Young Mongols and Vigilantes in Inner Mongolia's Interregnum Decades*; Jagchid, *The Last Mongol Prince*.

9. For an overview of the Go-West campaign, see Yue-man Yeung and Shen Jianfa, eds., *Developing China's West*; Goodman, ed., *China's Campaign to "Open Up the West*."

10. According to the National Bureau of Statistics, Inner Mongolia in 2016 has a GDP of 1.8 trillion CNY, ranking fifteenth in the nation, and a GDP per capita of 73,936 CNY, which is among top seven of the nation. See http://www.stats.gov.cn/tjsj/ndsj/2017/ind-exch.htm.

Bibliography

Adas, Michael. 1998. "Imperialism and Colonialism in Comparative Perspective," *The International History Review* 20.2 (June): 371–88.

Adelman, Jeremy, and Stephen Aron 1999. "From Borderlands to Borders: Empires, Nation-States, and the Peoples in Between in North American History," *The American Historical Review* 104.3 (June): 814–41.

Alitto, Guy. 1979. *The Last Confucian: Liang Shu-Ming and the Chinese Dilemma of Modernity*. Berkeley: University of California Press.

Amitai, Reuven, and Michal Biran, eds. 2005. *Mongols, Turks, and Others: Eurasian Nomads and the Sedentary World*. Leiden: Brill.

Andrade, Tonio 2008. *How Taiwan Became Chinese: Dutch, Spanish, and Han Colonization in the Seventeenth Century*. New York: Columbia University Press.

Anzai Kuraji 安斎庫治 1938–1939. "Shinmatsu ni okeru suien no kaikon" 清末に於ける綏遠の開墾 [Land reclamation in Suiyuan in the late Qing], *Mantetsu Chōsa Geppo* [Southern Manchuria Railway Research Monthly] 18.12: 1–43; 19.1: 14–62; 19.2: 36–68.

——. 1942. "Mōkyō ni okeru tochi bunkatsu shoyūsei no ichi ruikei—ikokushō mei junkatsujiki gatōchi ni okeru tochi kankei no tokushitsu" 蒙疆に於ける土地分割所有制の一類型——伊克昭盟準噶爾旗河套地に於ける土地関係の特質 [A form of divided land ownership in Mongolia: land relationship in Hetao of Jüüngar banner of Yekhe Juu league], *Mantetsu Chōsa Geppo* [SMR Research Monthly] 22.5: 31–98.

Aramusu アラムス [Almas]. 2009. "Shindai uchi mongoru ni okeru nōchi shoyu no jittai: kenryū nenkan kara dōchi nenkan ni itaru kikajō tometo qi no kokōchi wo chūshin ni" 清代内モンゴルにおける農地所有の実態－乾隆年間から同治年間に至る帰化城トッメト旗の戸口地を中心に－ [Actual conditions of land ownership in Inner Mongolia during the Qing: focusing on household plots of Tümed banners of Höhhot from the Qianlong to the Tongzhi era], *Nairiku ajia shi kenkyū* [Inner Asian Studies] 24: 61–82.

Atwood, Christopher Pratt. 2002. *Young Mongols and Vigilantes in Inner Mongolia's Interregnum Decades, 1911–1931*. Leiden: Brill.

——. 2004. *Encyclopedia of Mongolia and the Mongol Empire*. New York: Facts on File, Inc.

——. 2010. "How the Mongols Got a Word for Tribe—and What It Means." *Menggu shi yanjiu* [Studia Historica Mongolica] 10: 63–89.

——. 2012. "Banner, *Otog*, Thousand: Appanage Communities as the Basic Unit of Traditional Mongolian Society," *Mongolian Studies* 34: 1–76.

————. 2015. "The Administrative Origins of Mongolia's 'Tribal' Vocabulary," *Eurasia: Statum et Legem* (Ulan-Ude) 1.4: 7–45.

Avery, Martha. 2003. *The Tea Road: China and Russia Meet Across the Steppe*. Beijing: China Intercontinental Press.

Ayala, César J. 1999. American Sugar Kingdom: The Plantation Economy of the Spanish Caribbean, 1898-1934. Chapel Hill: University of North Carolina Press.

Ba Jingyuan 巴靖遠. 1986. "Tumochuan de 'Errentai' yu Lao Shuangyang" 土默川的'二人台'與老雙羊 [*Errentai* drama on Tümed plain and Old Shuangyang]. *Tumote shiliao* 土默特史料 [Historical materials of Tümed] 20: 288–93.

Bailadugeqi 白拉都格其 [Baildagchi], Jinhai 金海 [Altan-dalai], and Saihang 賽航 [Saikhan], eds. 2002. *Menggu mingzu tongshi* 蒙古民族通史 [General history of the Mongolian nation], volume 5. Hohhot: Niemenggu daxue chubanshe.

Bao Muping 包慕萍. 2005. *Mongoru ni okeru toshi kenchikushi kenkyū: yūboku to teijū no jūsō toshi fufuhoto* モンゴルにおける都市建築史研究：遊牧と定住の重層都市フフホト [A study on the history of urban architecture in Mongolia: Höhhot, a multi-layered city of nomadism and settlement]. Tokyo: Tōhō shoten.

————. 2006. "Trade Centres (Maimaicheng) in Mongolia, and their function in Sino-Russian Trade Networks," *The International Journal of Asian Studies* 3.2: 211–37.

"Baoxi gequ quwu qudao gaikuang" 包西各區渠務渠道概況 [A survey of irrigation canals west of Baotou]. 1983. *Bayannao'er shiliao* 巴彥淖爾史料 [Historical matierals of Bayan Nuur] 2: 42–49.

Baoyin寶音 [Buyan]. 1986. "Yikezhao meng 'duguilong' yundong gaishu" 伊克昭盟獨貴龍運動概述 [An overview of *duguilang* movement in Yekhe Juu league]. *Eerduosi shizhi yanjiu wengao* 鄂爾多斯史志研究文稿 [Draft of Ordos historical gazetteer] 5.

Baoyinchaoketu 寶音朝克圖 [Buyanchogtu]. 2005. *Qingdai beibu bianjiang kalun yanjiu* 清代北部邊疆卡倫研究 [A study of guard posts on Qing's northern frontiers]. Beijing: Zhongguo renmin daxue chubanshe.

Baoyu 寶玉. 1985. "Qingmo suiyuan kenwu" 清末綏遠墾務 [Land reclamation in Suiyuan during the late Qing]. *Nei Menggu shizhi ziliao xuan* 內蒙古史志資料選編 [Selected materials of historical gazetteers of Inner Mongolia] 1.2: 33–216.

————, ed. 1985–1986. "Mengqi kenwu dang'an shiliao xuanbian" 蒙旗墾務檔案史料選編 [Selected archives and historical materials on land reclamation in Mongol banners], *Lishi dang'an* [Historical Archives] 4: 34–59; 1: 51–58.

Barfield, Thomas J. 1989. *The Perilous Frontier: Nomadic Empires and China, 221 BC to AD 1757*. Oxford: Basil Blackwell.

Baud, Michiel, and Willem van Schendel. 1997. "Toward a Comparative History of Borderlands," *Journal of World History* 8.2 (Fall): 211–42.

Bawden, Charles R. 1958. "Two Mongol Texts concerning Obo-Worship," *Oriens Extremus* 5: 23–41.

————. 1961. *The Jebtsundamba Khutukhtus of Urga*. Weisbaden, Germany: Otto Harrassowitz.

————. 1968. *The Modern History of Mongolia*. New York: Frederick A. Praeger.

Bayanao'er meng zhi 巴彥淖爾盟志 [Bayan Nuur league gazetteer]. 1997. Hohhot: Nei Menggu renmin chubanshe.

Bello, David A. 2015. *Across Forest, Steppe, and Mountain: Environment, Identity, and Empire in Qing China's Borderlands*. Cambridge: Cambridge University Press.

Bickers, Robert, and R. G. Tiedemann, eds. 2007. *The Boxers, China, and the World*. Lanham, MD: Rowman & Littlefield Publishers.

Bold, Bat-Ochir. 2000. "The Death and Burial of Chinggis Khaan," *Central Asian Survey* 19.1: 95–115.

Bolton, Herbert E. 1921. *The Spanish Borderlands*. New York: Yale University Press.

Borjigin, Burensain ボルジギン・ブレンサイン. 2003. *Kingendai ni okeru mongoru jin nōkō sonraku shakai no keisei* 近現代におけるモンゴル人農耕村落社会の形成 [Formation of the Mongolian farming village society]. Tokyo: Kazama shobō.

———. 2004. "The Complex Structure of Ethnic Conflict in the Frontier: Through the Debates Around the 'Jindandao Incident' in 1891," *Inner Asia* 6.1: 41–60.

Borjigin, Huhbator. 2004. "The History and the Political Character of the Name of Nei Menggu," *Inner Asia* 6.1: 61–80.

Braudel, Fernand. 1980. *On History*. Translated by Sarah Matthews. Chicago: University of Chicago Press.

Brenner, Robert, and Christopher Isett. 2002. "England's Divergence from China's Yangzi Delta: Property Relations, Microeconomics and Patterns of Development." *Journal of Asian Studies* 61.2 (May): 609–62.

Brook, Timothy. 1999. *The Confusions of Pleasure: Commerce and Culture in Ming China*. Berkeley: University of California Press.

Buck, John Lossing. 1937. *Land Utilization in China: A Study of 16,786 Farms in 168 Localities, and 38,256 Farm Families in Twenty–two Provinces in China, 1929–1933*. Chicago: University of Chicago Press.

Bulag, Uradyn Erden. 1998. *Nationalism and Hybridity in Mongolia*. Oxford: Oxford University Press.

———. 2002. *The Mongols at China's Edge: History and the Politics of National Unity*. Lanham, MD: Rowman & Littlefield Publishers.

———. 2004. "Inner Mongolia: The Dialects of Colonization and Ethnicity Building," in Morris Rossabi ed., *Governing China's Multiethnic Frontiers*. Seattle: University of Washington Press.

Cao Shuji 曹樹基. 2001. *Zhongguo renkou shi, di wu juan, Qing shiqi* 中國人口史，第五卷：清時期 [A demographic history of China, volume 5: the Qing era]. Shanghai: Fudan daxue chubanshe.

Cao Yongnian 曹永年. 2002. *Menggu minzu tongshi* 蒙古民族通史 [General history of the Mongolian nation], volume 3. Hohhot: Nei Menggu daxue chubanshe.

———, ed. 2007. *Nei Menggu tongshi* 內蒙古通史 [General history of Inner Mongolia]. Six volumes. Hohhot: Nei Menggu daxue chubanshe.

Cartier, Carolyn. 2002. "Origins and Evolution of a Geographical Idea: The Macroregion in China," *Modern China* 28.1 (January): 79–143.

Casanova, Pablo Gonzalez. 1965. "Internal Colonialism and National Development," *Studies in Comparative International Development* 1.4: 27–37.

Chan, Wellington. 1977. *Merchants, Mandarins, and Modern Enterprise in Late Ch'ing China*. Cambridge, MA: Harvard University Asia Center.

Chang Fei 常非. *Tianzhujiao suiyuan jiaoqu chuanjiao jianshi* 天主教綏遠教區傳教簡史 [A short history of the Catholic missions in the Suiyuan vicariate]. Unpublished manuscript.

Chang Yin-T'ang. 1933. *The Economic Development and Prospects of Inner Mongolia*. Shanghai: The Commercial Press.

Chao, Kang. 1986. *Man and Land in Chinese History: An Economic Analysis*. Stanford: Stanford University Press.

———. 2005. *Zhongguo chuantong nongcun de diquan fenpei* 中國傳統農村的地權分配 [Distribution of land property in traditional rural China]. Taipei: Lianjing chuban gongsi.

Charleux, Isabelle. 2010a. "Qing Imperial Mandalic Architecture for Gelugpa Pontiffs Between Beijing, Inner Mongolia and Amdo," in Eric Lehner, Alexandra Harrer, and Hildegard Sint (dir.), *Along the Great Wall: Architecture and Identity in China and Mongolia*, 107–18. Vienna: IVEA-ICRA.

———. 2010b. "The Making of Mongol Buddhist Art and Architecture: Artisans in Mongolia from the Sixteenth to the Twentieth Century," in Elvira Eevr Djaltchinova-Malets, ed., *Meditation: The Art of Zanabazar and His School*, 59–105. Warsaw: The Asia and Pacific Museum.

———. 2015. *Nomads on Pilgrimage: Mongols on Wutaishan (China), 1800–1940*. Leiden: Brill.

Chen Bingrong 陳秉榮. 2011. "Hequ: Huashuo Zou Xikou" 河曲：話說走西口 [Hequ: tales of going beyond the Western Pass]. http://hequ.xinzhou.org/2011/0927/article_2415.html.

——— and Yuan Lu 原魯. 2000. "*Jiusi yisheng 'zou xikou*" 九死一生'走西口'[Going beyond the Western Pass: a close call], in Guo Yuhuai 郭裕懷 ed., *Shanxi shehui daguan* 山西社會大觀 [An overview of Shanxi society]. Shanghai: Shanghai shudian chubanshe.

Chen Chongzu 陳崇祖. 1965. *Waimenggu jinshi shi* 外蒙古近世史 [A modern history of Outer Mongolia]. Taipei: Wenhai chubanshe.

Chen Erdong 陳耳東. 1988. *Hetao guanqu shuili jianshi* 河套灌區水利簡史 [A brief history of irrigation in Hetao]. Beijing: Shuili dianli chubanshe.

Chen Xibo 陳喜波, Yan Tingzhen 顏廷真, and Han Guanghui 韓光輝. 2001. "*Lun qingdai changcheng yanxian waice chenzhen de xingqi*" 論清代長城沿線外側城鎮的興起 [On the rise of cities and towns outside the Great Wall during the Qing], *Beijing daxue xuebao* [Journal of Beijing University] 3: 12–18.

Chen Yuning 陳育寧. 1983. *E'erduosi shihua* 鄂爾多斯史話 [A history of the Ordos]. *Eerduosi shizhi yanjiu wengao* 鄂爾多斯史志研究文稿 [Draft of Ordos historical gazatteer] 1.

———. 1984. "Mingdai menggu zhi ruju Hetao" 明代蒙古之入居河套 [Mongol settlement in Hetao during the Ming period," *Shixue yuekan* [Journal of historical science] 2: 40–44.

Chia, Ning. 1992. "The Li-fan Yuan in the Early Ch'ing Dynasty." PhD dissertation, Department of History, Johns Hopkins University.

———. 1993. "The Lifanyuan and the Inner Asian Rituals in the Early Qing (1644–1795)," *Late Imperial China* 14.1 (June): 60–92.

Chuzo, Ichiko. 1980. "Political and Institutional Reforms, 1901–1911," in John K. Fairbank and Kwang-ching Liu, eds., *The Cambridge History of China*, volume 12, Late Ch'ing 1800–1911, 375–415. New York: Cambridge University Press.

Cleaves, Fráncis W., translated and ed. 1982. *The Secret History of the Mongols*. Cambridge: Cambridge University Press.

Cohen, Myron L. 2002. "Commodity Creation in Late Imperial China: Corporations, Shares, and Contracts in One Rural Community," in David Nugent ed., *Locating Capitalism in Time and Space: Global Restructurings, Politics, and Identity*. Stanford: Stanford University Press.

———. 2004. "Writs of Passage in Late Imperial China: The Documentation of Practical Understandings in Minong, Taiwan," in Madeleine Zelin, Jonathan K. Ocko, and Robert Gardella, eds., *Contract and Property in Early Modern China*, 37–93. Stanford: Stanford University Press.

Cohen, Paul A. 1963. *China and Christianity: The Missionary Movement and the Growth of Chinese Anti-Foreignism, 1860–1870*. Cambridge, MA: Harvard University Press.

———. 1984. *Discovering History in China: American Historical Writing on the Recent Chinese Past*. New York: Columbia University Press.

———. 1997. *History in Three Keys: The Boxers as Event, Experience, and Myth*. New York: Columbia University Press.

Cole, H. M. 1940. "Origins of the French Protectorate over Catholic Missions in China," *The American Journal of International Law* 34.3 (July): 473–91.

———. 2002. "Conquest Elite of the Ch'ing Empire," in Willard J. Peterson, ed., *The Cambridge History of China*, volume 9, The Ch'ing Dynasty to 1800, 310–59. Cambridge: Cambridge University Press.

Coxe, William. 1787. *Account of the Russian Discoveries between Asia and America to Which Are Added the Conquest of Siberia and the History of the Transactions and Commerce between Russia and China*. London: T. Cadell.

Cressey, George B. 1932. "Chinese Colonization in Mongolia: A General Survey," in Joerg W. L. G., ed., *Pioneer Settlement: Cooperative Studies by Twenty-Six Authors*, 273–87. New York: American Geographical Society.

———. 1933. "The Ordos Desert of Inner Mongolia," Reprint from Denison University Bulletin, *Journal of the Scientific Laboratories* XXVIII (October).

Crossley, Pamela Kyle. 1997. *The Manchus*. Oxford: Blackwell Publishers.

———. 1999. *A Translucent Mirror: History and Identity in Qing Imperial Ideology*. Berkeley: University of California Press.

———. 2006. "Making Mongols," in Pamela Kyle Crossley, Helen F. Siu, and Donald S. Sutton, eds., *Empire at the Margins: Culture, Ethnicity, and Frontier in Early Modern China*, 58–82. Berkeley: University of California Press.

Dai Xueji 戴学稷. 1982. "Xifang zhiminzhe zai hetao eerduosi dengdi de zuie huodong" 西方殖民者在河套鄂爾多斯等地的罪惡活動 [Criminal activities of Western colonizers in Hetao and the Ordos], in Zhonggong Nei Menggu diqu dangshi yanjiusuo, ed., *Nei Menggu jindaishi luncong* 內蒙古近代史論叢 [Collected papers on modern history of Inner Mongolia] 1: 59–105. Hohhot: Nei Menggu renmin chubanshe.

Dai, Yingcong. 2001. "The Qing State, Merchants, and the Military Labor Force in the Jinchuan Campaigns," *Late Imperial China* 22.2 (December): 35–90.

———. 2009. The Sichuan Frontier and Tibet: Imperial Strategy in the Early Qing. Seattle: University of Washington Press.

Dalizhabu 達力扎布 [Darijav]. 2003. "'Menggu lüli' ji qi yu 'Lifanyuan zeli' de guanxi" 《蒙古律例》及其與《理藩院則例》的關係 ["Mongol Statutes and Precedents" and its relations to the "Regulations and Precedents of the Lifanyuan"]. *Qingshi yanjiu* [Studies in History of the Qing Dynasty] 4 (November): 1–10.

———. 2005. "Qingdai Chaha'er zhasake qi kao" 清代察哈爾札薩克旗考 [A study on Chakhar jasag banner during the Qing]. *Lishi yanjiu* [Historical Research] 5: 47–59.

Da Qing huidian shili 大清會典事例 [Collected Statutes and Precedents of the Great Qing dynasty]. 1991[1899]. Beijing: Zhonghua shuju.

Da Qing lichao shilu 大清歷朝實錄 [Veritable records of successive reigns of the Great Qing dynasty, 1583–1912] 1985. 4484 juan. Beijing: Zhonghua shuju.

Da Qing yitong zhi 大清一統志 [Grand gazetteer of the Great Qing dynasty]. 2008 [1842]. Shanghai: Shanghai guji chubanshe.

David, Pére Armand. 1949. *Abbé David's Diary: Being an Account of the French Naturalist's Journeys and Observations in China in the Years 1866 to 1869*. Cambridge, MA: Harvard University Press.

Davis, Mike. 2000. *Late Victorian Holocausts: El Niño Famines and the Making of the Third World*. London: Verso.

De Vries, Jan. 1980. "Measuring the Impact of Climate on History: The Search for Appropriate Methodologies," *Journal of Interdisciplinary History* 10: 599–630.

Demidova (デミドワ), N. F. 2004. "*Fyōdoru baikof shisetsu no chūgoku hōmon 1654–1658 nen*" フョウドルバイコフ使節の中国訪問 1654–1658 年 [The F.I. Baikov mission's visit to China 1654–1658], translated by Seol Mal-Ja, *Hokkutō ajia bunka kenkyū* [Northeast Asian Cultural Studies] 20: 67–98.

Derevyanko, Anatoli P., and Lü Zun-E. 1992. "Upper Paleolithic Cultures," in Ahmad Hasan Dani and Vadim Mikhailovich Masson, eds., *History of Civilizations of Central Asia*, volume 1, 86–126. Paris: UNESCO Publishing.

Di Cosmo, Nicola. 1994. "Ancient Inner Asian Nomads: Their Economic Basis and Its Significance in Chinese History," *The Journal of Asian Studies* 53.4 (November): 1092–26.

———. 1998. "Qing Colonial Administration in Inner Asia," *The International History Review* 20.2 (June): 287–309.

———. 1999. "State Formation and Periodization in Inner Asian History," *Journal of World History* 10.1 (Spring): 1–40.

———. 2002. *Ancient China and Its Enemies: The Rise of Nomadic Power in East Asian History*. Cambridge: Cambridge University Press.

——— and Dalizhabu Bao. 2003. *Manchu-Mongol Relations on the Eve of the Qing Conquest: A Documentary History*. Leiden: Brill.

Di Cosmo, Nicola, Allen J. Frank, and Peter B. Golden, eds. 2009. *The Cambridge History of Inner Asia: The Chinggisid Age*. Cambridge: Cambridge University Press.

Dillon, Michael. 1999. *China's Muslim Hui Community: Migration, Settlement, and Sects*. London: Routledge.

Ding Xikui 丁錫奎, ed. 1970 [1899]. *Jingbian xianzhigao* 靖邊縣志稿 [Draft of Jingbian county gazetteer]. Taipei: Chengwen chubanshe.

Doi Takeo 土肥武雄. 1935. "Netsukashō ryōgenken jyūgoriho ni okeru tochi kankō" 熱河省凌源縣十五里堡に於ける土地慣行 [Land usage customs in Shiwulibu of Lingyuan county in Rehe province]. *Mantetsu Chōsa Geppō* [SMR Research Monthly] 15.9–10.

Du Halde, Jean-Baptiste. 1741. *The General History of China. Containing a Geographical, Historical, Chronological, Political, and Physical Description of the Empire of China, Chinese–Tartary, Corea, and Thibet*. London: J. Watts.

Du Hede 杜赫德 [J. B. Du Halde], ed. 2001 [1819]. *Yesu huishi zhongguo shujian ji: zhongguo huiyilu* 耶穌會士中國書簡集—中國回憶錄 [Lettres édifiantes et curieuses, écrites des missions étrangères mémoires de la Chine]. Translated by Zheng Dedi 鄭德弟, Lü Yimin 呂一民, Shen Jian 沈堅. Zhengzhou: Daxiang chubanshe.

Du Jiaji 杜家驥. 2003. *Qingchao manmeng lianyin yanjiu* 清朝滿蒙聯姻研究 [Manchu-Mongol intermarriage in the Qing dynasty]. Beijing: Renmin chubanshe.

Du Jingyuan 杜静元. 2012. "Qingmo Hetao diqu minjian shehui zuzhi yu shuili kaifa" 清末河套地區民間社會組織與水利開發 [Popular organizations and irrigation development in Hetao during the late Qing]. *Kaifang shidai* [Open Times] 3: 117–23.

Du Yasong 杜亞松. 1989. "Wang tongchun shilue" 王同春事略 [A sketch of Wang Tongchun], in Zhongguo renmin zhengzhi xieshang huiyi Nei Menggu zizhiqu weiyuanhui wenshi ziliao yanjiu weiyuanhui, ed., *Wang Tongchun yu Hetao shuili* 王同春與河套水利 [Wang Tongchun and irrigation of Hetao], *Nei Menggu wenshi ziliao* 內蒙古文史資料 [Literary and historical materials of Inner Mongolia] 36: 24–33.

Duan Shengwu 段繩武. 1936. "Kaifa Hetao de shangque" 開發河套的商榷 [Opinions on Hetao's development]. *Yu Gong banyuekan* [Evolution of Chinese Geography] 6.5.

Duara, Prasenjit. 1988. *Culture, Power, and the State: Rural North China, 1900–1942*. Stanford: Stanford University Press.

———. 1995. *Rescuing History from the Nation: Questioning Narratives of Modern China*. Chicago: The University of Chicago Press.

Eastman, Lloyd E. 1988. *Family, Field, and Ancestors: Constancy and Change in China's Social and Economic History, 1550–1949*. New York: Oxford University Press.

Edgerton-Tarpley, Kathryn. 2008. *Tears from Iron: Cultural Responses to Famine in Nineteenth-Century China*. Berkeley: University of California Press.

Elliott, Mark C. 2001. *The Manchu Way: Eight Banners and Ethnic Identities in Late Imperial China*. Stanford: Stanford University Press.

Elverskog, Johan. 2003. *The Jewel Translucent Sūtra: Altan Khan and the Mongols in the Sixteenth Century*. Leiden: E. J. Brill.

———. 2006. *Our Great Qing: The Mongols, Buddhism, and the State in Late Imperial China*. Honolulu: University of Hawai'i Press.

Elvin, Mark. 1973. *The Pattern of Chinese Past*. Stanford: Stanford University Press.

Esherick, Joseph. 1988. *The Origins of the Boxer Uprising*. Berkeley: University of California Press.

Fairbank, John King. 1968. *The Chinese World Order: Traditional China's Foreign Relations*. Cambridge, MA: Harvard University Press.

——— and Ssu-yü Teng. 1941. "On the Ch'ing Tributary System," *Harvard Journal of Asiatic Studies* 6.2 (June): 135–246.

Fan Rusen 樊如森. 2010. "Minguo yilai de huanghe hangyun" 民國以來的黃河航運 [Transport on the Yellow River since Republican period], *Lishi dili* [Historical Geography] 24: 285–300.

Faure, David. 2006. *China and Capitalism: A History of Business Enterprise in Modern China*. Hong Kong: Hong Kong University Press.

Feng Chuanyou 馮傳友, ed. *Meili Baotou* 魅力包頭 [Glamorous Baotou] 263. *Baotou renmin guangbo diantai* [Radio Baotou].

Feng Jilong 馮際隆, ed. 1919. *Diaocha hetao baogaoshu digao* 調查河套報告書底稿 [Manuscript of reports on the survey of Hetao].

———. 1991 [1921]. *Hetao xinbian* 河套新編 [A new editorial collection of Hetao]. Ten volumes. Beijing: Quanguo tushuguan wenxian suowei fuzhi zhongxin [Center of microfilms of national library documents].

Fieldhouse, D. K. 1981. *Colonialism 1870–1945: An Introduction*. London: Palgrave Macmillan.

Fletcher, Joseph. 1978a. "Ch'ing Inner Asia c. 1800," in Denis Twitchett and John K. Fairbank eds., *The Cambridge History of China*, volume 10, 35–107. Cambridge: Cambridge University Press.

———. 1978b. "The Heyday of the Ch'ing Order in Mongolia, Sinkiang and Tibet," in Denis Twitchett and John K. Fairbank eds., *The Cambridge History of China*, volume 10, 409–491. Cambridge: Cambridge University Press.

———. 1985. "Integrative History: Parallels and Interconnections in the Early Modern Period 1500–1800," *Journal of Turkish Studies* 9: 37–57.

———. 1986. "The Mongols: Ecological and Social Perspectives," *Harvard Journal of Asiatic Studies* 46.1 (June): 11–50.

Flynn, Dennis O., and Arturo Giráldez. 1995. "Born with a 'Silver Spoon': The Origin of World Trade in 1571," *Journal of World History* 6.2 (Fall): 201–220.

———. 2002a. "Cycles of Silver: Globalization as Historical Process," *World Economics* 3.2 (April-June): 1–16.

———. 2002b. "Cycles of Silver: Global Economic Unity through the Mid-Eighteenth Century," *Journal of World History* 13.2 (Fall): 391–427.

Follett, Richard, Sven Beckert, Peter Coclanis, and Barbara Hahn. 2016. *Plantation Kingdom: The American South and Its Global Commodities*. Baltimore: Johns Hopkins University Press.

Frank, Andre Gunder. 1972. "The Development of Underdevelopment," in James D. Cockcroft, Andre Gunder Frank, and Dale Johnson, eds., *Dependence and Underdevelopment*. Garden City, NY: Anchor Books.

——— and Barry K. Gills. 1992. "The Five Thousand Year World System: An Interdisciplinary Introduction," *Humboldt Journal of Social Relations* 18.1: 1–79.

———. 1996. *The World System: Five Hundred Years or Five Thousand?* London: Routledge.

———. 1998. *Re-Orient: Global Economy in the Asian Age*. Berkeley: University of California Press.

Friedmann, John R. 1966. *Regional Development Policy: A Case Study of Venezuela*. Cambridge, MA: Massachusetts Institute of Technology Press.

Fu Linxiang 傅林祥. 2007. "Qingdai fuminting zhidu xingcheng guocheng chutan" 清代撫民廳制度形成過程初探 [Study on the formation of the subprefecture system during the Qing], *Zhongguo lishi dili luncong* [Chinese Historical Geography Studies] 22.1: 32–38.

Gan Pengyun 甘鵬雲. 1916. *Diaocha guisui kenwu baogaoshu* 調查歸綏墾務報告書 [Report on Investigating reclamation affairs in Guisui]. Shahukou: Jinbei zhenshoushi shu.

Gangbagana ガンバガナ. 2015. "Senzenki ni okeru 'kusachi baibai'—keizai ni kansuru kikitori chōsa no katsuyō" 戦前期における＜草地売買＞ —経済に関する聞き取り調査の活用 ['Grassland trade' in early war period: practical use of economic-related inquiring surveys], *Kokuritsu minzokugaku hakubutsukan chōsa hōkoku* [Bulletin of the National Museum of Ethnology] 130: 55–79.

Gao Geng'en 高賡恩. 1968 [1908]. *Tumote qi (Suiyuan) zhi* 土默特旗（綏遠）志 [Gazetteer of Tümed banner (Suiyuan)]. Taipei: Chengwen chubanshe.

———. 2007 [1908]. *Guisui dao zhi* 歸綏道志 (Gazatteer of Guisui circuit). Hohhot: Yuanfang chubanshe.

Gaubatz, Piper. 1996. *Beyond the Great Wall: Urban Form and Transformation on the Chinese Frontiers*. Stanford: Stanford University Press.

Ge Shijun 葛士濬, ed. 1972 [1898]. *Huangchao jingshi wen xu bian* 皇朝經世文續編 [Sequel edition of collected essays on statecraft in the Qing dynasty]. Taipei: Wenhai chubanshe.

Geertz, Clifford. 1960. "The Javanese Kijaji: The Changing Role of a Cultural Broker," *Comparative Studies in Society and History* 2.2 (January): 228–49.

Geng Sheng 耿昇 and He Gaoji 何高濟 (transl.) 1985. *Bolang Jiabin Menggu xingji* 柏朗嘉賓蒙古行紀 [Histoire des Mongols]; *Lubuluke dong xingji* 魯布魯克東行紀 [The journey of William of Rubruck to the eastern parts of the world, 1253–1255]. Beijing: Zhonghua shuju.

Gerbillon, Jean-Francois. 1741. "The Travels of Father Gerbillon, A Jesuit and French Missionary in China, into Tartary: The First Travel in the Year 1688," in Jean Baptiste du Halde, ed., *The General History of China: Containing a Geographical, Historical, Chronological, Political, and Physical Description of the Empire of China, Chinese-Tartary, Corea, and Thibet*. London: J. Watts.

Gibbs, Levi S. 2018. *Song King: Connecting People, Places, and Past in Contemporary China*. Honolulu: University of Hawai'i Press.

———. 2019. "Going Beyond the Western Pass: Chinese Folk Models of Danger and Abandonment in Songs of Separation," *Modern China* 46.5: 1–31.

Giersch, C. Patterson. 2006. *Asian Borderlands: The Transformation of Qing China's Yunnan Frontier*. Cambridge, MA: Harvard University Press.

———. 2011. "Cotton, Copper, and Caravans: Trade and the Transformation of Southwest China," in Eric Tagliacozzo and Wen-Chin Chang, eds., *Chinese Circulations: Capital, Commodities, and Networks in Southeast Asia*, 37–61. Durham: Duke University Press.

———. 2014. "Commerce and Empire in the Borderlands: How Do Merchants and Trade Fit into Qing Frontier History?" *Frontiers of History in China* 9.3 (September): 361–83.

Gilmour, James. 1892. *Among the Mongols*. London: The Religious Tract Society.

Gō Mitoru 江実, ed. 1942. *Mōko rengō jichi seifu hagentōra mei shi shiryō shūsei: Tomokutoku tokubetsu ki no bu dai'ichi shū* 蒙古聯合自治政府巴彥塔拉盟史資料集成—土默特特別旗の部第一輯 [Collection of historical materials of Bayantala league of Mongolian United Autonomous Government: Tümed special banner, volume 1]. Kōwa 厚和 (Hohhot): Hagentōra kōsho 巴彥塔拉公署.

Gong Zizhen. 1959. "Xiyu zhi xingsheng yi" 西域置行省議 [On establishment of province in Western Region]. In Wang Peizheng 王佩諍, ed., *Gong Zizhen quanji* 龔自珍全集 [Completed works of Gong Zizhen], 105–12. Beijing: Zhonghua shuju.

Goodman, David S. G., ed. 2004. *China's Campaign to "Open Up the West": National, Provincial and Local Perspectives*. Cambridge: Cambridge University Press.

Gotō Tomio 後藤十三雄 (後藤富男). 1942. "Kusachi ni okeru shina shōnin" 草地における支那商人 [Chinese merchants in the grasslands], *Nairiku Ajia* [Inner Asia] 2: 96–126.

———. 1958. "Kindai uchimōko ni okeru kanjin shōnin no shishutsu" 近代内蒙古における漢人商人の進出 [Advance of Chinese merchants in Inner Mongolia in modern times], *Shakai keizai shigaku* [Socio-Economic History] 24.4: 401–33.

Grupper, Samuel M. 1984. "Manchu Patronage and Tibetan Buddhism during the First Half of the Ch'ing Dynasty," *Journal of the Tibetan Society* IV: 47–75.

Gu Jiegang 顧頡剛. 1935. "Wang Tongchun kaifa hetao ji" 王同春開發河套記 [Wang Tongchun's development in Hetao]. *Yu Gong banyuekan* 2.12: 2–15.

Gugong bowuyuan 故宮博物院 [The Palace Museum], ed. 2000. *Qing gaozong yuzhi shi* 清高宗御製詩 [Anthology of imperial poems of Qianlong emperor of the Qing]. Nineteen volumes. Haikou: Hainan chubanshe.

Guo Gai 郭蓋. 2005. "Gensui 'Zou Xikou' zou Xikou" 跟隨《走西口》走西口 [Crossing the Western Pass along with the folk song 'Crossing the Western Pass'], *Nanfang zhoumo* [Southern Weekly] (April 14).

Guo Juanjuan 郭娟娟. 2016. *Lümeng shanxi shangren yu neimenggu chengshi jingji jindaihua (1860–1937): yi Guisui, Baotou wei zhongxin de kaocha* 旅蒙山西商人與内蒙古城市經濟近代化 (1860–1937): 以歸綏, 包頭為中心的考察 [Shanxi merchants in Mongolia and modernization of Inner Mongolia's urban economy: an investigation focusing on Höhhot and Baotou, 1860–1937]. Beijing: Jingji guanli chubanshe.

Guojia dang'anju mingqing dang'anguan [Ming and Qing Archives of National Archival Bureau], ed. 1959. *Yihetuan dang'an shiliao* 義和團檔案史料 [Historical materials on the Yihetaun from the archives, YHTDA], two volumes. Beijing: Zhonghua shuju.

Guy, R. Kent. 2002. "Who were the Manchus? A Review Essay," *The Journal of Asian Studies* 61.1 (February): 151–64.

Haizhong 海忠 and Lin Congjiong 林從烱, eds. 1968 [1887]. *Chengde fuzhi* 承德府志 [Chengde prefecture gazetteer]. Taipei: Chengwen chubanshe.

Hamashita Takeshi 浜下武志. 1990. *Kindai Chūgoku no kokusaiteki keiki—chōkō bōeki shisutemu to kindai ajia* 近代中国の国際的契機——朝貢貿易システムと近代アジア [Modern China's international opportunity: the tribute trade system and modern Asia]. Tokyo: University of Tokyo Press.

———. 1994. "The Tribute System of Modern Asia," in A. J. H. Latham and Heita Kwaakatsu, eds., *Japanese Industrialization and the Asian Economy*, 91–103. London: Routledge.

Han Meipu 韓梅圃. 1934. *Suiyuansheng hetao diaochaji* 綏遠省河套調查記 [Investigation of Hetao in Suiyuan]. Hohhot: Suiyuansheng minzhong jiaoyuguan.

Han Rulin 韓儒林. 1982. "Qingdai Menggu yizhan" 清代蒙古驛站 [Postal relay system of Mongolia in the Qing dynasty], in *Qionglu Ji: Yuan shi ji xibei minzu shi yanjiu* 穹廬集——元史及西北民族史研究 [Collection from the Domed Studio – research on the history of the Yuan and the northwest minorities]. Shanghai: Shanghai renmin chubanshe.

Han Xiangfu 韓相符. 1989. "Wo suo zhidao de Wang Tongchun" 我所知道的王同春 [Wang Tongchun as I knew], in *Wang Tongchun yu Hetao shuili* 王同春與河套水利 [Wang Tongchun and irrigation in Hetao], *Nei Menggu wenshi ziliao* 36: 96–110.

Han Yanru 韓燕如. 1953. *Pashange xuan* 爬山歌選 [Selected folk songs]. Beijing: Renmin wenxue chubanshe.

Hang, Xing. 2015. *Conflict and Commerce in Maritime East Asia: The Zheng Family and the Shaping of the Modern World, c. 1620–1720.* Cambridge: Cambridge University Press.

Hangin, Gombojab. 1980. "The Mongolian Titles *Jinong* and *Sigejin*," *Journal of the American Oriental Society* 100.3: 255–66.

Hao Chongli 郝崇理. 2007. *E'erduosi geming laoqu xubian* 鄂爾多斯革命老區續編 [Sequel to the Ordos revolutionary district]. Hohhot: Yuanfang chubanshe.

Hao Wanhu 郝萬虎. 2009. "Zou xikou mantan" 走西口漫談 [Random talk on immigration beyond the Western Pass]. *Zhongguo rencai* [Chinese Talents] 2: 73–75; 3: 72–73.

Hao Weimin 郝維民, ed. 1991. *Nei menggu zizhiqu shi* 内蒙古自治區史 [A history of Inner Mongolia Autonomous Region]. Hohhot: Nei menggu daxue chubanshe.

Harrell, Stevan, ed. 1995. *Cultural Encounters on China's Ethnic Frontiers.* Seattle: University of Washington Press.

Hasibagen 哈斯巴根 [Khasbaghana]. 2007. *E'erduosi nongmu jiaocuo quyu yanjiu (1697–1945)—yi zhunga'er qi wei zhongxin* 鄂爾多斯農牧交錯區域研究 (1697–1945) —以準噶爾旗為中心 [Research on areas of interpenetration of agriculture and pastoralism in Ordos (1697–1945): focusing on Jüüngar banner of Yekhe Juu league]. Hohhot: Neimenggu daxue chubanshe.

He Yangling 賀揚靈. 1935. *Chasui mengmin jingji de jiepou* 察綏蒙民經濟的解剖 [An analysis of Mongolian economy in Chakhar and Suiyuan]. Shanghai: The Commercial Press.

Hechter, Michael. 1975. *Internal Colonialism: The Celtic Fringe in Britich National Development*. Berkeley: Routledge.

Hecken, Joseph van, CICM. 1949. *Les Missions Chez Les Mongols* [Missions among the Mongols]. Peiping: Imprimerie des Lazaristes.

———. 1957. *Les réductions catholiques du pays des Ordos: Une méthode d'apostolat des missionnaires de Scheut* [Catholic reductions in the land of the Ordos: a method of the apostolate of the Scheut missionaries]. Schöneck-Beckenried: Administration der Neuen Zeitschrift für Missionswissenschaft.

———. 1958. "Les réductions catholiques du pays des Alasha" [Catholic reductions in the land of Alasha]. *Neue Zeitschrift für Missionswissenschaft* 14: 29–40, 131–44.

———. 1960. "Une dispute entre deux bannières mongoles et le rôle joué par les missionnaires catholiques" [A dispute between two Mongolian banners and the role played by Catholic missionaries]. *Monumenta Serica* 19: 276–305.

Heissig, Walther. 1980. *The Religions of Mongolia*. Translated by Geoffery Samuel. Berkeley: University of California Press.

Herman, John E. 2007. *Amid the Clouds and Mist: China's Colonization of Guizhour, 1200–1700*. Cambridge, MA: Harvard University Asia Center.

Hertslet, Godfrey E. P. 1908. *Treaties, &c., between Great Britain and China; and between China and Foreign Powers; and Orders in Council, Rules, Regulations, Acts of Parliament, Decrees, &c., Affecting British Interests in China*, volume 1. London: Harrison & Sons.

Heshen 和珅 and Liang Guozhi 梁國治. 2003 [1781]. *Qinding Rehe zhi: jiaodian ben* 欽定熱河志:校點本 [Imperial gazetteer of Jehol: a revised version]. Tianjin: Tianjin guji chubanshe.

"Hetao jiaoqu chuanjiao yange" 河套教區傳教沿革 [History of Catholic missions in Hetao]. 1983. In *Bayannao'er shiliao* 巴彥淖爾資料 [Historical materials of Bayan Nuur] 1: 233–56.

Hevia, James L. 1993. "Lamas, Emperors, and Rituals: Political Implications in Qing Imperial Ceremonies," *Journal of the International Association of Buddhist Studies* 16.2: 243–78.

———. 1995. *Cherishing Men from Afar: Qing Guest Ritual and the Macartney Embassy of 1793*. Durham, NC: Duke University Press.

———. 2003. *English Lessons: The Pedagogy of Imperialism in Nineteenth-Century China*. Durham, NC: Duke University Press.

Heylen, Ann. 2004. *Chronique du Toumet-Ortos: Looking through the Lens of Joseph Van Oost, Missionary in Inner Mongolia, 1915–1921*. Louven: Leuven University Press & Ferdinand Verbiest Foundation.

High, Mette M., and Jonathan Schlesinger. 2010. "Ruler and Rascals: The Politics of Gold in Mongolian Qing History," *Central Asian Survey* 29.3 (September): 289–304.

Hirokawa Saho 広川佐保. 2005. *Mōchi bujo—"Manshūkoku" no tochi seisaku* 蒙地奉上—"満州国"の土地政策 [Presentation of Mongol lands: land policy of Manchukuo]. Tokyo: Kyūko shoin.

Ho, Ping-ti. 1967. "The Significance of the Ch'ing Period in Chinese History," *Journal of Asian Studies* 26.2 (February): 189–195.

———. 1998. "In Defense of Sinicization: A Rebuttal of Evelyn Rawski's 'Reenvisioning the Qing'," *Journal of Asian Studies* 57.1 (February): 123–155.

Hoang, Pierre 黃保祿. 1904. *Zhengjiao fengbao* 正教奉褒 [Imperial commendation of Christianity]. Shanghai: Cimutang.

Hostetler, Laura. 2001. *Qing Colonial Enterprise: Ethnography and Cartography in Early Modern China*. Chicago: The University of Chicago Press.

Hsiao Ch'i-ch'ing 蕭啟慶. 1983. "Beiya youmu minzu nanqin gezhong yuanyin de jiantao" 北亞遊牧民族南侵各種原因的檢討 [The Causes of Nomadic Invasions: A Synthesis], *Yuandaishi xintan* 元代史新探 [New research on Yuan history], 303–22. Taipei: Xinwenfeng chuban gongsi.

Hu Huanyong 胡煥庸. 1935. "Zhongguo renkou zhi fenbu" 中國人口之分佈——附統計表與密度圖 [The distribution of Chinese population, with statistics and maps], *Dili xuebao* [*Acta Geographica Sinica*] 2.2: 33–74.

———. 1990. "Zhongguo renkou de fenbu, quhua, he zhanwang" 中國人口的分佈，區劃和展望 [The distribution, regionalization, and prospect of China's population], *Dili xuebao* [*Acta Geographica Sinica*] 45.2: 139–45.

Huang Fensheng 黃奮生. 1936. *Mengzang xinzhi* 蒙藏新志 [A new gazetteer of Mongolia and Tibet], volume 1. Hong Kong: Zhonghua shuju.

Huang Li-Sheng 黃麗生. 1995. *You junshi zhenglue dao chengshi maoyi: Nei Menggu guisui diqu de shehui jingji bianqian (14 shiji zhong zhi 20 shiji chu)* 由軍事征掠到城市貿易：內蒙古歸綏地區的社會經濟變遷（14世紀中至20世紀初）[From wars and plundering to cities and trade: changes in the society and economy of the Guisui region in Inner Mongolia (from the mid-14th century to the beginning of the 20th century)]. Taipei: Guoli Taiwan shifan daxue lishi yanjiusuo.

Huang, Philip C. C. 1985. *The Peasant Economy and Social Change in North China*. Stanford: Stanford University Press.

———. 1990. *The Peasant Family and Rural Development in the Yangzi Delta, 1350–1988*. Stanford: Stanford University Press.

———. 2002. "Development or Involution in Eighteenth-Century Britain and China? A Review of Kenneth Pomeranz's *The Great Divergence: China, Europe, and the Making of the Modern World Economy*." *Journal of Asian Studies* 61.2 (May): 501–38.

Huang Shijian 黃時鑒. 1964. "Lun qingmo qingzhengfu dui Nei Menggu de 'yimin shibian' zhengce," 論清末清政府對內蒙古的'移民實邊'政策 [On the late Qing policy of "moving people to solidify the frontier" in Inner Mongolia], *Nei Menggu daxue xuebao* [Journal of Inner Mongolia University] 2: 65–77.

Huang Yanpei 黃炎培 and Pang Song 龐淞, eds. 1917. *Zhongguo shangzhan shibai shi: Zhongguo sishinian haiguan shangwu tongji tubiao, 1876–1915* 中國商戰失敗史——中國四十年海關商務統計圖表 [The history of the defeat of China in commercial warfare: statistical charts and tables and graphs on Chinese commerce in a forty-year period (1876–1915)]. Shanghai: The Commercial Press.

Huc, Évariste-Régis, and Joseph Gabet. 1987 [1857]. *Travels in Tartary, Thibet and China, 1844–1846*. New York: Dover Publications.

Huidian guan 會典館, ed. 2005 [1764]. *Qinding daqing huidian shili "lifanyuan"* 欽定大清會典事例：理藩院 [Lifanyuan section of Imperially Authorized Collected Statutes and Precedents of the Great Qing dynasty]. Annoted by Zhao Yuntian. 1220 juan. Beijing: Zhongguo zangxue chubanshe.

Humphrey, Catherine. 1995. "Chiefly and Shamanist Landscapes in Mongolia," in E. Hirsch and M. O'Hanlon, eds., *The Anthropology of Landscape: Perspectives on Place and Space*, 135–62. Oxford: Clarendon Press.

Huonder, Anthony. 1911. "Reductions of Paraguay." In *The Catholic Encyclopedia*, volume 12. New York: Robert Appleton Company. Retrieved from New Advent: http://www.newadvent.org/cathen/12688b.htm.

Hyer, Paul. 1977. "The Chin-Tan-Tao Movement: A Chinese Revolt in Mongolia (1891)," *Proceedings of Permanent International Altaistic Conference*: 105–12.

———. 1981. "The Dalai Lama and the Mongols," *The Tibet Journal* 6.4: 3–12.

———. 1982. "An Historical Sketch of Koke-Khota City, Capital of Inner Mongolia," *Central Asiatic Journal* 26: 56–77.

Imahori Seiji 今堀誠二. 1953. *Chūgoku no shahai kōzō: anshan rejimu ni okeru 'kyōdōtai'* 中国の社会構造——アンシャンレジームにおける「共同体」[The social structure of China: "community" in ancient régime]. Tokyo: Yuhikaku.

———. 1955. *Chūgoku hōken shakai no kikō: kisui (fufuhoto) ni okeru shakai shūdan no jitai chōsa* 中國封建社會の機構—帰綏(呼和浩特)における社会集団の実態調査 (The structure of the Chinese feudal society: a survey of social groups in Guisui). Tokyo: Nihon gakujutsu shinkōkai.

———. 1978. *Chūgoku hōken shakai no kōzō: so no rekishi to kokumei zenya no genjitsu* 中国封建社会の構造——その歴史と革命前夜の現実 [The social structure of feudal China: its history and the immediate reality before the revolution]. Tokyo: Nihon gakujutsu shinkōkai.

Isett, Christopher Mills. 2007. *State, Peasant, and Merchant in Qing Manchuria, 1644–1862*. Stanford: Stanford University Press.

Isobe Kensan 磯部検三. 1937. "Katō to ōdōshun: kindai shina yūichi no imin kaitakusha" 河套と王道春——近代支那唯一の移民開拓者 [Hetao and Wang Tongchun: lone pioneer of modern China], *Zenrin kyōkai chōsa getsupō* [Mongolia Friendship Association Monthly Survey] 67: 13.

Jagchid, Sechin. 1988. *Essays in Mongolian Studies*. Provo: Brigham Young University.

———. 1999. *The Last Mongol Prince: The Life and Times of Demchugdongrob, 1902–1966*. Bellingham, WA: Western Washington University Press.

——— and Paul Hyer 1979. *Mongolia's Culture and Society*. Boulder, CO: Westview Press.

——— and Van Jay Symons 1989. *Peace, War, and Trade Along the Great Wall: Nomadic-Chinese Interaction through Two Millennia*. Bloomington: Indiana University Press.

Ji Huang 嵇璜 et al. 1965 [1787]. *Qinding huangchao wenxian tongkao* 欽定皇朝文獻通考 [Imperial encyclopedia of the records of the august dynasty]. Taipei: Xinxing shuju.

———. 1983 [1785]. *Qinding huangchao tongdian* 欽定皇朝通典 [Comprehensive canon of the august dynasty]. Taipei: Taiwan shangwu yinshuguan.

Jia Hanqing 賈漢卿. 1989. "Hetao shuili kenzhi yu Wang Tongchun" 河套水利墾殖與王同春 [Irrigation and colonization of Hetao and Wang Tongchun], in *Wang Tongchun yu Hetao shuili* 王同春與河套水利 [Wang Tongchun and irrigation in Hetao], *Nei Menggu wenshi ziliao* 36: 10–23.

Jin Feng 金峰 [Altan-orgil]. 1979a. "Qingdai Nei Menggu wulu yizhan" 清代內蒙古五路驛站 [Five-route postal relay stations of Inner Mongolia during the Qing], *Neimenggu shifan xueyuan xuebao* [Journal of Inner Mongolia Normal University] 1: 20–33.

———. 1979b. "Qingdai Wai Menggu beilu yizhan" 清代外蒙古北路驛站 [Northern-route postal relay stations of Outer Mongolia during the Qing], *Neimenggu daxue xuebao* [Journal of Inner Mongolia University] 3.4: 77–102.

———. 1980. "Qingdai xinjiang xilu juntai" 清代新疆西路軍台 [Western-route military relay stations of Xinjiang during the Qing], *Xinjiang daxue xuebao* [Journal of Xinjiang University], 1–2.

Jin Fuzeng 金福增. 1872. *Hequ xianzhi* 河曲縣誌 [Hequ county gazetteer].

Jin Hai 金海 [Altan-dalai]. 2002. "Menggu jindai lishi dang'an ziliao shulue" 蒙古近代歷史檔案資料述略 [Brief survey of archives on modern Mongolian history], *Neimenggu daxue xuebao* [Journal of Inner Mongolia University] 34.1: 94–102.

Jin Yufu 金毓黻, ed. 1934. *Daqing xuantong zhengji* 大清宣統政記 [Political records of the Xuantong reign of the Great Qing dynasty]. Fengtian: Liaohai shushe.

Jin Zhizhang 金志章 and Huang Kerun 黃可潤. 1968 [1758]. *Koubei santing zhi* 口北三廳志 [Gazetteer of three counties beyond the Great Wall]. Taipei: Chengwen chubanshe.

Jing Su 景甦 and Luo Lun 羅崙. 1959. *Qingdai Shandong jingying dizhu di shehui xingzhi* 清代山東經營地主底社會性質 [Social nature of managerial landlordism of Shandong during the Qing]. Jinan: Shandong renmin chubanshe.

———. 1978. *Landlord and Labor in Late Imperial China: Case Studies from Shandong*. Translated by Endymion Wilkinson. Cambridge, MA: Council on East Asian Studies, Harvard University.

Keehn, Martha McKee, ed. 1993. *Y.C. James Yen's Thought on Mass Education and Rural Reconstruction: China and Beyond: Selected Papers from an International Conference Held in Shijiazhuang, China, May 27-June 1, 1990*. New York: International Institute of Rural Reconstruction.

Khan, Almaz. 1996. "Who Are the Mongols? State, Ethnicity, and the Politics of Representation in the Peoples' Republic of China," in Melissa Brown, ed., *Negotiating Ethnicities in China and Taiwan*. Berkeley: Routledge.

Khazanov, Anatoly M. 1994. *Nomads and the Outside World*. Second edition. Madison: University of Wisconsin Press.

Kikuchi Morio 菊地杜夫. 1941. "Orudosu kanjin shokuminshi (gōtō hen)" オルドス漢人植民史（後套篇）[History of Han colonization in Ordos: the case of Houtao], in Mōko zenrin kyōkai ed., *Nairiku ajia* [Inner Asia] 1.

Kim, Kwangmin. 2016. *Borderland Capitalism: Turkestan Produce, Qing Silver, and the Birth of an Eastern Market*. Stanford: Stanford University Press.

Kotkin, Stephen, and Bruce A. Elleman, eds. 1999. *Mongolia in the Twentieth Century: Landlocked Cosmopolitan*. Armonk, NY: M. E. Sharpe.

Ku Wei-ying 古偉瀛. 2002. *Saiwai chuanjiao shi* 塞外傳教史 [Catholic missions beyond the Great Wall]. K. U. Leuven: Ferdinand Verbiest Foundation and Kuangchi Cultural Group.

Kuhn, Philip A. 1980. *Rebellion and Its Enemies in Late Imperial China: Militarization and Social Structure, 1796–1864*. Cambridge, MA: Harvard University Press.

———. 2009. *Chinese Among Others: Emigration in Modern Times*. Lanham, MD: Rowman & Littlefield Publishers.

Lan, Meihua. 1999. "China's 'New Administration' in Mongolia," in Stephen Kotkin and Bruce A. Elleman, eds., *Mongolia in the Twentieth Century: Landlocked Cosmopolitan*, 39–58. New York: M. E. Sharpe.

Lane, George. 2009. *Daily Life in the Mongol Empire*. Westport: Greenwood Press.

Lary, Diana. 2012. *Chinese Migrations: The Movement of People, Goods and Ideas Over Four Millennia*. Lanham: Rowman & Littlefield Publishers.

Latourette, Kenneth. 1929. *A History of Christian Missions in China*. New York: The Macmillan Company.

Lattimore, Owen. 1928. "Caravan Routes of Inner Asia: The Third 'Asian Lecture,'" *The Geographical Journal* 72.6: 497–528.

———. 1932. "Chinese Colonization in Inner Mongolia: Its History and Present Development," in W. L. G. Joerg, ed., *Pioneer Settlement: Cooperative Studies by Twenty-Six Authors*, 288–312. New York: American Geographical Society.

———. 1934. *The Mongols of Manchuria: Their Tribal Divisions, Geographical Distribution, Historical Relations with Manchus and Chinese and Present Political Problems*. New York: The John Day Company.

———. 1937a. "Inner Mongolia: Chinese, Japanese, or Mongol?" *Pacific Affairs* 10.1: 64–71.

———. 1937b. "Origins of the Great Wall of China: A Frontier Concept in Theory and Practice," *Geographical Review* 27.4: 529–549.

———. 1962a. *Inner Asian Frontiers of China*. Boston: Beacon Press.

———. 1962b. *Studies in Frontier History: Collected Papers 1929–58*. London: Oxford University Press.

Lee, Erika. 2015. *The Making of Asian America: A History*. New York: Simon & Schuster.

Lesdain, Jacques. 1908. *From Pekin to Sikkim: Through the Ordos, the Gobi Desert, and Tibet*. London: John Murray.

Li, Bozhong. 1998a. *Agricultural Development in Jiangnan, 1620–1850*. New York: St. Martin's Press.

———. 1998b. "Changes in Climate, Land, and Human Efforts: The Production of Wet-Field Rice in Jiangnan during the Ming and Qing Dynasties," in Mark Elvin and Liu Ts'ui-jung, eds., *Sediments of Time: Environment and Society in Chinese History*, 447–86. Cambridge: Cambridge University Press.

Li Dahai 李大海. 2013. "Qingdai yikezhaomeng changcheng yanxian 'jinliudi' zhu gainian kaoshi" 清代伊克昭盟長城沿線'禁留地'諸概念考釋 [Analysis of several notions concerning 'reserved land' along the Great Wall in Yekhe Juu league during the Qing], *Zhangguo lishi dili luncong* [Chinese Historical Geography Studies] 28.2: 36–47.

Li Di 李杕. 1923. *Quanfei huojiaoji* 拳匪禍教記 [Records of Boxer bandits scourging the Church]. Shanghai: Tushanwan yinshuguan.

Li, Lillian M. 2007. *Fighting Famine in North China: State, Market, and Environmental Decline, 1690s–1990s*. Stanford: Stanford University Press.

Li Narangoa. 2004. "Sōryo dōin to bukkyō kaikaku" 僧侶動員と仏教改革 [Mobilization of monks and Buddhist reform], *Hokutō ajia kenkyū* [Journal of Northeast Asian Studies] 7: 69–82.

Li Xiling 李熙齡. 1841. *Yulin fuzhi* 榆林府志 [Yulin district gazetteer], fifty juan.

Liang Bing 梁冰. 1983. "*Lamajiao zai e'erduosi de chuanbo ji yingxiang*" 喇嘛教在鄂爾多斯的傳播與影響 [Spread and impact of Tibetan Buddhism in Ordos], in *E'erduosi shizhi yanjiu wengao* 鄂爾多斯史志研究文稿 [Draft of Ordos historical gazetteer] 3: 1–142.

———. 1991. *Yikezhao meng de tudi kaiken* 伊克昭盟的土地開墾 [Land reclamation in Yekhe Juu league]. Hohhot: Nei menggu daxue chubanshe.

Liang Xiaowen 梁瀟文. 2018. "Qingdai guihuacheng tumote hukoudi tanxi" 清代歸化城土默特戶口地探析 [A study of household plots of the Tümeds of Höhhot during the Qing], *Zhongguo jingjishi yanjiu* [Researches in Chinese Economic History] 3: 75–88.

Lievens, Sara. 2003. "The Spread of the CICM Mission in the Apostolic Vicariate of Central Mongolia (1865–1911): A General Overview," in W. F. Vande Walle, *The History of the Relations Between the Low Countries and China in the Qing Era (1644–1911)*, 301–324. K. U. Leuven: Leuven University Press and Ferdinand Verbiest Foundation.

Limerick, Patricia Nelson, Clyde A. Milner II, and Charles E. Rankin, eds. 1991. *Trails: Toward a New Western History*. Lawrence: University Press of Kansas.

Lin Jing 林競. 1933. *Xibei congbian* 西北叢編 [Northwest miscellany]. Shanghai: Shenzhou guoguangshe.

Lin Qian 林謙. 1877. *Guodi yiming lu* 國地異名錄 [Records of various names of nations and places], in Wang Xiqi 王錫祺, ed., *Xiao fanghu zhai yudi congchao* 小方壺齋輿地叢鈔 [Collected books on geography from the Xiaofanghu Studio]. Shanghai: Zhuyitang.

Lin, Wen-Kai. 2008. "Land Property and Contract in Taiwan during the Qing and Japanese Colonial Period." Paper presented at the 68th Economic History Association annual meeting, "The Engines of Growth: Innovation, Creative Destruction, and Human Capital Accumulation." New Haven: Economic History Association.

Lipman, Jonathan N. 1997. *Familiar Strangers: A History of Muslims in Northwest China*. Seattle: University of Washington Press.

Liu Haiyuan 劉海源, ed. 1990. *Nei menggu kenwu yanjiu* 內蒙古墾務研究 [Research on reclamation of Inner Mongolia]. Hohhot: Nei menggu renmin chubanshe.

Liu Jingshan 劉靜山. "Hetao jiaoqu chuanjiao jianshi" 河套教區傳教簡史 [A brief history of Catholic missions in Hetao]. Unpublished manuscript.

Liu Shiming 劉士銘. 1968 [1733]. *Shuoping fuzhi* 朔平府志 [Shuoping prefecture gazetteer]. Taipei: Taiwan xuesheng shuju.

Liu Wenpeng 劉文鵬. 2004. *Qingdai yichuan jiqi yu jiangyu xingcheng guanxi zhi yanjiu* 清代驛傳及其與疆域形成關係之研究 [A study of postal relay system and territorial formation during the Qing]. Beijing: Zhongguo renmin daxue chubanshe.

Liu Xianpu 劉先普. 2010. "Errentai tianxia yijue 'fengjiaoxue' qianxi" 二人台天下一絕"風攬雪"淺析 [An analysis of 'fengjiaoxue,' a unique style of *errentai* drama], *Quyi* [Chinese folk art] 1: 44–45.

Liu Zhonghe 劉忠和. 2010. *Zou xikou lishi yanjiu* 走西口歷史研究 [History of Han migration across the Western Pass]. Hohhot: Neimenggu daxue chubanshe.

———. 2017. "Shahukou yizhan gujin diming yanjiu" 殺虎口驛站古今地名研究 [A study of ancient and current names of postal relay stations of Shahukou pass], in Liu Menglin 劉蒙林 and Yun Guang 雲廣, eds., *Shuofang luncong* [Symposium on the north] 6.

——— and Boyinhu 薄音湖. 2007. "'Xikou' bian" '西口'辨 [On the Western Pass]. *Nei menggu daxue xuebao* [Journal of Inner Mongolia University] 3: 3–8.

Lu Minghui 盧明輝. 1986. "Qingmo 'yimin shibian' dui menggu shehui de yingxiang" 清末'移民實邊'對蒙古社會的影響 [Impact of the late Qing policy of "moving people to strengthen the border" on Mongolian society], *Nei Menggu shehui kexue* [Social Sciences of Inner Mongolia] 5: 55–60.

———, ed. 1994. *Qingdai beibu bianjiang minzu jingji fazhan shi* 清代北部邊疆民族經濟發展史 [A history of economic development of nationalities in northern frontiers during the Qing]. Harbin: Heilongjiang jiaoyu chubanshe.

——— and Liu Yankun 劉衍坤. 1995. *Lümengshang: 17 shiji zhi 20 shiji zhongyuan yu Menggu diqu de maoyi guanxi* 旅蒙商——17世紀至20世紀中原與蒙古地區的貿易關係 [Chinese merchants in Mongolia: trade relationships between China and Mongolia from the seventeenth to the twentieth century]. Beijing: Zhongguo shangye chubanshe.

Maejima Shigeo 前島重男. 1941. "Uchimōko ni okeru kitokukyō – kōwa wo chūshin suru sono gaikyō" 内蒙古に於ける基督教——厚和を中心するその概況 [Christianity in Inner Mongolia: an overview focusing on Hohhot], in Mōko zenrin kyōkai, ed., *Nairiku ajia* [Inner Asia] 1.

Mancall, Mark. 1971. *Russia and China: Their Diplomatic Relations to 1728*. Cambridge, MA: Harvard University Press.

Mantetsu shomubu chōsaka 満鉄庶務部調査課, ed. 1927. *Gaimo kyōwakoku* 外蒙共和国 [Republic of Outer Mongolia]. Two volumes. Osaka: Osaka mainichi shinbunsha.

March, G. Patrick. 1996. *Eastern Destiny: Russia in Asia and the North Pacific*. Westport: Praeger.

Masui Yasuki 真水康樹. 1995. "Yongzheng nianjian de zhilizhou zhengce" 雍正年間的直隸州政策 [Policies regarding autonomous prefectures during Yongzheng reign], *Lishi dang'an* [Historical archives] 3: 86–91.

———. 1996. "Qingdai 'zhiliting' yu 'santing' de 'dingzhi'hua ji qi mingdai qiyuan" 清代"直隸廳"與"散廳"的"定制"化及其明代起源 [The system of "autonomous sub-prefectures" and "ordinary sub-prefectures" during the Qing and its origin in the Ming dynasty], *Beijing daxue xuebao* [Journal of Beijing University] 33.3: 98–103.

———. 2007. "Kenryūki ni okeru chokureichō • chō no seidoka" 乾隆期における直隸庁・庁の制度化 [Autonomous sub-prefectures in the Qianlong reign: formation of sub-prefecture system], *Hōsei riron* [Journal of Law and Politics] 39.4: 631–49.

McCaffrey, Cecily. 2011. "From Chaos to a New Order: Rebellion and Ethnic Regulation in Late Qing Inner Mongolia," *Modern China* 37.5: 528–61.

McKeown, Adam. 2001. *Chinese Migrant Networks and Cultural Change:* Peru, Chicago, Hawaii, 1900–1936. Chicago: University of Chicago Press.

———. 2008. *Melancholy Order: Asian Migration and the Globalization of Borders*. New York: Columbia University Press.

Megowan, Anne Splingaerd. 2008. *The Belgian Mandarin*. Philadelphia: Xlibris.

Meirong 梅榮. 2009. "Gengzi nian yikezhaomeng dalateqi jiao'an xintan" 庚子年伊克昭盟達拉特旗教案新探 [New study on missionary cases in Dalad banner of Yekhe Juu league in 1900." Unpublished paper presented in "Beyond the Great Wall: Christianity and Chinese-Western Cultural Exchange in Modern China" Conference, 156–62.

Melckebeke, Carlo von, CICM [Wang Shouli 王守禮]. 1949. *Bianjiang gongjiao shehui shiye* 邊疆公教社會事業 (Service social de l'Eglise en Mongolie) [Social service of the Church in Mongolia]. Translated by Fu Mingyuan. Beijing: Puaitang and Shangzhi Editorial and Translation Center.

Meng Siming 蒙思明. 1936. "Hetao nongken shuili kaifa de yange" 河套農墾水利開發的沿革 [History of land reclamation and irrigation in Hetao], *Yu Gong banyuekan* 6.5: 33–49.

Menggu lianhe zizhi zhengfu dizheng zongshu tudi zhidu diaochashi 蒙古聯合自治政府地政總署土地制度調查室 [Land survey office, headquarter of land administration, Mongolia Autonomous Government], ed. 1940. *Qian suiyuan kenwu zongju ziliao* 前綏遠墾務總局資料 [Materials from the former Bureau of Land Reclamation, Suiyuan province]. Hohhot: Menggu lianhe zizhi zhengfu dizheng zongshu.

Mengzang weiyuanhui diaochashi 蒙藏委員會調查室 [Research office of Mongolian and Tibetan Affairs Commission], ed. 1988 [1939]. *Yimeng zuoyi sanqi diaocha baogaoshu* 伊盟左翼三旗調查報告書 [Survey on three left-wing banners of Yekhe Juu League], *Yikezhao meng wenshi ziliao* 伊克昭盟文史資料 [Literary and historical materials of Yekhe Juu league] 3: 184–226.

———, ed. 1990 [1939]. *Yimeng youyi siqi diaocha baogaoshu – bianjian diaocha baogao zhi er* 伊盟右翼四旗調查報告書——邊疆調查報告之二 [Survey of four right-wing banners of Yekhe Juu League: frontier survey, part two], *Yikezhao meng wenshi ziliao* [Literary and historical materials of Yekhe Juu league] 5.

Mi Chenfeng 米辰峰. 2000. "Cong Ershisiqingdi jiao'an riqi de fenqi kan jiaohui shiliao de juxian" 從二十四頃地教案日期的分歧看教會史料的局限 [Dating of martyrdom of Mgr. F. Hamer and the limitations of missionary archives of C.I.C.M.-Scheut]. Unpublished paper presented at the Symposium Commemorating the Centenary of the Boxer Movement, Shandong University, October 9–12.

Miaozhou 妙舟. 1988 [1935]. *Mengzang fojiao shi* 蒙藏佛教史 [A history of Tibetan Buddhism in Mongolia and Tibet]. Taipei: Wenhai chubanshe.

Miller, Robert J. 1959. *Monasteries and Culture Change in Inner Mongolia*. Wiesbaden: Otto Harrassowitz.

———. 1961. "Buddhist Monastic Economy: The Jisa Mechanism," *Comparative Studies in Society and History* 3.4 (July): 427–38.

Millward, James A. 1998. *Beyond the Pass: Economy, Ethnicity, and Empire in Qing Central Asia, 1759–1864*. Stanford: Stanford University Press.

———. 1999. "'Coming onto the Map': 'Western Regions' Geography and Cartographic Nomenclature in the Making of Chinese Empire in Xinjiang," in *Late Imperial China* 20.2 (December): 61–98.

———. 2007. *Eurasian Crossroads: A History of Xinjiang*. New York: Columbia University Press.

Millward, James A., Ruth W. Dunnell, Mark C. Elliott, and Philippe Forêt, eds. 2004. *New Qing Imperial History: The Making of Inner Asian Empire at Qing Chengde*. London: Routledge.

Mingshilu 明實錄 [Veritable records of the Ming dynasty]. 1940. Changle Liang Hongzhi.

Morgan, David. 1986. *The Mongols*. Oxford: Basil Blackwell.

Mostaert, Antoine. 1956. "Introduction," in Sa γ ang Sečen, *Erderni-yin Tobči* [Precious Summary: Mongolian Chronicle of 1662]. Cambridge, MA: Harvard University Press.

Mote, Frederic. 1974. "The T'u-mu Incident of 1449," in Frank Kierman, Jr. and John K. Fairbank, eds., *Chinese Ways in Warfare*, 243–272. Cambridge, MA: Harvard University Press.

Mouly, Joseph-Martian. 2002. *Xue Madou shenfu* 薛瑪竇神父 [Father Mathieu Sué], in Ku Weiying 古偉瀛 ed., *Saiwai chuanjiao shi* 塞外傳教史 [Catholic mission beyond the Great Wall], 95–123. K. U. Leuven: Ferdinand Verbist Foundation and Kuangchi Cultural Group.

Myers, Ramon. 1970. *The Chinese Peasant Economy: Agricultural Development in Hopei and Shantung, 1890–1949*. Cambridge, MA: Harvard University Press.

Nagata Shigeshi 永田稠. 1939. *Mōkyō konshoku to taishi imin* 蒙疆墾殖と對支移民 [Colonization of Mongolia and immigration to China]. Tokyo: Rikyōsha.

Nakami Tatsuo 中見立夫. 1999. "Russian Diplomats and Mongol Independence," in Stephen Kotkin and Bruce Elleman, eds., *Mongolia in the Twentieth Century: Landlocked Cosmopolitan*, 69–78. Armonk, NY: M. E. Sharpe.

———. 2005. "Mongolia from the Eighteenth Century to 1919," in Chahryar Adle, ed., *History of Civilizations of Central Asia*, volume VI: Toward the Contemporary Period: From the Mid Nineteenth to the End of the Twentieth Century, 347–62. Paris: UNESCO.

Nakamura Atsushi 中村篤志. 2018. "Shinchō chika haruha Monguru shakai ni okeru hito no yidō to ekitan" 清朝治下ハルハ＝モンゴル社会における人の移動と駅站 [Human mobility and postal stations in Khalkha Mongol society under the Qing rule], *Hokutō ajia kenkyū* [Journal of northeast Asian studies] 4: 163–81.

Nei Menggu dang'anguan [Inner Mongolia Archives], ed. 1999. *Qingmo Nei Menggu kenwu dang'an huibian* 清末內蒙古墾務檔案彙編 [Compilation of archives on reclamation affairs in Inner Mongolia in the late Qing]. Hohhot: Nei Menggu renmin chubanshe.

Nei Menggu daxue menggu xue yanjiu zhongxin [Center for Mongolian Studies of Inner Mongolia University], ed. 2007–2008.*Zhunge'er qi zhasake Yamen dang'an yibian* 准格爾旗札薩克衙門檔案譯編 [A compiled translation of archives from Administrative Office of Jüüngar banner]. Three volumes. Hohhot: Nei Menggu renmin chubanshe.

Nei Menggu zizhiqu tongjiju [Inner Mongolia Bureau of Statistics]. 2011. *Nei menggu zizhiqu 2010 nian diliuci quanguo renkou pucha zhuyao shuju gongbao* 內蒙古自治區2010年第六次人口普查主要數據公報 [Communique of main statistics of the sixth national census of 2010 in the Inner Mongolia Autonomous Region]. http://www.stats.gov.cn/tjsj/tjgb/rkpcgb/dfrkpcgb/201202/t20120228_30397.html

Newby, Laura J. 2005. *The Empire and the Khanate: A Political History of Qing Relations with Khoqand c. 1760–1860.* Leiden: Brill Academic Publishers.

Oidtmann, Max. 2018. *Forging the Golden Urn: The Qing Empire and the Politics of Reincarnation in Tibet.* New York: Columbia University Press.

Oost, Joseph van, CICM [Peng Songshou 彭嵩壽]. 1922. *Notes sur le T'oemet* [Notes on the Tümed]. Shanghai: Imprimerie de la Mission Catholique.

———. 1932. *Au Pays des Ortos* [In the land of the Ordos]. Paris: Dillen & Cie.

———. 1964 [1932] *Min Yuqing zhuan* 閔玉清傳 (Monseigneur Bermyn, apôtre des Ordos) [Monsignor Bermyn, apostle of Ordos]. Translated by Hu Ruhan and Wang Xueming. Hohhot: Nei Menggu tianzhujiao aiguohui.

Osborne, Anne. 2004. "Property, Taxes, and State Protection of Rights," in Madeleine Zelin, Jonathan K. Ocko, and Robert Gardella, eds., *Contract and Property in Early Modern China*, 120–58. Stanford: Stanford University Press.

Parkes, Harry. 1854. "Report on the Russian Caravan Trade with China," *Journal of the Royal Geographical Society of London* 24: 306–12.

Perdue, Peter C. 1998a. "Comparing Empires: Manchu Colonialism," *The International History Review* 20.2 (June): 255–62.

———. 1998b. "Boundaries, Maps, and Movement: Chinese, Russian, and Mongolian Empires in Early Modern Central Eurasia," *The International History Review* 20.2 (June): 263–86.

———. 2005. *China Marches West: The Qing Conquest of Central Eurasia.* Cambridge, MA: The Belknap Press of Harvard University Press.

———. 2015. "The Tenacious Tributary System," *Journal of Contemporary China* 24.96 (May): 1007–11.

Pereira, George. 1911. "A Journey across the Ordos," *The Geographical Journal* 37.3: 260–64.

Perkins, Dwight. 1969. *Agricultural Development in China, 1368–1968.* Chicago: Aldine.

Polanyi, Karl. 1957. *The Great Transformation: The Political and Economic Origins of Our Time.* Boston, Beacon Press.

Pomeranz, Kenneth. 1997. "'Traditional' Chinese Business Forms Revisited: Family, Firm, and Financing in the History of the Yutang Company of Jining, 1779–1956," *Late Imperial China* 18.1 (June): 1–38.

———. 2000. *The Great Divergence: China, Europe, and the Making of the Modern World Economy.* Princeton: Princeton University Press.

————. 2002. "Beyond the East-West Binary: Resituating Development Paths in the Eighteenth-Century World." *Journal of Asian Studies* 61.2 (May): 539–590.

Pozdneyev, Aleksei M. 1971 [1892]. *Mongolia and the Mongols*, volume 1, translated by John Roger Shaw and Dale Plank. Bloomington: Indiana University and Mouton & Co.

————. 1977 [1896]. *Mongolia and the Mongols*, volume 2, translated by W. Dougherty. Bloomington: Indiana University and Mouton & Co.

————. 1978 [1887]. *Religion and Ritual in Society: Lamaist Buddhism in Late 19th-Century Mongolia*, translated by Alo Raun and Linda Raun, edited by John R. Krueger. Bloomington: The Mongolia Society.

Pratt, Mary Louise. 1992. *Imperial Eyes: Travel Writing and Transculturation*. London: Routledge.

Prejevalsky, N. 1876. *Mongolia, the Tangut Country, and the Solitudes of Northern Tibet: Being a Narrative of Three Years' Travel in Eastern High Asia*, translated by E. Delmar Morgan, two volumes. London: Sampson Low, Marston, Searle, & Rivington.

Qi Meiqin 祁美琴. 1991. "Yikezhao meng de mengdi kaiken" 伊克昭盟的蒙地开墾 [Reclamation of Mongolian lands in Yekhe Juu League], *Nei Menggu jindaishi luncong* 內蒙古近代史論叢 [Collected papers on the modern history of Inner Mongolia] 4: 1–54.

————. 2004. *Qingdai queguan zhidu yanjiu* 清代榷關制度研究 [Research on the system of Qing tollhouses]. Hohhot: Neimenggu daxue chubanshe.

————. 2007. "Lun qingdai changcheng biankou maoyi de shidai tezheng" 論清代長城邊口貿易的時代特徵 [Features of border trade along the Qing Great Wall], *Qingshi yanjiu* [Studies in Qing history] 3: 73–86.

————. 2011. "Gongzhu gege xiajia waifan menggu suixing renyuan shixi" 公主格格下嫁外藩蒙古隨行人員試析 [Analysis of entourage of Manchu princesses marrying Mongol vassals]. *Manzu yanjiu* [Manzu Minority Research] 1: 28–33.

Qinding lifanbu zeli 欽定理藩部則例 [Imperially Commissioned Collected Statutes of the Court of Dependency Affairs]. 1998. Tianjin: Tianjin guji chubanshe.

Qinming duban mengqi kenwu dachen dang'an 欽命督辦蒙旗墾務大臣 [Archives of Imperial Commissioner Supervising Reclamation Affairs in Mongol banners]. 1901–1910. Nei Menggu dang'an guan 內蒙古檔案館 [Inner Mongolia Archives], Record Group No. 433, 536 juan.

Qu Zhisheng 曲直生. 1935. "Fuji er" 附記二 [Appendix II], in Gu Jiegang, "Jieshao sanpian guanyu wang tongchun de wenzi" 介紹三篇關於王同春的文字 [Introducing three pieces of writing on Wang Tongchun]. *Yugong banyuekan* 4.7.

Rasidongdug, Sh., in collaboration with Veronika Veit (transl.). 1975. *Petitions of Grievances Submitted by the People* (18th–Beginning of 20th Century). Wiesbaden: Otto Harrassowitz.

Rawski, Evelyn S. 1996. "Presidential Address: Reenvisioning the Qing: The Significance of the Qing Period in Chinese History," *Journal of Asian Studies* 55.4 (November): 829–850.

Reardon-Anderson, James. 2005. *Reluctant Pioneers: China's Expansion Northward, 1644–1937*. Stanford: Stanford University Press.

Reid, Anthony, ed. 2001. *Sojourners and Settlers: Histories of Southeast Asia and the Chinese*. Honolulu: University of Hawai'i Press.

Relyea, Scott. 2010. *Gazing at the Tibetan Plateau: Sovereignty and Chinese State Expansion in the Early Twentieth Century*. PhD dissertation, University of Chicago.

Reynolds, Douglas 1993. *China, 1989–1912: The Xinzheng Revolution and Japan*. Cambridge, MA: Harvard University Asia Center.

Rhoads, Edward J. M. 2000. *Manchus and Han: Ethnic Relations and Political Power in Late Qing and Early Republican China, 1861–1928*. Seattle: University of Washington Press.

Rong Xiang 榮祥 and Rong Genglin 榮賡麟. 1981. *Tumote yange* 土默特沿革 [History of Tümed]. Höhhot.

Rossabi, Morris. 1975. *China and Inner Asia: From 1368 to the Present Day*. London: Thames and Hudson.

———. 1998. "The Ming and Inner Asia," in Denis Twitchett and Frederick W. Mote, eds., *The Cambridge History of China*, volume 8, 233–35. New York: Cambridge University Press.

———, ed. 2004. *Governing China's Multiethnic Frontiers*. Seattle: University of Washington Press.

Rowe, William T. 2009. *China's Last Empire: The Great Qing*. Cambridge, MA: Belknap Press of Harvard University Press.

Sagang Sechen. 1991. *Erdeni-yin Tobči/Precious Summary: A Mongolian Chronicle of 1662*. Transcribed and edited by M. Gō, I. de Rachewiltz, J.R. Kreuger and B. Ulaan. Canberra: Australian National University Faculty of Law.

Sagaster, Klaus, ed. 1999. *Antoine Mostaert (1881–1971), C.I.C.M. Missionary and Scholar*. Leuven: Ferdinand Verbiest Foundation.

Sahlins, M. 1972. *Stone Age Economics*. Abingdon: Routledge.

Sands, Barbara, and Ramon Myers. 1986. "The Spatial Approach to Chinese History: A Test," *Journal of Asian Studies* 45.4: 721–46.

Sanjdorj, M. 1980. *Manchu Chinese Colonial Rule in Northern Mongolia*, translated and annotated by Urgunge Onon. New York: St. Martin's Press.

Schlesinger, Jonathan. 2017. *A World Trimmed with Fur: Wild Things, Pristine Places, and the Natural Fringes of the Qing Rule*. Stanford: Stanford University Press.

Schwieger, Peter. 2015. *The Dalai Lama and the Emperor of China*. New York: Columbia University Press.

Sen, Sudipta. 2002. "The New Frontiers of Manchu China and the Historiography of Asian Empires: A Review Essay," *The Journal of Asian Studies* 61.1 (February): 165–77.

Serruys, Henry. 1945. Pei-lou fong-sou: Les coutumes des esclaves septentrio-naux de Siao Ta-heng" [Beilu fengsu: The Customs of the Northern Slaves by Xiao Daheng], *Monumenta Serica* 10: 117-164.

———. 1959a. "Chinese in Southern Mongolia during the Sixteenth Century," *Monumenta Serica* 18: 26–66.

———. 1959b. *Sino-Mongol Relations During the Ming*, volume 1: *The Mongols in China During the Hung-Wu Period*. Bruxelles: Institut Belge Des Hautes Etudes Chinoises.

———. 1967. *Sino-Mongol Relations during the Ming*, volume 2: *The Tribute System and Diplomatic Missions, 1400–1600*. Bruxulles: Institut Belge des Hautes Études Chinoises.

———. 1975. *Sino-Mongol relations during the Ming*, volume 3: *Trade Relations: The Horse Fairs, 1400–1600*. Bruxulles: Bruxulles: Institut Belge des Hautes Études Chinoises.

———. 1976. "*Jinong: Ch'ün-wang* or *Ch'in-wang?*" *Acta Orientalia Academiae Scientiarum Hungaricae* 30: 199–208.

———. 1977. "Documents from Ordos on the 'Revolutionary Circles,' Part I," *Journal of the American Oriental Society* 97.4: 482–507.

———. 1978a. "Documents from Ordos on the 'Revolutionary Circles,' Part II," *Journal of the American Oriental Society* 98.1: 1–19.

———. 1978b. "The Chakhar Population during the Ch'ing," *Journal of Asian History* 12.1: 58–79.

———. 1978c. "Twelve Mongol Letters from Ordos," *Zentralasiatische Studien* 12: 255–72.

————. 1979. "A Question of Land and Landmarks between the Banners Oto γ and Üüsin (Ordos)," *Zentralasiatische Studien* 13: 215–37.

————. 1980. "Letter of Apology from a Troublesome Lama, 1905," *Central Asiatic Journal* 24: 117–28.

————. 1982. "Place Names Along China's Northern Frontier," *Bulletin of the School of Oriental and African Studies* XLV.2: 271–83.

Shang Hong 尚虹, Wei Qi 衛奇 and Wu Xiaohong 吳小紅. 2006. "Guanyu salawusu yizhi diceng ji renlei huashi niandai de wenti" 關於薩拉烏蘇遺址地層及人類化石年代的問題 [Issues on the date of strata and human fossils of the Sjara-osso-gol site], *Renleixue xuebao* [*Acta Anthropologica Sinica*] 25.1 (February): 82–86.

Shang Yue 尚鉞. 1956. *Zhongguo ziben zhuyi guanxi fasheng ji yanbian de chubu yanjiu* 中國資本主義關係發生及演變的初步研究 [Preliminary studies of the origins and development of Chinese capitalist relations]. Beijing: Sanlian shudian.

Shangwu yinshuguan bianyisuo 商務印書館編譯所, ed. 1910. *Daqing xuantong xin faling* 大清宣統新法令 [New laws and decrees of the Xuantong reign of the Great Qing]. Eight volumes. Shanghai: Shangwu yinshuguan.

Sharula 莎茹拉 [Saruul] and Sude 蘇德 [Sodbilig]. 2002. "1900 nian Nei Menggu xibu de mengqi jiao'an" 1900 年內蒙古西部的蒙旗教案 [Religious cases in Mongol banners of western Inner Mongolia in 1900], *Lishi dang'an* [Historical archives] 4: 114–117.

Shen Tongsheng 潘桐生. 1909. *Guangxu zhengyao* 光緒政要 [Administrative compendium of the Guangxu reign]. Thirty-four juan. Shanghai: Chongyitang.

Sheng Kang 盛康, ed. 1966 [1897]. *Huangchao jingshi wen xubian* 皇朝經世文續編 [Sequel to the statecraft writings of our august dynasty]. 120 juan. Taipei: Wenhai chubanshe.

Shepherd, John. 1993. *Statecraft and Political Economy on the Taiwan Frontier, 1600-1800*. Stanford: Stanford University Press.

Shu Xilong 舒習龍. 2007. "Yao Xiguang shengping jiqi chengjiu chutan" 姚錫光生平及其成就初探 [Preliminary explorations of Yao Xiguang, his life and his achievements], *Changjiang luntan* [Yangtze Tribune] 1: 74–78.

Sichuan sheng minzu yanjiusuo 四川省民族研究所 [Sichuan Nationality Institute], ed. 1989. *Qingmo chuandian bianwu dang'an shiliao* 清末川滇邊務檔案史料 [Historical materials from the late Qing Sichuan-Yunan frontier archives]. Beijing: Zhonghua shuju.

Sima Qian 司馬遷. 1959. *Shi Ji* 史記 [Records of the historian]. Beijing: Zhonghua shuju.

————. 1961. *Records of the Grand Historian of China*, volume 2. Translated by Burton Watson. New York: Columbia University Press.

Siu, Helen. 1989. *Agents and Victims in South China: Accomplices in Rural Revolution*. New Haven, CT: Yale University Press.

Skinner, G. William. 1964. "Marketing and Social Structure in Rural China," Part I, *Journal of Asian Studies*, 24.1: 3–43.

————, ed. 1977. *The Cities of Late Imperial China*. Stanford: Stanford University Press.

Sneath, David. 2000. *Changing Inner Mongolia: Pastoral Mongolian Society and the Chinese State*. Oxford: Oxford University Press.

————. 2007. *The Headless State: Aristocratic Orders, Kinship Society & Misrepresentations of Nomadic Inner Asia*. New York: Columbia University Press.

Song Naigong 宋廼工. 1987. *Zhongguo renkou nei menggu fence* 中國人口內蒙古分冊 [China's population: Inner Mongolia]. Beijing: Zhongguo caizheng jingji chubanshe.

Steenackers, Jan-Baptist. 1893. "Aperçu sur le Vicariat de la Mongolie Sud–Ouest (Ortos)" [Overview of the Vicarite of Southwest Mongolia (Ordos)], *Missions en Chine et au Congo*, 59: 353–58.

Su Xixian 蘇希賢. 1989. "Wang Tongchun—Hetao shuili kaifa de jiechu rencai" 王同春——河套水利開發的傑出人才 [Wang Tongchun: mastermind in irrigation development in Hetao], in *Wang Tongchun yu Hetao shuili* [Wang Tongchun and irrigation in Hetao], *Nei Menggu wenshi ziliao* 36: 43–91.

———. 1998. "Longxingchang shanghao xinshuai shimo" 隆興長商號興衰始末 [Rise and fall of the firm Longxingchang], in *Wuyuan wenshi* 五原文史 [Literature and history of Wuyuan] 6: 36–38.

Sude 蘇德 [Sodbilig]. 1998. "*Shaangan huimin qiyi qijian de yikezhaomeng*" 陝甘回民起義期間的伊克昭盟 [Yekhe Juu league during the Chinese Muslim Rebellion of Shaanxi and Gansu], *Nei menggu shifan daxue xuebao* [Journal of Inner Mongolia Normal University] 5: 65–70.

Sudebilige 蘇德畢力格 [Sodbilig]. 2005. *Wanqing zhengfu dui Xinjiang, Menggu he Xizang zhengce yanjiu* 晚清政府對新疆，蒙古和西藏政策研究 [A study of the late Qing policies toward Xinjiang, Mongolia and Tibet]. Hohhot: Neimenggu renmin chubanshe.

———. 2008. "Reclamation of Pastureland in Chakhar: Regional and Environmental Transformation," *Mengguxue wenti yu zhenglun* [Quaestiones Mongolorum Disputatae] 4: 33–44.

———. 2009. "Tianzhujiao yu qingchao jinken mudi zhengce de feichi" 天主教與清朝禁墾牧地政策的廢弛 [Catholicism and the cessation of Qing policies prohibiting reclamation of Mongol pasturelands]. Unpublished paper presented in Conference on "Beyond the Great Wall: Christianity and Chinese-Western Cultural Exchange in Modern China."

———, ed. 2014. *Jüüngar khoshuun no jasag yamon no dangan* (Ch: Zhunge'er qi zhasake yamen dang'an 准格爾旗扎薩克衙門檔案) [Archives of administrative office of the *Jüüngar* banner], forty-two volumes. Hohhot: Neimenggu keji chubanshe.

Suiyuan minzhong jiaoyuguan 綏遠民眾教育館 [Mass Educational Bureau of Suiyuan], ed. 1934. *Suiyuan sheng fenxian diaocha gaiyao* 綏遠省分縣調查概要 [Summary of county-level investigation of Suiyuan province].

Suiyuan sheng zhengfu 綏遠省政府 [Suiyuan provincial government], ed. 1933. *Sunyuan gaikuang* 綏遠概況 [An overview of Suiyuan].

Suiyuan Tongzhiguan 綏遠通志館 [Suiyuan office of comprehensive gazetteer], ed. 2007. *Suiyuan tongzhigao* 綏遠通志稿 [Draft of the comprehensive gazetteer of Suiyuan], twelve volumes. Hohhot: Nei menggu renmin chubanshe.

Sulian kexueyuan 蘇聯科學院 [Akademiya Nauk SSSR/Academy of Sciences of the USSR] and Menggu renmin gongheguo kexue weiyuanhui 蒙古人民共和國科學委員會 [Komitet Nauk Mongol'skoi Narodnoi Respubliki/Committee of Sciences of the Mongolian People's Republic]. 1958 [1954]. *Menggu renmin gongheguo tongshi* 蒙古人民共和國通史 [Istoriya Mongoliskoi Narodnoi Respubliki/History of the Mongolian People's Republic]. Translated by Bagen and Yu Jinxiu. Beijing: Kexue chubanshe.

Sun Zhe 孫喆. 2003. *Kang yong qian shiqi yutu huizhi yu jiangyu xingcheng yanjiu* 康雍乾時期輿圖繪制與疆域形成研究 [A study of cartography and territorial formation in the Kangxi, Yongzheng, and Qianlong reigns]. Beijing: Zhongguo renmin daxue chubanshe.

Tagliacozzo, Eric, and Wen-Chin Chang, eds. 2011. *Chinese Circulations: Capital, Commodities, and Networks in Southeast Asia*. Durham: Duke University Press.

Taiyichiwuti Manchang 泰亦赤兀惕•滿昌 [Taichiud Mansang]. 2004. *Menggu zu tongshi* 蒙古族通史 [General history of the Mongolian nationality]. Shenyang: Liaoning minzhu chubanshe.

Takakura Shinichirō高倉新一郎. 1960. *The Ainu of Northern Japan: A Study in Conquest and Acculturation*. Translated by John A. Harrison. Philadelphia: The American Philosophical Society.

Tamura Hideo 田村英男. 1942. "*Mōkō shakai kōsei no kisō tan'i somoku: ikokushō mei junkatsujiki gatōchi (gahoku) wo chūshin toshite*" 蒙古社会構成の基礎単位蘇木——伊克昭盟準噶爾旗河套地(河北)を中心として——[Sumun, basic unit of Mongol social formation: focusing on the Hetao area (north of the river) of Jüüngar banner of Yekhe Juu league]. *Mantetsu Chōsa Geppo* [SMR Research Monthly] 22.2.

Tao Jing-shen 陶晉生. 1971. "Bianjiang minzu zai zhongguo lishi shang de zhongyaoxing" 邊疆民族在中國歷史上的重要性 [Significance of frontier nationalities in Chinese history], in *Bianjiangshi yanjiu ji: Song Jin shiqi* 邊疆史研究集—宋金時期 [Collected papers on frontier history: Song and Jin periods], 190–201. Taipei: Taiwan shangwu yinshuguan.

Taobuxin 陶布新 [Tubshin]. 1983. "Nei Menggu de 'xiao Beijing' – Dingyuanying" 內蒙古的'小北京' ——定遠營 ["Dingyuanying: 'little Beijing' in Inner Mongolia"], in *Nei Menggu wenshi ziliao* [Literary and historical materials of Inner Mongolia] 10: 139–50.

Taveirne, Patrick. 2003. "The Religious Case of Fengzhen District: Reclamation and Missionary Activities in Caqar during the Late Qing Dynasty," in W. F. Vande Walle and Noel Golvers, eds., *The History of the Relations between the Low Countries and China in the Qing Era (1644–1911)*, 369–416. K. U. Leuven: Leuven University Press and Ferdinand Verbiest Foundation.

———. 2004. *Han-Mongol Encounters and Missionary Endeavors: A History of Scheut in Ordos [Hetao] 1874–1911*. K. U. Leuven: Leuven University Press, Ferdinand Verbiest Foundation.

Tayama Shigeru 田山茂. 1954. *Shin jidai ni okeru mōko no shakai seido* 清時代に於ける蒙古の社会制度 [The social system of Mongolia during the Qing]. Tokyo: Bunkyō shoin.

Teimole 忒莫勒 (Tuimer). 1998. *Jianguo qian nei menggu fangzhi kaoshu* 建國前內蒙古方志考述 [Commentary on local gazetteers of Inner Mongolia before 1949]. Hohhot: Nei Menggu daxue chubanshe.

———. 2009. "Guihuacheng fei 'xikou' kao" 歸化城非"西口"考 ["Study on Höhhot being no 'Western Pass'"], *Xikou wenhua* [Culture of Western Pass] 6.

Temule, Temur 特木勒. 2016. "The Great Wall as Perilous Frontier for the Mongols in 16th Century: Reconsidering Nomadic-Sedentary Relations in Premodern Inner Asia," *International Journal of Korean History* 21.1: 121–56.

T'eng, Ssu-yü. 1944. "Sêng-ko-lin-ch'in," in Arthur William Hummel, ed., *Eminent Chinese of the Ch'ing Period (1644–1912)*, volume 2, 632–34. Washington: U.S. Government Publishing Office.

Tetsuyama Hiroshi 鉄山博. 1995. "Uchi mōko no kindaika to chishō keizai" 內蒙古の近代化と地商経済 [Modernization and land merchant economy in Inner Mongolia], in Regional Institute of Kakojima Economic University, ed., *Kindai higashi ajia no shosō* 近代東アジアの諸相 [Multiple dimensions of modern Eastern Asia]. Tokyo: Keisō shobō.

———. 1999. *Shindai nōgyō keizaishi kenkyū: kōzō to shūhen no shikaku kara* 清代農業経済史研究——構造と周辺の視角から [A study of agricultural economical history during the Qing: from a structural and peripheral perspective]. Tokyo: Ochanomizu shobō.

Tian Mi 田宓. 2012. "Qingdai guihuacheng tumote diqu de tudi kaifa yu cunluo xingcheng" 清代歸化城土默特地區的土地開發與村落形成 [Land development and village formation in the Tümed area of Höhhot during the Qing], *Minzu yanjiu* [Journal of nationality studies] 6: 86–99.

Tiedaobu caiwusi diaochake 鐵道部財務司調查科 [Survey Division, Treasury Department of the Ministry of Railway], ed. 1931. *Baoningxian baolinduan jingji diaocha baogaoshu* 包寧線包臨段經濟調查報告書 [Survey on economy along the Baotou-Linhe section of the Baotou-Ningxia railway].

"Treaty of Tianjin between the Queen of Great Britain and the Emperor of China," Tianjin, June 26, 1858. http://en.wikisource.org/wiki/Treaty_of_Tien-Tsin_between_the_Queen_of_Great_Britain_and_the_Emperor_of_China.

Tsai, Sheng Luen. 1983. *Chinese Settlement of Mongolian Land: Manchu Policy in Inner Mongolia: A Case Study of Chinese Migration in Jerim League*. PhD dissertation, Brigham Young University.

Tumote zuoqi tumote zhi biancuan weiyuanhui 土默特左旗《土默特志》編纂委員會 [Editorial committee of Tümed gazetter, Tümed Left Banner], ed. 1997. *Tumote zhi* 土默特志 [Tümed gazetteer]. Hohhot: Nei Menggu renmin chubanshe.

Turner, Frederick Jackson. 1972. "The Significance of the Frontier in American History," in George Rogers Taylor, ed., *The Turner Thesis: Concerning the Role of the Frontier in American History*, 1–18. Third edition. Lexington, MA: Heath & Co.

Underdown, Michael. 1980. "Banditry and Revolutionary Movements in Late 19th and Early 20th Century Mongolia," *Mongolian Studies* 6: 109–16.

Verhelst, Daniel. 2002. "Th. Verbist and CICM Pioneers," in Ku Weiying 古偉瀛 ed., *Saiwai chuanjiao shi* 塞外傳教史 [Mission Beyond the Great Wall], 125–280. K. U. Leuven and Taipei: Ferdinand Verbiest Foundation and Kuangchi Cultural Group.

Vladimirtsov, Boris Yakovlevich. 1934. *Obshestvennii Stroi Mongolov: Mongolskii Kochevoi Feodalism* [Social organization of the Mongols: Mongolian nomadic feudalism]. Leningrad: Academy of Science.

——— [Wuladimi'erzhuofu 物拉底迷爾卓夫]. 1957. *Menggu shehui zhidu shi* 蒙古社會制度史 [Social systems of the Mongols: Mongolian nomadic feudalism]. Translated by Zhang Xingtang and Wu Zhankun. Taipei: Zhonghua wenhua chuban shiye weiyuanhui.

Vlastos, Stephen. 1986. *Peasant Protests and Uprisings in Tokugawa Japan*. Berkeley: University of California Press.

Von Glahn, Richard. 1996. *Fountains of Fortune: Money and Monetary Policy in China, 1000–1700*. Berkeley: University of California Press.

Wada Sei 和田清. 2015 [1959]. *Mingdai Menggu shi lunji* 明代蒙古史論集 [A collection of essays on Mongol history in the Ming period]. Translated by Pan Shixian. Hohhot: Neimenggu remin daxue chubanshe.

Waldron, Arthur. 1990. *The Great Wall of China: From History to Myth*. Cambridge: Cambridge University Press.

Waley-Cohen, Joanna. 1998. "Religion, War, and Empire-Building in Eighteenth-Century China," *The International History Review* 20.2 (June): 336–52.

———. 2004. "The New Qing History," *Radical History Review* 88 (Winter): 193–206.

Walker, Brett L. 2001. *The Conquest of Ainu Lands: Ecology and Culture in Japanese Expansion, 1590–1800*. Berkeley: University of California Press.

Wallerstein, Immanuel. 1974. *The Modern World-System: Capitalist Agriculture and the Origins of the European World-Economy in the Sixteenth Century*. New York: Academic Press.

————. 1980. *The Modern World-System II: Mercantilism and the Consolidation of the European World-Economy, 1600–1750.* New York: Academic Press.

————. 1989. *The Modern World-System III: The Second Era of Great Expansion of the Capitalist World-Economy, 1730–1840.* New York: Academic Press.

Wang Binming 汪炳明 [Baildogchi]. 1989. "Shi 'fangken mengdi' haishi 'yimin shibian'" 是‘放墾蒙地’還是‘移民實邊’ ['Official sale of Mongol land' or 'moving people to solidify the frontier'?], *Menggushi yanjiu* [Studia historica Mongolica] 3: 189–97. Hohhot: Nei menggu daxue chubanshe.

Wang, Gungwu. 1996. "Sojourning: The Chinese Experience in Southeast Asia," in Antony Reid, ed., *Sojourners and Settlers: Histories of Southeast Asia and the Chinese.* Honolulu: University of Hawai'i Press.

————. 2002. *The Chinese Overseas: From Earthbound China to the Quest for Autonomy.* Cambridge, MA: Harvard University Press.

Wang Guojun 汪國鈞. 2006 [1919]. *Menggu jiwen* 蒙古紀聞 [Recollections of Mongolia]. Annotated by Maxi and Xu Shiming. Hohhot: Nei Menggu renmin chubanshe.

Wang Guangzhi 王廣智. 1995. "Jin shaan meng jierangchu shengtai huanjing bianqian chutan" 晉陝蒙接壤處生態環境變遷初探 [Study on the ecological changes along the borders of Shanxi, Shaanxi, and Inner Mongolia], *Zhongguo nongshi* [Agricultural history of China] 4: 78–86.

Wang Han 王晗. 2006. "Qingdai shaanbei changcheng wai huopandi de jianci kuozhan" 清代陝北長城外伙盤地的漸次擴展 [Advance of agricultural settlements outside the Great Wall in northern Shaanxi during the Qing], *Xibei daxue xuebao* [Journal of Northwest University] 2: 89–93.

Wang Jiange 王建革. 2001. "Qingmo hetao diqu de shuili zhidu yu shehui shiying" 清末河套地區的水利制度與社會適應 [Irrigation system and its social adaption in Hetao during the late Qing], *Jindaishi yanjiu* [Modern Chinese History Studies] 6: 127–52.

————. 2003. "Qingdai mengdi de zhanyou quan, gengzhong quan yu menghan guanxi" 清代蒙地的占有權、耕種權與蒙漢關係 [Mongol land ownership and tenure rights and Mongol-Han relations during the Qing], *Zhongguo shehui jingjishi yanjiu* [Journal of Chinese social and economic history] 3: 81–89.

Wang Jianxun 王建勳. 1982. "Chongxiu zhushenmiao bing kaiqu zhuti bei beiwen" 重修諸神廟並開渠築堤碑碑文 [Stele inscriptions on the restoration of the Temple of Various Gods and the construction of irrigation canals and levees], in Yao Xuejing 姚學鏡, ed. *Wuyuanting zhigao* [Draft of Wuyuan sub-prefecture gazetteer] 2: 43–46. Yangzhou: Jiangsu guanglin keyinshe.

Wang Laigang 王來剛. 2004. "Zou'xikou' jianxi" 走西口簡析 [An analysis of migration across the 'Western Pass']. *Xinzhou shifan xueyuan xuebao* [Journal of Xinzhou Teacher's University] 20.1: 41–45.

Wang, Liping. 2014. "The State, Relational Governance, and Nomad Sedentarization: Land Reform in Inner Mongolia, 1900–1911," *Comparative Studies in Society and History* 56.3 (July): 714–44.

————. 2015. "From Masterly Brokers to Compliant Protegees: The Frontier Governance System and the Rise of Ethnic Confrontation in China–Inner Mongolia, 1900–1930," *American Journal of Sociology* 120.6: 1641–89.

Wang Ming-ke 王明珂. 1997. *Huaxia bianyuan: lishi jiyi yu zuqun renting* 華夏邊緣-歷史記憶與族群認同 [The frontiers of Huaxia: historical memory and ethnic identity]. Taipei: Yunchen wenhua.

———. 2008. *Youmuzhe de jueze: miandui Han diguo de beiya youmu buzu* 遊牧者的抉擇：面對漢帝國的北亞遊牧部族 [The choice of nomads: northern nomadic groups that faced the Han empire]. Guilin: Guangxi shifan daxue chubanshe.

Wang Tao 王陶. 1921. "Hetao wuyuan xian diaocha ji" 河套五原縣調查記 [Survey of Wuyuan county in Hetao], *Dixue zazhi* [Journal of Earth Studies] 12.2.

Wang Weidong 王衛東. 2000. "E'erduosi diqu jindai yimin yanjiu" 鄂爾多斯地區近代移民研究 [A study on migration to the Ordos area in modern times], *Zhongguo bianjiang shidi yanjiu* [China's Borderland History and Geography Studies] 10.4: 70–84.

———. 2007. *Ronghui yu jiangou: 1648–1937 nian suiyuan diqu yimin yu shehui bianqian yanjiu* 融會與建構—1648–1937年綏遠地區移民與社會變遷研究 [Integration and construction: a study on migration and social transformation in Suiyuan, 1648–1937]. Shanghai: Huadong shifan daxue chubanshe.

Wang Wenchi 王文墀. 1968 [1931]. *Linhe xianzhi* 臨河縣誌 [Linhe county gazatteer]. Taipei: Chengwen chubanshe.

Wang, Xiuyu. 2011. *China's Last Imperial Frontier: Late Qing Expansion in Sichuan's Tibetan Borderlands.* Lanham: Lexington Books.

Wang Xueming 王學明. 1984. *Nei Menggu tianzhujiao chuanjiao jianshi* 內蒙古天主教傳教簡史 [A brief history of Catholic missions in Inner Mongolia]. Hohhot: Tianzhujiao Nei Menggu huhehaote shi shenzhe xueyuan.

Wang Yanping 王艷萍. 1990. "Qingmo chaha'er baqi mengdi de fangken" 清末察哈爾八旗蒙地的放墾 [Official reclamation of Mongol pasturelands of the Chakhar eight banners during the late Qing], in Liu Haiyuan 劉海源, ed., *Nei Menggu kenwu yanjiu* 內蒙古墾務研究 [Researches on land reclamation in Inner Mongolia], 209–34. Hohhot: Nei Menggu renmin chubanshe.

Wang Yi 汪毅 and Zhang Chengqi 張承啟, eds. 1974. *Xianfeng tiaoyue* 咸豐條約 [Treaties of the Xianfeng era], in Shen Yunlong 沈雲龍, ed. *Jindai zhongguo shiliao congkan xubian* 近代中國史料叢刊續編 [Sequel edition of the collection of historical materials on modern China]. Taipei: Weihai chubanshe.

Wang Yuhai 王玉海. 1997. "Guihuacheng tumote erqi de neishu wenti" 歸化城土默特二旗的內屬問題 [A study on the problem of incorporation of two Tümed banners of Höhhot], *Menggu shi yanjiu* [Studia Historica Mongolica] 5: 232–38. Hohhot: Neimenggu daxue chubanshe.

Wang Zemin 王澤民. 2007. *Shahukou yu zhongguo beibu bianjiang* 殺虎口與中國北部邊疆 [Shahukou and China's northern frontier]. Höhhot: Nei menggu daxue chubanshe.

Wang Zhe 王喆. 1935. "Wang Tongchun xiansheng yiji" 王同春先生軼記 [Anecdotal accounts on Wang Tongchun]. *Yu Gong banyuekan* 4.7. Beijing: Yugu xuehui.

———. 1937. "Houtao qudao zhi kaijun yange" 後套渠道之開濬沿革 [History of canal development in Houtao], *Yu Gong banyuekan* 7.8/9 (July): 123–151.

Wang Zhiyun 王致雲. 1841. *Shenmu xianzhi* 神木縣誌 [Shenmu county gazetteer].

Wang Zhongmin 王忠民. 2003. "Dashengkui yu luotuo 'fangzi': 'dashengkui xianxiang' zhi si" 大盛魁與駱駝'房子' —— '大盛魁現象'之四 [Dashengkui and camel 'houses': the 'Dashengkui phenomenon,' part four]. *Huhehaote jingji* [Hohhot economy] 4: 54–56.

———. 2004. "Dashengkui yu tongshihang/si: dashengkui xianxiang zhi er" 大盛魁與通事行（司）——'大盛魁現象'之二 [Dashenkui and translating agencies: the 'Dashengkui phenomenon," part two]. *Nei Menggu difangzhi* [Inner Mongolia gazetteer] 6.

Wanner, Michal. 2013. "First Russian-Chinese Diplomatic Relations and Business Relationship 1689–1728," *Prague Papers on the History of International Relations* 2: 66–76.

———. 2014. "The Russian-Chinese Trade in Kyakhta—Its Organisation and Commodity Structure 1727–1861," *Prague Papers on the History of International Relations* 2: 35–49.

———. 2015. "Russian-Chinese Trade in Kyakhta—Trade Development and Volume Indicators 1727–1861," *Prague Papers on the History of International Relations* 1: 17–27.

Waseda daigaku Mongoru kenkyūsho 早稲田大学モンゴル研究所 [Institute for Mongolian Studies of Waseda University], ed. 2007. *Kingendai uchi mongoru tōbu no henyo* 近現代内モンゴル東部の変容 [Transformation of eastern Inner Mongolia in modern times]. Tokyo: Yūzankaku.

Weber, Max. 1978. *Economy and Society*. Berkeley: University of California Press.

Wei Shu 魏樞, and Lü Yaozeng 呂耀曾. 1736. *Shengjing tongzhi* 盛京通志 [Comprehensive gazetteer of Shengjing].

Wei Yuan 魏源. 1984 [1842]. *Shengwu ji* 聖武記 [Records of august military achievements]. Beijing: Zhonghua shuju.

Wenqing 文慶, Jia Zhen 賈楨, and Baoyun 寶鋆, eds. 1929–1931. *Chouban yiwu shimo* 籌辦夷務始末 [Complete records on managing barbarian affairs]. Beijing: Gugong bowuyuan.

White, Richard. 1991. *The Middle Ground: Indians, Empires, and Republics in the Great Lakes Region, 1650–1815*. Cambridge: Cambridge University Press.

Wilkinson, Endymion. 1978. *Landlord and Labor in Late Imperial China: Case Studies from Shandong by Jing Su and Luo Lun*. Cambridge, MA: Council on East Asian Studies, Harvard University.

Will, Pierre-Étienne, and R. Bin Wong, with James Lee. 1991. *Nourish the People: The State Civilian Granary System in China, 1650–1850*. Ann Arbor: Center for Chinese Studies, University of Michigan.

Williams, Dee Mack. 1996. "The Barbed Walls of China: A Contemporary Grassland Drama," *The Journal of Asian Studies* 15.3: 665–91.

———. 2002. *Beyond Great Walls: Environment, Identity, and Development on the Chinese Grasslands of Inner Mongolia*. Stanford: Stanford University Press.

Willis, John E. Jr. 1988. "Tribute, Defensiveness, and Dependency: Uses and Limits of Some Basic Ideas about Mid-Qing Dynasty Foreign Relations," *American Neptune* 48: 225–29.

Winichakul, Thongchai. 1997. *Siam Mapped: A History of the Geo-body of A Nation*. Honolulu: University of Hawai'i Press.

Winterhalder, Bruce P. 1994. "Concepts in Historical Ecology," in Carole L. Crumley, ed., *Historical Ecology: Cultural Knowledge and Changing Landscapes*, 17–41. Santa Fe: School for Advanced Research Press.

Wolf, Eric. 1956. "Aspects of Group Relations in a Complex Society," *American Anthropologist* 58.6: 1065–78.

Wolpe, Harold. 1975. "The Theory of Internal Colonialism: The South African Case," in I. Oxaal, et al, *Beyond the Sociology of Development*. London: Routledge & Kegan Paul.

Wong, Roy Bin. 1997. *China Transformed: Historical Change and the Limits of European Experience*. Ithaca: Cornell University Press.

Woodhead, H. G. W, and H. T. Montague Bell. 1914. *The China Year Book*. London: George Routledge & Sons Ltd.

Wu Meifeng 吳美鳳. 2007. "*Qingdai de shahukou shuiguan*" 清代的殺虎口稅關 ["Shahukou customs during the Qing dynasty"], *Shanxi daxue xuebao* [Journal of Shanxi University] 30.2: 13–18.

Wu Shengrong 武生榮. 1990. "Woguo xibei pimao jisan zhongzhen Baotou de pimao hangye" 我國西北皮毛集散重鎮包頭的皮毛行業 [Skin and pelt business in Baotou, distribution center of northwest China], *Nei Menggu gongshang shiliao* 內蒙古工商史料 [Historical materials on industry and commerce of Inner Mongolia] 39: 215–62.

Wulan 烏蘭 [Ulaan]. 1990. "Cong chaha'er fangken zhangcheng kan chaha'er kenwu" 從察哈爾放墾章程看察哈爾墾務 [reclamation of Chahar as seen from the Regulations on Chahar Reclamation], in Liu Haiyuan 劉海源, ed., *Nei menggu kenwu yanjiu* 內蒙古墾務研究 [Researches on land reclamation in Inner Mongolia], 193–208. Hohhot: Nei Menggu renmin chubanshe.

Wulijitaogetao 烏力吉陶格套 [Öljeitogtoh]. 2007. *Qing zhi minguo shiqi menggu fazhi yanjiu—yi zhongyang zhengfu dui menggu de lifa ji qi yanbian wei xiansuo* 清至民國時期蒙古法制研究—以中央政府對蒙古的立法及其演變為線索 [Research on the Mongol legal system during the Qing and Republican eras: based on the legislation of central government on Mongolia and its evolution]. Hohhot: Nei Menggu daxue chubanshe. Hohhot: Nei Menggu daxue chubanshe.

Wulsin, Frederick Roelker. 1979. *China's Inner Asian Frontier: Photographs of the Wulsin Expedition to Northwest China in 1923*. Cambridge, MA: The Peabody Museum of Archaeology and Ethnology, Harvard University.

Wurenqiqige 烏仁其其格 [Uranchecheg]. 2008. *18–20 shijichu guihuacheng tumote caizheng yanjiu* 18–20 世紀初歸化城土默特財政研究 [Financial studies in Tümed banners of Höhhot from the eighteenth to the early twentieth century]. Beijing: Minzu chubanshe.

———. 2010. "Qingdai guihuacheng tumote liangyi qiquan xiaoruo wenti yanjiu" 清代歸化城土默特兩翼旗權削弱問題研究 [Study on the reduction of power of two Tümed banners of Höhhot during the Qing], *Neimenggu caijing xueyuan xuebao* [Journal of Inner Mongolia University of Finance and Economics] 10.4: 82–87.

Wuyuan xian difangzhishi bianxiu bangongshi 五原縣地方誌編修辦公室 [Editorial office of local gazetteers of Wuyuan county], ed. 1984. "Wuyuan diqu ziran zaihai shiliao" 五原地區自然災害史料 [Historical materials on natural disasters in the Wuyuan area], in *Wuyuan shiliao huiyao* 五原史料薈要 [Collection of historical materials on Wuyuan] 7.

Wuyuan xianzhi biancuan weiyuanhui 《五原縣志》編纂委員會 [Editorial committee of the Wuyuan county gazetteer], ed. 1996. *Wuyuan xian zhi* 五原縣志 [Wuyuan county gazetteer]. Hohhot: Nei Menggu renmin chubanshe.

Wuyunbilige 烏雲畢力格 [Oyunbilig], Cheng Chongde 成崇德, and Zhang Yongjiang 張永江. 2002. *Menggu minzu tongshi* 蒙古民族通史 [General history of the Mongolian nation], volume 4. Hohhot: Nei Menggu daxue chubanshe.

Wuyungerile 烏雲格日勒 [Oyungerel]. 1998. "Qingmo Nei Menggu de difang jianzhi yu chouhua jiansheng 'shibian'" 清末內蒙古的地方建置與籌劃建省'實邊'[On the establishment of local administrative units and the plan to create provinces in Inner Mongolia during the late Qing to "strengthen the border"], *Zhongguo bianjiang shidi yanjiu* [China's Borderland History and Geography Studies] 1: 15–22.

———. 2005. *Shiba zhi ershi shiji chu neimenggu chengzhen yanjiu* 十八至二十世紀初內蒙古城鎮研究 [Inner Mongolian urban studies from the eighteenth to the early twentieth centuries]. Hohhot: Neimenggu daxue chubanshe.

Xi Huidong 席惠東. 2011. "Qingdai tingzhi chutan" 清代廳制初探 [A preliminary investigation on sub-prefecture system during the Qing], *Zhongguo lishi xiehui shixue jikan* [Bulletin of the Historical Association of the Republic of China] 43: 85–110.

Xia Zhengnong 夏徵農, ed. 2009. *Ci Hai* 辭海 [Word-ocean dictionary]. Shanghai: Shanghai cishu chubanshe.

Xiao Daheng 蕭大亨. 1972 [1594]. "Beilu fengsu" 北虜風俗 [Customs of the northern slaves], in *Shiliao sibian* 史料四編 [Collection of four historical documents]. Taipei: Guangwen shuju.

Xiao Ruiling 蕭瑞玲, Cao Yongnian 曹永年, Zhao Zhiheng 趙之恆, and Yu Yong 于永. 2006. *Mingqing Neimenggu xibu diqu kaifa yu tudi shahua* 明清內蒙古西部地區開發與土地沙化 [Land development and desertification in western Inner Mongolia during the Ming and Qing periods]. Beijing: Zhonghua shuju.

Xiaoguang 曉光. 2003. *Ganzhuer miao* 甘珠爾廟 [Ganjuur sume]. Hohhot: Nei Menggu wenhua chubanshe.

Xiaoke 曉克, ed. 2008. *Tumote shi* 土默特史 [A history of the Tümed]. Hohhot: Neimenggu jiaoyu chubanshe.

Xiaoyuan Liu. 2006. *Reins of Liberation: An Entangled History of Mongolian Independence, Chinese Territoriality, and Great Power Hegemony, 1911–1950*. Stanford: Stanford University Press.

Xibei kenwu diaochaju 西北墾務調查局, ed. 1969 [1910]. *Xibei kenwu diaocha huice* 西北墾務調查彙冊 [Collected survey reports on reclamation affairs of the northwest]. Taipei: Chengwen chubanshe.

Xie Bingxin 謝冰心. 1936. *Pingsui yanxian lüxingji* 平綏沿線旅行記 [*Travel records along the Beijing-Hohhot Railway*]. Beijing: Pingsui tielu guanli ju.

Xiehua shuju 擷華書局. ed. 1891–1907. *Guangxu yuzhe huicun* 光緒諭摺匯存 [A collection of edicts and memorials during the Guangxu reign]. Beijing: Xiehua shuju.

Xing Ye 邢野. 2006. "Youguan nei menggu difangxi errentai de tianye diaocha" 有關內蒙古地方戲二人台的田野調查 [Fieldwork on *Errentai*, a local drama of Inner Mongolia], *Nei menggu daxue yishu xueyuan xuebao* [Journal of Art College of Inner Mongolia University] 3: 31–38.

Xing Yichen 邢亦塵, ed. 1981. *Qingji menggu shilu* 清季蒙古實錄 [Veritable records on the Mongols during the Qing], three volumes. Hohhot: Nei Menggu shehui kexueyuan menggushi yanjiusuo.

———. 1986. "Luelun qingmo menggu diqu de 'xinzheng'" 略論清末蒙古地區的'新政' [On the New Policies reform in Mongolia during the late Qing], *Nei Menggu shehui kexue* [Social sciences of Inner Mongolia] 3: 37–42.

Xu Chonghao 許崇灝, ed. 1945. *Monan menggu dili* 漠南蒙古地理 [The geography of southern Mongolia]. Shanghai: Zhengzhong shuju, 1945.

Xu Dixin 許滌新 and Wu Chengming 吳承明. 1985. *Zhongguo zibenzhuyi de mengya* 中國資本主義的萌芽 [The sprouts of capitalism in China], 3 volumes. Beijing: Renmin chubanshe.

Yan Kemin 閻克敏. "Chilege yu pashandiao" 敕勒歌與爬山調 [Song of Chile and Pashandiao folk song], in *Wuchuan wenshi ziliao* 武川文史資料 [Literary and historical materials of Wuchuan].

Yan Tianling 閻天靈. 2004a. *Hanzu yimin yu jindai Nei Menggu shehui bianqian yanjiu* 漢族移民與近代內蒙古社会變遷研究 [Research on Han immigrants and social transformation in modern Inner Mongolia]. Beijing: Minzu chubanshe.

———. 2004b. "*Zou xikou' yu jinshan nei menggu piliandai mingequan de shengcheng*," "走西口"與晉陝內蒙古毗連帶民歌圈的生成 ["Going beyond the Western Pass" and the formation of a folk song circle along the border of Shanxi, Shannxi and Inner Mongolia], Xibei minzu yanjiu [Journal of Northwest Ethnography] 2: 157–174.

Yan Zhiguo 燕治國. 2007.*Xikou qingge* 西口情歌 [Love songs from the Western Pass]. Taiyuan: Shanxi guji chubanshe.

Yang, Bin. 2009. *Between Winds and Clouds: The Making of Yunnan*. New York: Columbia University Press.

Yang Bin 楊賓. 1968 [1707].*Liubian jilue* 柳邊紀略 [Notes from the willow palisade]. Taipei: Guangwen shuju.

Yang Haiying 楊海英 [Oghonos Chogtu], ed. 2001. *Guowai kanxing de e'erduosi menggu zu wenshi ziliao* 國外刊行的鄂爾多斯蒙古族文史資料 [Historical materials published abroad on Ordos Mongols]. Hohhot: Nei Menggu renmin chubanshe.

———. 2004. *Chinggisu haan saishi: kokoromi toshite no rekishi jinruigakuteki zaikōsei* チンギス・ハン祭祀：試みとしての歴史人類学的再構成 [The worship of Chinggis Khan: a historical-anthropological study]. Tokyo: Fukyōsha.

Yang Jiang 楊江. 1934 [1857]. *Hetao tukao* 河套圖考 [An illustrated study on Hetao]. Xi'an: Shaanxi tongzhi guan.

Yang Zhilin 楊值霖. 1951. "Errentai fanshen" 二人台翻身 [Emancipation of the *errentai* drama], *Suiyuan wenxun*.

Yanō Jin'ichi 矢野仁一. 1925. *Kinsei mōkoshi kenkyū* 近世蒙古史研究 [Study of Mongol history in early modern times]. Tokyo: Kōbundō.

Yao Minghui 姚明煇. 1966 [1903]. *Menggu zhi* 蒙古志 [Mongolia gazetteer]. Taipei: Wenhai chubanshe.

Yao Xiguang 姚錫光. 1935 [1908]. *Choumeng chuyi* 籌蒙芻議 [Preliminary suggestions on managing Mongolia]. Tokyo: Manmō sōsho kankōkai.

Yao Xuejing 姚學鏡, ed. 1982 [1907]. *Wuyuanting zhigao* 五原廳志稿 [Draft of Wuyuan sub-prefecture gazetteer]. Yangzhou: Jiangsu guangling guji keyinshe.

Yeung, Yue-man, and Shen Jianfa, eds. 2004. *Developing China's West: A Critical Path to Balanced National Development*. Hong Kong: The Chinese University Press.

Yi Baozhong 衣保中 and Zhang Liwei 張立偉. 2011. "Qingdai yilai neimenggu diqu de yimin kaiken jiqi dui shengtai huanjing de yingxiang" 清代以來內蒙古地區的移民開墾及其對生態環境的影響 [Migration and reclamation in Inner Mongolia since the Qing and its impact on ecological environment], *Shixue jikan* [Collected Papers of History] 5: 88–96.

Yigu 貽穀. 1974a. *Kenwu zouyi* 墾務奏議 [Memorials on reclamation affairs]. Taipei: Wenhai chubanshe.

———. 1974b. *Suiyuan Zouyi* 綏遠奏議 [Memorials from Suiyuan]. Taipei: Wenhai chubanshe.

———. 1974c.*Mengken xugong* 蒙墾續供 [Subsequent confessions on reclamation affairs of Mongolia]. Taipei: Wenhai chubanshe.

Yikezhao meng defang zhi biancuan weiyuanhui 《伊克昭盟地方志》編纂委員會 [Editorial committee of local gazetteers of Yekhe Juu league], ed. 1997. *Yikezhao meng zhi* 伊克昭盟志 [Yekhe Juu league gazetteer]. Beijing: Xiandai chubanshe.

Yilinzhen 亦鄰真 [Irinchin], et al. 1993. *Nei Menggu lishi dili* 內蒙古歷史地理 [Historical geography of Inner Mongolia]. Hohhot: Nei menggu daxue chubanshe.

Yixiang 奕湘. 1990. *Dingbian jilüe* 定邊紀略 [Records on Dingbian], in Wu Fengpei 吳豐培, ed., *Qingmo menggu shidi ziliao huicui* 清末蒙古史地資料彙萃 [A collection of Mongolian historical and geographical materials of the late Qing]. Beijing: Quanguo tushuguan wenqian suowei fuzhi zhongxin.

Yoshida Junichi 吉田順一. 2004. "Uchi mongoru ni okeru dentō nōgyō to kanshiki nōgyō no jyuyō" 内モンゴルにおける伝統農業と漢式農業の受容 [Traditional farming and acceptance of Chinese farming in Inner Mongolia]. Paper presented at the COE International Symposium of the 21st Century on the Transformation of Eastern regions of Inner Mongolia during the modern period, Waseda University.

Yuan Senpo 袁森坡. 1986. "Saiwai Chengde senlin lishi bianqian de fansi" 塞外承德森林歷史變遷的反思 [Reflections on historical change of forests in Chengde beyond the Great Wall], *Hebei xuekan* [Hebei Academic Journal] 2: 26–31.

———. 1991. *Kang Yong Qian jingying yu kaifa beijiang* 康雍乾經營與開發北疆 [On Kangxi, Yongzheng, and Qianlong's rule and exploitation of the northern frontier]. Beijing: Zhongguo shehuikexue chubanshe.

Zelin, Madeleine. 1988. "Capital Accumulation and Investment Strategies in Early Modern China: The Case of the Furong Salt Yard," *Late Imperial China* 9.1: 79–122.

———, Jonathan K. Ocko, and Robert Gardella, eds. 2004. *Contract and Property in Early Modern China*. Stanford: Stanford University Press.

Zeng Guoquan 曾國荃, et al. 1892. *Guangxu Shanxi tongzhi* 光緒山西通志 [Comprehensive gazetteer of Shanxi].

Zhang Erjie 張爾傑. 1989. "Tumote tudi wenti shihua" 土默特土地問題史話 [History of the problem of Tümed lands], *Tumote wenshi ziliao* 土默特文史資料 [Literary and historical materials of Tümed] 4.

Zhang Jinli 張晉俐. 2006. "Errenttai 'Zou Xikou' de yishu tese fenxi" 二人台《走西口》的藝術特色分析 [Analysis of the artistic characteristics of the Errentai drama 'Going beyond the Western Pass,'" *Zhongguo yinyue* [Chinese music] 2: 173–79.

Zhang Liren 張力仁. 2018. "Qingdai yikezhaomeng nanbu 'jinliudi' xintan" 清代伊克昭盟南部'禁留地'新探 [New investigation on the 'reserved land' of southern Yekhe Juu league during the Qing], *Zhongguo lishi dili luncong* [Chinese Historical Geography Studies] 33.4: 87–94.

Zhang Mu 張穆. 1938 [1867]. *Menggu youmu ji* 蒙古遊牧記 [Records of the Mongol nomads]. Changsha: The Commercial Press.

Zhang Penghe 張鵬翮. 1868. *Fengshi eluosi riji* 奉使俄羅斯日記 [Diary of a mission to Russia], in Wu Zhenfang 吳震方 ed., *Shuo Ling* 說鈴 [Speaking of bells].

Zhang Pengyi 張鵬一. 1922. *Hetao tuzhi* 河套圖志 [Illustrated Hetao gazetteer]. Zaishan caotang.

Zhang Qixiong 張啟雄. 2010. "Qingting dui zhengfu guanyuan menggu choubian lunshu de jueze: yi guangxudi zhupi zouzhe wei zhongxin" 清廷對政府官員蒙古籌邊論述的抉擇——以光緒帝硃批奏摺為中心 [The Qing court's choice on official expositions on managing the Mongol frontier: focusing on rescripted palace memorials of Guangxu emperor], *Mengzang jikan* [Mongolia and Tibet Quarterly] 20.1: 34–53.

Zhang Rui 張睿. 1988. "Guzhen hekou" 古鎮河口 [Old market town Hekou], in *Nei Menggu wenshi ziliao* [Literary and historical materials of Inner Mongolia] 33: 215–9.

Zhang Shiming 張世明. 2005. "Qingdai 'shaohuang' kao" 清代'燒荒'考 [On "burning the wilderness" during the Qing], *Qingshi yanjiu* [Studies in Qing history], 3: 85–88.

——— and Gong Shengquan 龔勝泉. 2006. "Linglei shehui kongjian – zhongguo bianjiang yimin shehui zhuyao teshuxing toushi, 1644–1949" 另類社會空間——中國邊疆移民社會主要特殊性透視 [Alternative social space: investigation of main particularities of immigrant societies in China's frontier], *Zhongguo bianjiang shidi yanjiu* [China's Borderland History and Geography Studies] 1: 78–87.

Zhang Shuli 張淑利. 2004. "'Jinliudi' chutan'" 禁留地'初探 [A preliminary study of 'reserved land'], *Yinshan xuekan* [Yinshan Academic Journal] 17.1: 92–95.

Zhang Tingyu 張廷玉, et al. 2000 [1739]. *Ming shi* 明史 [History of the Ming dynasty]. Bejing: Zhonghua shuju.

Zhang Xiangwen 張相文. 1974 [1935]. *Nanyuan conggao* 南園叢稿 [Collected works of Zhang Xiangwen]. Taipei: Wenhai chubanshe.

Zhang Yongjiang 張永江. 1998. "Lun qingdai monan menggu diqu de eryuan guanli tizhi" 論清代漠南蒙古地區的二元管理體制 [On the dual administrative system in the Mongol territory south of the Gobi desert in the Qing dynasty], *Qingshi yanjiu* [Studies in Qing history] 2: 29–40.

———. 2001. *Qingdai fanbu yanjiu – yi zhengzhi bianqian wei zhongxin* 清代藩部研究——以政治變遷為中心 [A study on the outer dependencies during the Qing: focusing on the political transformation]. Harbin: Heilongjiang jiaoyu chubanshe.

Zhang Yu 張彧. 2006. *Wanqing shiqi shengmu shengxin hui zai Nei Menggu diqu chuanjiao huodong yanjiu, 1865–1911* 晚清時期聖母聖心會在內蒙古地區傳教活動研究 [Study on the CICM's missionary activities in Inner Mongolia during the late Qing, 1865–1911]. PhD dissertation, Guangzhou: Jinan University.

Zhang Zhengming 張正明. 1989. "Qingdai jinshang de gufengzhi" 清代晉商的股份制 [Shareholding system of Shanxi merchants during the Qing], *Zhongguo shehui jingjishi yanjiu* [Journal of Chinese social and economic history] 1.

———. 1995. *Jinshang xingshuai shi* 晉商興衰史 [The rise and decline of Shanxi merchants]. Taiyuan: Shanxi guji chubanshe.

Zhang Zhidong 張之洞. 1970 [1900]. *Zhang wenxianggong quanji* 張文襄公全集 [Completed works of Zhang Zhidong]. Taipei: Wenhai chubanshe.

Zhang Zhihua 張殖華. 1983. "Qingdai zhi minguo shiqi nei menggu diqu mengguzu renkou gaikuang" 清代至民國時期內蒙古地區蒙古族人口概況 [A survey of Mongol population in Inner Mongolia from the Qing to the Republican period], in *Nei Menggu jindaishi luncong* 內蒙古近代史論叢 [Collected papers on modern history of Inner Mongolia], volume 2, 221–51. Hohhot: Nei menggu daxue chubanshe.

———. 1990. "Lüelun hetao dishang" 略論河套地商 [A brief inquiry on the land merchants of Hetao], in Liu Haiyuan 劉海源 ed. *Nei Menggu kenwu yanjiu* 內蒙古墾務研究 [Studies on land reclamation in Inner Mongolia], 81–99. Hohhot: Nei Menggu renmin chubanshe.

Zhao Chizi 趙尺子. 1965 [1939]. *Yikezhao meng zhi* 伊克昭盟志 [Yekhe Juu league gazetteer]. Taipei: Mengzang weiyuanhui [Mongolian and Tibetan Affairs Commission].

Zhao Erxun 趙爾巽, et al. 1977. *Qing shi gao* 清史稿 [Draft History of the Qing]. Fortyeight volumes. Beijing: Zhonghua shuju.

Zhao Kuanren 趙寬仁. 1962. "Hequ minjian liuchuan de 'errentai'" 河曲民間流傳的"二人台"[Popular *errentai* drama circulated in Hequ],in Zhongyang yinyue xueyuan zhongguo yinyue yanjiusuo, ed., *Hequ minjian gequ* 河曲民間歌曲 [Folk songs of Hequ]. Beijing: Yinyue chubanshe.

Zhao Yuntian 趙雲田. 1982. "*Qingdai lifanyuan chutan*" 清代理藩院初探 [Investigation of the Court of Dependency Affairs during the Qing], *Zhongyang minzu xueyuan xuebao* [Journal of the Central Institute for Nationalities] 1: 18–26.

———. 1989. *Qingdai menggu zhengjiao zhidu* 清代蒙古政教制度 [Mongolian political and religious institutions in the Qing dynasty]. Beijing: Zhonghua shuju.

———. 1995. *Qingdai zhili bianchui de shuniu: Lifanyuan* 清代治理边疆的枢纽—理藩院 [Axis of Qing's frontier rule: the Lifanyuan]. Ürümqi: Xinjiang renmin chubanshe.

———. 2002. "Qingmo xinzheng qijian de 'choumeng gaizhi'" 清末新政期間的'籌蒙改制' ["Reforming Mongolian institutions" during the late Qing New Policies], *Minzu yanjiu* [Journal of nationality studies] 5: 83–90.

———. 2004. *Qingmo xinzheng yanjiu: ershi shiji chu de Zhongguo bianjiang* 清末新政研究—二十世纪初的中国边疆 [A study of the late Qing New Policies: China's frontiers in the early twentieth century]. Harbin: Heilongjiang jiaoyu chubanshe.

Zhao Zhiheng 趙之恆. 2009. *Nei Menggu tongshi* 內蒙古通史 [General history of Inner Mongolia], volumes 3. Hohhot: Nei Menggu daxue chubanshe.

Zheng Juzhong 鄭居中. 1970 [1783]. *Fugu xianzhi* 府谷縣志 [Fugu county gazetteer]. Taipei: Chengwen chubanshe.

Zhongguo diyi lishi dang'anguan bianjibu [First Historical Archives of China, comp], ed. 1984. Kangxichao hanwen zhupi zouzhe huibian 康熙朝漢文硃批奏摺彙編 [A complication of Chinese language rescripted palace memorials of the Kangxi reign]. Beijing: Dang'an chubanshe.

———, ed. 1990. *Yihetuan dang'an shiliao xubian* 義和團檔案史料續編 [Sequel to historical materials on the Yihetuan from the archives]. Beijing: Zhonghua shuju.

———, ed. 1996. *Guangxuchao zhupi zouzhe* 光緒朝硃批奏摺 [Rescripted palace memorials of the Guangxu reign]. Beijing: Zhonghua shuju.

"Zhongguo gancao zhi shuchu ji shengchan qingxing" 中國甘草之輸出及生產情形 [Export and production of licorice in China]. 1923. *Zhongwai jingji zhoukan* [Sino-foreign Economic Weekly] 7.

Zhongguo renmin zhengzhi xieshang huiyi Nei Menggu zhizhiqu weiyuanhui wenshi ziliao weiyuanhui [Research committee of Literary and Historical Materials, CPPCC Inner Mongol Autonomous Region Committee], ed. 1984. *Lümengshang dashengkui* 旅蒙商大盛魁 [Dashengkui, a trading firm in Mongolia], *Nei Menggu wenshi ziliao* [Literary and historical materials of Inner Mongolia] 12.

———, ed. 1989. *Wang Tongchun yu Hetao shuili* 王同春與河套水利 [Wang Tongchun and irrigation in Hetao], *Nei Menggu wenshi ziliao* [Literary and historical materials of Inner Mongolia] 36.

Zhongyang yanjiuyuan jindaishi yanjiusuo 中央研究院近代史研究所 [Institute of Modern History, Academia Sinica], ed. 1974–1981. *Jiaowu jiao'an dang* 教務教案檔 [The Zongli Yamen Archives on Christian affairs and religious cases]. Seven series, twenty-one volumes. Taipei: Zhongyang yanjiuyuan jindaishi yanjiusuo.

Zhongyang yinyue xueyuan zhongguo yinyue yanjiusuo 中央音樂學院中國音樂研究所 [Institute of Chinese Musicology, Central Conservatory], ed. 1962. *Hequ minjian gequ* 河曲民間歌曲 [Folk songs of Hequ]. Beijing: Yinyue chubanshe.

Zhou Tiezheng 周鐵錚 and Shen Mingshi 瀋鳴詩, eds. 1930. *Chaoyang xianzhi* 朝陽縣志 [Chaoyang county gazetteer].

Zhu Jinfu 朱金甫, ed. 1998. *Qingmo jiao'an* 清末教案 [Religious cases in the late Qing]. Beijing: Zhonghua shuju.

Zhu Kezhen 竺可楨. 1973. "Zhongguo jin wuqian nian lai qihou bianqian de chubu yanjiu" 中國近五千年來氣候變遷的初步研究 [Preliminary investigations into the changes in China's climate during the last five thousand years], *Scientia Sinica* 3.2: 168–189.

Zhu Qiqian 朱啟鈐, ed. 1920. *Dongsansheng mengwu gongdu huibian* 東三省蒙務公牘彙編 [A collection of official documents on Mongolian affairs in the three eastern provinces]. Tokyo: Manmō sōsho kankōkai.

Zhu Shoupeng 朱壽朋, ed. 1958. *Guangxu chao donghua lu* 光緒朝東華錄 [The Donghua Gate records for the Guangxu reign]. Beijing: Zhonghua shuju.

Zhukov, Ye M., and Aleksandr Andreevich Guber. 1973. *History of the Mongolian People's Republic*. Moscow: Nauka Publishing House.

Zhusa 珠颯 [Jusaal]. 2006. "*Lifanyuan yu dongbu mengqi: yi lishi siyuan wei zhongxin*" 理藩院與東部蒙旗：以理事司員為中心 [The Lifanyuan and eastern Mongol banners: focusing on the judicial superintendent]. *Mengguxue jikan* [Collected papers on Mongolian studies] 4: 1–12.

———. 2009. *18–20 shiji chu dongbu neimenggu nonggeng cunluohua yanjiu* 18–20世紀初東部內蒙古農耕村落化研究 [Study on farming villages of eastern Inner Mongolia from the eighteenth to the early twentieth century]. Hohhot: Neimenggu renmin chubanshe.

———. 2010. "Youguan cangchu zhidu fangmian de jifen menggu wen dang'an wenshu" 有關倉儲制度方面的幾份蒙古文檔案文書 [On Mongolian language documents concerning the granary system]. *Mengguxue jikan* [Collected papers on Mongolian studies] 4: 1–17.

Zuo Zongtang 左宗棠. 1979 [1890]. *Zuo wenxianggong quanji* 左文襄公全集 [Completed works of Zuo Zongtang]. Taipei: Wenhai chubanshe.

Glossary

Abagha 阿巴噶
Abaghanar 阿巴哈納爾
Aihun-Tengchong *xian* 璦琿-騰衝線
aimag / *bu* 部
Ajirma 爾駕馬梁
Alasha 阿拉善
albatu / *qiding* 旗丁
Altai 阿爾泰
Altan Khan 俺答汗 / 阿勒坦汗
altan-urugh / *huangjin jiazu* 黃金家族
amban / *banshi dachen* 辦事大臣 / *zongguan* 總管
amban khoshuu / *zongguan qi* 總管旗
Amdo 安多
Amur / Heilongjiang 黑龍江
Amur-Bayasqulangtu keyid / Qingningsi 慶寧寺
Anbian 安邊
Anda 安達
Anguang 安廣
an tu zhong qian 安土重遷
Aokhan 敖汗
Ar Monggol / Bei Menggu 北蒙古 / Wai Menggu 外蒙古
arban / *paijia* 牌甲
Aru Khorchin 阿魯科爾沁
Baarin 巴林
baaz / *bazi* 把子
Bachang 霸昌
Bagha Nuur / Xiaonao'er 小淖爾
Bagha Shibar / Xiaoshibian 小石砭
Bagha Turgen ghol / Xiaohei he 小黑河

301

Bagou 八溝 / Pingquan 平泉
baishing / *bansheng* 板升
Balagai 巴拉蓋
banbei bandiu 半背半丢
bandi renqing 辦地人情
banzhong 伴種
Baode 保德
baojia 保甲
baoxiao 報效
Barghu / Barga 巴爾虎
baruun ghar / *youyi* 右翼
Bayandai / Huining cheng 惠寧城
Bayan Nuur 巴彥淖爾
beigong 背工
Beiniuju 北牛犋
beise / *beizi* 貝子
Beitang 北堂
Bermijn, Alfons / Min Yuqing 閔玉清
bianwai 邊外
bogino duu / *duandiao* 短調
Boro-Balgasun / Chengchuan 城川
bu 堡
Bugutu / Baotou 包頭
Bulung Nuur 補隆淖爾
bunkatsu shoyūsei 分割所有制
bupiao 部票 / *yuanpiao* 院票 / *zhaopiao* 照票
Buryat 布里亞特
caigu 財股
Cao Runtang 曹潤堂
Cen Chunxuan 岑春煊
Chakhar 察哈爾
Changchun 長春
Changgeng 長庚
Changji qu 長濟渠
Changling 長嶺
changpingcang 常平倉
Changsheng qu 長勝渠 / Changji qu 長濟渠
Changtu 昌圖
Changzi 長子
Chanjin qu 纏金渠 / Yongji qu 永濟渠
chaogong 朝貢
Chaoyang 朝陽
Chayija boro tala / Chanjindi 纏金地

Chengde 承德
Chengqi 承啟
Chifeng 赤峰
Chinggis Khan 成吉思汗
Chongli 崇禮
Choros 綽羅斯
choubian 籌邊
chuanhua 串話
chuulghan / *meng* 盟
chuulghan darugha / *mengzhang* 盟長
Dabsun Nuur 達布遜淖爾
daghachin 達慶
da huoji 搭夥計
Daidu 大都
Daihaichuan 岱海川
Daizhou 代州
Dalad 達拉特
Dalai 大賚
Dalai Lama 達賴喇嘛
Dalan Terigün / Dalan khara uul / Daqingshan 大青山 / Yinshan 陰山
daliang guandi 大糧官地
Daming 大名
damnuurchin 貨郎
Dampil 丹丕爾
dao 道
Daqiangpan 大搶盤
darugha 達爾古
Dashengchuan 大盛川
Dashengkui 大盛魁
Dashetai 大佘太
Datong 大同
Dayan Khan 達延汗
Dayao 大窯
dayinglu 大營路
Da Yu 大禹
Dehui 德惠
Demaoyong 德茂永
Dengkou 磴口
Devos, Alfons / De Yuming 德玉明
Di 狄
dian 典
dianmai 典賣
dijia 地價

Dingbian 定邊
Dingyuanying 定遠營
Dingzhou 定州
dishang 地商
diugong 丟工
Dolonnuur 多倫諾爾 / Lamamiao 喇嘛廟
Donghu 東胡
Dongsheng 東勝
Dörbed 杜爾伯特
Dörben Keüked / Siziwang 四子王
Dotood Jasag Monggol / Nei zhasake Menggu 內扎薩克蒙古
Dotood Monggol / Nei Menggu 內蒙古 / Neishu Menggu 內屬蒙古
Duanfang 端方
Duan Tai 段泰
duguilang 獨貴龍
Dushikou 獨石口
dutong 都統
Ejei Khan 額哲汗
Ejene 額濟納
Enze 恩澤
en wei bing shi 恩威並施
Erdeni Juu / Guangxian si 光顯寺
errentai 二人台
Ershisanhao 二十三號
Ershisiqingdi 二十四頃地
Etügen Ekhe 地母
Fakumen 法庫門
fanfeng 藩封
fangzi 房子
fangzu 放租
fen 分
Fenghua 奉化
fenghuan 奉還
Fengji qu 豐濟渠
fengjian 封建
fengjiaoxue 風攪雪
fengjin 封禁
Fengtian 奉天
Feng Yuxiang 馮玉祥
Fengzhen 豐鎮
fentu 分土
fenzhuang 分莊
Fiyanggû 費揚古

fu 府
fudutong 副都統
Fugu 府谷
fuqing mieyang 扶清滅洋
Fuxin 阜新
Fuzhou 福州
Fu Zuoyi 傅作義
Gadaad Jasag Monggol / Wai zhasake Menggu 外扎薩克蒙古
Gadaad Monggol / Wai Menggu 外蒙古 / *Waifan Menggu* 外藩蒙古
Gadaad monggol-un törü-yi jasakhu yabudal-un yamun / Lifanyuan 理藩院
gaitu guiliu 改土歸流
gaizhi 改制
Galdan 噶爾丹
Galdan Tsering 噶爾丹策零
gancao 甘草 / *genzi* 根子
Gangmuhe qu 剛目河渠
Gangyi 剛毅
ganqu 幹渠
Gansu 甘肅
Gelugpa 格魯派
ghajar khagalakhu / *kaihuang* 開荒
Gerbillon, Jean-Francois / Zhang Cheng 張誠
Ghorlos 郭爾羅斯
Giuseppe Ma Zhongmu Tegüsbilig 馬仲牧
gongdi 公地
Gongyiyuan 公義源
gongzhong 公中
gongzhong miao 公中廟
Gong Zizhen 龔自珍
guandi 官地
guandu 官渡
Guanhekou 關河口
guanshang heban 官商合辦
guanzhuang 官莊
Gubeikou 古北口
Gu Jiegang 顧頡剛
Guifang 鬼方
Guisui 歸綏
Güshi Khan 固始汗/顧實汗
hai 害
Hamer, Ferdinand / Han Moli 韓默理
handi 旱地
hangshe 行社

Hankou 漢口
Hecken, Joseph van / He Genan 賀歌南
Heheyuan 和合源
Hehui 河會
hehuoyue 合夥約
Heilongjiang 黑龍江
Hekou 河口
Helanshan 賀蘭山
Hequ 河曲
Hetao 河套
Hinggan 興安
Höhhot / Guihuacheng 歸化城
Hongdong 洪洞
Hongsheng 洪升
Hong Taiji 皇太極
Houba 後壩
houlu 後路
Houtao 後套
Hu 胡
Hu Huanyong 胡煥庸
Hu Pinzhi 胡聘之
hua 華 / *xia* 夏
Huaide 懷德
Huaiyuan 懷遠
Huangfukou 皇甫口
huanghe bai hai, wei fu yi tao 黃河百害，惟富一套
huangjia 荒價
Huang Siyong 黃思永
Huangyu quanlan tu 皇輿全覽圖
Huangyuwa 黃榆窊
huangzhuang 皇莊
Huayansi 華嚴寺 / Buzimiao 堡子廟
Huc, Évariste-Régis / Gu Bocha 古伯察
huiguan 會館
huizhang 會長
hukoudi 戶口地
Hulun 呼倫
Hulun Buir 呼倫貝爾
huopan 伙盤
huopandi 伙盤地
huzong 戶總
jakirugchi janggi / *guanqi zhangjing* 管旗章京
Jalaid 扎賚特

Jangjiya Khutugtu 章嘉呼圖克圖
Jaruud 扎魯特
jasag / *zhasake* 扎薩克
Jasagtu Khan 札薩克圖汗
Jebtsundamba Khutugtu 哲布尊丹巴呼圖克圖
Jehol / Rehe 熱河
Jerim 哲里木
jiangjun 將軍
Jianchang 建昌 / Lingyuan 凌源
Jianping 建平
jiao'an 教案
Jiazhou 葭州
jiedi yangmin 借地養民
Jilin 吉林
Jindandao 金丹道
Jing'an 靖安
Jingbian 靖邊
jingdi 淨地
Jining 集寧
jinliudi 禁留地
jinong 濟農 / 吉囊 / 吉能
Jinyonghe 錦永和
Jishengtang 吉盛堂
jiubian 九邊
Jiujiang 九江
jiyun wang / *junwang* 郡王
Jiyun Wang (*khoshuu*) / Junwang (*qi*) 郡王（旗）
Josotu 卓索圖
juemai 絕賣
junhu 軍戶
juntun 軍屯
junxian 郡縣
Jurchen / *nüzhen* 女真
jüün gaar / *zuoyi* 左翼
Jüüngar (*khoshuu*) / Zhunge'er (*qi*) 準格爾（旗）
Juu Uda 昭烏達
Kaifeng 開封
Kailu 開魯
Kaitong 開通
kaizhongfa 開中法
Kalgan / Zhangjiakou 張家口
Kalmyk 卡爾梅克
kang 炕

Kangping 康平
Kangyoufang 康油房
Kanjur 甘珠爾
kanshou 勘收
kao tian tian 靠天田
kenwu gongsi 墾務公司
kenwu zongju 墾務總局
Keshigten 克什克騰
khadag 哈達
Khalkha 喀爾喀
Kham 康 / 喀木
khan 汗
Khanggai 杭蓋
Khanggin 杭錦
Khangkha 杭哈
Kharachin 喀喇沁
Khara Khote 喀喇河屯 / Luanping 灤平
Khara Narin / Langshan 狼山
khara paisa / *heijie* 黑界
kharuul / *kalun* 卡倫
Khasar 哈薩爾
Khauchit 浩齊特
khereg shüükh tushimel / *lishi siyuan* 理事司員
Khingan 興安
Khobdo 科布多
Khöbchi 庫布齊
khoboot chaghan / *xiangbai* 鑲白
khoboot khökhe / *xianglan* 鑲藍
khoboot shira / *xianghuang* 鑲黃
khoboot ulaan / *xianghong* 鑲紅
Khökhe Ergi 可可以力更 / Wuchuan 武川
Khökhe Nuur / Qinghai 青海
Khökhe Nuur Monggol / *Deed Monggol* / *Qinghai Menggu* 青海蒙古
Khökhe süme / Huizongsi 匯宗寺
Khorchin 科爾沁
Khoringer 和林格爾
Khoshut 和碩特
khoshuu / *khoshuun* / *qi* 旗
khoshuu-yi jakirugchi said / *dutong* 都統
khubilgan / *huofo* 活佛
Khüriye 庫倫
khutugtu 呼圖克圖
Koubei 口北

kouwai 口外
kuai wu man liu, jin qi man ba 快五慢六，緊七慢八
Kulja / Ili 伊犁
Kumbum Jampa Ling / Ta'ersi 塔爾寺
Kurultai 忽里勒台
Kyakhta 恰克圖
lama-yin khoshuu / *lama qi* 喇嘛旗
Lansuo qu 蘭鎖渠
Lao Guo qu 老郭渠
li 釐
li 利
Li Bing 李冰
Li Hongzhang 李鴻章
Li Yourun 李有潤
lianbing chu 練兵處
Liangcheng 涼城
liangdi 糧地
Liang Shuming 梁漱溟
liangzhuang 糧莊
Liaodong 遼東
Liao he 遼河
Liaoyuan 遼源
Lifanbu 理藩部
Ligangbu 李崗堡
Lighden Khan 林丹汗
Lingyuan 凌源
Linhe 臨河
Linhu 林胡
Linxi 林西
Linxiang 臨湘
Liquan 醴泉
lishi tongpan 理事通判
lishi tongzhi 理事同知
liuchengdi 六成地
liuchenhang 六陳行
liutiaobian 柳條邊
longpiao 龍票
Longxingchang 隆興長
Loufan 樓煩
Lubin 臚濱
Lu Chuanlin 鹿傳霖
Lu Dianying 陸殿英
Luan he 灤河

Luanping 灤平
lümengshang 旅蒙商
lunjiaofa 輪澆法
Maimaachin / Maimaa khota / *maimaicheng* 買賣城
manhandiao 漫瀚調
Manzhouli 滿洲里
mashang xingguo 馬上行國
mashi 馬市
mazei 馬賊
Mazha 馬柵
meiren-ü janggi / *fuduiong* 副都統
meiren-ü janggi / *meilin zhangjing* 梅林章京
mengdingdi 蒙丁地
Meng-Han diao 蒙漢調
Monggol naiman khoshuu / *Menggu baqi* 蒙古八旗
Monggol jurghan / *Menggu yamen* 蒙古衙門
Monggol / *Menggu* 蒙古
miao 廟
minzu quyu zizhi 民族區域自治
mizi jiaoyou 糜子教友
Mobei 漠北
Monan 漠南
Möngkhe Tengri 長生天
Mostaert, Antoine / Tian Jingbo 田靜波
Mouly, Joseph-Martian / Meng Zhensheng 孟振生
Mukden / Shengjing 盛京 / Fengtian 奉天
Muni uul / Sheiten-ula / Wulashan 烏拉山
Muumingghan 茂明安
myangat / *qianhu* 千戶
Naiman 奈曼
namug tariya / *mansazi* 漫撒子
Nanhaoqian 南壕塹
Nanshawa 南沙窩
neidi 內地
Nei Menggu zizhiqu 內蒙古自治區
Neishu Menggu 內屬蒙古
neiwufu 內務府
nianban 年班
Ningchengkou 寧城口
Ningtiaoliang 寧條梁
Ningxia 寧夏
Ningyuan 寧遠
niuju 牛犋

niujudi 牛犋地
Nong'an 農安
nongzhengsi 農政司
noyan 諾顏
Nyingmapa 寧瑪派
oboo 鄂博
Öbör Monggol / Nan Menggu 南蒙古 / Nei Menggu 內蒙古
Oirat 瓦剌 / 衛拉特 / 厄魯特
Olan bohereg / Wu-lan-bu-er 烏蘭卜爾
Ongniut 翁牛特
Oost, Joseph van / Peng Songshou 彭嵩壽
Ordos 鄂爾多斯
otog 鄂托克
Otog (*khoshuu*) / Etuoke (*qi*) 鄂托克（旗）
örtöö / *yizhan* 驛站 / *taizhan* 台站
paijiedi 牌界地
paisa / *paijie* 牌界
paitou 牌頭
Pantaokou 蟠桃口
pao kouwai 跑口外
paoqing 跑青
pashange 爬山歌
peijiaodi 賠教地
penggu 朋股
penghuo 朋夥
Pereira, Thomas / Xu Risheng 徐日昇
Pianguan 偏關
piaohao 票號
piaozhuang 票莊
pingfan shuomo 屏藩朔漠
Pingjibu 平集堡
pingkou liushui 平口流水
Pinglu 平魯
Pingluo 平羅
Pingquan 平泉
Puqi 蒲圻
Qianshihui 遣使會
Qikou 磧口
qingfengsi 慶豐司
qingmiao 青苗
Qingshuihe 清水河
qinwang 親王
Qixian 祁縣

Qizhou 祁州 / Anguo 安國
qudizu 渠地租
qugong fenju 渠工分局
qutou 渠頭
quzu 渠租
Ricci, Matteo / Li Madou 利瑪竇
Rong 戎
saiwai 塞外
Sarachi 薩拉齊
Samdanjamba 桑達欽巴
Sandaohe 三道河
sankin kōtai 參勤交代
Sanshenggong 三盛公
santing 散廳 / *shuting* 屬廳
Sanyuchuan 三玉川
sanzhou 散州 / *shuzhou* 屬州
Sanzuota 三座塔 / Chaoyang 朝陽
Sayin Noyan Khan 賽音諾顏汗
Scheut 司各特
Schram, Louis / Kang Guotai 康國泰
Sechen Khan 車臣汗
Sengge Rinchen 僧格林沁
Shaanxi 陝西
shabinar / *miaoding* 廟丁
Shahe qu 沙河渠
Shahubu 殺胡堡
Shahukou 殺虎口
shangdi 上地
Shangdu 商都
shangsiyuan 上駟院
shangtun 商屯
Shangyi 尚義
shanqu 山曲
Shanxi 山西
Shanyin 山陰
shaohuang 燒荒
Shaoqi 紹祺
Shaoying 紹英
sheng 省
shengchan jianshe bingtuan 生產建設兵團
shengjidi 生計地
shengke 升科
Shengmu shengxin hui 聖母聖心會

shengu 身股
Shenmu 神木
Shi-da-gu qu 十大股渠
Shilinghol 錫林郭勒
shilu 實錄
Shira Muren / Zhaohe 召河
Shira Muren / Xiliao he 西遼河
Shira süme / Shanyinsi 善因寺
Shireetü Juu 席力圖召 / Yanshousi 延壽寺
Shizuizi 石嘴子
shuiguan 水關
shuili junzhan 水利均霑
shuiliyin 水禮銀
shuluun chaghan / *zhengbai* 正白
shuluun khökhe / *zhenglan* 正藍
shuluun shira / *zhenghuang* 正黃
shuluun ulaan / *zhenghong* 正紅
Shunde 順德
Shunyi Wang 順義王
Shuoping 朔平
Shuozhou 朔州
Sichengbudi 四成補地
Sichengdi 四成地
Si-da-gu qu 四大股渠 / Lao Guo qu 老郭渠 / Tongji qu 通濟渠
sidi 私地
Sima Qian 司馬遷
Siqi 四旗 / Fengning 豐寧
sishi 私市 / *minshi* 民市
sizhi 四至
Sjara-osso-gol (Shar usun ghol) / Salawusu he 薩拉烏蘇河 / Wuding he 無定河
Solon 索倫
Sonam Gyatso 索南嘉措
sōyūsei 総有制
Splingaerd, Paul / Lin Fuchen 林輔臣
Steenackers, Jan-Baptist / Si Fuyin 司福音
Suidong 綏東
sui menggu 隨蒙古
suiquedi 隨缺地
Suiyuancheng 綏遠城
suizu 歲租
sumu / *sumun* 蘇木 / *niru* 牛彔 / *zuo* 佐
Sünit 蘇尼特
süreg / *muqun* 牧群

Tabin-u khelkhiy-e-yin ghajar / *wushili paijie* 五十里牌界
Tabuhe canal 塔布河渠
Taigu 太谷
taipusi 太僕寺
Taiyuan 太原
taizhan 台站
Tangjiahui 唐家會
Tannu Uriankhai 唐努烏梁海
Taolin 陶林
Taonan 洮南
Tarbagatay 塔爾巴哈台
tayiji / *taiji*
Tazigou 塔子溝 / Jianchang 建昌
tebie qu 特別區
Tenjur / Danjuur 丹珠爾
tiandi 田底
Tianjin 天津
tianmian 田面
Tianyide 天義德
Tieliang 鐵良
ting 廳
Togtokhu 托克托
Tongji qu 通濟渠
tongshihang 通事行
Torghut 土爾扈特
törö / *guozheng* 國政
Tsong-kha-pa 宗喀巴
Tuchengzi 土城子
tui 推
Tümed 土默特
tümen / *wanhu* 萬戶
Tumubu 土木堡
tunken si 屯墾司
tünsh / *tongshi* 通事
tuntian 屯田
tuozhishi 拓殖使 / *kaitakushi* 開拓使
tusalagchi tayiji / *xieli taiji* 協理台吉
Tüshiyetü khan 土謝圖汗
Tuva 圖瓦
Üjümchin 烏珠穆沁
Ulaanchab 烏蘭察布
Ulaan Khada 烏蘭哈達 / Chifeng 赤峰
Ulaan Oboo 烏蘭腦包

Ulanhu 烏蘭夫
Uliasutai 烏里雅蘇台
ulus 兀魯思
ulus-tur tusalakhu gung / *fuguogong* 輔國公
ulus-un tushiye gung / *zhenguogong* 鎮國公
Urad 烏喇特
Uriyankhan 兀良哈
urtiin duu / *changdiao* 長調
Üüshin 烏審
Verbist, Ferdinand / Nan Huairen 南懷仁
Verbist, Théophile / Nan Huaiyi 南懷義
Verlinden, Remi / Fei'erlindun 費爾林敦
wailu 外路
Wandeyuan 萬德元
Wang 郡王
Wang Tongchun 王同春
Wang Xiangqing 王相卿
Wang-un Juu 王愛召
wanshoudi 萬壽地
Wantaigong 萬泰公
wanyi'er 玩藝兒
wanyou zhenyuan 萬有真元
weiban 圍班
Weichang 圍場
wei pengyou 為朋友
Wei Yuan 魏源
Wenzhehun 文哲琿
Wuchuan 武川
Wu-da-gu qu 五大股渠
Wuhuan 烏桓
Wujia he 烏加河
wu lu yizhan 五路驛站
Wushengmen 無生門
Wu Shengxiang 鄔聖祥
wushi wuzhong zhenzhuzai, xuanren xuanyi daquanheng 無始無終大主宰，宣仁
　宣義大權衡
Wutai shan 五台山
Wuyuan 五原
Wuyuntang Wanyiban 五雲堂玩意班
xiadi 下地
Xiajiadian 夏家店
xian 縣
Xianbei 鮮卑

xiangcun jianshe yundong 鄉村建設運動
xianghuodi 香火地
Xianyun 玁狁/獫狁
Xiao Daheng 蕭大亨
xiaohao 小號
Xiaoqiaopan 小橋畔
Xiaoshetai 小佘太
xiaoshi 小市 / *yueshi* 月市
Xiayingzi 下營子
xibu dakaifa 西部大開發
Xiechenghe 協成和
xieli tongpan 協理通判
Xifengkou 喜峰口
Xihuofang 西伙房
xikou 西口
xikouwai 西口外
xilu 西路
Xinghe 興和
Xingtai 邢台
Xinjiang 新疆
Xinqin 信勤
xintianyou 信天遊
Xinyi yanghang 信義洋行
xinzheng 新政
Xiongnu 匈奴
Xiqiang 西羌
Xiwanzi 西灣子
Xiyingzi 西營子 / Nanhaoqian 南壕塹
Xuanfu 宣府
Xuanhua 宣化
Xunyu 獯鬻/葷粥/薰育
yadiyin 押地銀
yahuangju 押荒局
yahuangyin 押荒銀
yaji 牙紀
Yande 彥德
yangma dian 羊馬店
Yanping 雁平
yanxing 雁行
Yan Xishan 閻錫山
Yanyusui 延榆綏
yaoban 遙辦 / *yaozhi* 遙治
yaodong 窯洞

Yao Xiguang 姚錫光
Yao Xuejing 姚學鏡
Y. C. James Yen 晏陽初
Yekhe Baishing / Da Bansheng 大板升
Yekhe Juu / Dazhao 大召 / Wuliangsi 無量寺
Yekhe Juu / Yikezhao 伊克昭
Yekhe Khüriye / Da Kulun 大庫倫
Yekhe Nuur / Danao'er 大淖爾
Yekhe Turgen ghol / Dahei he 大黑河
yesun chaghan-u alban / jiu bai gong 九白貢
yi 夷
Yigu 貽谷
Yihe qu 義和渠
yimin shibian 移民實邊
yinpiao 印票
yinpiao zhuang 印票莊
Yinshan gusha 陰山古剎
yi tian er zhu 一田二主
yi yang san pi 一羊三皮
Yongde 永德
yongdian 永佃
Yonghe qu 永和渠 / Shahe qu 沙河渠
Yongji qu 永濟渠
Yongshenghe 永盛和
Yongshengxing 永盛興
Yöngshiyebü 永謝布
yongzu 永租
Yongzudi 永租地
youyi 右翼
Youyu 右玉
Yu Gong 禹貢
Yuanshengde 元盛德
Yue Zhonglin 岳鍾麟
Yulin 榆林
Yun Shuangyang 雲雙羊
Yuxian 毓賢
Zaili 在理
Zenrin kyōkai 善隣協会
zhangfang 丈放
Zhang Genzong 張根宗
Zhang Penghe 張鵬翮
Zhangwu 彰武
Zhang Xiangwen 張相文

Zhang Zhidong 張之洞
Zhao Erfeng 趙爾豐
Zhaozhou 肇州
zhen 鎮
Zhendong 鎮東
Zhili 直隸
zhili ting 直隸廳
zhili zhou 直隸州
zhiqu 枝渠
zhiyuan bianjiang jianshe 支援邊疆建設
Zhonghe qu 中和渠 / Fengji qu 豐濟渠
zhou 州
zhuancha 磚茶
zhuangtou 莊頭
zhuangtoudi 莊頭地
zhugudi 祝嘏地 / *wanshoudi* 萬壽地
Zhukaigou 朱開溝
ziqu 子渠
zongguan qi 總管旗
zonggui 總櫃
zongjia 總甲
Zongli Yamen 總理衙門
zouxikou 走西口
Zunghar (Jüünghar) 準噶爾
Zuo Shaozuo 左紹佐
Zuoyun 左云
Zuo Zongtang 左宗棠
zuut / *baihu* 百戶

Index